The Jews of Europe

and the

Inquisition of Venice,

1550-1670

The Jews of Europe
and the
Inquisition of Venice,
1550-1670

BRIAN PULLAN

BARNES
&NOBLE
BOOKS
NEW YORK

Contents

v

Acknowledgments

In writing this book I have become deeply indebted to many scholars in Italy, in America and in Great Britain for their generosity in sharing and discussing ideas and in drawing attention to valuable material. Pier Cesare Ioly Zorattini made available to me the first page proofs of his meticulous edition of the trials of Jews and judaizers before the Holy Office in Venice, of which two volumes have now appeared. He and others, including Eliahu Ashtor, Gaetano Cozzi, Paul Grendler, Giovanni Scarabello and Elena Vanzan Marchini, have presented me with important printed materials difficult to obtain in this country. Benjamin Ravid allowed me to read and refer in print to his Harvard doctoral thesis, parts of which have been published, while others are being prepared for publication. He has read and commented on certain parts of this book in draft, and I have benefited from his learning and his precise attention to detail. Those who work in the Venetian archives have a splendid habit of trooping out to coffee to exchange ideas and swap references, in the best traditions of the academic republic; let me record my particular thanks to two fellow workers on the Inquisition, Nicholas Davidson and Ruth Martin, for my debt to them is greater than they will ever know.

Without the patience and courtesy of the staff of the Archivio di Stato in Venice none of this research could have been undertaken, and it also owes much to the Fondazione Giorgio Cini's magnificent collection of microfilms of materials in foreign archives concerning the affairs of the Venetian Republic. With unfailing kindness and consideration Signor Giuseppe Ellero guided me through the newly opened archive of I.R.E. at Cannaregio 187/A, which contains among much else the surviving papers of the Pia Casa dei Catecumeni. Father Fulvio Parisotto gave me access to the Inquisition trials housed in the archive of the Curia Patriarcale in Venice.

As always, I have the happiest memories of the hospitality and cordiality of friends in Venice and elsewhere, and I thank all those who have been generous enough to hear, and gently criticize, my tentative theories at seminars in Cremona, Udine and Venice, and at several universities in England, Scotland and Wales. I am indebted to the University of Manchester for travel grants which defrayed the expenses of research in Venice, and to colleagues and pupils for their interest.

My hope is that the book may provide a modest companion to Paul Grendler's admirable thematic study of the Inquisition in Venice and its attempts to control the press, that it may add a little to the accounts of obscure but interesting people which Carlo Ginzburg has drawn from the records of the Inquisition in Friuli, and that it may provide a supplement to Cecil Roth's classic account of the Jews of Venice by describing some of those people who moved uneasily back and forth across the dangerous border country between the Jewish and the Christian faiths.

George Orwell said that one of the four great motives for writing was 'sheer egoism'. I am grateful to everyone who has tolerated mine, and especially to my family.

Brian Pullan
Manchester

Abbreviations

Ad Limina Venezia	Archivio Segreto del Vaticano, Archivio della Sacra Congregazione del Concilio, Relazioni dei vescovi dopo le visite ad limina: Venezia (available on microfilm at the Fondazione Giorgio Cini, Venice): accounts of the diocese of Venice submitted to Rome by the Patriarchs and their deputies
Albèri	E. Albèri, ed., *Relazioni degli ambasciatori veneti al Senato* (15 vols., Florence, 1839–63)
A.S.V.	Archivio di Stato, Venice
A.S.Vat.	Archivio Segreto del Vaticano
b.	*busta*
Barozzi–Berchet	N. Barozzi and G. Berchet, eds., *Relazioni degli stati europei lette al Senato dagli ambasciatori veneti nel secolo decimosettimo* (10 vols., Venice, 1856–78)
B.A.V.	Biblioteca Apostolica del Vaticano
B.R.	Bullarium Romanum: i.e., *Bullarium diplomatum et privilegiorum sanctorum Romanorum pontificum Taurinensis editio locupletior facta* (24 vols., Aosta, 1857–72)
C.D.	A.S.V., Consiglio dei Dieci: records of the Council of Ten, the standing committee of public safety in Venice
C.E.R.	A.S.V., Collegio Esposizioni Roma: these registers describe the encounters between the nuncio and the Collegio, which consisted of the Doge of Venice and his principal ministers of state, and

ix

	their debates on matters concerning the Church of Rome
C.J.	A.S.V., Consultori in Jure: the archive preserving the written opinions of the official legal consultants to the Venetian state
C.S.I.	Archivio della Curia Patriarcale di Venezia, Criminalia Sanctae Inquisitionis: the location of the small number of Inquisition trials kept in the diocesan archives rather than in the state archive of Venice
C.S.M.	A.S.V., Cinque Savii alla Mercanzia: papers of the Venetian board of trade
den.	denunciation by
D.M.S.	*I Diarii di Marino Sanuto*, ed. R. Fulin and others (58 vols., Venice, 1879–1903)
D.N.	A.S.Vat., Dispacci del Nunzio a Venezia alla Segreteria di Stato (available on microfilm at the Fondazione Giorgio Cini, Venice): unpublished correspondence of the nuncio in Venice
E.B.	A.S.V., Esecutori contro la Bestemmia: records of the sub-committee of the Council of Ten which was charged with the suppression of blasphemy, gambling and other forms of loose behaviour, and also with the registration of foreigners
Eymeric	Nicolau Eymeric, *Directorium Inquisitorum, cum scholiis seu annotationibus eruditissimis D. Francisci Pegnae Hispani, S. Theologiae et Iuris Utriusque Doctoris* (Rome, 1578): the contributions of Eymeric and Peña are separately paginated
fasc.	*fascicolo*
H.C.	*Hierarchia catholica medii et recentioris aevi*, ed. C. Eubel and others (6 vols., Munich and Padua, 1898–1958)
I.R.E.C.	Archivio degli Istituti di Ricovero e di Educazione, Venezia, Pia Casa dei Catecumeni: papers of the house of catechumens and converts in Venice
I.Z.	P.C. Ioly Zorattini, ed., *Processi del S. Uffizio di Venezia contro ebrei e giudaizzanti (1548–60)* (Florence, 1980)

I.Z. II	P.C. Ioly Zorattini, ed., *Processi del S. Uffizio di Venezia contro ebrei e giudaizzanti (1561–70)* (Florence, 1982)
Not.	Notatorio: a minute-book
N.V.	*Nunziature di Venezia*, vols. V–XI, ed. F. Gaeta and others (Rome, 1967 onwards)
Peña	The notes by the canonist Peña, appended to the treatise by Eymeric, listed above, and separately paginated
proc.	*processo*
Q.C.	A.S.V., Quarantia Criminal: records of the high court of ordinary criminal justice in Venice
reg.	*registro*
S.D.R.O.	A.S.V., Senato, Deliberazioni Roma Ordinaria: resolutions of the Venetian Senate on matters concerning the Church of Rome, often consisting of instructions to the Venetian ambassador at the papal curia
S.S.D.R.	A.S.V., Senato III Secreta, Dispacci Roma: despatches of the Venetian ambassador in Rome
S.T.	A.S.V., Senato, Terra: resolutions of the Venetian Senate on domestic affairs of the city and *Terra Ferma*, with the information submitted to enable them to reach their decisions
Stella–Bolognetti	The account of the Church and the religious life of Venice compiled by the nuncio Alberto Bolognetti, who served in Venice from 1578 to 1581, and printed in A. Stella, *Chiesa e Stato nelle relazioni dei nunzi pontifici a Venezia: ricerche sul giurisdizionalismo veneziano dal XVI al XVIII secolo* (Vatican City, 1964), pp. 105–318
S.U.	A.S.V., Santo Uffizio: records of the Inquisition in Venice, consisting chiefly of the transcripts of trials and inquiries
test.	testimony of
U.C.	A.S.V., Ufficiali al Cattaver: papers of the magistrates whose duties included supervising the Ghetto Nuovo and enforcing the wearing of distinctive clothing by Jews

Note on Venetian Dates

In Venice the year ran from the beginning of March to the end of February. So 23 February 1623 Venetian style means 23 February 1624.

Introduction

This book is about people on the frontier between Christianity and Judaism, who lived in Venice or passed through the city at some time between the mid-sixteenth century and the year 1670. It spans the period between the beginnings of Tridentine Catholicism, which gave a new impetus to the Venetian Inquisition, and the end of the Cretan war, when the economic and fiscal contribution of the Jews to the Venetian state was fully acknowledged and their permanence in the city seemed assured. Its main concern is with travellers and rootless men who were not born in Venice, ranging in social status from the international merchant to the professional beggar, and bringing to the city problems and troubled histories which originated in other countries from Poland to Portugal, from Antwerp to Salonica.

Prominent in the book are Marranos, immigrants from Portugal and Spain who had Jewish blood and some experience of living, at least outwardly, as Catholics. Equally prominent are Jews from Italy and the Levant who turned to Christianity in Italy, and were converted by processes which had little in common with the mass baptisms imposed by King Manoel in 1497. Some space, but rather less, is devoted to a few Jews who had never been Christians, but attracted the attention of the Inquisition by allegedly insulting the Christian faith; some, too, to a few Christians who had no Jewish ancestry, but flirted dangerously with the doctrines or customs of the Jews. At this time Venice was one of the chief points of departure from Europe to the Levant, and one of the chief points of re-entry to the West from the Ottoman Empire. Inevitably it served as a transit town for people on a spiritual journey between two faiths and on a physical voyage between the monolithically Catholic states of western Europe and the religious pluralism of the Ottoman lands. It was often in Venice that Europeans of Jewish blood made their final choice between Christianity and Judaism; those who hesitated and faced both ways, neither conforming fully nor vowing themselves permanently to either creed, were most likely to suffer at the Inquisition's hands.

Seeking to understand such people, the book analyses about a hundred *processi*, many of them trials for apostasy, suspicion of heresy or heretical blasphemy, which were conducted by the Roman Inquisition in Venice between 1548 and 1594, and between 1619 and 1670. Few relevant proceedings survive for the interval of twenty-five years between these two half-centuries; in that interval came the interdict imposed on the Venetians by Pope Paul V, the expulsion of the Jesuits, and the open disruption of good relations between the Papacy and the Venetian state. No serious attempt will be made at any statistical approach, both because the figures – strongly affected by the accidental survival or destruction of evidence – would in any case be too small to prove very much, and because no two trials can be treated as equivalent units; the important thing about them is the individual, but not unrelated, stories which they tell.

For many of these people, the Inquisition is the only known recorder of their existence, and there is an obvious need to inquire into its religious, social and political ends, and into its relationship both with the Church and with the host state of Venice. Only then may it become possible to assess the quality of the evidence it transmits, to know when and why judaizing is thought to threaten state as well as Church, and to sense why some people are prosecuted and others escape. Something must be said, not only about those Jews who suffered because they tried to be men of two worlds, but also about those who, being content to accept the state's notions of order and economic planning, earned its protection against the Inquisition. By examining a fairly sharply defined group of offences and offenders, the book may help the reader to understand something of the general principles to which the Inquisition subscribed, and to appreciate the nature and extent of religious toleration in a particular type of society – a closely regulated international port faced with economic decline. Turning from judges to prisoners, it will try to convey something of the attitudes, speech and biographies of people – some of them rich but unlearned, others poor and barely literate – who, but for their encounters with the Inquisition, would have left only the most impersonal traces on the documentary records of the past.

For these purposes, the book is divided into three parts. The first deals with the Inquisition, its constitution, records and procedures. The second discusses the Jews as groups, legal categories, 'nations' or corporations, dealing with the place within the religious, social and economic orders assigned to them by the Church and by the Venetian government, and examining, too, the changing policies towards them both of the Inquisition and of the Venetian state. Moving from collectivities to individuals who would not fit into categories, the third part of the book discusses the central concern of the Inquisition – the problems created by the conversion of the Jews to Christianity; and it attempts to reconstruct the mentality and behaviour of those converts who offended against the conceptions of right order held dearest by Church and state alike.

PART I

The Recording Institution

I

The Tasks of the Inquisition
in Venice

By decree of the Doge and his six councillors, on 22 April 1547, the Republic of Venice strove to impart new vigour to an old institution. Three · Venetian patricians, described as discreet and Catholic men of integrity, were to join with the papal legate, the Patriarch of Venice and the Franciscan Inquisitor in the common enterprise of pursuing and punishing heresy.[1] Half Holy Office linked to Rome, half board of magistrates accountable to the Ten, the Senate and the Collegio, this tribunal was designed to deal with the religious problems of one of the most variegated city populations in Christian Europe. Occasionally, too, it would judge cases brought to it from elsewhere within the sprawling mainland and island empires of the Venetian lordship. Venice was a point of contact, and sometimes of collision, between Catholic and Protestant, westerner and Greek, Christian and Jew, Christendom and Islam. Unambiguously Catholic but famed for its 'liberty', it sheltered believer and unbeliever, atheist and zealot, the hesitant and the convinced.

In the midst of its dominant Catholic population, Venice gave room to a large colony of German traders and immigrant workers, seemingly infected with Lutheranism and concentrated in the parishes near Rialto and round the German Exchange on the Grand Canal. Students from France and the Empire attended the University of Padua in numbers

---

[1] For the text of the decree, see Cardinal Francesco Albizzi, *Risposta all' historia della sacra Inquisitione composta già dal R. P. Paolo Servita* (second edition, probably of Rome, ca. 1680), pp. 42–3; G. Sforza, 'Riflessi della Controriforma nella Repubblica di Venezia', *Archivio Storico Italiano*, anno 93 (1935), vol. I, pp. 195–6. On the establishment of the Inquisition in its new form, A. Santosuosso, 'Religious orthodoxy, dissent and suppression in Venice in the 1540s', *Church History*, 42 (1973), pp. 476–85; P. F. Grendler, *The Roman Inquisition and the Venetian press, 1540–1605* (Princeton, 1977), pp. 39–42.

large enough to alarm those who feared outbreaks of 'scandal' and the contagion of Lutheran and Huguenot beliefs.[2] Soon after the renewal of the Inquisition, Venice became the site of a secret conference of religious radicals, lumped together loosely under the name of Anabaptists, who questioned not only the sacraments of the Catholic Church but also the divinity of Christ and the authenticity of the New Testament. With the Pope's approval, the state allowed rights of public worship to a Greek population (including many immigrants from its own colonies) which numbered several thousands. Some toleration was extended even to those among them who did not subscribe to the union of churches agreed in Florence in 1439, and the authorities had occasionally to repel attacks from clergymen who objected to Greek opinion on Purgatory or the Trinity.[3]

Poised between the enforcement of strict Catholicism and the granting of liberty of conscience, the city was to become the uneasy refuge of Portuguese New Christians or Marranos, often hesitating between Christianity and Judaism. For some of them Venice would be their point of departure for Ottoman Turkey and an open return to the law of their fathers; others would settle in the Ghetto of Venice, turning their backs on their Christian past in Lisbon, or Oporto, or Antwerp. Economic conservatism, and distrust of the municipal Christian banks and pawnshops called *monti di pietà*, contributed to the Venetian decision to solve the problem of cheap credit for the poor by the employment of Jewish bankers and the protection of a large community of Germanic and Italian Jews. The Ghetto in Cannaregio sheltered not only European Jews from as far afield as Poland and Bohemia, not only immigrants from Spain, Portugal and the Low Countries, but also Sephardim from Constantinople, Salonica or Cairo who enjoyed the protective status of subjects of the Turkish Sultan. Ancient commercial links with the Levant and reciprocal agreements with the Turk attracted Islamic merchants from his Asiatic and Balkan provinces, though no mosque was built in Venice to compete with the synagogues of the Jews.

Broadly speaking, the task of the Inquisition was to guarantee the supremacy of the Catholic religion in a city where other creeds were often tolerated for economic advantage or reason of state. Striving to protect the faith by a mixture of disciplinary and pastoral action, it shared this task with a number of secular magistracies. The Inquisition set out to save

[2] On the German communities in Venice and Padua, see H. Šimonsfeld, *Der Fondaco dei Tedeschi in Venedig und die deutsch-venetianischen Handelsbeziehungen* (2 vols., Stuttgart, 1887); Stella–Bolognetti, pp. 277–86; D.N., filza 19, fol. 504–5, 522r.–v., 21 Nov., 5 Dec. 1579. For French students at Padua, D.N., filza 2, fol. 74v., 81, 17 Oct. 1562, 30 Jan. 1563.

[3] See G. Fedalto, *Ricerche storiche sulla posizione giuridica ed ecclesiastica dei greci a Venezia nei secoli XV e XVI* (Florence, 1967); D.N., filza 32, fol. 251r.–252v., 13 April 1596.

the native and resident populations from the corruption of heresy, and, if it could do no more, to prevent the foreigners from giving scandal. In suitably optimistic tones, even after the outbreak and precarious settlement of a spectacular conflict between the Papacy and the Venetian state, the Ad Limina report submitted to Rome in 1612 declared:

> By the grace of God the city of Venice lives in the manner of Catholics. Although men of various nations and men from far-flung countries dwell therein, they cause no public scandal, and do not dare to speak of the faith, much less dispute about it. A tribunal of the Holy Inquisition has been established in the city, and with all due diligence the most illustrious Papal Nuncio, the most reverend Patriarch and the reverend father Inquisitor keep watch to prevent any outbreak of heresy, and when the need arises they are most readily supported by the secular arm.[4]

The early months of 1547 had seen the collapse of hopes that Venice's independence of Rome and the Habsburgs might enable it to ally with England, the Lutheran princes of Germany and the King of France, and so become a protector of the reformed religion. Warned by the Imperial ambassador of the danger of flirting with heretics, reminded that to court distant friendships was to incur the enmity of Habsburg neighbours, discouraged by the deaths of Henry VIII and Francis I, the Venetian Republic retreated into strict neutrality in western Europe.[5] Its repression of heresy was not ostentatious and was still too moderate to satisfy certain zealots.[6] But it became more determined and efficient than in previous years. Attacks on Protestant heresy were accompanied by other, more open, moves to defend the faith against contamination by the presence of judaizing heretics and against the blasphemous abuse supposedly contained in the Talmud.

Giovanni Della Casa, papal nuncio in Venice from 1544 to 1549, greeted the new arrangements with undisguised relief that they had been so smoothly made – 'God has shown immense favour in allowing me to introduce the Inquisition into this dominion peacefully and without disturbance.'[7] Perhaps he had in mind the alarm and resentment festering in

---

[4] Ad Limina Venezia, *relazione* of Giovanni Andrea Salice on behalf of the Partiarch Francesco Vendramin, fol. 19.

[5] A. Stella, 'Utopie e velleità insurrezionali dei filoprotestanti italiani (1545–1547)', *Bibliothèque d'humanisme et Renaissance: travaux et documents*, 27 (1965), pp. 134–58; also his 'La società veneziana al tempo di Tiziano', in *Tiziano nel quarto centenario della sua morte (1576–1976)* (Venice, 1977), pp. 103–21.

[6] N.V., V, p. 160 ff., 15 Nov. 1550.

[7] Sforza, 'Riflessi ...', I, pp. 196, 212.

Naples in the early months of 1547 at rumours of the intrusion into the Viceroyalty of a foreign inquisition, actually Roman but thought to be Spanish.[8] Venice's alternative, though implying heavy concession to the principle of lay participation, seemed greatly to be preferred. Within three or four years, however, Pope Julius III became deeply uneasy at the invasion of the Inquisition by lay authorities, especially the governors of subject cities and provinces, not only in the Venetian Dominion but also in Milan and Lombardy: the pursuit of heresy must not be allowed to prejudice the jurisdiction of the Church, for the crime of heresy was 'purely ecclesiastical'.[9] When the Council of Ten tried to extend a version of the Venetian system to the bishoprics of the Dominion, the ensuing argument called in question the existing arrangements in Venice itself. But in 1551 a compromise was reached, with the Pope insisting that if laymen took part in arrest, trial and sentence they must do so only as auxiliaries and observers, and with Rome acknowledging a certain difference between the dominant city of Venice and the dioceses of the Venetian state.[10] In Venice there were three lay members of the Congregation of the Inquisition, and they were, at least in theory, chosen for their piety and proven loyalty to the Catholic faith. In other bishoprics, the only layman entitled as of right to attend trials, and the only one whose presence was indispensable, was the Venetian governor or his deputy; and he – as a nuncio was later to observe – was not chosen for his piety, but rather for his abilities in the field of temporal government.[11]

In essence, then, the Venetian Holy Office was a specially composed tribunal serving a diocese of exceptional importance. Most mainland bishoprics acquired their own inquisitions, each consisting of the diocesan bishop or his vicar and of a Franciscan or Dominican inquisitor, with the attendance of the Venetian *Podestà* and of such local doctors of law as the ecclesiastical members of the court might choose to summon and con-

---

[8] Cf. L. Amabile, *Il Santo Officio della Inquisizione in Napoli* (2 vols., Città di Castello, 1892), I, pp. 196–211; also S. Miccio, 'Vita di Don Pietro di Toledo, Marchese di Villafranca', ed. F. Palermo in *Archivio Storico Italiano*, 9 (1846), pp. 54–73, and H. C. Lea, *The Inquisition in the Spanish dependencies* (London, 1908), pp. 70–7.

[9] See L. Fumi, 'L'Inquisizione romana e lo Stato di Milano: saggio di ricerche nell' Archivio di Stato', *Archivio Storico Lombardo*, serie iv, anno 37 (1910), vol. 13, pp. 349–68; cf. also A. Battistella, *Il Santo Officio e la riforma religiosa in Bologna* (Bologna, 1905), pp. 49–50.

[10] N.V., V, pp. 160, 198, 279–81, 302; Albizzi, *Risposta* ..., p. 53; P. Paschini, *Venezia e l'Inquisizione romana da Giulio III a Pio IV* (Padua, 1959), pp. 53–8, 60, 65, 66–7.

[11] From a letter of Giovanni Antonio Facchinetti describing a speech in the Collegio, 2 Aug. 1567, N.V., VIII, p. 255.

[12] See especially N.V., V, p. 302. For the example of the Inquisition of Aquileia and Concordia, based upon Udine, see A. Battistella, *Il Santo Officio e la riforma religiosa in Friuli: appunti storici documentati* (Udine, 1895), and L. De Biasio, 'Note storiche sul Santo Officio di Aquileia e Concordia', in G. C. Menis, ed., *Mille processi dell' Inquisizione in Friuli (1551–1647)* (Udine, 1976), pp. 83–100.

sult.[12] Some difficulties arose concerning the role of these doctors and the degree of trust to be placed in them.[13] In relation to these courts, Venice's tribunal was not, like the Supreme Council of the Inquisition in Spain, intended to be a central directory for the whole state, much less to be used regularly as a higher court of appeal.[14] But it did possess a special reserve authority which entitled it to repair the deficiencies of local machinery, in that the papal nuncio in Venice had a general responsibility for ecclesiastical affairs (including those of Inquisition tribunals) in the Venetian dominions to seaward or landward, and in that – at least from the appointment of Felice Peretti in 1557[15] – the office of Inquisitor in Venice began to be combined with that of Inquisitor-General throughout the Venetian dominions.

Hence, in certain circumstances, it was possible to call cases from the provinces to Venice itself for investigation or even retrial, especially perhaps where diocesan administration had been weakened by the absence of bishops and their failure to appoint efficient vicars to rule in their stead.[16] When, in 1553, the Lieutenant of Cyprus and his councillors sent to Venice a Franciscan Observant, accused *inter alia* of apostatizing in Cairo and resuming his priestly functions in Cyprus without reconciliation with the Church, they did so on the grounds that the island contained no inquisitor and no superior within the man's order competent to judge him. The Heads of the Ten duly referred him to the Inquisition in Venice, which read the text of the investigations already conducted by the Vicars-General of Paphos and Nicosia, heard his confession, and sentenced him among much else to serve eight years in the penal galleys.[17] With the improvement of local arrangements for judging heresy, the importance of Venice's reserve powers would naturally dwindle. In Friuli, which is unlikely to have been unique in this respect, there was much resistance, both on the part of locals and on that of Venetian governors, to the practice of dragging accused persons out of their own jurisdic-

---

[13] Paschini, *Venezia e l'Inquisizione romana* ..., p. 140; N.V., IX, pp. 119–20, 123, 127, 214, and Battistella, *Il Santo Officio ... in Friuli*, docs. V–VI, pp. 119–21 (concerning disputes in Friuli in 1569–70); N.V., XI, pp. 328, 346, 360–1 (concerning Vicenza in 1575).

[14] A letter of the nuncio Beccadelli of 30 April 1552 reports attempts to use the Venetian tribunal as an appeal court which might review the sentence of one Piccinino, who had been condemned at Rovigo; the nuncio said this was wrong in principle, 'because appeals cannot be granted in matters of heresy' (N.V., VI, p. 95).

[15] Cf. G. Cugnoni, 'Documenti chigiani concernenti Felice Peretti, Sisto V, come privato e come pontefice', *Archivio della Società Romana di Storia Patria*, 5 (1882), pp. 300, 301. Earlier Franciscan inquisitors in Venice are described simply as *inquisitor della heretica pravità* – e.g., I.Z., pp. 75, 90, 139, 219, 245.

[16] N.V., V, p. 160, and Paschini, *Venezia e l'Inquisizione romana* ..., pp. 54–5, for the case of the priest Calcagno of Brescia (Nov. 1550).

[17] I.Z., pp. 101–43, proc. Pietro de Nixia.

tions.[18] The Inquisitor-General could use his authority, as Felice Peretti attempted to do in the bishopric of Feltre in 1558, by appointing a deputy to deal with the case *in situ*, and some twenty years later Rome issued an instruction that similar measures should become normal practice.[19]

Emphasis began to fall on the sparing use of the nuncio's and Inquisitor's powers, although they were admitted to exist. In 1567 the nuncio Facchinetti had occasion to explain that he had not yet called a case of heresy from any mainland diocese to Venice, although in one instance he had passed on to the Bishop of Brescia instructions received from Rome for a retrial, and had asked for a transcript of the proceedings to help him persuade the Venetian government to put the convicted man to death.[20] Twenty years later there were signs that the Congregation of Cardinal Inquisitors-General was anxious to protect its own direct relationship with the mainland tribunals of the Inquisition, and not to allow the Venetian Inquisitor to assume an intermediate authority over them; indeed, in 1591, the Inquisitor in Venice was instructed that his powers 'do not extend outside Venice, save to those parts of the dominions in which no special inquisitors have been appointed'.[21] Some cases had none the less arisen during the previous few years in which the tribunal tried offences allegedly committed outside the diocese of Venice – as in 1584, when it judged those of Mandolino or Mendlin, the Jewish banker at the seaside township of Muggia, which lay within Venetian territory but was subject in ecclesiastical affairs to the foreign bishopric of Trieste.[22] In such circumstances, the reserve powers of the Venetian Inquisition were still of use.

A very rough impression of the overall activity of the Inquisition in Venice, and of its shifting preoccupations, can be formed from the valuable statistics compiled by the archivists Pasini and Giomo after indexing the records of the Holy Office, and subsequently published by Cecchetti in 1874.[23] It must be said that the statistic, like the archival inventory, is concerned with enumerating and classifying *processi*, the dossiers of Inquisition proceedings, and that the term *processo* covers a great variety of phenomena. It ranges from denunciations which were never followed up, to elaborate trials on charges of heresy which lasted a year or more. It can

[18] N.V., V, p. 198, 16 Jan. 1551; Battistella, *Il Santo Officio ... in Friuli*, doc. VI, pp. 120–1, 27 July 1569.

[19] Cugnoni, 'Documenti chigiani ...', pp. 548–50; L. von Pastor, 'Allgemeine Dekrete der römischen Inquisition aus den Jahren 1555–1597. Nach dem Notariatsprotokoll des S. Uffizio zum erstenmale veröffentlicht', *Historisches Jahrbuch*, 23 (1912), p. 513.

[20] N.V., VIII, pp. 206–7, 26 April 1567.

[21] B.A.V., Vaticanus Latinus 10945, fol. 85r.–v., 15 July 1589, 7 Dec. 1591.

[22] S.U., b. 52, proc. Mandolino da Muggia.

[23] I.Z., pp. 61–3; B. Cecchetti, *La Republica di Venezia e la Corte di Roma nei rapporti della religione* (2 vols., Venice, 1874), II, pp. 4–7.

include such matters as inquiries into the authenticity of conversions from Judaism to Christianity,[24] or the refusal of the Holy Office in 1555 to allow the export to Jerusalem of the bones of a Jewess who had died in Ferrara.[25] The statistic does not distinguish between proceedings against individuals and prosecutions involving groups of accused persons, such as the complicated trial which began in 1579 with delations of judaizing and ended early in 1580 with the condemnation of half a dozen people for necromancy.[26] All attempts at classifying trials by subject matter are inevitably somewhat arbitrary, especially as many cases involved a number of charges, some of which were abandoned whilst others were pursued. Some proceedings have disappeared; certain Inquisition records were already, by the 1690s, suffering sadly from rain and damp,[27] and one shady official, the Commissario Guiotti, filched a substantial number of documents for sinister purposes of his own at about that time.[28] And the figures probably take no account of a small number of procedural records now located in the archive of the Curia Patriarcale of Venice.

For all these qualifications, the outlines of a rough sketch emerge quite clearly. From the sixteenth century, approximately 1,550 *processi* survive, most of them packed into the second half of the century, since a sharp increase of activity occurred in and after 1547, when the Inquisition was given teeth and claws. Some 800 of these were concerned with offences loosely classified as 'Lutheranism'. Comparatively few accused persons were called Calvinists or Huguenots, although there were some thirty-five proceedings against Anabaptists, resulting in a disproportionately large number of sentences to death by drowning.[29] Approximately 150 *processi*, some 10 per cent of the whole, were concerned with the possession, production or dissemination of prohibited books.[30] Cases of sorcery, witchcraft, magic, healing or mere superstitious practice seem to have accounted for about one-eighth of the total number of proceedings. Those involving 'Judaism' in some guise or other numbered, according to Pasini and Giomo, forty-three. Recent research has shown that this figure can be increased to over seventy, nearly 5 per cent of the whole, by taking

[24] See below, p. 296.

[25] I.Z., pp. 145–50, proc. David Malagino.

[26] S.U., b. 44, proc. 'Negromanti'; see also Stella–Bolognetti, pp. 287–8.

[27] C.E.R., reg. 20, fol. 94, 31 March 1623.

[28] See A. Zanelli, 'Di alcune controversie tra la Repubblica di Venezia ed il Sant' Officio nei primi anni del Pontificato di Urbano VIII (1624–1626)', *Archivio Veneto*, serie v, vol. 6 (1929), pp. 202–4.

[29] On Anabaptism in Venice, see A. Stella, *Dall' Anabattismo al Socinianesimo nel Cinquecento Veneto: ricerche storiche* (Padua, 1967), and A. Stella, *Anabattismo e antitrinitarismo in Italia nel XVI secolo: nuove ricerche storiche* (Padua, 1969).

[30] For thorough treatment of this theme in the sixteenth century, see Grendler, *Roman Inquisition* . . . .

account of some other cases involving Jews or recent converts from Judaism charged with offences such as repetition of baptism or heretical blasphemy which were arguably related to their Judaism.[31]

For the seventeenth century, approximately 1,480 *processi* survive. Analysis of the figure suggests a decisive shift in the Inquisition's ruling concerns. For the place of 'Lutheranism' has been seized by witchcraft, sorcery and magic, which between them account for 695 surviving transcripts, or nearly 50 per cent of the whole.[32] Lutheranism shrinks to a mere 125 cases, but Calvinism has increased to 46, and Lutheranism and Calvinism together score 11 or 12 per cent. Another 10 per cent of cases are described as 'heretical propositions, discourses and blasphemies'. There is a steep decline in delations or prosecutions involving prohibited books; the proportion falls to some 4 per cent only. 'Mohammedanism', insignificant in the sixteenth century, rises to nearly 5 per cent in the seventeenth; most of these proceedings entailed the reconciliation to the Church of persons who, captured by Muslims, had outwardly embraced Islam with (or so they said) inward reservations, and were now presenting themselves spontaneously to the Holy Office to confess their fault.[33] And the seventeenth-century Inquisition seems to have shown a stronger concern with the morals, as distinct from the beliefs, of the clergy, since it had brought to its attention not less than seventy-eight cases of abuse of the confessional for the purposes of seduction.[34] There was no very dramatic change, at least up to the close of the 1630s, in the Inquisition's relations with Jews and judaizers, which were not subject to crazes or sudden accesses of zeal. Thirty-four such cases, according to Pasini and Giomo, arose in the course of the century. Analysis in this book of known and surviving trials involving Jews will, perhaps, reveal a greater concern with Levantines (who had seldom, if ever, been touched in the sixteenth century); a stronger concentration upon poor Jews, as distinct from persons of merchant rank; and a tendency to prosecute for 'suspicion of heresy', rather than for manifest heresy or apostasy as in the 1570s and 1580s.[35]

The Pasini–Giomo statistic distinguishes only between the sixteenth

[31] See P. C. Ioly Zorattini, 'Note sul S. Uffizio e gli ebrei a Venezia nel Cinquecento', *Rivista di Storia della Chiesa in Italia*, anno 33 (1979), pp. 500–8; English version as 'The Inquisition and the Jews in sixteenth-century Venice', *Proceedings of the Seventh World Congress of Jewish Studies* (Jerusalem, 1981), pp. 83–92. These are now the best guide to sixteenth-century trials involving Jews in the archive of the Holy Office in Venice.

[32] Ruth Martin of the University of Manchester is writing a thesis on this subject for the Ph.D. degree.

[33] See P. Preto, *Venezia e i Turchi* (Florence, 1975), p. 187 ff.

[34] For one example, the case of Father Michele Zanardi of Orgnano, see Zanelli, 'Controversie . . .', pp. 199–200.

[35] See below, pp. 62–4, 300–7.

and the seventeenth centuries; it seems likely, from contemporary comment, that the shift of emphasis began to take place about 1580, when the nuncio Bolognetti, in the course of an extensive report on the state of the Venetian Church, described how

> the tribunal of Venice has been continuously engaged upon various matters of heresy. Among these the most recurrent, or at least those which have kept it most fully occupied, are two: the superstition of incantations, and the faithlessness of judaizing Christians.[36]

Prosecution of the Portuguese and Spanish Jews to whom he alluded was, within nine years, to be inhibited by the guarantees offered them by the Senate.[37] But the preoccupation with sorcery and superstition was to be a lasting one, its concerns ranging from demonolatry and the conjuring of spirits through healing and the concoction of love-philtres to mere fortune-telling and the casting of beans.

Symptomatic of the change, and of a certain slowing down of the activity of the Inquisition in the early seventeenth century, was the brief remark in a report of the Patriarch Tiepolo on his diocese in 1622: the Inquisition was then said to meet twice a week and to direct its actions *adversus sortilegos et haereticos*, 'against sorcerers and heretics'.[38] In Bolognetti's day, as in the mid-sixteenth century, the congregation of the Inquisition had been accustomed to meet every alternate day, three times a week.[39] In 1622, also, the state's most famous legal consultant, Paolo Sarpi, argued that the heretics of Venice were no more than a memory.

> By the grace of God there are no heretics in this city, and for decades there has been no trial for formal heresy, but only for some looseness of speech indulged in by persons who have spoken of the Christian religion without due veneration and understanding, and for some outbreaks of herbal magic and sorcery.[40]

But the state did not act on his suggestion that the Inquisition was no longer vital, and that the few remaining cases could be heard by the Patriarch and by the Council of Ten's standing commission against blasphemers.

[36] Stella–Bolognetti, p. 286.
[37] See below, pp. 187–8, 192–4.
[38] Ad Limina Venezia, fol. 43v.
[39] Stella–Bolognetti, p. 290; cf. Santosuosso, 'Religious orthodoxy ...', pp. 480–1; N.V., V, p. 279, 5 Sept. 1551; Cugnoni, 'Documenti chigiani ...', p. 301.
[40] P. Sarpi, 'In materia di crear novo inquisitor di Venezia. 29 ottobre 1622', in his *Opere*, ed. G. and L. Cozzi (Milan–Naples, 1969), p. 1210.

The punishment of offences actually committed against the faith was not the sole concern of the Inquisition, for it had, or at least claimed, certain powers of admonition or censorship to prevent religious crime. At times the state found these powers useful and adapted them to its own purposes; at others – particularly in the late sixteenth and early seventeenth centuries – it challenged and tried to curb them. Even so, in the course of a heated debate in 1622, the lay members of the Venetian Inquisition reminded an over-zealous cleric that 'what we are to believe has been established and ordained by the Church, and that the sole business of this court is the salutary and charitable correction, without malice, of individuals who have made mistakes.'[41]

Over the previous sixty years, however, the Inquisition had been trying to anticipate error rather than merely correct it, and to check the spread of heretical opinions and dietary practices. Censorship of books was an important personal responsibility of the Inquisitor, who found himself, from the 1560s onwards, ingeniously absorbed into a system of censorship, at once religious and political, supervised both by the Council of Ten and by the magistrates called the *Riformatori dello Studio di Padova*. The objects of this system were to inspect manuscripts destined for publication and to exercise control over foreign and imported books with the aid of a small army of fifty monastic auxiliaries drafted into service in 1569–70.[42] Despite attempts to involve other members of the Holy Office in the serious decision to ban books, censorship was often treated as the responsibility of the Inquisitor alone, the specialist in diagnosing heresy: in 1623, for example, it was discovered that the late Inquisitor had refused to delegate his authority in the matter of licensing books to any other member of the Holy Office, and that the Patriarch was reluctant to take on the job.[43]

In other fields, however, the Inquisition seems to have exercised corporately its powers to anticipate attacks on the faith. By the end of the sixteenth century it was attempting to exercise some disciplinary control, if only through admonition, over two bodies of men – preachers and victuallers, whose activities became of special interest during Lent, the season of sternest austerity and most intensive sermonizing. The government successfully resisted the proposal that printers, publishers and booksellers should swear before the Bishop and Inquisitor an oath to obey the new Clementine Index of Prohibited Books, and ban probable heretics from their guild.[44] In 1596 the Lenten preachers could expect much good advice from the Holy Office, including a salutary warning not to cast

[41] C.E.R., reg. 20, fol. 28v., 14 July 1622.
[42] Grendler, *Roman Inquisition* . . . , pp. 151–4, 162–9.
[43] Ibid., pp. 273–8; D.N., filza 42I, fol. 11v.–12v., 14 Jan. 1623.
[44] Grendler, *Roman Inquisition* . . . , pp. 264–78.

aspersions on the Greeks.[45] It is clear that by 1623 the Holy Office was accustomed to hold an annual congregation to receive an oath and a profession of faith from the preachers.[46] Like all actions which might establish a claim to control over laymen, the admonitions of the Holy Office to the victuallers proved in the end to be more controversial than their dealings with the clergy. Since the foreign communities of Venice, and particularly the Germans of Rialto, caused grave disquiet by violating the Church's dietary laws, the nuncio Bolognetti arranged about 1580 for the Holy Office to take over from the Patriarch the task of inspecting the kitchens of German inns on Fridays, Saturdays and vigils, to ensure that at such times they contained no prohibited foodstuffs.[47] It was probably then that the Holy Office developed the habit of issuing admonitions about the observance of Lent to innkeepers and other persons particularly concerned with the preparation or bulk purchasing of food – including butchers, confectioners and the house manager of the German Exchange. The practice was certainly challenged, and probably not allowed to continue, beyond the early 1620s: for the government, increasingly aware of a need to prevent the clerical wing of the Holy Office from expanding their powers, objected to their admonishing laymen who had as yet done no wrong.[48]

In general, it is probably true that the Inquisition's didactic or pastoral activity, its authority to guide, warn and censor suffered in the seventeenth century more than did its powers of punishment, though its jurisdiction, too, was circumscribed. In the eyes of the state its posture should be one of defence, for its proper role was not to instruct and exhort those as yet without guilt.

Professing Jews, former Jews and people of Jewish descent were seldom – save briefly in the 1580s and perhaps in the 1630s – a spectacular preoccupation of the Inquisition in Venice. But they did represent a steady, recurrent concern which survived the curtailment of the Inquisition's powers in the early seventeenth century by an increasingly jealous state. The story of their encounters with the Inquisition can provide a kind of paradigm of its history, since they became involved with its activity at many different points. They formed one of several alien communities, or rather they formed a cluster of foreign nations united by belief in Judaism, and enjoying protection from a state which claimed to be de-

[45] D.N., filza 32, fol. 252, 13 April 1596.
[46] D.N., filza 42I, fol. 89v., 25 Feb. 1623.
[47] Stella–Bolognetti, p. 285.
[48] C.E.R., reg. 20, fol. 94r.–95r., 31 March 1623; D.N., filza 42I, fol. 133v.–136, 152v.–153, 1, 15 April 1623. The nuncio then said that surviving records enabled him to trace back the practice for at least thirty-seven years (i.e. to about 1586). Cf. C.E.R., reg. 21, fol. 1r.–2v., 1 March 1624.

voutly Catholic; at the same time they were open to charges of corrupting, insulting or otherwise threatening the progress of the Catholic faith. Tolerated partly for economic reasons, they were also regarded as a target for evangelical campaigns which would bring a few converts within the pale of the Holy Office's jurisdiction over baptized Christians.

Jurisdiction over the Jews, even if they had been nominal Christians abroad, became a matter for dispute between Church and state, and called into play the negotiating machinery built into the Inquisition itself through the association of laymen with the pursuit of heresy. Jewish dietary practices and Jewish rejection of images at times overlapped perilously with those of Protestant heresy; Purim, the Jewish carnival, offered to a few Christians relief from the austerities of Lent; and loose links were sometimes traceable between Judaism and Anabaptism, the most anarchic and iconoclastic of subversive creeds. In so far as they attacked the Christian faith, or impinged upon the common faith of Christians and Jews, Hebrew books were subject to the censorship of the Inquisition. At one time or another, Jews or former Jews were denounced for, investigated for or actually charged with many of the offences within the Inquisition's purview – with heresy or apostasy, suspicion of heresy, heretical blasphemy, misuse of the sacraments, insults to converts or clergy, or involvement in superstitious practices ranging from the unorthodox exorcism of evil spirits to the detection of thieves by supernatural means.

2

Heresy, the State and the Inquisition

To Paolo Sarpi, writing his treatise on the Inquisition in response to instructions from the Senate in 1613, the Holy Office in Venice was, or ought to have been, an autonomous Venetian institution. His thesis, upheld by selective historical argument, sprang from his own sense of expediency, from his conviction of the need to guard the sovereignty of the Republic against encroachments committed by the Roman curia under cover of religion and piety. For him the Congregation of Cardinal Inquisitors-General, established in 1542 by Pope Paul III, could claim no authority over institutions which antedated it, among them the Inquisitions of Venice and of Spain.[1] Venice's Inquisition, he argued, was originally a creation of the state in the year 1289, to which Pope Nicholas IV merely gave his approval, and it had at first been financed by a 'deposit of moneys of the commune'.[2] Arrangements concluded between the Venetian state and the Papacy, whether in the thirteenth century or in the sixteenth, were concordats or bilateral agreements between equal powers, and could be altered by common consent.[3]

To Francesco, Cardinal Albizzi, sometime assessor of the Holy Office in Rome, who wrestled with Sarpi's ghost, the Venetian Inquisition was a subordinate branch of a hierarchical organization subject to Roman com-

---

[1] P. Sarpi, 'Sopra l'Officio dell' Inquisizione (18 novembre 1613)', in his *Scritti giurisdizionalistici*, ed. G. Gambarin (Bari, 1958), p. 163. The Senate had invited Sarpi to draw up a capitulary, or book of rules made by the state concerning the Inquisition, in October 1613; there is one reference, presumably added later, to an event of 1617. The work, not designed by Sarpi for publication, was printed in two editions in 1638, one bearing the imprint of Serravalle, the other without date or place of publication, but generally held to be of Geneva (see pp. 186, 312–14, and B.A.V., MS Vaticanus Latinus 10945, fol. 106).

[2] Sarpi, 'Inquisizione', pp. 140–1.

[3] Ibid., pp. 127, 183–4.

mand. There had been a Cardinal Inquisitor-General, if not a congregation of such dignitaries, since 1263, and the original Inquisition of 1289
had been established in belated obedience to papal orders which had been
respected by all other Italian princes.[4] Universal and absolute as it was,
the authority of the Pope could not enter into concordats; if he had made
concessions to the Venetian Republic, as in 1551, these were revocable
graces or privileges, and not binding agreements.[5] In the affairs of the
Inquisition, the state should act only as a willing auxiliary force. Should
the Roman Inquisition choose to call a case to Rome, thereby removing it
from the jurisdiction of any tribunal within the Venetian Dominion, it
was not for the Venetian government to question or resist.[6]

In practice the character of the Venetian Inquisition, and its behaviour
towards Jews and towards Christians of Jewish stock, was shaped by a
mixture of Venetian and Roman elements. It was not, like the Spanish
Inquisition, essentially of the state; nor, like the Neapolitan, essentially of
the Church. Though Sarpi, maintaining the tension of the post-interdict
years, portrayed them as conflicting interests engaged in a contest for
sovereign power, Venice and Rome were frequently joined in the middle
and later sixteenth century in the common enterprise of putting down
heresy and impiety, the state's enthusiasm for the task being greatest at
the points where heresy seemed to threaten public order and state security. It might stir up rebellion, it might inspire treason and espionage,
or it might provoke the wrath of God to punish a state impure in faith,
tolerant of blasphemy and divided against itself.

As ardently as any sixteenth-century monarchy, the collective abso-

---

[4] Albizzi, *Risposta* ..., pp. 20–42, 152–4. According to A. Monticone, 'Albizzi, Francesco',
in *Dizionario biografico degli Italiani*, II (Rome, 1960), pp. 23–6, Albizzi's *Risposta* appeared at
Rome in 1678 and its publication was probably a response to the second edition of Sarpi's
work in 1675. It is at least possible that the bulk of it was actually written soon after
Albizzi's nineteen years as assessor of the Holy Office in Rome from 1635 to 1654; he refers
to his 'nineteen long years in Rome' (pp. 160–1) as if these had recently passed. In any case
it seems likely that most of his arguments are founded on material accessible to him during
that period of service (note his detailed discussion of a case of 1653, involving the Inquisitor
of Vicenza, pp. 99–102). Albizzi also refers (pp. 219–20) to 'a certain Dr Pinto Pereira, who
in the guise of a Christian was Auditor of the Rota in Florence and public lecturer in the
University of Pisa; a few months ago he died as a Jew in the city of Verona, or else of
Brescia.' A Dr Pinto, formerly Auditor of the Rota in Florence, had arrived in Verona by
1651 (see the delation of him by his former servant, Giovanni Battista Magini Romito of
Moncelese, in S.U., b. 106, 9 Dec. 1651). There is a note in b. 107, in the papers labelled
'Valenza, D'Acosta', to the effect that Dr Pinto died on 3 May 1654. A. Rotondò suggests,
though without convincing evidence, that an early draft was written as an 'instruction' to
Venetian inquisitors in response to the first edition of Sarpi – see 'La censura ecclesiastica e
la cultura', in *Storia d'Italia*, ed. C. Vivanti and R. Romano, V (Turin, 1973), pp. 1476–7.

[5] Albizzi, *Risposta* ..., pp. 60, 280–3.

[6] Ibid., pp. 154–60.

lutism of the Venetian aristocracy, personified by the Doge and Signory, claimed authority from God and demanded obedience by virtue of its character as a Catholic state. Difficulties arose not from any Venetian claim to be a secular (as distinct from a lay) state; but rather from the government's ambition to wield, like some Byzantine Caesar, the swords both of temporal and of spiritual power.[7] Religious bonds were too essential to protecting established patterns of order for the state to welcome innovation in the sphere of religion; any challenge to Catholicism became, almost automatically, a challenge to the state itself. In the mid-sixteenth century, heresy was linked with fears of popular disturbance and of factionalism; Venetian authorities were confronted with visions of iconoclastic mobs and peasant rebels, not regaled with reassuring accounts of the state-controlled churches of the German cities and principalities, or of clergymen compelled to be ordinary citizens and taxpayers in their towns. By 1543, officials of the bakers' guild in Venice were attributing the violent, rebellious acts of their immigrant journeymen not just to sottishness but to heresy, and remarking with considerable bathos that 'they follow in the footsteps of the Lutherans, and, boasting of having flung once-most-Christian Germany into confusion and converted it to their own superior faith, are now sparing no effort to ruin the bakers' guild here.'[8]

Should the lords of Venice show any signs of forgetting the message, foreign diplomats were quick to remind them that heresy was implacably hostile to established order and authority. Don Diego Hurtado de Mendoza, Charles V's ambassador, warned the heads of the government that by flirting with heretics they would attract 'the enmity of princes for the sake of winning the friendship of peoples . . . for they wish no vassal to give obedience to his prince, and they seek to destroy all dominion and to make peoples free.'[9] Recalling these events some sixty years later, Sarpi was to say in secret conversation with a German visitor that 'News of the wars of Charles V made them believe that the reformed religion brought in its train both war and mutations of state; and this opinion has taken deep root in the minds of the Venetian government.'[10] The Pope himself and a Dominican emissary warned the Venetians of the virulently anar-

---

[7] Cf. P. Prodi, 'The structure and organisation of the Church in Renaissance Venice: suggestions for research', in *Renaissance Venice*, ed. J. R. Hale (London, 1973), pp. 409–30. On this theme, cf. the later remark of the nuncio Offredi on 7 Sept. 1602: 'in matters spiritual or temporal the Council of Ten has always done as it chooses without hindrance.' Should Rome attempt to destory the Ten's freedom altogether, 'they would become heretics rather than submit to us' (D.N., filza 37, fol. 151v.–152).

[8] Simonsfeld, *Fondaco dei Tedeschi* . . . , II, doc. 77, pp. 338–40, 19 Sept. 1543.

[9] Stella, 'Utopie . . .', pp. 137–8.

[10] P. Sarpi, *Lettere ai protestanti*, ed. M. D. Busnelli (2 vols., Bari, 1931), II, p. 123 – record of his conversation with the Burgrave Christoph von Dohna, 4 Aug. 1608.

chic streak in Anabaptism.[11] In May 1547 the governors of Vicenza promptly recognized the threat to public order from the presence of heretics attacking images and the Eucharist; this might lead to something far worse than brawls on the piazza, and the sect might cause 'scandal and disorder, not only of words, but of weapons also'.[12] Some years later, the *Podestà* of Capodistria added a new article to the indictment against Anabaptists when he accused them of weakening the state by encouraging emigration of its subjects to Moravia, the promised land of the Hutterite communities.[13] Significantly, the council most intimately involved in the pursuit of heresy in these early years was Venice's standing committee of public safety, the Ten, which was often found not restraining provincial inquisitions, but reproving their laxity and urging them to cleanse the state of 'the evil species of men that follow the new opinions in religion'.[14] Outbreaks of civil war to the north, first in France and then in the Spanish Low Countries, provided further lessons on the bonds between dissent and disturbance.

Judaism was not in itself a heresy, but the act of forsaking Christianity for it was a peculiarly heinous form of heresy or apostasy, and in these years there were several potential links between Judaism and subversion. Judaism could provide, to restless, curious young men who might never have heard of Protestantism, an inspiration for argument about the very foundations of Christianity. Some Anabaptist sects in the Veneto, drawing on immigrants of Marrano stock from Naples, created an alarming mixture of Christian and Judaic belief.[15] Pietro of Naxos, a wandering Franciscan sent from Cyprus for judgement in Venice, had had himself circumcised in Cairo; perhaps it was part of his disguise on a dangerous journey through Ottoman lands in search of Prester John, or perhaps he was flirting with Judaism in order to 'understand the laws and writings of the Jews, though not to deny his faith'.[16] Whatever his motives, his acquaintance with Judaism led him to contest the Virgin Birth, to mock the images of saints in churches, to attack Christian interpretations of Scripture and extol Jewish interpretations at their expense. To the painter of icons who reminded him that the Church had ordained that saints be adored, Pietro of Naxos replied: 'Those who so commanded were men,

---

[11] Paschini, *Venezia e l'Inquisizione romana* ..., p. 91; Stella, *Anabattismo al Socinianesimo*, pp. 88–9.

[12] Stella, 'Utopie', docs. XX–XXIII, pp. 181–2.

[13] Stella, *Anabattismo al Socinianesimo*, pp. 111–12.

[14] Stella, *Anabattismo e antitrinitarismo*, pp. 126–7, 157, 161.

[15] Cf. Stella, *Anabattismo al Socinianesimo*, pp. 33 ff., 81–2; Stella, *Anabattismo e antitrinitarismo*, pp. 15 ff., 30 ff., 79–81, 97.

[16] I.Z., pp. 118–20, 132–3, proc. Pietro de Nixia, test. the accused, 11 Dec. 1552, 16 May 1553; test. 'Ser Antonio Flogotomo' of Famagosta, ship's purser, 11 Dec. 1552.

even as you are. Why trust in them? Fix your mind on God, for all the rest is vanity.'[17] He seemed to exemplify perfectly that dangerous individual who sets up his own judgment against authority, for he had once declared 'that he said and did such things to provoke argument and discover the truth'.[18]

In these years, too, the Talmud was bitterly attacked, and was burned in Venice (as elsewhere) not only for the blasphemies ascribed to it but also for its antisocial qualities, in that, for example, it destroyed the force of the oaths on which loyalties, contracts, and testimony in law courts depended: 'the Talmuds teach them it is lawful to swear a false oath with the mouth, yet break it in the heart, and a hundred thousand other things to the detriment of Christians.'[19] Such notions of faithlessness and unreliability developed, in connexion with crypto-Jews from Spain and Portugal, into fears of treachery towards Christian countries and of alliance with the Turk. Returning from his embassy to Spain in 1573, Leonardo Donà portrayed the crypto-Jews of that country as potential rebels, who might ally 'with Moors, Huguenots and all other disaffected persons in order to return to life under their ancient law . . .'[20] The treachery of these Marranos need not be confined to Spain, but could, in time of war with Islam, extend to all Christendom. At the time of the war of Cyprus fear of Jewish espionage based on Venice reached formidable proportions, and the Turkish attack upon the island was often ascribed to João Miquez Mendes, Duke of Naxos and the Archipelago, the most influential of ex-Christian Jews, whose presence at the right hand of the Sultan gave substance to uneasy belief about a Marrano conspiracy.[21] Willingly enough, in 1570, the Council of Ten handed over to the Inquisition Enriques Nuñes, otherwise Abraham called Righetto, alternately Christian and Jew, and believed to be a relative of the Duke bent on departure for the Levant.[22] Not long after the war ended, the nuncio Castagna promoted in Venice a revised edition of an inquisitor's handbook originally composed in the Spain of Ferdinand and Isabella. This would remind its readers that secret judaizers must be savagely punished 'not only because of the horrendous nature of their crime, but also because of the danger of betrayal' (periculum proditionis), quoting in support of its argument the axiom of the Council of Toledo: 'No man who is

[17] Ibid., p. 126, test. Master Gabriel, painter, 22 May 1553.
[18] Ibid., p. 122, test. 'Venerabilis hieromonacus de Antrio', 19 May 1553.
[19] I.Z., p. 169, proc. Elena de' Freschi Olivi, petition of Giovanni Battista de' Freschi Olivi, 18 April 1555.
[20] Albèri, I/vi, pp. 404–5.
[21] See below, pp. 179–80.
[22] See B. Pullan, ' "A ship with two rudders": "Righetto Marrano" and the Inquisition in Venice', The Historical Journal, 20 (1977), pp. 25–28.

faithless to God can ever keep faith with man.'[23] Such adages offered the state a powerful inducement to repress heresy, thus seen as a symptom of general unreliability, or readiness to challenge all authority, not merely that of the Church.

Facchinetti, Pius V's nuncio during the war of Cyprus, did not fail to appeal to the Republic to put down heresy, for the sakes both of Christian duty and of reason of state. Eloquently, he stressed the peculiar vulnerability of the Republic to 'the sedition and discord that heresy brings', and exploited to the full the common metaphor of heresy as insidious disease, as the plague that strikes from within and disunites the people, more terrible than any foreign foe.[24] At intervals over the last thirty years of the century, the nuncios repeated in the Collegio, as though for the benefit of the less devout statesmen, the commonplace that civil obedience could be instilled into subjects only by 'religion and the fear of God', and that the ecclesiastical power would always bring great profit to the secular.[25] Such sentiments were not confined to sermonizing churchmen, for they entered the store of maxims which were handed down in ambassadorial *relazioni* on foreign countries and designed to contribute to the collective political wisdom of members of the ruling estate. Francesco Soranzo repeated most of them on returning in 1602 from a five-year embassy to Spain, saying that false religion was the perfect shield for those planning 'innovations' (*novità*) and plotting to disrupt the peace of states. For him, too, heresy was a *piaga*, a boil or sore which threatened to poison the body politic.[26]

Moralists did not associate the presence of heresy and impiety merely with rebellion. Disaster could strike the state from above, no less than from below; the wrath of God, immediate divine punishment in a physical form, could be deserved by the toleration of heresy, blasphemy or moral laxity.[27] In 1566 Facchinetti had urged the Collegio that to protect heretics, or accord them any kind of safe-conduct, would be to call down

---

[23] See the *Repertorium Inquisitorum pravitatis haereticae in quo omnia quae ad haeresum cognitionem ac S. Inquisitionis forum pertinent continentur. Correctionibus et annotationibus praestantissimorum iurisconsultorum Quintilliani Mandosii ac Petri Vendrameni decoratum et auctum* (Venice, 1588), p. 54. On the authorship, and on Castagna's part in promoting the work – first published in this edition in 1575 – see the dedicatory epistle. The passage refers to Canon 64 of the Fourth Council of Toledo, 633 (see J. D. Mansi, ed., *Sacrorum Conciliorum nova et amplissima collectio*, X, Florence, 1764, col. 634).

[24] N.V., X, pp. 221–2, 229, 234, 21, 28 June, 5 July 1572.

[25] E.g. the remarks of the Bishop of Amelia in D.N., filza 32, fol. 249v.–250, 6 April 1596.

[26] Barozzi–Berchet, I/i, p. 74; cf. also p. 447, the remarks of Girolamo Soranzo in 1611.

[27] On the tendency of blasphemy to provoke the wrath of God against the city and its subject peoples, see the preamble of the decree of the Council of Ten on 30 Dec. 1523, and that of the Ten's decree against blaspheming on ships, 28 March 1553, E.B., b. 54, Capitolare, fol. 1, 6.

the wrath of God upon the state,[28] which could, like a private individual, acquire both merit and disfavour. Five years later, he had good reason to return to the theme:

> Private persons examine their consciences and seek to placate the Lord God when they are admonished by his scourges. This Republic should do the same. Well knowing that it is really God and not the Turk who is making war upon us, they should carefully reflect upon the question, 'Why should the Majesty of God think itself offended by this state?'[29]

And a denunciation addressed to the Inquisition in April 1572 observed trenchantly:

> No wonder the Turk cuts deeply into Christendom, for the true worship of God is trodden underfoot and driven forth from the city of Udine, and many families have begun to live as Huguenots . . .[30]

As offences, indeed as acts of treason towards God, heretical beliefs were evil in themselves, even if the perpetrator could not be convicted of subversive acts; and in the shape of the Turk, God had an instrument of vengeance ready to hand. Venice's mission, to serve as the shield and buckler of Christendom against the infidel, could only be performed if it were itself in a state of high moral and religious purity. In a less tense atmosphere, some years later, Nuncio Matteucci, arguing the contentious case of the Jew Nemias of Ferrara, strove to impress upon the Venetians that the extraordinary longevity of their state was tied to their impeccable Catholicism, which was, however, constantly under threat from

> the great number of suspect persons from Germany, France, Flanders and England, from the Fondaco dei Tedeschi and from others, as well as from the Turks, Jews and Marranos. For the preservation of this city is truly a miracle of God. It surpasses every other commonwealth in the world, chiefly in being born, bred and maintained Christian. I most humbly drew attention to the responsibility of the Doge and state for supporting the tribunal of the Holy Office, for they have before them examples of the swift ruin of provinces and kingdoms from changes in the Christian religion and failure to observe it.[31]

[28] N.V., VIII, pp. 82–3, 27 July 1566.
[29] N.V., X, p. 81, 29 Aug. 1571.
[30] Battistella, *Il Santo Officio . . . in Friuli*, doc. VII, pp. 121–2.
[31] From his letter to the Cardinal of Santa Severina, 2 July 1588, in D.N., filza 26.

None the less, in the last quarter of the sixteenth century, the attitudes of ecclesiastical and lay authorities towards heresy showed signs of diverging, especially on such matters as the toleration to be extended to foreign heretics entering the Venetian state for the sake of trade or travel or study. As Professor Grendler has suggested, the serious political menace of Protestant heresy now seemed to have been removed,[32] and since the peace with Ottoman Turkey the heresy of crypto-Judaism seemed less dangerous. Content to secure the economic services of foreign communities, the Republic practised a degree of toleration which amounted to granting liberty of conscience to foreigners who caused no scandal by proselytizing to their faith or by showing open disrespect for Catholic dietary laws, images or places of worship. Venice seemed confident of its ability to contain foreign heterodoxy or infidelity and to prevent them from infecting the host population. It was the unenviable task of the nuncio Bolognetti to persuade the government that true reason of state could never point in the direction of such toleration; however superficially attractive the economic arguments that might be urged in its favour, heresy would always threaten the good order of the community, and foreign heretics could never fail to cause scandal.[33] But Protestants in Venice at this time were for the most part heretics born into heresy: they were not dissenters who had made conscious decisions to adopt a new faith, but rather persons who had conformed willingly to the official religion of their own country, and they did not represent the free-thinkers and nonconformists whom the government had most reason to fear. And Venetian policy was prepared, by 1589, to go much further, and to grant toleration even to Portuguese or Spaniards of Jewish descent who had once been Christians, but had retreated into Judaism.[34]

More seriously, events in France and later in Italy suggested that militant Catholicism – the ultra-Catholicism ascribed to the Catholic League, to certain Jesuits, to the Spanish monarchy and its allies abroad – might develop into a threat to the state's cohesion at least as powerful as Protestant heresy. For its conciliatory acts towards Protestant rulers, nations or factions, and for its anxiety to defend its own jurisdiction against a legalistic and inflexible Papacy, the Republic might itself be charged with heresy and its defenders be arraigned before the Holy Office. An early sign of the state's sensitivity on the point was the case of Fra Alberto da Lugo, Inquisitor in Verona in 1591. He was accused of having 'laid charges against our Republic' by collecting evidence from low and despicable persons concerning cavalry said to have been despatched, with the Venetian government's aid and consent, to the service

[32] Grendler, *Roman Inquisition* ... , pp. 208–9, 292.
[33] Stella–Bolognetti, pp. 282–3.
[34] See below, pp. 187 ff.

of Henry of Navarre, the still-heretical claimant to the throne of France. Arrested and brought in disgrace to Venice, the Inquisitor was threatened for a few days with ignominious expulsion from the state.[35] This incident provided one among many debating points in polemical literature written after the interdict in 1606–7.[36]

During its conflict with Paul V in those years, the Republic sought to retain its subjects' obedience by insisting that its quarrel was purely juris-dictional. But the fear that schism might develop into heresy, that the Pope by his intransigence might be 'founding twenty Genevas in Italy', was undoubtedly helpful to reaching a settlement;[37] and in the aftermath of the interdict the schemes of the English ambassador Wotton and his circle for impressing on the Venetians the political benefits of the Anglican Church, were not wholly far-fetched.[38] Despite the unshakable caution of the patriciate, the government's antipathy towards Protestant heresy was none too clear. After the settlement the theologians who had defended the Republic's cause were highly vulnerable, and had strong moral claims to the protection of the state. The Pope instructed the nuncio Gessi to ensure that 'Fra Paolo of the Servites, . . . Giovanni Marsiglio' and the other 'seducers who pass for theologians . . . shall be abandoned by the Republic, deprived of their stipends, and handed over to the Holy Office.' Not less than three of them, Ribetti, Manfredi and Cappello, became entangled with the Inquisition in Rome, though only those who had gone to Rome to exculpate themselves actually suffered penalties at its hands.[39] A Vatican manuscript, compiled in 1625, sug-gested that after the interdict the Venetians began to exercise much closer vigilance over the Inquisition, 'fearing the punishment of many who had unjustly taken the Republic's side and had thus fallen into the gravest of errors, and even into heresy itself'.[40] The long spell of uneasy relations, which culminated in serious disputes over the appointment of the Inquisi-tor and in renewed efforts by the Venetian government to return the post

[35] S.D.R.O., reg. 8, fol. 82v.–86r., 91r.–v., 93r.–v., 98, 99, 2 March to 13 April 1591; Grendler, *Roman Inquisition* . . . , pp. 216–18.

[36] Sarpi, 'Inquisizione', pp. 123, 161; B.A.V., MS Barberino Latino 5195, fol. 16v.–17; Albizzi, *Risposta* . . . , pp. 147–50.

[37] Cf. the letter of Cardinal du Perron Davy to Henry IV, 5 April 1607, in P. Pirri, ed., *L'Interdetto di Venezia del 1606 e i Gesuiti: silloge di documenti con introduzione* (Rome, 1959), p. 349.

[38] Cf. the letters of William Bedell to Adam Newton from Venice, 1 Jan. 1608, 1 Jan. 1609, printed as Letters V and VI in E. S. Shuckburgh, ed., *Two biographies of William Bedell, Bishop of Kilmore* (Cambridge, 1902), pp. 226–251; L. P. Smith, *The life and letters of Sir Henry Wotton* (2 vols., Oxford, 1907), I, p. 87 ff.

[39] See G. Benzoni, 'I "teologi" minori dell' Interdetto', *Archivio Veneto*, serie v, vol. 91 (1970), pp. 47–8, 56–9, 67–78, 88–89; also Sarpi, *Lettere ai protestanti*, I, pp. 65–6; II, pp. 82, 130–2; Shuckburgh, *Two biographies* . . . , pp. 246–7.

[40] B.A.V., MS Barberino Latino 5195, fol. 1v.

to the hands of its own subjects, extended well into the 1620s; after about 1625, the tension probably relaxed, following the deaths of most of the theologians or jurisconsults formerly involved in the defence of the state against the censures of Paul V.

However unorthodox the sentiments he confided to his private note-books,[41] however willing he may have been to correspond and converse with Protestants, Sarpi still stressed in his official statements the state's obligation to control heresy. He argued, indeed, that the magistrate must have a stake in the Holy Office precisely because of the importance of orthodoxy to public order.

> Inquisitors must strive to keep the people free of heresy for the service of God alone; the magistrate must do so both for the service of God and for the sake of good government.[42]

But he departed from convention in treating the Inquisition itself as a threat to public order scarcely less menacing than Protestant heresy and equally prone to introduce *novità*. Some inquisitors had disrupted peace and order by high-handed and oppressive conduct towards the subject, others by presuming to censure governments or aristocracies.[43] In his opinion the state must provide the *via media*, the conservative force determined to maintain the Catholic faith where the Roman appetite for power would pervert and corrupt it.

> Like other Catholic states, the Venetian Republic is placed between two opposing forces: the Protestants, who seek only to reduce the authority of the Church, and the Roman curia, which strives only to increase it and to enslave the temporal power. Hence Catholic realms and states must, to preserve themselves, oppose any innovation on either hand and maintain the Catholic faith unimpaired, for we see clearly by experience that either novelty is deeply harmful. The veneration we rightly owe to the Christian religion is the reason why abuses can so easily creep in under cover of that sacred cloak. For the protection of the faith we respect the Holy Office against heresy; and hence, when Rome seeks to introduce some novelty, it readily resorts to that office, in the belief that its true purpose will not appear.[44]

---

[41] On the nature of Sarpi's personal opinions, see the forthcoming book by D. Wootton, *Paolo Sarpi, atheism and the social order: a case study in early modern irreligion.*

[42] Sarpi, 'Inquisizione', pp. 149–50.

[43] Ibid., pp. 123, 148–9, 161; for Albizzi's rejoinder, *Risposta* ..., pp. 86–8, 147–50.

[44] Sarpi, 'Inquisizione,' p. 188.

Sarpi's was an express rationalization of a policy of fostering the Inquisition as an important instrument of public order, but at the same time scrutinizing it closely lest it become disruptive in itself. In his own time, the emphasis fell more heavily upon the restraint, rather than the encouragement, of the Inquisition. But the position was not a constant one, and varied by the decade in response to a broad political and economic situation. Venice's Inquisition was founded in about equal measure upon the state's need for legitimation by the Catholic faith and on the Church's need for sanctions which would secure the repression of heresy; the two powers entertained overlapping but ultimately distinguishable concepts of right order in the world, and the constitution of the Inquisition itself was designed to reconcile them. Where Jews were concerned, the Inquisition was no menace to public order, but it could inadvertently threaten the economic interests of the Venetian state.

3

Venetian and Roman Elements
in the Inquisition

In all probability, the mixed constitution of the revived Inquisition of the 1540s was designed to lock together three authorities which could easily have become rivals or failed to co-ordinate their efforts to put down heresy. Central authority within the Church was represented by the nuncio and the Inquisitor, and by their respective deputies, the auditor and the *commissario*. The authority of the diocese was upheld by the Patriarch of Venice or his vicar-general. The interests and power of the state were guarded by the three noblemen known either as the *Tre Savii sopra l'Eresia* or (more modestly) as the *Assistenti*.

At the time of Della Casa's appointment in 1544, the Venetian government feared that the judicial powers wielded by a papal legate and his authority over heresy might begin to compete with those of the ordinaries – of the bishops who had jurisdiction of their own right, and not by special deputation, in ecclesiastical cases. Such misgivings were not unreasonable; in the past sixty years the Spanish Inquisition had threatened to supplant the authority of the bishops in the matter of heresy.[1] Within the next three years the Neapolitans would strive to defend the authority of the ordinary – which they associated with fair and 'ordinary' procedures – against the intrusion of an alien Inquisition into the Viceroyalty.[2] As though well aware of the issue, the Council of Ten instructed its ambassador in Rome to plead – in vain, as it happened – that the nuncio should be granted only the powers of a normal diplomat representing a head of state, without the judicial authority of a legate.[3] Armed

---

[1] See H. C. Lea, *A history of the Inquisition of Spain* (4 vols., New York, 1906), II, pp. 5–18.
[2] Amabile, *Il Santo Officio ... in Napoli*, I, pp. 198–9.
[3] Sforza, 'Riflessi ...', I, pp. 19–29.

none the less with this authority, Della Casa feared that the Venetians might counter by establishing their own state tribunal to judge heretics. Good in itself, the move could seriously trespass upon the jurisdiction of the Church.[4] Fusion of the three authorities in April 1547 offered a practical solution to the problem, and the legate-nuncio became far more closely associated with the Inquisition than did his colleagues in Naples or Bologna or, for that matter, in Spain.[5] It was his presence, above all, that made the Inquisition in Venice a Roman tribunal.

Corresponding both with the Cardinal Secretary of State and with the president of the Congregation of Cardinal Inquisitors-General, the nuncio had ultimate responsibility under Rome for all tribunals of the Inquisition within the Venetian dominions. It was his duty to intercede with the Doge, in the presence of the Collegio, on behalf of any which got into difficulties. Beccadelli was granted in 1550 a commission of the supreme tribunal of the Inquisition over and above his authority as legate, since he was 'head of all our other commissaries' in the Venetian state.[6] Years later, the Procurator Donà observed in the Collegio that the Holy Office in Venice 'acts with the authority of His Holiness himself, because his most illustrious nuncio is present at its judgments and joins with the other members of the holy tribunal.'[7] Certain nuncios displayed a special interest in the affairs of the Inquisition that went far beyond the call of duty, as witness Castagna's decision, circa 1575, to sponsor a new edition of a Spanish inquisitor's handbook, the *Repertorium Inquisitorum*.[8]

Since high-level negotiation and questions of policy were his special responsibilities, the nuncio was not always a diligent attender of trials, and in the first decade or so he did not invariably sign the sentences, which could be left to his auditor-general.[9] Auditors were important servants, providing a much needed element of continuity, for they sometimes outlasted several nuncios – as did Rocco Cataneo, canon of Pola, who was serving Beccadelli and Archinto in the 1550s and was still being reappointed in 1561, to assist the Bishop of Fano.[10] The auditor Anteo Claudi wrote in 1590 of the departing nuncio that 'he has left to me, as

---

[4] Ibid., I, pp. 194–5.

[5] Battistella, *Il Santo Officio ... in Bologna*, pp. 50–3, 71–2; cf. Amabile, *Il Santo Officio ... in Napoli*, I, pp. 221, 225–6; Lea, *Inquisition of Spain*, I, p. 322.

[6] N.V., V, pp. 130–1, 137–8.

[7] Proceedings in the Collegio in the case of Giordano Bruno, 22 Dec. 1592, among the documents in V. Spampanato, *Vita di Giordano Bruno, con documenti editi e inediti* (2 vols., Messina, 1921), II, p. 757.

[8] See above, pp. 19–20.

[9] Cf. Sforza, 'Riflessi ...', I, pp. 214–15; N.V., V, pp. 125, 199, 279, 14 Sept. 1550, 16 Jan., 5 Sept. 1551; I.Z., pp. 75–7, 90–1, 139–43, 218–20, 244–6. In 1560 the nuncio Ferreri signed the resolution to release Giovanni Battista Moretto – ibid., pp. 334–5.

[10] D.N., filza 2, fol. 8, 32r.–v., 13 March, 13 Dec. 1561.

his auditor, the responsibility for ordinary cases' both in the Holy Office
and in the nuncio's own tribunal, which had much to do with judging
disputes among the regular clergy.[11] But the nuncios' practice of dele-
gating did not prevent their taking a personal interest in particular
accused or forming decided opinions concerning their guilt. Facchinetti
claimed personal credit for having had the case of Enriques Nuñes,
accused of apostatizing to the Jewish faith, transferred from the Council
of Ten to the Holy Office, and he acted as his own detective, in seeking
information from Florence and Ferrara, and in writing to the Cardinal-
Bishop of Pisa.[12] In the contentious case of Nemias in 1588, the nuncio
expressed a personal conviction to the Collegio: 'I am sure that he is a
Marrano, and I have been assured of this by certain Ferrarese with whom
I am friendly because I lived in Ferrara as a young man.'[13]

Techniques and attitudes adopted by the nuncio swung dramatically in
the first twenty years of the rejuvenated Inquisition from the cautious,
even deferential, approach adopted by Della Casa and Beccadelli to the
assertiveness of Facchinetti. The earlier nuncios were obviously wary of
prejudicing the future of the Inquisition by offending its host state.[14]
Confident of its retention, Facchinetti plainly believed that he could
threaten the Republic by alluding darkly to probable losses of ecclesiastical patronage if it failed to co-operate with the Pope.[15] During his seven-
year tenure of office, from 1566 to 1573, he pressed for the public
execution of relapsed and pertinacious heretics;[16] he recovered the right
of the Inquisition to sentence guilty men to strenuous service on board the
dreaded penal galleys;[17] he succeeded in procuring the extradition of one
prisoner, Guido da Fano, for trial in Rome;[18] and he asserted his right to
send friars and other religious for trial in that city without consulting the
Assistenti or any representative of the Venetian state.[19] He agitated effectively for strict control of imported books, including works of law, literature and history printed in Germany or France. In principle he favoured
the expulsion, or at least the very strict control, of the German community focused on the Fondaco de' Tedeschi, though resigning himself pri-

[11] Ibid., filza 28, fol. 262, 6 Jan. 1590; on the nuncio's own court, ibid., filza 27, fol. 291,
7 Sept. 1591.
[12] N.V., X, pp. 60–1, 14–18 July 1571.
[13] C.E.R., reg. 4, fol. 21, 28 June 1588; D.N., filza 26, fol. 268, 2 July 1588.
[14] Sforza, 'Riflessi ...', I, p. 212; N.V., V, p. 122, 13 Sept. 1550.
[15] N.V., VIII, pp. 77–80.
[16] N.V., VIII, pp. 119, 166–7, 363–4; IX, p. 88, 12 Oct. 1566 to 6 July 1569.
[17] N.V., VIII, p. 455, 4 Nov. 1568; cf. Battistella, Il Santo Officio ... in Friuli, p. 66.
[18] N.V., VIII, various entries from p. 75 to p. 96, 20 July to 24 August 1566.
[19] N.V., VIII, pp. 226–7, 233–4, 238, 245, 249, 7 June to 19 July 1567.

vately to the belief that Venetian commercial interests would surely frustrate any such drastic moves.[20]

After Facchinetti, the nuncios became less aggressive. Advocacy of the Inquisition's interests, generally couched in suitably diplomatic language, was accompanied by a realistic acknowledgment in their correspondence that there were some things to which the Venetian state would never give its consent.[21] The accent now fell upon maintaining respect for the Holy Office, rather than on seeking to increase its severity or extend its concerns. In disputed cases, such as those of Giacomo Castelvetro in 1611, or the Diaz in 1621, or Fulgenzio Camaldolese in 1622, the nuncio and his auditor were noticeably firmer than other members of the tribunal in their championship of the Roman standpoint.[22] Over Castelvetro and his release by the *Assistenti* 'the Nuncio and his crewe of Inquisitors did storme very much' – thus Sir Dudley Carleton, the triumphant English ambassador.[23] In fact the Inquisitor, like the Patriarch, proved far readier than the nuncio to accept the government's solution.[24]

While the nuncio's special concern was to represent the interests of the Holy Office to the world outside it, the Inquisitor was chiefly responsible for the diagnosis of heresy, the conduct of trials, and the censorship of books and of manuscripts destined for publication. At first the office rested in the hands of the Franciscan Conventuals, although in 1550 attempts were made to increase the tribunal's ardour by sending in a second wave of commissars recruited from the Dominican order. One of these, Fra Giulio da Brescia, bore the title of Inquisitor-General and was reluctantly and briefly attached by Beccadelli to the Holy Office in Venice.[25] Permanent transfer of the post to the Dominicans came about in 1560, partly in consequence of the intrigues of fellow Franciscans against Fra Felice Peretti da Montalto, a zealous inquisitor also unpopular with the government. The convent of the Frari in Venice, whose Guardian had been involved in the affair, may well have seemed too unstable, too deeply riven by jealousies and *persecuzioni fratesche*, to perform the tasks laid upon it. Pius IV fulfilled his promise to send another inquisitor, 'but not of those friars who are now in Venice', and the

[20] N.V., X, p. 222, 21 June 1572.

[21] Cf. for example the study of Berlinghiero Gessi, nuncio from 1607 to 1618, in P. Savio, 'Il nunzio a Venezia dopo l'Interdetto', *Archivio Veneto*, serie V, vol. 56 (1955), pp. 55–110.

[22] For Castelvetro, see K. T. Butler, 'Giacomo Castelvetro, 1546–1616', *Italian Studies*, 5 (1950), pp. 1–42; for the Diaz, S.U., b. 77, and C.E.R., reg. 19, fol. 52–3, 23 July 1621; for Fulgenzio Camaldolese, ibid., reg. 20, fol. 28v., 31, 32, 14, 23 July 1622.

[23] Butler, 'Castelvetro ...', pp. 29–30.

[24] H. F. Brown, ed., *Calendar of state papers and manuscripts Venetian*, XII (London, 1905), docs. 331 and 343, pp. 210–11, 219–20, 13 Sept., 1 Oct. 1611.

[25] N.V., V, pp. 122, 125, 160 ff., 198, from 13 Sept. 1550 to 16 Jan. 1551; N.V., VI, pp. 57–9, 27 Feb. 1552.

Dominicans moved into the Venetian tribunal[26] – although several of the diocesan inquisitions on the mainland rested in Franciscan hands.[27]

An inquisitor should be no less than forty years of age. Such was the view of Nicolau Eymeric, the fourteenth-century Aragonese inquisitor whose manual or *Directorium* was republished at Rome as a standard guide in 1578, equipped with scholarly apparatus and with massive notes by the canonist Peña. The status of an inquisitor was that of a judge delegate of the Pope, a specialist in the realm of heresy, 'because he has no jurisdiction, over persons or over crimes or over cases, save in so far as our lord Pope confers it upon him'.[28] His duties demanded that he be qualified first and foremost as a theologian, rather than be learned in canon law; Peña would have preferred qualifications in both disciplines, but conceded that it was the general practice for Italian inquisitors to be trained in theology alone.[29] Not all candidates for the post in Venice met all these requirements; Felice Peretti was only thirty-five at the time of his appointment in 1557, although his personal library did come to include law books as well as theological works. Nor, before coming to Venice, had he acquired experience as an inquisitor; his rapid promotion seems to have been due to his reputation as a preacher and to his acquaintance with Michele Ghislieri, the Commissary-General of the Holy Office in Rome.[30]

But in the maturer years of the institution Venice was recognized as a late and honourable stage in the career of an inquisitor who ought to have proved himself elsewhere. A regular pattern of professional promotion, if not a *cursus honorum*, began to be established. The careers of Venetian inquisitors came roughly to resemble those in at least one other major Italian city, Bologna, for they often began with an assistant–inquisitorship in some modest provincial town and culminated in promotion to a minor bishopric.[31] Side-stepping from one major post to another was sometimes possible; Giovanni Battista da Milano had served

[26] See Cugnoni, 'Documenti chigiani ...', pp. 300–3; L. von Pastor, *The history of the Popes from the close of the Middle Ages*, XXI, ed. R. F. Kerr (London, 1932), pp. 29–34; Sforza, 'Riflessi ...', I, pp. 190–1; Paschini, *Venezia e l'Inquisizione romana ...*, pp. 126–32; Grendler, *Roman Inquisition ...*, p. 115 ff.

[27] Battistella, *Il Santo Officio ... in Friuli*, pp. 44–5, 65; De Biasio, 'Aquileia e Concordia', p. 86; Grendler, *Roman Inquisition ...*, p. 48, n. 70.

[28] N. Eymeric, *Directorium Inquisitorum, cum scholiis seu annotationibus eruditissimis D. Francisci Pegnae Hispani, S. Theologiae et Iuris Utriusque Doctoris* (Rome, 1578): Eymeric, p. 348 (the main text and the commentaries are paginated separately, and will henceforth be cited as Eymeric and Peña). See also the useful abridged French translation, *Le manuel des inquisiteurs*, ed. L. Sala–Molins (Paris–The Hague, 1973), with an extensive introduction.

[29] Peña, p. 194.

[30] Pastor, *History of the Popes ...*, XXI, pp. 24–5, 29–31, 32–3, 36.

[31] Battistella, *Il Santo Officio ... in Bologna*, pp. 42–3.

as Inquisitor in Milan itself before his translation to Venice in 1578, and his successor, Angelo Mirabino of Faenza, was very likely the 'Angelo Marabini' of Faenza who had served as Inquisitor of Bologna from 1574 to 1578.[32] When the appointment of inquisitors became in the 1620s matter for acrimonious debate the nuncio would occasionally describe the careers of promising candidates. Giovanni Lodovico Sechiario, a native of Ravenna or nearby, was for several years deputy or vicar to the Inquisitors in Rimini and later in Ferrara; for six years he was *commissario* or assistant to his countryman, Giovanni Domenico Vignuzio, Inquisitor of Venice, and on Vignuzio's death in 1622 he was unavailingly backed by the nuncio to succeed him. Commending Sechiario, the nuncio pointed out that he was over forty years of age and a Doctor of Theology – as though to demonstrate that he met the requirements laid down in Eymeric–Peña.[33] Paolo Canevari da Gabbiano, Inquisitor in Venice in 1623, had previously served in Faenza.[34] Silvestro Ugoletti da Castiglione made his career entirely within the Venetian dominions. Professed in Brescia, where he had studied, he was for six years vicar or deputy to the Inquisition in Bergamo, and then succeeded to the inquisitorship in that city for a further eight. Another eight were spent as Inquisitor of Verona, before the Papacy chose to press him, as a candidate of twenty-two years' experience, for the inquisitorship in Venice.[35] The position of deputy inquisitor, whether called vicar or *commissario*, was sometimes regarded as a stepping-stone to promotion in the same city; the *commissario* in Venice in the 1620s would be considered for the job when a vacancy occurred, although his chances of actually obtaining it were not robust.[36] It seems reasonably certain that by the late sixteenth and the early seventeenth centuries the Inquisitor's chair in Venice was usually occupied by highly experienced professional judges, guided – if they chose to consult Eymeric's authoritative manual or the slimmer works that derived from it – by a very elaborate corpus of procedural rules.

Should an inquisitor bear himself discreetly and prove conciliatory towards the state, he might – if he were a Venetian subject – expect the Republic within a few years to intercede with the curia and try to get him

---

[32] Ibid., p. 200; Cecchetti, *Republica di Venezia* ..., II, pp. 10–11.

[33] D.N., filza 42H, fol. 247v.–248v., 27 Aug. 1622.

[34] C.E.R., reg. 21, fol. 8v.–9, 22 March 1624.

[35] C.E.R., reg. 20, fol. 176v.–177, 23 Feb. 1623 Venetian style; reg. 21, fol. 10r.–v., 15v.–16, 29 March, 12 April 1624; Zanelli, 'Controversie ...', p. 216.

[36] For the case of Commissario Francesco Guiotti, Zanelli, 'Controversie ...', pp. 198–204. Among the compromising papers removed from the Holy Office in Venice by Guiotti was, it seems, a letter from Cardinal Mellini to the late Inquisitor, exhorting him to choose a *commissario* from the Papal States who could then succeed him.

a bishopric.[37] In 1552 an important patrician said of a Franciscan inquisitor, Fra Marino da Venezia, that 'it had been said several times that he would earn himself a bishopric.'[38] It was true that no such person would ever be preferred to any of those lucrative mainland sees, such as Padua, Aquileia or Vicenza, which were monopolized by Venetian noblemen and sometimes held for several generations by dynasties of patrician churchmen.[39] But for an ambitious man without distinguished antecedents a see such as Capodistria, Chioggia or Sebenico was not to be despised. Chioggia was deemed especially useful for this purpose; the nuncio wrote in 1596 that

> the see is a modest one, not worth more than five or six hundred crowns, and it has for the most part served as an honourable reward for inquisitors. The present bishop is a Franciscan and was formerly Inquisitor of Padua.[40]

The current Inquisitor of Venice, Vincenzo Arrigoni of Brescia, was considered for this bishopric after less than two years' service when the incumbent bishop was thought to be dying; in fact he recovered, and Arrigoni succeeded to Sebenico in 1599.[41] These tactics on the part of the Ten or the Senate were not merely a form of crude patronage politics designed to hold out rewards to the flexible. They were probably also intended to guarantee a reasonably brisk turnover in office, allowing no inquisitor, even if he were a subject, to entrench himself too deeply or to acquire the self-confidence bred of many years in the same place. Between 1560 and 1600, ten inquisitors served in Venice, and the average tenure of four years was noticeably shorter than the six years generally served over that period both in Friuli and in Bologna. After a mere three years, Felice Peretti was accused of staying in office too long. In Venice the pattern was decisively broken by the prolonged reign of Vignuzio of Ravenna from 1600 to 1622; the Papacy was probably reluctant to move him for

[37] See Cecchetti, *Republica di Venezia* ... , II, pp. 10–11; Grendler, *Roman Inquisition* ... , pp. 48–9.

[38] N.V., VI, p. 72, 19 March 1552; on Fra Marino, cf. also P. Grendler, 'The *Tre Savii sopra Eresia*, 1547–1605: a prosopographical study', *Studi Veneziani*, nuova serie, 3 (1979), p. 303, n. 28.

[39] On these, see B. Pullan, 'Service to the Venetian state: aspects of myth and reality in the early seventeenth century', *Studi Secenteschi*, 5 (1964), pp. 125–34.

[40] D.N., filza 32, fol. 352r.–v., 21 Sept. 1596. See also N.V., IX, pp. 51, 103, 27 April, 3 Aug. 1569, where the Inquisitor Valerio Faenzi is considered for the see of Chioggia, and H.C. III, pp. 170–1, which shows that the former Venetian Inquisitor Marco Medici of Verona was Bishop of Chioggia from 1578 to 1583. Massimiliano Benjamini of Crema, formerly Inquisitor in Padua, was Bishop of Chioggia from 1585 to 1601.

[41] D.N., filza 33, 19 Sept. 1598; filza 42H, fol. 250r.–v., 3 Sept. 1622; H.C., III, p. 299.

fear of provoking, in the post-interdict years, controversy over the succession. After the swift rotation of office which accompanied the disputes between the Venetian government and the Papacy in 1622–24, there was a move towards significantly longer spells in the inquisitorial chair, when service for periods of seven or eight years became the rule. This was probably a reflexion of the declining political importance of the Inquisition, combined with the renewed success of the Venetian Republic in obtaining as inquisitors natives of its own provinces whom it was now less eager to have moved: from 1639 to 1670, all inquisitors in Venice were of Brescian origin.[42]

From 1560 onwards, the Dominican Inquisitors to Venice were generally appointed by apostolic brief; in theory at least they were direct representatives of Roman authority on Venetian soil, though the Venetian government tried to allay misgivings by urging the appointment of Venetian subjects. Describing the developed system in 1624, the nuncio explained to the Collegio that inquisitors were chosen by the Congregation of Cardinal Inquisitors-General in Rome and then subjected to confirmation by the Pope.[43] But the Ten, Senate and Collegio could influence the appointment both positively and negatively: positively, by making representations to the Pope through the ambassador in Rome, and negatively, by delaying the formal grant to the Inquisitor by the Doge in the Collegio of permission to carry out his duties.[44] On occasion they could suspend inquisitors and demand their replacement, though they stopped short of deposing them on the authority of the state alone.

Venetian resistance to foreign inquisitors was one symptom of a general reluctance to allow alien clergy to hold positions of authority.[45] Felice Peretti was an early victim of the suspicion that attached to them. There were others. Between 1560 and 1578, as though by tacit agreement, the Dominican inquisitors were all Venetian subjects, natives of the great cities of the *Terra Ferma*. Then precedent was breached by the appoint-

---

[42] For lists of Dominican inquisitors in Venice, see S.U., b. 153; B.A.V., MS Vaticanus Latinus 10945, fol. 106r.–v.; Cecchetti, *Republica di Venezia* ..., II, pp. 10–11. Cf. also Battistella, *Il Santo Officio ... in Friuli*, pp. 126–8, and Battistella, *Il Santo Officio ... in Bologna*, pp. 198–200; Sforza, 'Riflessi ...', I, pp. 190–1. On Vignuzio, see also B.A.V., MS Barberino Latino 5195, fol. 17. See H.C., IV, p. 283, for the appointment of Ambrogio Fracassini of Brescia, Inquisitor in Venice from 1651 to 1663, to the bishopric of Pola in 1663.

[43] C.E.R., reg. 20, fol. 176v.–177, 23 Feb. 1623 Venetian style; D.N., filza 44, fol. 123–4, 24 Feb. 1624.

[44] Cf. C.E.R., reg. 20, fol. 86r.–v., 25 Feb. 1622 Venetian style; D.N., filza 42I, fol. 89r.–v., 25 Feb. 1623.

[45] For example, as heads of religious houses – see D.N., filza 37, fol. 151v.–152, 7 Sept. 1602, for an example. The parallel between inquisitors and religious superiors is expressly drawn by the nuncio in C.E.R., reg. 21, fol. 7v.–8, 15 March 1624.

ment of Giovanni Battista da Milano. According to the Venetians' own version, they protested to Rome and obtained assurances that the Inquisitor would be replaced within six months. When, in March 1581, the promise had still not been honoured, the Council of Ten made capital out of a mysterious incident between the Inquisitor and one of the lay deputies, accusing the friar of interfering in 'matters not appropriate to his office, but only to laymen' and also of using improper language to a representative of the state. It seems likely that he had shown Antonio Tiepolo, one of the *Assistenti*, a papal Bull which spoke in general terms of excommunication, telling Tiepolo that he 'wanted to show him what condition he was in' – possibly, though this was never made clear, on account of the lay deputies' failure to enforce some order of the Inquisition. Tiepolo, himself a member of the Ten, described the conversation to that council; to his dismay, they took it upon themselves to forbid the Inquisitor to attend the tribunal. Disclaiming any intention of dismissing him themselves, they still used their veto as a device to procure his removal by the Pope. The Inquisitor decided to lie low in his friary, lest he smirch the dignity of his office by becoming the subject of an open brawl, and the *commissario* took over his duties for perhaps three weeks.[46] Three months after the incident, the Papacy did in fact appoint a successor, but refused to give away the principle, and for the next forty years, with only a single exception, Venetian inquisitors were foreigners.

Arguments for the appointment of Venetian subjects as inquisitors were strongly urged in the early seventeenth century by Sarpi, his attitude apparently hardening over the nine years which separated his general treatise of 1613 from his *consulta* of 1622. At first he merely stressed the need to appoint persons well informed of local events, customs and conditions, and thus equipped to perform duties which called for exceptional qualities of 'charity and discretion'.[47] Later, he chose to emphasize the sinister power an inquisitor might choose to wield, not only over his fellow religious, but also, through his instructions to confessors, over the world at large. It was essential that such authority – if, in the absence of any serious danger from manifest heresy, it needed to exist at all – should rest in the hands of a Venetian subject.[48] Curialists, from the ex-nuncio Gessi to Sarpi's opponent Albizzi, believed that such a person would be too easily manipulated by Venetian interests, would become a respecter of persons and of social rank, and would never have the courage to resist the

[46] D.N., filza 22, fol. 99r.–v., 102r.–v., 11 March 1581; C.D., Parti, Roma, reg. 2, fol. 70, 70v., 71v., 72, 73, 8 March to 7 April 1581; A.S.V., Capi del Consiglio dei Dieci, Lettere degli ambasciatori da Roma, b. 27, letter from Giovanni Correr, 25 March 1581. Cf. also Grendler, ' *Tre Savii* ...', p. 311, n. 41.

[47] Sarpi, 'Inquisizione', pp. 122, 155.

[48] Sarpi, 'In materia di crear ...', pp. 1208–9.

Venetian authorities.[49] Such problems could only partly be solved by uneasy compromises such as that of 1624, when Urban VIII pressed on the Venetian state a candidate who was not actually a Venetian subject but had a Brescian mother, and had lived out his professional life in the Veneto.[50] By the 1630s, the office had passed once more into the hands of Venetian subjects.

In general, the Inquisition formed a vital part of the elaborate machinery for procuring compromise and regulating conflict which enabled Church and state, as two claimants to ultimate sovereignty, not only to coexist but actively to aid each other in matters of common concern. The conduct of the Inquisition in Venice was not one of the issues which provoked the interdict, though collisions of principle over the Inquisitor's appointment could arguably have provoked another showdown at about the time of Sarpi's death.[51] Within the tribunal, there was no simple alignment of clerics against lay deputies; the Inquisitor might be the nominee of Rome, but the state manoeuvred to attract him into its orbit and to discourage high-handed action on his part. Not surprisingly, Nuncio Zacchia, outlining the qualities of the ideal inquisitor in the 1620s, chose to demand not zeal but diplomatic skills. He should be a confidant of the Pope and the Holy See, and should not 'provoke the distrust of the Republic, for he would find it obstructive or suspicious of him in everything he tried to do. And, finally, he should be of such graceful and pleasing manners that he may perform the service of God without breaking with anyone, even in the midst of opposition and frustration, so far as in him lies.'[52]

Towards 1580, the canonist Peña reminded his readers:

There are two kinds of judges in matters of faith, the first being ordinaries, such as the Supreme Pontiff of Rome and the bishops of the various places, who receive power and jurisdiction over heretics by divine right when they are ordained or consecrated.[53]

Venetian actions in the 1540s were designed, as we have seen, to protect the jurisdiction of the ordinaries, and the decree of 1547 established the principle of the Patriarch's involvement in the affairs of the Holy Office. Early descriptions of the tribunal and early trial records suggest, however,

[49] Cozzi, in Sarpi, *Opere*, pp. 1198–200; Albizzi, *Risposta* ..., pp. 121–2.

[50] See above, n. 35, and Zanelli, 'Controversie ...', pp. 205–6, 223.

[51] Note, for example, Urban VIII's remark that 'The Republic, then, will seek to become a limb cut off from Holy Church' ('Dunque vorrà la Repubblica esser membro diviso da Santa Chiesa') – D.N., filza 44, fol. 58r.–v., 27 Jan. 1624.

[52] D.N., filza 42H, fol. 247v.–248v., 27 Aug. 1622.

[53] Peña, p. 194.

that the diocesan authorities were not actively involved in the Inquisition until the late 1550s – very likely on account of the long absence from the city of the Patriarch Querini, who died in 1554.[54]

Accounts of inquisitions have revealed bishops more ardent than inquisitors in the pursuit of heresy.[55] They have brought to light vicars such as Maracco of Friuli, who inspired the revival of the Inquisition in the dioceses of Aquileia and Concordia,[56] and vicars such as those of Naples who provided the barely concealed link between an ostensibly diocesan Inquisition and the Congregation of the Holy Office in Rome.[57] It seems unlikely that either the patriarchs of Venice or their vicars were inclined to play any such part, although there is no reason to doubt their piety. In the sixteenth and seventeenth centuries, the Patriarch of Venice, elected by the Senate, was invariably a Venetian patrician. His appointment was subject to confirmation by the Pope, who did not apply stringent criteria of his own; his most intrusive acts were to subject Zane and Vendramin, in the early seventeenth century, to interviews dangerously resembling examinations.[58] In the mid-sixteenth century the practice of electing laymen to the office was first tentatively tried, and by about 1600 lay candidates for the dignity – prepared to take holy orders on election – had come to outnumber clerical. Successful contenders at this time had gathered much of their experience in major embassies abroad, including those of Spain and Rome; they had had the opportunity to observe the workings of the Spanish Inquisition and to form some impression of its advantages and pitfalls; above all they had been imbued with the aristocratic tradition of service to the Venetian state.[59] A rather different career was followed by Giovanni Tiepolo, who served first in a number of minor magistracies, then took to the priesthood and became *Primicerio* of St

[54] Santosuosso, 'Religious orthodoxy ...', pp. 480–1; N.V., V, pp. 125, 279, 14 Sept. 1550, 5 Sept. 1551; A. Niero, *I Patriarchi di Venezia da Lorenzo Giustinian ai nostri giorni* (Venice, 1961), p. 87. Down to 1555 the sentences in trials involving Jews or Judaism are signed by the nuncio's auditor and the Franciscan Inquisitor alone (see above, n. 9); the vicar-general of the diocese was involved in the case of Gian Giacomo de' Fedeli – see I.Z., pp. 284, 296, 25 Aug., 19 Sept. 1558; in October 1560, the Patriarch joined the nuncio and the Inquisitor's deputy in ordering the release of Giovanni Battista Moretto – ibid., pp. 334–5.

[55] E.g. Jacques Fournier – see E. Le Roy Ladurie, *Montaillou. Cathars and Catholics in a French village, 1294–1324*, transl. B. Bray (London, 1978), p. xiii.

[56] Battistella, *Il Santo Officio ... in Friuli*, pp. 43–6 and doc. III, pp. 117–18.

[57] Amabile, *Il Santo Officio ... in Napoli*, I, pp. 213–15, 224–6, 264–7, 288, 297, 302; P. Villani, ed., *Nunziature di Napoli*, I (Rome, 1962), pp. 188, 326, 26 Feb. 1573, 13 May 1575.

[58] Niero, *I Patriarchi* ..., pp. 14–15, 108, 113–15; G. Benzoni, 'Una controversia tra Roma e Venezia all' inizio del' 600: la conferma del Patriarca', *Bollettino dell' Istituto di Storia della Società e dello Stato Veneziano*, 3 (1961), pp. 121–38. Cf. also Prodi, 'The structure ...', pp. 415–17.

[59] Niero, *I Patriarchi* ..., pp. 88–90, 100, 107, 110–12.

Mark's at the age of thirty-two in 1603; sixteen years later he became Patriarch.[60] Justifying its policies in 1600, the Senate declared: 'We have seen clearly from the past that those who have held secular appointments and offices, and have experience of worldly affairs, have proved to be better prelates than those recruited from libraries and bare monastic cells.'[61] However, after Tiepolo's death in 1631 it returned to recruiting its patriarchs from the great ecclesiastical dynasties of Cornaro and Morosini.[62]

In general, the patriarchs were willing enough to collaborate with the state, in matters concerning the Holy Office as in other affairs. This rule applied to monkish prelates, as well as to former ambassadors and magistrates. Giovanni Trevisan, a Benedictine, Patriarch from 1560 to 1590, was despised by the intransigent Carlo Borromeo as a mere state official incapable of giving independent leadership; he was said in 1580 to consult with the Doge and Signory about everything, and to employ as his secretary one of the secretaries of the Senate.[63] There is plainly a risk of exaggerating the complaisance of the patriarchs. Several of them – Priuli in 1596, Vendramin in 1615, Cornaro in 1626 while still Bishop of Bergamo – were sufficiently highly regarded by Rome to obtain cardinals' hats.[64] Priuli provoked complaint from the Signory in 1596 by telling the 'Heads of the Clergy' (Capi del Clero) in the Patriarchate to observe the controversial Clementine Index of Prohibited Books, and by doing so without a word to the Doge and Collegio, and without the presence of the Assistenti.[65] On the other hand, Giovanni Tiepolo in the 1620s was plainly regarded by those lay deputies as a safe collaborator: in the case of the Diaz, arrested for judaizing, Michele Priuli and the Cavalier Procurator Agostino Nani said of him that

> on account of his goodness, and because he is generally very well disposed to fall in with the state's wishes, we may hope that it will be easy to make him agree to whatever Your Serenity may judge expedient.[66]

And in an important case the following year the Doge and Collegio in

[60] Ibid., pp. 117–18.

[61] Quoted in Benzoni, 'Una controversia ...', p. 127.

[62] Niero, I Patriarchi ..., pp. 121–30.

[63] G. Soranzo, 'Rapporti di San Carlo Borromeo con la Repubblica Veneta', Archivio Veneto, serie V, vol. 27 (1940), pp. 23–5, 36–7; Prodi, 'The structure ...', pp. 416, 427.

[64] H.C., IV, pp. 4, 12, 20.

[65] D.N., filza 32, fol. 329v., 331r.–v., 17, 24 Aug. 1596; on this affair, see Grendler, Roman Inquisition ..., pp. 257–78, especially pp. 269–73.

[66] C.E.R., reg. 19, fol. 51, 16 July 1621.

fact relied, not only on the *Assistenti,* but also on the Patriarch to give them a frank account of what had occurred in the Congregation of the Holy Office; in its subsequent meeting, the Patriarch urged moderation, and mildly opposed the hard line taken by the nuncio's auditor.[67] Tiepolo consulted with the nuncio more, perhaps, than the Signory knew.[68] But in general the presence of the Patriarch or his vicar, if it did not constantly remind the tribunal of the state's interests, would at least make it sensitive to local custom.

Though plainly anxious to draw both the Patriarch and the Inquisitor into its sphere of influence, the state was not perpetually concerned with neutralizing or actively frustrating the Holy Office, and it made reciprocal concessions, especially in the conciliatory character of most appointments to the office of *Assistente* in the second half of the sixteenth century. The lay attachés were not merely a control or check on its activities, but a means of enhancing respect for its authority and providing it with sanctions. Indeed, the legislation of 1547 assigned the *Assistenti* an active rather than a cautionary role in the campaign against heresy: they should seek out heretics in the city, receive complaints or denunciations against them, urge the legate, Patriarch and Inquisitor to proceed wherever appropriate, attend trials and ensure that sentence was passed upon the guilty. Hints of a duty to impose controls on the Holy Office appeared only at the end of the decree, which obliged them to inform the Doge from time to time of their actions.[69] In the early years the nuncios themselves were happy to argue that the authority of the 'three gentlemen' was more feared than their own, and that they above all made the Inquisition formidable.[70] Thirty years after, during the debates on the apostolic visitation of 1580, Doge Nicolò da Ponte was to maintain that the association of lay deputies with any enterprise of the Church would help its execution, 'and on this matter the Prince said that when he was ambassador in Rome he had persuaded Pope Julius III of holy memory to agree that three noblemen be present at the tribunal of the Inquisition – for the same reason, that is, to help enforce its decisions.'[71]

In one respect the *Assistenti* were an emanation of the Doge's personal authority in matters concerning the Holy Office, of which da Ponte made the nuncio Bolognetti fully aware.[72] For the pursuit of heresy was a duty

[67] Ibid., reg. 20, fol. 22v.–24, 28v., 1, 14 July 1622.

[68] D.N., filza 42I, fol. 11v.–12v., 14 Jan. 1623.

[69] Albizzi, *Risposta* ..., pp. 42–3; Sforza, 'Riflessi ...', I, pp. 195–6.

[70] N.V., V, pp. 137–8, 4 Oct. 1550, 279–80, 5 Sept. 1551.

[71] D.N., filza 21, fol. 441, 10 Dec. 1580. On the visitation in general, see S. Tramontin, 'La visita apostolica del 1581 a Venezia', *Studi Veneziani*, 9 (1967), pp. 453–533.

[72] Stella–Bolognetti, p. 168 – 'in matters relating to the Holy Office the laws give to the Doge authority to do by himself alone things which he could not otherwise do without the

enjoined upon him by his coronation oath or ducal promise at least since 1249 (an oath, said Sarpi, to God and the Republic, not to the Inquisition).[73] And this obligation was partially fulfilled in the sixteenth century by the nomination of the *Assistenti*. Between 1547 and 1595, they were elected first by the ducal councillors and then by the Collegio, who would vote on candidates proposed by the Doge.[74] More specifically, the *Assistenti* were also said, at least up to the early 1580s, to represent the Council of Ten, of which, being elderly men of prolonged experience in high governmental office, they often were or had been members. In 1572, Righetto Marrano, arraigned before the tribunal, was sharply told that 'The *Signori Clarissimi Assistenti* are here present by the orders of the Most Excellent Council of Ten, and they represent that Council. . . .'[75] They marked the extension into the sphere of heresy of the Council's elastic commission to protect public safety and eliminate all treasonable acts; for similar reasons it had also, since 1537, been responsible through a weighty sub-committee for the punishment of blasphemers.[76] In 1579 two persons entangled with the Inquisition mentioned rumours that the Ten had blocked the prosecution of certain Portuguese immigrants accused of judaizing and had indeed 'made it a matter of state' (*cosa del stato*). But it was dismissed as unthinkable that the Ten should behave in such a way – 'no one could possibly believe this of such Catholic lords and such zealous defenders of the Christian religion.'[77]

In the middle and later sixteenth century, the *Assistenti* generally met the requirement that they be good Catholics, actively respectful towards the ecclesiastical hierarchy. Their age – a typical lay attaché would then be past sixty – doubtless made for caution. Notorious anticlericals, who might have made dialogue and compromise impossible, were seldom chosen before 1600.[78] Appointed *Assistente* in 1574, Giovanni Soranzo went out of his way to profess himself the devoted servant of the Cardinal

---

Senate or Council of Ten ...' Note also his remark on p. 288 about winning over the Doge in the Collegio to his ideas about a solemn public abjuration.

[73] Sarpi, 'Inquisizione', pp. 138–40, 152; cf. the Doge's reply to Facchinetti on 21 June 1572, N.V., X, pp. 221–2. For Albizzi's view of the Doge's authority, see his *Risposta* ..., pp. 24–5.

[74] Grendler, *Roman Inquisition* ..., pp. 44–8, 219–21, and (more fully) his '*Tre Savii* ...', pp. 285–6.

[75] S.U., b. 36, proc. Righetto, 29 May 1572. Also Stella–Bolognetti, p. 291, and Grendler, *Roman Inquisition* ..., p. 46.

[76] On the *Esecutori contro alla Bestemmia*, see below, pp. 79–80.

[77] S.U., b. 44, proc. Antonio Saldanha and others: interrogations of Saldanha and of Francisco Oglies, 1, 2, 16 Sept.; 28 Dec. 1579.

[78] For examples, see Grendler, *Roman Inquisition* ..., pp. 44–6; Grendler, '*Tre Savii* ...', pp. 289–90; 311–12, n. 41; 336, n. 95.

Secretary of State.[79] Nuncio Bolognetti said of the Procurator Grimani that he was 'most ardent in the service of the Apostolic See while in my time he was *Assistente* at our tribunal of the Inquisition'.[80] Antonio Tiepolo, *Assistente* in 1581, took pains to discuss with the nuncio not only the affairs of the Inquisition but also the difficulties arising between the Holy See and the state over the contentious apostolic visitation.[81] And the Procurator Federico Contarini seems to have become so vigorous a partisan of the Holy See that discovery of his bias might well have brought him to ruin.[82]

None the less the moderating, restraining role of the *Assistenti* was always noticeable in some degree, even from the early days. They were less than enthusiastic about some of the penalties the nuncios would have liked to see imposed on convicted persons.[83] They objected in 1567 to the imposition of public penance on a person of citizen rank, a professional man condemned to wear the penitential *habitello* outside the church of San Gimignano.[84] By 1580, Bolognetti was aware of their reluctance to execute orders for arrest or to act on information transmitted from abroad – even, perhaps especially, if the instructions and the intelligence came from the Congregation of Cardinal Inquisitors-General. The *Assistenti*, too, were liable to deny the Inquisition the use of its police force where arrests might 'impede the course of trade'.[85] On that occasion Bolognetti was referring to Protestant Grisons; the problem of Portuguese Marranos would soon prove no less intractable.

However, it was in the first quarter of the seventeenth century, and particularly in the 1620s, that the restrictive actions of the *Assistenti* became most apparent. From 1595, they had been appointed not by the Doge and Collegio, but rather by the Senate – on the grounds that ducal appointments produced mild and good men, but no one forceful enough to defend the jurisdiction of the laity.[86] There had been a marked increase in the number of individuals entitled to the state's protection against the Inquisition, from the Sephardic Jews who benefited from the

[79] N.V., XI, p. 130, 16 Jan. 1574.
[80] D.N., filza 21, 24 Sept. 1580.
[81] D.N., filza 22, fol. 35v., 28 Jan. 1581.
[82] D.N., filza 30, fol. 59r.–v., 27 Feb. 1593; filza 31, fol. 72v.–73, 24 May 1595; G. Cozzi, 'Federico Contarini: un antiquario veneziano tra Rinascimento e Controriforma', *Bollettino dell' Istituto di Storia della Società e dello Stato Veneziano*, 3 (1961), pp. 195–7; Grendler, *Roman Inquisition* . . . , pp. 220–1.
[83] Sforza, 'Riflessi . . .', I, pp. 211–12, 214–15.
[84] N.V., VIII, p. 217, 17 May 1567.
[85] Stella–Bolognetti, p. 292.
[86] G. Cozzi, *Il Doge Nicolò Contarini: ricerche sul patriziato veneziano agli inizi del Seicento* (Venice–Rome, 1958), p. 31; Grendler, *Roman Inquisition* . . . , p. 219; Grendler, '*Tre Savii* . . .', pp. 287–8.

privileges of 1589 and subsequent safe-conducts to the theologians who had upheld the state's cause during the interdict.[87] Sarpi had provided the *Assistenti* with an up-to-date book of rules,[88] which amounted to far more than the usual collection of legislation designed to instruct magistrates in the scope of their office, for it was accompanied by an exhortation to keep constant watch on the naturally expansive authority of the Inquisitor. As though fortified by this authority, the *Assistenti* reported diligently to the Collegio, released more than one prisoner of the Inquisition, and strove to deprive it of certain of its non-judicial functions.[89] Meanwhile the state campaigned with vigour for the appointment of a subject inquisitor, and allowed the ducal printer to put out the second volume of Andrea Morosini's official history, covering the interdict years, despite the Inquisitor's refusal to license it. There was no hope that the *Assistenti* would collaborate in any proceedings launched against printers, publishers or booksellers responsible for producing and distributing the work.[90] Stabler relations were, however, shortly afterwards restored – to judge, at least, by the paucity of references in Albizzi's 'Anti-Sarpi' to contentious issues arising after 1625 within the city of Venice itself. 'Throughout the nineteen long years I have been in Rome (1635–54) I have observed that the *Assistenti* in Venice have borne themselves with great discretion towards the Holy Tribunal. Would I could say the same of the governors of the Venetian state and of their officials'.[91] The defensive attitudes of the 1620s were not characteristic of the *Assistenti* in all decades; the Venetian patriciate was no phalanx of anticlericals, though it did, perhaps at all times, contain a loose collection of persons with little access to Church patronage and a deep suspicion of Rome, capable of forming, if not a regular political party, at least an intermittent pressure group.

Fundamental to the system in Venice was the principle that the *Assistenti* should be present at the examination of accused persons and witnesses, indeed throughout the whole judicial process except for the preliminary taking of information from delators.[92] They were not willing merely to execute orders issued to them by churchmen, or to put in an appearance only at the moment when sentences came under discussion. True, they were not supposed to be judges, even in the opinion of the state's most ardent defender. Sarpi maintained that laymen could quite

[87] See above, p. 23, and below, p. 187 ff.
[88] Sarpi, 'Inquisizione', pp. 130, 312. On the need for vigilance, see especially pp. 120–1, 148–9.
[89] See above, pp. 12–13.
[90] D.N., filza 42I, fol. 384v.–386,, 395r.–v., 21 Oct. 1623.
[91] Albizzi, *Risposta* ..., pp. 160–1; above, p. 16, n. 4.
[92] B.A.V., MS Barberino Latino 5195, fol. 8.

properly serve as judges of fact in matters of heresy: a clerical expert might be required in order to determine whether an opinion was or was not heretical, but a layman could decide whether or not the accused had held or uttered it.[93] However, he did not suggest that it was the business of the *Assistenti* in his own day to act as judges, and contented himself with arguing that when the clergy judged matters of fact they were exercising a power which had once belonged to the state and could be reclaimed.[94] On the other side, during the disputes of 1551, it had been recognized by Rome and its representatives that the *Assistenti* would in fact utter opinions on the cases before them, and that this was 'not wholly undesirable', so long as trials were conducted and sentences pronounced in the names of the ecclesiastical judges alone. *Assistenti* were said by Beccadelli to 'defer to' the auditor and inquisitor.[95] But the possibility of exerting strong informal influence on the trial was open to them.

The power of the *Assistenti* was most clearly manifested in their control over the arrest and custody of prisoners, which continued even after the Holy Office acquired prisons of its own, between about 1580 and 1590. Admittedly the nuncio could circumvent them when arresting members of religious orders and sending them for trial in Rome, so long as he used monasteries as places of confinement.[96] Otherwise there were few gaps in the state's defences. At first the *Assistenti* would, after evidence had been considered in the Congregation of the Inquisition, issue instructions by word of mouth to the constable of the Holy Office for the detention of a suspect. Soon after 1600, written warrants subscribed by at least two of the three *Assistenti* became necessary.[97] The ecclesiastical members of the tribunal were not permitted to form any independent police force or bodyguard.[98] The state would assign constables to the Holy Office, but they remained state employees controlled by the *Assistenti*.

It was in the discretion of the *Assistenti* to refuse the aid of the 'secular arm' on grounds of expediency, on the grounds that an accused person had been granted immunity by the state, or – and in this they were effectively acting as judges – on the grounds that the evidence presented was too flimsy to justify an arrest. Where privileges issued by the state to Sephardic Jews, collectively or individually, were in question, the

[93] Sarpi, 'Inquisizione', pp. 120, 130–9. But cf. Albizzi, *Risposta* ..., p. 108, rejecting the distinction: 'it is not enough that a man utter heretical words, which is the fact, unless it appears that he who puts them forward has done so knowing his error and obstinately persisting in his belief.'

[94] Sarpi, 'Inquisizione', p. 150.

[95] N.V., V, pp. 279–80, 5 Sept. 1551; Albizzi, *Risposta* ..., p. 53.

[96] N.V., VIII, pp. 234, 238 (21, 28 June 1567).

[97] B.A.V., MS Barberino 5195, fol. 62v.–63; MS Vaticanus Latinus 10945, fol. 39.

[98] See below, pp. 100–1.

Assistenti might (as in the cases of Simon Gomez in 1616 and of Jorge and Diogo Diaz in 1621) seek the advice of the Republic's official legal consultants, the *Consultori in Jure*.[99] In 1622, Fulgenzio Camaldolese was released from gaol (though not spared confinement in his own monastery) on the grounds that the case against him had proved too feeble to justify arrest. On this occasion the *Assistenti* Marc'Antonio Cornaro and Sebastiano Venier said 'that we did not want to discuss doctrine, for that was not our business. . . . We wished only to consider the defects of the case against him, and various occurrences in connexion with this affair.'[100]

Apart from the Congregation of the Holy Office there was another forum for debate, the Collegio, through which the *Assistenti* were responsible to the Ten or, in later years, to the Senate. As a nuncio once complained, in 1577, 'they want to hear in the Collegio cases belonging to the Inquisition, allowing the parties to argue before temporal lords. . . .'[101] Where some questionable arrest had been made, an aggrieved or interested party (other than the accused himself) could complain to the Collegio; should it take the matter up, the nuncio and the *Assistenti* would be likely to debate it in the Collegio's presence. Since this, in Sir Henry Wotton's words, was a place 'of distribution and not of determination of affairs',[102] it might then prove necessary to refer the matter for decision either to the Council of Ten or to the Senate. After the famous constitutional crisis of 1582–83, the responsibility for resolving matters concerning the Inquisition clearly shifted towards the Senate.[103] Alternatively, the *Assistenti*, although themselves quite capable of taking independent action, might report their misgivings about some particularly delicate case to the Collegio, in the hope of obtaining firm guidance from higher authority, or they might be summoned before the Collegio to give some account of their actions. The nuncio himself, having been apprised of the Republic's arguments, would often take instructions from Rome; he would sometimes end by formally expressing the Pope's dissatisfaction,

[99] C.J., filza 12, fol. 384r.–v., 386–7, 17–20 Dec. 1616; C.E.R., reg. 19, fol. 50v.–51, 16 July 1621. On the *Consultori*, see G. Maranini, *La costituzione di Venezia* (2 vols., Venice, 1927–31; reprint, Florence, 1974), II, pp. 352–3.

[100] Ibid., reg. 20, fol. 26–28v., 13–14 July 1622.

[101] D.N., filza 18, fol. 211v., 5 Oct. 1577.

[102] Wotton to Salisbury, 22 Feb. 1608, in Smith, *Life* . . . , I, p. 413. Cf. Maranini, *La costituzione* . . . , II, p. 345 ff.

[103] It was, for example, the Senate which issued a decree in the matter of Nemias (C.E.R., reg. 4, fol. 20, 28 June 1588); the Senate which resolved to hand over Giordano Burno to the nuncio 'to gratify the Pope' on 7 Jan. 1593 (Spampanato, *Vita di Giordano Bruno* . . . , II, pp. 761–2); the Senate which debated the case of Castelvetro and ordered his release in 1611 (Butler, 'Castelvetro . . .', pp. 26–9, and H. F. Brown, ed., *Calendar of state papers and manuscripts Venetian*, XII, doc. 327, p. 208, 10 Sept. 1611).

but would enjoy a certain comforting sense of having done all that he decently could. Some compromise could often be achieved. The nuncio would not release the Jew Nemias outright as the state requested in 1588, but he allowed him bail against his better judgment and despite unfortunate precedents; the state would not agree to the prosecution of Castelvetro in 1611 or the Diaz family in 1621, but it promptly expelled them from its dominions.[104]

The structure of the Holy Office put a premium on diplomatic skills. Conflict was regulated by providing a theatre for the formal discussion of delicate points and by observing, at least for substantial stretches of time, conventions such as the state's own obligation to appoint good Catholics as *Assistenti*. The composition of the tribunal was calculated to secure some moderation and a degree of sensitivity to political expediency and the economic interests of the commonwealth. It seems, in retrospect, a thing half Roman and half Venetian, born of the adaptation of a would-be universal institution to the specific conditions of a city state ruling two empires. Although in many respects the interests of Church and state coincided, and they acknowledged an equally powerful interest in the defence of a disciplined and moral society cemented by the unity of a dominant Catholic faith, their concepts of right order in the world were ultimately separable. Only those who offended against the interests both of the Church and of the state were likely to suffer sustained prosecution at the hands of the Inquisition.

[104] For a full example of such negotiations, see the Nemias case of 1588, C.E.R., reg. 4, fol. 4v.–6v., 20–1, 23v., 140v.; D.N., filza 26, fol. 268–9, 2 July 1588. On the Diaz case, see below, p. 194.

4

Venetian, Roman and Other Inquisitions

Classic histories of the Inquisition in other Italian states have often portrayed local tribunals as mere limbs of a Roman organism or agents of the papal monarchy, made to depend for minute instruction on a distant corpus of cardinals and assessors. The historian Amabile saw the Neapolitans protesting and even arming against the threat of the Spanish Inquisition, but somehow failing to recognize in the Roman an equally pernicious intrusion of foreign authority into their midst.[1] Battistella recalled the 2,576 letters sent by the Congregation to the Inquisitor in Bologna between 1571 and 1695, and declared that it 'reduced these tribunals almost to becoming mere executors of its decisions, depriving them of all liberty and pedantically regulating every move they made.'[2] In his discussion of the Inquisition in Milan and Lombardy, Fumi reached a very similar conclusion.[3]

In the Jewish trials which provide the core of this book, and in other known cases, evidence of Roman intervention is strongest for the 1570s, 1580s and early 1590s. Soon after 1570 the nuncio was supplying detailed information to Rome about the case of Righetto, which seems to have been referred there for advice on the sentence.[4] The Venetian tribunal might consult Rome on such specific points as the application of torture or the nature of the sentence.[5] For its part Rome could demand that the

---

[1] Amabile, *Il Santo Officio ... in Napoli*, I, pp. 39–40, 191–2.

[2] Battistella, *Il Santo Officio ... in Bologna*, pp. 64–8, 174.

[3] Fumi, 'L'Inquisizione ... e lo Stato di Milano', XIII, p. 43.

[4] N.V., X, pp. 60–1, 14, 18 July 1571; Pullan, ' "A Ship ..." ', pp. 51–2.

[5] Cf. N.V., XI, pp. 318, 319, 328–9, 29 Jan., 12 Feb. 1575, where Cardinal Scipione Rebiba advises the nuncio Castagna on the application of torture to a suspected heretic, the physician Hieronimo Donzellino.

entire transcripts of judicial proceedings be submitted to it for the advice of the Congregation. In 1581 the Cardinal Inquisitors-General stipulated that in so-called 'difficult cases' (*in arduis causis*) the complete record should be sent to them, and even when dealing with simpler matters inquisitors were expected to send in a summary of the case and to await a reply. All proposed sentences were to be submitted to the Holy Office in Rome.[6] Albizzi, eager to prove prompt compliance with Rome's wishes, was able to cite two examples from 1582.[7] The best-known extradition from Venice, that of Giordano Bruno in 1593, seems to have resulted from the Inquisitor sending to the Cardinal of Santa Severina a full transcript of all the depositions taken and all the acts of the Holy Office in Venice.[8]

Roman advice was clearly received in three important cases involving judaizing in Venice in 1583, 1586 and 1588. The first of these concerned João Batista of Lisbon, a much travelled youth vacillating between Christianity and the Jewish faith. In December 1582 he presented himself in Venice and sought reconciliation with the Church – having, by his own account, twice lapsed from Christianity. On this occasion, Cardinal Savello wrote to the Inquisitor in Venice in the tone of one who communicates firm instructions, as if the Cardinals were judging the case and the Inquisitor was merely their agent.

> We have seen the examination of Giovanni Battista, alias Abram, which your reverence sent to us; and, although this man's error deserves severe punishment, none the less my most illustrious lords are content to show mercy and charity towards him. And so your reverence may deal with him and receive him back into the bosom of Holy Church if it be known that he has sincerely repented; and you shall impose whatever salutary penance you may deem appropriate, and shall also seek to persuade him, once his case has been despatched, to come to Rome, where he may be instructed and strengthened in the faith and in the service of the Lord God.

The stiff penance duly laid upon him is recorded, but there is no mention – perhaps because this was exhortation and no part of the sentence – of any encouragement to go to Rome.[9] The Inquisitor was given orders, but not deprived of all discretion.

In 1585, members of a household known as the Filippi were arrested in

---

[6] Pastor, 'Allgemeine Dekrete ...', p. 515.

[7] Albizzi, *Risposta* ..., pp. 161–2, referring to the cases of Aurelio Vergerio and of one N. Savorgnana.

[8] See L. Firpo, *Il processo di Giordano Bruno (Quaderni della Rivista Storica Italiana*, I, Naples, 1949), p. 35.

[9] S.U., b. 32, 18 Dec. 1582 to 8 Feb. 1583. Savello's letter is dated 29 Jan. 1583.

Venice for judaizing. Their case was described to Rome by the nuncio, Inquisitor and Patriarch, and Cardinal Savello again sent a reply on behalf of the Roman Congregation. It began by reassuring the Venetian tribunal that a certain law decreed by Pope Paul IV did indeed apply to the case, and would serve to convict Filipe de Nis, the head of the family. This substantive point made, Savello's advice on the conduct of the trial became tentative, provisional, almost platitudinous, going no further than an inquisitor's textbook:

> . . . having offered him the chance to make his defence, if you have not done so already (and indeed you may choose not to do so), and having given him the cord in the usual manner *pro ulteriori veritate habenda* (unless there is some just impediment to so doing) he should be allowed a sufficient period in which to repent. If this elapses and the proper admonitions are made to him and he still does not return to the faith, you should then proceed against him in the manner customary with heretics and pertinacious and impenitent apostates by relaxing him to the judgment of the secular arm. But if he wishes to repent of his Jewish perfidy and errors and to return to the bosom of Holy Church he should be received and admitted as a formal apostate with the usual public abjuration and the penalty of perpetual imprisonment and such other salutary punishments and penalties as may seem good to you, though you should reserve the right to commute and modify these penalties . . .[10]

Roman intervention in this case did not reduce the inquisitors to the condition of automata, or make them mere executors of a distant will.

In the third case, Giovanni Battista Capponi, a young Christian of choleric temperament, was accused by fellow prisoners in the gaols at Rialto of making a great variety of heretical remarks. He eventually decided to confess in full to having spoken these words and to trace their inspiration to certain conversations he had had with Jews. On this occasion, the Holy Office in Venice received advice from Rome in two separate instalments, first concerning the application of torture, and then concerning the sentence; letters from Cardinal Santa Severina were mentioned in the trial records, but they do not appear to survive. In sentencing him to galley service, the Holy Office in Venice spoke of 'holding to

[10] S.U., b. 54. Systematic inquiries, some time after the receipt of denunciations, began on 28 Sept. 1585; Filipe de Nis abjured and was sentenced on 17 Oct. 1586, at which time he was the only member of his household still in the custody of the Inquisition. The evidence against him had been assembled by mid-November 1585, and it was probably at this point that the ecclesiastical members of the Holy Office wrote to Rome. Savello's letter is dated 1 Feb. 1586. For the decree of Paul IV, see below, p. 180.

the letters (*adherendo alle lettere*) of the most illustrious Cardinal Santa Severina in the name of the sacred tribunal of the Inquisition of Rome'. And it also 'reserved to the holy tribunal of Rome the authority to increase, diminish, or wholly or partially alter' the penance laid upon him.[11]

After the 1580s records of Roman intervention disappear from the known trials concerning Jews. This fact proves neither that communication ceased nor that Roman influence collapsed, but it does suggest a reluctance in the post-interdict period to seem to be acting on Roman instructions. Sarpi once wrote that 'The inquisitors of Italy minutely inform Rome by every courier of everything that goes on in the Holy Office',[12] but later admitted that this statement applied rather less to the Venetian than to other Italian inquisitions. Some correspondence, however, was inevitable, especially where inquisitors were trying to use Roman pronouncements to disarm opposition from their colleagues. Sarpi's own fairly moderate attitude was that communications from Rome could be respectfully received and even acted upon, but that they must not be treated in the text of the *processo* as actual orders.[13] There was certainly, at least in 1613–15, considerable Roman interest in collecting and filing summarized information about trials conducted, denunciations received, sentences imposed and abjurations made in Venice.[14]

The President of the Congregation of Cardinal Inquisitors-General could underline the subordinate position of the Venetian Holy Office by demanding that a prisoner arrested in Venice be removed for trial to Rome, and he might also ordain that a case which, like that of Giordano Bruno, had already been opened in Venice should be concluded in Rome. In practice such commands were swiftly transmuted into negotiations through the Collegio with the Council of Ten or – towards the close of the sixteenth century – with the Senate. These government organs had an interest both in maintaining the autonomy of the Venetian tribunal and in guaranteeing their own subjects and foreigners temporarily resident in the city against deportation: the liberty of Venice, which sometimes implied studied indifference to a man's past history and any crimes he might have committed outside the city, could be one of its greatest assets.[15]

[11] S.U., b. 61. Capponi confessed on 11 Aug. 1588; the letters of Santa Severina were apparently dated 10 Sept. and 5 Nov. 1588 – see the entry for 11 Oct. and the sentence promulgated on 22 Nov.

[12] Sarpi, 'Inquisizione', pp. 122, 154–5.

[13] Ibid., pp. 123–4, 162–3.

[14] B.A.V., MS Vaticanus Latinus 10945, fol. 28r.–v.

[15] Cf. N.V., VI, pp. 72–3, 19 March 1552 – 'Essentially it does not please them that their subjects be summoned to any tribunal outside the state [*Dominio*]' (Beccadelli to Cervini on the cases of Fra Marino da Venezia and two Vicentines); also N.V., VIII, pp. 76, 82, in the case of Guido Giannetti of Fano, summer 1566.

Several prisoners of the Venetian Inquisition were in fact relaxed to Rome, but the process was usually treated, not as the transfer of a culprit from a lower to a higher court, but rather as the extradition of a prisoner from one state to another. In the sixteeenth century, those who experienced this treatment fell into two main categories, which consisted first of persons subject to the temporal authority of the Church who were accused of heinous crimes against the faith, and second of members of religious orders who had not been born subject to the Venetian Dominion.[16] The Pope was often treated as a fellow sovereign asking for the surrender of a subject.[17] Sixteen extraditions are known to have been granted between 1544 and 1589; over the same period twelve requests for removal to Rome were certainly denied.[18] Prisoners were occasionally shipped under heavy guard to Ancona, but there was no equivalent to the 'frigate of the Holy Office' which regularly plied between Naples and Rome.[19]

Jews cited before the Venetian Inquisition were in the end little affected by extradition procedures. Few of the Marranos, in whom the Holy Office of the sixteenth century was chiefly interested, could have been claimed as temporal subjects of the Pope. When Cardinal Savello suggested the removal of Filipe de Nis from Venice to Rome in 1586, he did so on two rather different grounds. He thought it possible that the Sultan might intervene on the prisoner's behalf, and the Venetian state be pressed to surrender him, especially if his case was dragged out at length in Venice. Rich Portuguese New Christian emigrés, bent on judaizing, were a sought-after prize, and the Venetians were known to have permitted the export in part of a huge New Christian fortune to Turkey – that of the Mendes family some thirty years earlier; more recently, in the trial of an aged Portuguese merchant, Gaspar Ribeiro, they had shown their willingness to respond to Turkish exhortations, this time for the prosecution of the prisoner.[20] Furthermore, Rome was systematically collect-

---

[16] C. De Frede, 'L'estradizione degli eretici dal Dominio Veneziano nel Cinquecento', *Atti dell' Accademia Pontaniana*, nuova serie, vol. 20 (1970–71), pp. 264–5.

[17] Cf. the instructions of the Cardinal Secretary to the nuncio in Venice concerning the extradition of Cornelio Soccino: '... to speed the matter you may say that Soccino his father, although a Sienese, took a wife in Bologna, where this Cornelio was born. Since we are dealing with a subject of the Church, their most illustrious lordships must be even readier to oblige His Holiness' – D.N., filza 20, 15 Nov. 1578. Also Stella, *Anabattismo al Socinianesimo*, pp. 154–8.

[18] De Frede, 'L'estradizione ...', pp. 282–3.

[19] References in Villani, ed., *Nunziature di Napoli*, I, pp. 227, 292, 387; cf. also Amabile, *Il Santo Officio ... in Napoli*, I, pp. 213, 221, 225, 265, 273–4; II, doc. 10, p. 74; I, pp. 312, 315–16.

[20] See below, pp. 99–100, 179.

ing evidence about New Christian merchants,[21] and Savello believed that
the interrogation of de Nis in Rome might be 'of greater service to the
holy faith'. Members of the Portuguese community in Rome could perhaps throw light on his past; and the prisoner might be induced to
contribute, not only to his own conviction, but to that of other apostates
from the Christian faith – 'if he were to confess to having other Marrano
accomplices, of whom there are such numbers in that city of yours and in
Italy at large'.[22] But Savello was not insistent, and the state was unlikely
to sympathize with these arguments. Filipe de Nis and his family had
offended too blatantly to escape punishment in Venice itself, but there
can have been little incentive to alarm the Jewish and Portuguese mercantile communities by an extradition as well as an arrest.

For controversialists bent on proving the subordination of the Venetian
tribunal to its head office in Rome, every authentic case of a prisoner sent
to Rome for judgment was a point gained. Examples of extradition were
thin on the ground in the seventeeth century, and Rome's champions
seemed inclined to stretch the concept to include informal arrangements
which had not apparently been the subject of diplomatic negotiations or
debate in the Collegio. Curialists seem at once to have recognized the case
of Mariana, a Polish Jewess, as a precedent which could be cited to
induce the Venetians – more recalcitrant in this matter than all other
Italian sovereigns save the Duke of Savoy – to surrender other prisoners
to Rome.[23] Mariana was arrested in the Venetian Ghetto in 1624; she
had been living for some years as the wife of Giovanni Domenico
Brochaldo, a Christian by profession, a Neapolitan by birth and a hatter
by trade, who had now settled in Rome. By her own account she was of
Jewish birth and had lived as a Christian out of sheer necessity, but had
never been baptized, and could not therefore, in returning to the Jewish
faith, be guilty of heresy or apostasy. But she was willing to receive
baptism if she could be reunited with her husband, and she clearly felt
herself in need of protection from his brothers. She was eventually sent to
the inquisitors in Rome by way of Ancona, and once arrived there was
delivered to the house of Ascanio Tomati, with a recommendation that
she be charitably treated.[24] The intention was not, apparently, to send
her to Rome for judgment or punishment, and her custody was at least
partially protective. This, coupled with the fact that her husband was a
papal subject, probably accounted for the complaisance of the *Assistenti*
and for the smoothness with which the affair passed off. Such consider-

[21] S.S.D.R., filza 22, fol. 166v. – despatch of Giovanni Gritti from Rome, 9 July 1588.
[22] See Savello's letter of 1 Feb. 1586, in S.U., b. 54.
[23] B.A.V., MS Vaticanus Latinus 10945, fol. 40v., 92; MS Barberino Latino 5195, fol.
17v.–18, 64r.–v.
[24] S.U., b. 79, 18 April to 6 July 1624.

ations did not prevent Cardinal Albizzi from including the case in his treatise as one of five instances of extradition from Venice to Rome between 1600 and 1625;[25] and it seems, indeed, that the Inquisition in Rome acted as if it were still trying the case – it made further inquiries and elicited the new information that the woman had been baptized in Ragusa, after which she was reunited with her husband.[26]

In its pursuit of heresy and of lesser crimes against the faith, the Venetian Inquisition had to relate, not only to a senior authority in Rome, but also to a sisterhood of diocesan inquisitions under Rome's wing. It could be argued that the Venetian Inquisition ought to be concerned solely with offences committed within the city and its dominions: such a principle, making it national rather than international in scope, would enhance the city's reputation as a haven for religious refugees, and might increase its prosperity as a port or even as a tourist attraction which could be safely visited by the discreet Protestant or Marrano prepared to cause no scandal. Venice's reputation for freedom, said Sir Dudley Carleton in 1611, 'is world-wide, and has secured for the place the title of microcosmos rather than city'.[27] But would the Inquisition look beyond the microcosmos? Other inquisitions were known to do this; before the protective Alva–Cobham agreement of 1576, the Inquisition in Seville would interrogate English sailors to discover if 'Lutheran' services had been held on board even before the ship entered a Spanish port.[28] In theory, inquisitions should form part of a universal police force engaged in a common struggle against heresy, and entitled to call on each other's assistance. The faith was without bounds or inner divisions; offences against it could be judged in any place where evidence was available, without regard to the nationality or allegiance of the accused person; the Inquisition should review the entire religious life of the person before it, and not merely that part of it which had been lived in Venice. Some international cooperation was surely vital to striking down heretics, who were notoriously mobile. The prospects of, say, a Sephardic merchant in Venice would be gravely affected if it were thought desirable to prove, by systematic con-

[25] Albizzi, *Risposta* ..., p. 157.

[26] MS Barberino Latino 5195, fol. 64r.–v., 79v.–80. Both this MS and Albizzi couple the case of Mariana with that of Ludovico Ludovisio, who was, it seems, a young Turkish convert to Christianity who had absconded from the Collegio de' Neofiti in Rome. This, again, was hardly a straightforward case of extradition – he was handed over to the nuncio, who put him in the Casa de' Catecumeni (see below, p. 255 ff.) and subsequently sent him on to his godfather, Cardinal Ludovisio. It was Ludovisio, Archbishop of Bologna, who took him to Rome and had him tried by the Holy Office there, and there seems to have been no direct link between the Venetian and the Roman Inquisitions.

[27] H. F. Brown, ed., *Calendar of state papers and manuscripts Venetian*, XII, doc. 323, pp. 205–6, 9 Sept. 1611.

[28] See P. Croft, 'Englishmen and the Spanish Inquisition, 1558–1625', *English Historical Review*, 87 (1972), p. 259.

sultation with the Inquisitions of Lisbon or Coimbra or Oporto, or even with others in Italy, that he had been baptized and had lived as a Christian in some other place.

When trying a Jew charged with apostasy during the war of Cyprus and Lepanto, with Pius V taking some personal interest in the case and Facchinetti serving as his nuncio, the Venetian Inquisition proved quite capable of seeking information from as far afield as Lisbon. On 12 April 1572, Don Diego Guzman de Silva, Philip II's ambassador, released to the Holy Office in Venice eighteen pages of proceedings conducted in the name of the Cardinal Infante, Inquisitor-General in Portugal, and containing the depositions of nine witnesses who had testified in Lisbon in the matter of Enriques Nuñes, otherwise Abraham, called Righetto.[29] The accused was felt to threaten the security of the state in time of war, and the state was unlikely to object to the man being held in custody whilst an exceptionally prolonged investigation of his life history was carried out. Unusually, he seems to have been prosecuted on the strength, not of any particular scandal or heresy perpetrated in Venice or its dominions, but rather of his way of life in several European countries, of his shifting allegiances between Christianity and the Jewish faith: much of the evidence gathered related to his conduct in Spain, the Low Countries and Florence.

After this important case, which ended anticlimactically with Righetto's escape in the summer of 1573,[30] the Venetian Inquisition seems to have narrowed its focus. At least two other major cases of Marranism were tried, that of Gaspar Ribeiro in 1580–81 and that of the Filippi in 1585–86. But both clearly rose out of misconduct committed in Venice itself, for Ribeiro was accused of consenting to an illicit marriage on the island of Murano, and the Filippi of creating scandal within the parishes bordering on the Ghetto.[31] It was true that the lives and careers of the prisoners before their arrival in Venice were in question, but chiefly on the basis of their own testimony, and without attempts to find witnesses abroad. In 1588 the Collegio interceded strongly on behalf of Nemias, whose offence seems to have lain in posing as a nominal Christian in the Low Countries but declaring himself a Jew in Ferrara and Venice: there was no suggestion in the debates of misconduct committed in Venice itself, and the state plainly indicated its lack of enthusiasm for prosecutions of this kind.[32] The following year, Portuguese and

[29] S.U., b. 36, April 1571, late July, early August, 18 Sept. 1571, 12 April 1572; witnesses' testimony dated 11–14 Jan. 1572.

[30] Pullan, ' "A ship ..." ', pp. 42–5.

[31] S.U., b. 45, proc. Gaspar Ribeiro; b. 54, proc. Filippi.

[32] C.E.R., reg. 4, fol. 4v.–6v., 20–1, 23v., 140v.–141r., 26 March, 28 June, 15 July 1588, 28 Dec. 1590; D.N., filza 26, fol. 268–9, 2 July 1588.

Spanish Jews were assured against prosecution based merely on their having adhered to Christianity outside Venice or its dominions: such was the effective meaning of crucial clauses in their contract of 1589.[33]

It fell to Sarpi to state most clearly the principle that the Venetian Inquisition should function like any lay magistracy, concerning itself with actions committed within the frontiers of the state. In September 1616, Carlo da Romulo noticed Simon Gomez wearing the red hat of a professing Jew in Venice; this perturbed him, for he knew that Gomez had lived as a Christian in Pisa, where he had two baptized daughters. But Carlo did not denounce the man immediately, and waited till his own return to Pisa, where he put in a report to the Inquisition on 7 October. About three months later, the matter had been referred back to Venice, and the nuncio Gessi was pressing urgently for the arrest of Gomez, especially because the souls of his two daughters, now living with him in the Ghetto, were at stake. But the *Assistenti* had meanwhile consulted Sarpi, and he had replied:

> My respectful opinion would be that the *Assistenti* should reply that if Simon Gomez, a Portuguese Jew living in the Ghetto, had created any scandal or was on the point of causing it, or had committed or was about to commit some fault in this Dominion, then he should be severely punished by the magistrates. But to proceed on the strength of things which happened in other dominions would be to undermine privileges which, for just and necessary reasons, have for several decades been granted to that nation by the Republic and by other Christian princes, and which cannot be violated without breaking [the prince's] word.

He had also criticized the Inquisitor of Pisa for accepting a delation for an offence committed outside his jurisdiction, and for omitting to question the motives of a delator who failed to put in an immediate report. Perhaps the delation had been sent from Pisa to Rome quite deliberately, to give it the chance to assert its authority by ordering the Venetian Inquisition to proceed:

> This would permit the Holy Office of Venice to receive laws from others, a thing most prejudicial to it, and it would also open the way to numberless undesirable consequences.[34]

It seems unlikely that Gomez was arrested and tried.

In the late sixteenth and early seventeenth centuries, therefore, the Venetian Inquisition would clearly encounter difficulties in proceeding

---

[33] See below, pp. 187–90, 192–4.

[34] C.J., filza 12, fol. 384r.–v., 386–7, 17 to 20 Dec. 1616; C.E.R., reg. 18, fol. 128v.–129r., 130v., 13, 27 Jan. 1616 Venetian style.

against Sephardic Jews leading double lives, unless it could be proved that they had adhered both to the Christian and to the Jewish faith in Venice itself: the man who went straight to the Ghetto was usually safe enough. And after 1600, as the cases of the brothers Masaod and the brothers Diaz show, the Venetians showed some indulgence even towards a few Portuguese immigrants who had lived both as Christians and as Jews in Venice itself.[35] German, Italian or Levantine Jews, and persons baptized on Italian, rather than Iberian, soil did not enjoy such explicit guarantees. Proceedings against Mariana the Pole began, not because she had committed any offence in Venice, but because she was denounced by her husband in Rome; the Jews were said (by Roman documents) to have stormed at the violation of their privileges by her arrest and deportation, but to no avail, and indeed it was doubtful whether Ashkenazim (Italian, German and central European Jews lumped together in the Venetian official mind as *Tedeschi*) could have claimed the same immunities as their Sephardic brothers.[36] It was easier to obtain the crucial information from neighbour states than to seek it from Spain or Portugal; it would generally be easier to prove a suspect's baptism, and more difficult for him to plead forced conversion. Several cases involving Italian converts were tried in Venice between 1629 and 1637, although in each of them there was in fact some evidence of scandalous or ambiguous behaviour within Venice or its dominions. A fair example is the trial of Felice Magalotti, otherwise Felice Sassatelli, formerly the Jew Samuel, son of Abram Levi of Salonica, and also known as Joseph Sabai. The proceedings began in August 1629 with his arrest by lay magistrates, the *Ufficiali al Cattaver*, for wearing at different times both the red hat of the Jew and the black hat of a Christian. Information was also supplied by the Inquisition of Ferrara, which soon afterwards sent important evidence of his conversion to Christianity and baptism in that city the previous November. Proof of misconduct in Venice was the gateway to investigation of Felice's whole way of life, which revealed him as a person who treated religious frontiers very cavalierly. Where an offence had been committed in the Venetian Dominion, it was quite proper for the tribunal to take account of similar offences committed outside it. In 1636–37, the fate of Iseppo Bon was determined by evidence that he had been baptized not only in Vicenza but also in Bologna and Rome – clear evidence of religious crime committed, not inadvertently, but systematically.[37]

---

[35] See below, pp. 193–4.

[36] B.A.V., MS Barberino Latino 5195, fol. 64r.–v., 79v.–80r.

[37] S.U., b. 87, 17 Aug. 1629 to 7 May 1630; cf. also the cases of Pier Vincenzo Maria Sandoval, b. 89, 26 Aug. to 5 Oct. 1632; of Andrea Nunciata, b. 91, from about 26 April 1633 to 24 Jan. 1636; of Iseppo Bon, b. 94, 9 Jan. 1636 to 29 Jan. 1637.

In general, the seventeenth-century Venetian Inquisition did not take instruction from tribunals abroad, and would seldom act on the suggestion that it ought to arrest persons living as Jews in the Ghetto merely for offences committed in other states. Its attitude to information transmitted from the Venetian empire could be more receptive; Carlo Labia, Archbishop of Corfu in 1660, passed information to Venice about the misconduct on the island of Nicolò Dolfin, formerly the Jew Nathan Cohen. Cohen had been converted to Christianity in Venice in 1658, but his behaviour roused the suspicion that he had been attracted to Christianity for material ends, and it seemed that he was cutting no ties either with Jews or with Judaism. The Holy Office in Venice resolved to issue warrants for the arrest of Dolfin, believed to have returned to the capital, though there is no record of their having found him.[38]

For all this, the Venetian Inquisition could not have functioned efficiently without co-operation from tribunals abroad, and without giving them reciprocal help. The bulk of the testimony might be available in Venice, but there were often a few witnesses who had gone to live or travel abroad. They could be examined by other inquisitions, and their sworn testimony sent to Venice to form part of the dossier. At various times, in its encounters with Jews and Judaism, the Holy Office drew on information supplied from Bologna in the Papal States,[39] from Milan and its subject city of Alessandria della Paglia,[40] from Modena in the Estense dominions,[41] and even from Gaeta in the Viceroyalty of Naples.[42] Rome, not always cast in the role of supreme authority or adviser, could also act as an informant of Venice.[43] But the closest links in these investigations were with the Inquisition of Ferrara, a city which sheltered a large and flourishing Jewish community. In the Righetto case the Inquisitor of Ferrara scribbled his reports for Venice heroically if agitatedly as earth tremors reduced buildings in the city to rubble, and – though not quite

[38] S.U., b. 114, from about 2 Feb. to 22 June 1660.

[39] S.U., b. 45, proc. Gaspar Ribeiro, examination of Domingo de Paz, 30 Sept. 1580, 17 May 1581; b. 94, proc. Iseppo Bon, correspondence with ecclesiastical authorities in Bologna concerning a baptism in the cathedral, 1624.

[40] I.Z. II, pp. 114–23, proc. Marc' Antonio degli Eletti, testimony of witnesses examined in Alessandria, 28 Feb. to 9 March 1570; S.U., b. 44, proc. 'Negromanti', interrogation of Estevão Nogueira, 27 Jan. 1579.

[41] S.U., b. 91, proc. Andrea Nunciata, two depositions of Joseph Teseo, 2 May 1633, 3 Jan. 1634.

[42] S.U., b. 107, papers of 'Valenza, Da Costa', deposition of Don Carlo Francisco da Costa, 20 July 1664.

[43] S.U., b. 33, papers on Solomon Dardero, 18 Dec. 1571 (information laid against him by a Florentine living in Rome); b. 36, proc. Righetto, test. Emanuel de Rocha, 30 Aug., 17 Sept. 1571; b. 45, proc. Ribeiro, den. in Rome by Enriques de Mello, 31 Oct., 15–16 Nov. 1575, and test. Samuel Abudent, formerly João Lopez, 27 April 1582; b. 107, papers on Emanuel Monis and others, a a deposition of Francesco di Giovanni Careton, 15 Oct. 1658.

impartially – he served the defence as well as the prosecution.[44] Venice could be expected, from time to time, to repay Ferrara's services. In 1622, the Inquisitor in Venice received from his colleague a list of nine questions to put to witnesses in the affair of Isaac Spagnoletto and his stepfather, arrested in Ferrara with Christian objects of worship in their possession.[45] And in 1670 the Venetian inquisitor responded, though ineffectively, to requests to seek out Bona Carpi, a young Jewess spirited by her brother away from the Ghetto of Ferrara, where she had shown interest in becoming a Christian and in marrying a young artisan.[46]

At all times, the conduct of the Venetian Inquisition was subject to influence by the rival claims of the universal and the local, of Christian idealism, reason of state and commercial commonsense. Tension between these things was modified by the composition of the tribunal, by the emphasis laid for a time on diplomatic skills on the part of inquisitors as well as of nuncios, and also on conventional piety in lay deputies. Clashes of interest were inevitable, but conflict was contained and regulated, and the famous stability of the Venetian Republic can perhaps be traced in part to its ability to control the Inquisition and to restrain it from provocative behaviour. It was not allowed to advertise its presence as some of the Lombard inquisitions did by parading their henchmen and familiars, and it was not allowed to develop, as did the Spanish Inquisition, into a self-contained and privileged jurisdiction accountable to none but itself. Unlike certain of their colleagues, Venetian inquisitors rarely attracted personal vengeance or violence; nor do they seem to have invited, as in Naples, open demonstrations of popular or noble suspicion and resentment.[47] It is true that Paolo Canevari da Gabbiano died in mysterious circumstances in 1623, when poisoning was suspected and traced to his refusal to license the official history of Andrea Morosini.[48] But his fate was a rare and uncertain exception to the rule.

If the Inquisition in Venice acted with moderation, it would be wrong to ascribe this solely to the anxiety of a pragmatic state to resist religious fanaticism. Jews were not leniently treated by the Inquisition of Spain,

---

[44] S.U., b. 36, proc. Righetto, 1 Dec. 1570, 22 May, July 1571. Cf. also b. 31, proc. Miguel Vaz; b. 39, proc. Gomez, 10 Sept. 1575; b. 92, proc. Carlo Antonio Barberini, test. Giovanni di Francesco Balla of Mantua, the courier whose boat plied between Ferrara and Venice, 15 Sept. 1636.

[45] S.U., b. 77, proc. Isacco Spagnoletto, 3 Aug. 1622.

[46] S.U., b. 115, proc. Salomone Carpi, 17 Aug. 1670.

[47] Cf. Fumi, 'L'Inquisizione ... e lo Stato di Milano', XIII, pp. 18–19, 24–5; XIV, pp. 148–53; Amabile, *Il Santo Officio ... in Napoli*, I, pp. 103–21, 196–211, 312–14; Villani, ed., *Nunziature di Napoli*, I, pp. 330, 331, 396, 8, 10 July 1575, 14 Feb. 1577.

[48] Zanelli, 'Controversie ...', pp. 198, 201–2; D.N., filza 42I, fol. 109v.–112v., 121r.–v., 182v.–184, 201, 356v.–358v., 384v.–386, 395r.–v., 412, 423r.–v.

which was free of regular supervision by Roman agents. In the prolonged debate on the procedures to be adopted in the new Inquisition of Portugal during the second quarter of the sixteenth century, the Papacy and the curia stood for restraint.[49] In his defence Righetto pleaded in 1572 that the savage acts of Paul IV towards Iberian Jews were out of key with the far more tolerant tradition of his predecessors.[50] Analogies were drawn – first in the Collegio and then in Sarpi's treatise – between the policies of toleration adopted by the Venetians and those followed in the papal port of Ancona in the later sixteenth century.[51] Much later, in the mid-seventeenth century, Rome was to exert a sobering influence on prosecutions for witchcraft.[52] It was, at most times, a champion of regular procedures, reinforcing the rules enshrined in the vast compilation of Eymeric and Peña with its own written advice on specific cases. Pedantry, rather than sadism, credulity or arbitrary conduct, was the besetting vice of inquisitors and their colleagues.

In 1631 Alvise Mocenigo, returning from his embassy in Madrid, remarked that the authority of the Inquisition in Castile was on the wane. It was, he said, a fitting punishment ordained by God for those who had cynically used religion in the service of the state. 'For the state is bound to serve the ends of religion; it is superstitious governments that invent religions to benefit the state.'[53] For Venice the Inquisition was an instrument of state in that to destroy heresy was to eliminate rebels and placate the wrath of God. Venetian observers saw the Spanish Inquisition being employed by the monarchy as an engine of centralization, charges of heresy being used to break regional privilege or violate personal immunities;[54] had the Venetian state wished to exploit the institution in that way, the churchmen involved would hardly have connived at it. Such clemency and caution as the Inquisition showed was the product of a balance between interests, and it was to some extent guaranteed by Roman surveillance of the court and its procedures, by Roman legalism as well as by Venetian reason of state.

[49] Cf. A. Herculano, *History of the origin and establishment of the Inquisition in Portugal*, transl. J. C. Branner in *Stanford University Publications in History, Economics and Political Science*, 1 (1926), pp. 346, 380–1, 417, 444–6; Lea, *Inquisition of Spain*, III, p. 257 ff.

[50] Pullan, ' "A ship ..." ', pp. 50–1.

[51] Sarpi, 'Inquisizione', p. 175, and below, pp. 188–9.

[52] Cf. C. Ginzburg, *I Benandanti: ricerche alla stregoneria e sui culti agrari tra Cinquecento e Seicento* (Turin, 1966), pp. 130–8.

[53] Barozzi–Berchet, I/i, p. 630.

[54] Albèri, I/v, pp. 21–2 (Paolo Tiepolo, 1563); pp. 85–6 (Giovanni Soranzo, 1565); p. 144 (Antonio Tiepolo, 1567); I/vi, pp. 366–7, 371–2 (Leonardo Donà, 1573); I/v, pp. 392–3 (Vincenzo Gradenigo, 1586); pp. 401–2 (Tommaso Contarini, 1593); Barozzi–Berchet, I/i, pp. 42, 144 (Francesco Soranzo, 1602); p. 306 (Simone Contarini, 1605); pp. 446–7 (Girolamo Soranzo, 1611); pp. 627–8 (Alvise Mocenigo III, 1631).

5

Jurisdiction, Crime and Punishment: the Heresy of the Baptized

By virtue of the canon law, of recent papal legislation and of instructions contained in their own manuals, inquisitors were entitled to claim jurisdiction over baptized Christians who flirted with Judaism, who mingled Judaism with Christianity, who alternated between Christianity and Judaism, or who withdrew from Christianity altogether and transferred their allegiance to the Jewish faith. They could also claim to judge professing Jews, never baptized, who offended against the 'law', the code of religious belief and observance, common to both Christians and Jews. In principle their jurisdiction further extended to Jews who attacked, insulted or otherwise harmed Christians and the Christian Church. At various times the Venetian Inquisition claimed authority to judge offenders charged with all these crimes, though it did not invariably get the cooperation of the *Assistenti* and the Collegio in the arrest and detention of prisoners. Charges of heresy and apostasy seem to have been laid against Jews and judaizers only in the second half of the sixteenth century, and it was only in the 1580s that the Inquisition made repeated attempts to judge and punish Jews who had not known baptism. Baptized Jews were convicted of grave spiritual offences in the 1620s and 1630s, but were sentenced for incurring suspicion of heresy rather than for heresy itself. The nature of the charges and the sentences imposed seem to have varied considerably according to the wealth, education and country of origin of the accused person: all these things had some bearing on the degree of responsibility attributed to him for his crime, and it was this responsibility, as much as the crime itself, that the Inquisition sought to assess.

The actions of the tribunal were consonant with the corpus of theology and canon law which was reaffirmed and summarized in Peña's edition of Eymeric's textbook for inquisitors. By this authority Judaism was not a heresy in itself, but was generally called *perfidia*. But it was closer to heresy than were the beliefs of pagans, since Jews, through their intimate knowledge of the Old Testament, had been exposed to the truths recognized by Christians. St Thomas Aquinas, duly quoted in Eymeric–Peña, had argued that Judaism represented a middle state between paganism and heresy. Jews were said to struggle against the Christian faith or Gospel which they had received through the Old Testament *in figura* – that is, in an implicit or symbolic form, rather than in the shape of a fully revealed truth.[1] And his sixteenth-century commentator, Caietanus, explained that the distinction between a Jew and a heretic was the difference between one who opposes the implicit and one who opposes the explicit faith.[2]

Although Judaism was in no strict sense a heresy, a deliberate switch of allegiance from Christianity to Judaism was without doubt a heretical act. About 1300, a directive of Pope Boniface VIII to inquisitors, preserved in the canon law as the decretal *Contra christianos*, laid it down that all born Christians who went over to Judaism and all converts who dared to return to it should be treated as heretics. This rule was to apply to all persons baptized Christians, with the sole exception of those who had suffered *absoluta coactio* and been dragged protesting to the font. Only the use of such physical force invalidated a baptism; threats, including the threat of death, did not. Nor did ignorance of the meaning and implications of the sacrament. Those who aided, abetted, or sheltered judaizers would be liable to prosecution as supporters, receivers or accessories of heretics. Pope Nicholas IV had already called the apostasy of Jews doubly distressing, because those made familiar with the name of Christ would be the better equipped to blaspheme against it.[3] In the words of Caietanus, at the start of the sixteenth century, 'If a Christian turns Jew, he becomes a heretic through denying the faith of the Gospel which he has once professed, and he becomes guilty of the Jewish perfidy by professing Judaism, which corrupts the image [*figura*] of the Gospel.'[4] Judaizers, suggested Peña towards 1580, deserved to be dealt with not merely as heretics but even as apostates. The difference between heresy and apostasy was one of degree rather than of principle, in that apostasy meant

---

[1] Thomas Aquinas, *Summa Theologica*, with the *Commentaries* of Thomas de Vio Caietanus, in *Opera omnia iussu impensaque Leonis XIII P.M. edita* (16 vols., Rome, 1882–1948), VIII, 2.2 qu. 10 art. 5 and 6, pp. 84–7; Eymeric, pp. 245, 246; Peña, pp. 74–5.

[2] Caietanus, *Commentaries*, in Aquinas, *Opera omnia*, VIII, pp. 85–6.

[3] E. Friedberg, ed., *Corpus Juris Canonici, Pars Secunda: Decretalium Collectiones* (Leipzig, 1922), col. 1075; Eymeric, pp. 66, 138, 158–9, 241–3; Peña, pp. 37–8; also E. Masini, *Sacro Arsenale, overo Prattica dell' Officio della S. Inquisitione ampliata* (Genoa, 1625), pp. 13, 336; B.R., IV, p. 88.

[4] Caietanus, *Commentaries*, p. 86.

rejection of the Christian faith in its entirety, whereas heresy might imply departure from it only in certain details.[5]

In Venice in the second half of the sixteenth century most of those expressly accused of heresy or apostasy through judaizing were Portuguese immigrants of Jewish descent. Righetto was informed in 1572 that he had been 'judged by the sacred tribunal an apostate from the Christian faith'.[6] Judges trying Gaspar Ribeiro in 1580 clearly described the process as a trial for heresy.[7] João Batista of Lisbon, who sought reconciliation with the Church in 1582 after twice departing from Christianity, was told that 'should he fall again into so grave a sin he would no longer be pardoned but be put to death as a relapsed heretic.'[8] And the instructions of Cardinal Savello in the case of Filipe de Nis, already quoted, envisaged his being treated as a heretic or apostate.[9]

To be accused in this unqualified fashion was, in a sense, a mark of social and intellectual distinction, an inverted reward of intelligence and determination. Detractors of Portuguese New Christians taxed them with conspiracy to accumulate great riches by pretending to be genuine Christians and then to export their wealth to the Ottoman Empire; theirs were no momentary lapses into Judaism.[10] The Inquisition strove to punish not only the act itself, not only the will and the intention behind it, but also the intellect and the sense of responsibility. Righetto, Ribeiro and Filipe de Nis were far from youthful: Righetto gave his age as forty, Filipe de Nis was in his middle fifties and Gaspar Ribeiro was eighty-seven at the time of his trial, though his extreme old age might, as the defence pleaded, suggest diminished responsibility. All three had been merchants, or came of mercantile families; all were, or had once been, rich. Righetto was famous for the extravagance with which he had staked and lost the family's fortunes on the gaming tables of the Duchess of Florence, Gaspar Ribeiro for the parsimony with which he preserved his substantial capital. All had social aspirations, which lured Righetto to the courts of Spain and Tuscany, tempted the Ribeiros to contrive aristo-cratic marriages, and caused Filipe de Nis — as though emulating the ostentation of Jewish bankers in pre-Ghetto days — to rent a large house from a noble family. Righetto gave at his trial ample proof of tenacity in argument, Ribeiro of stubbornness, Filipe de Nis of rather clumsy sub-terfuge. Since none could be excused by ignorance, youthful impulse or lifelong poverty, and since their social rank implied full awareness of the

[5] Peña, pp. 38, 93, 98–9; *Repertorium Inquisitorum* ..., pp. 52, 54; Masini, *Sacro Arsenale*, pp. 352–3.
[6] S.U., b. 36, proc. Abraham detto Righetto, 2 Nov. 1572.
[7] S.U., b. 45, proc. Gaspar Ribeiro, 16 Aug. 1580.
[8] S.U., b. 32, proc. Giovanni Battista da Lisbona, 18 Dec. 1582.
[9] See above, p. 47.
[10] See below, pp. 177–9, 232.

implications of their actions, they faced – as humbler judaizers did not – the full charge of heresy or apostasy. But since such charges promised to strike at increasingly valued members of the mercantile community, and to threaten their families with confiscation of their inheritance, the Venetian state became, by 1589, most reluctant to see them brought.[11]

In the second half of the sixteenth century, a few born Christians who had no Jewish blood were convicted of offences which entailed flirtations with Judaism. They were not treated as heretics of the same calibre as the Portuguese merchants; their crimes, though grave enough, sprang from frivolity, from iconoclasm or from a spirit of adventure and experiment. For Pietro of Naxos and Giovanni Battista Capponi, Judaism was a thing encountered on travels that were at once spatial and intellectual voyages of discovery. For Giorgio Moretto, born in the nearby parish of Madonna dell' Orto, the Ghetto was a place at once familiar and forbidden. Capponi's challenge to Christianity smelt of the Anabaptist heresy, at least of those versions which disputed the authority of the New Testament and the divinity of Christ. In his mouth, Judaism seemed a source of pernicious legends which demoted Christ to the rank of a prophet, or a magician and trickster, certainly to that of a mere man. For Giorgio Moretto, indifferent to ideas, Judaism was just an alternative sequence of feast days and celebrations which could offer relief from the austerities of the Christian Lent; he happened to admire a Jewish girl; and he proved incapable of respecting a solemn command from the Inquisition to stay out of the Ghetto. Pietro of Naxos and Giovanni Battista Capponi had been led astray, not by an inherited tradition of heresy, but by their own curiosity.[12] Capponi was drawn like a jackdaw to anything flashily unorthodox and had a fondness for possessing prohibited books if not for reading them. He chose to attribute most of the wilder statements he had made to conversations he had held with Jews – whether this was really true, or whether it merely seemed to be the simplest method of clearing the slate once he had resolved to confess. He was reported for saying that Christ was not the true Messiah, that his miracles had all been accomplished with the aid of the cabbalah, that all who believed in Christ were lost and damned, that the Gospel was untrue, and that the Virgin and saints were incapable of interceding for humankind. He had told a notary that 'the law of the Jews was better than ours, because the law was given to the Jews by God himself and to us by the apostles only.'[13]

---

[11] Pullan, ' "A Ship ..." '; B. Pullan, 'The Inquisition and the Jews of Venice; the case of Gaspare Ribeiro, 1580–81', *Bulletin of the John Rylands Library of Manchester*, 62 (1979), pp. 207–31; S.U., b. 54, proc. Filippi; below, p. 187 ff.

[12] I.Z., p. 132, proc. Pietro da Nixia, test. 'Ser Antonio Flogotomo famagostano', 11 Dec. 1552.

[13] S.U., b. 61, proc. Giovanni Battista Capponi, test. Giovanni Alvise Zaffardo, 12 July 1588.

Extravagant or frivolous offences of this kind, committed by young men of no social position who subsequently declared themselves contrite, did not incur the full penalties of heresy. Where Filipe de Nis was sentenced to perpetual imprisonment and the heirs of Gaspar Ribeiro, who had died of natural causes while under investigation, were threatened with the confiscation of his property, Pietro of Naxos, aged twenty-six, said to have confessed to 'apostasies', was sentenced to eight years' galley service, perpetual suspension from holy orders and dignities and perpetual deprivation of his Franciscan habit. His vocation, and the fact that he had resumed his priestly office in Cyprus without reconciliation with the Church, doubtless made his offence more serious than that of Capponi, a layman whose misconduct was essentially verbal. Capponi, who gave his age as twenty-one, had last been employed as agent to the Procurator Dolfin, and – although he claimed considerable knowledge of business practice – was certainly no independent merchant. He was sentenced to five years' galley service. Giorgio Moretto, a sailor and a pedlar who spent much time 'broking' or acting as an unofficial go-between for miscellaneous purposes in the Ghetto, was sentenced to three years in the galleys. As persons of less maturity and consequence, whose severance from Christianity was less complete, they incurred charges and penalties of smaller weight.[14]

Capponi was found 'vehemently suspect of heresy'. He had admitted to making various heretical remarks out of the 'looseness of speech which I have', but not to believing them. Despite the scepticism of the court, and its declaration that it 'presumes that every person believes in his soul the things he expresses in words, for the mouth is the organ of everyone's heart', he had held firmly to his position.[15] Hence, sufficient proof of heretical intentions behind his words was lacking. 'Suspicion of heresy' was in itself an offence punishable both by spiritual and by physical penalties designed to purge it, and it was a charge suitable to persons who (however compelling the judges' belief in their guilt) could not be conclusively shown to have realized the import of their words or deeds, or to have done or spoken them with an altogether evil intent.[16] Hence it was often applied – certainly in the seventeenth century – to the relatively

[14] For the three cases, I.Z., pp. 101–43, proc. Pietro da Nixia, 10 Dec. 1552 to 4 Nov. 1553; S.U., b. 61, proc. Giovanni Battista Capponi, 1588; S.U., b. 64, proc. Giorgio Moretto, 8 April to 10 June 1589.

[15] S.U., b. 61, 11 Aug., 20 Sept. 1588.

[16] On suspicion of heresy, see Eymeric, pp. 258–62, 318–19; Peña, p. 170; Masini, *Sacro Arsenale*, pp. 13–14; Zanelli, 'Controversie ...', pp. 213–14; Albizzi, *Risposta ...*, pp. 167–73. On the growing use of the *Verdachtsstrafe* or punishment for suspicion in secular law courts, cf. J. H. Langbein, *Torture and the law of proof: Europe and England in the Ancien Regime* (London, 1977), p. 47 ff.

large class of offenders who had been converted from Judaism to Christianity on Italian soil, and had subsequently lapsed into Judaism or otherwise defaulted on their promises to become pious Christians. In the early days of the revived Inquisition, it was usual when sentencing prisoners simply to describe the offence committed. By the seventeenth century, it was customary also to classify it in terms of suspicion of heresy, of which there were three degrees – 'mild' or 'slight' (*levis*), 'vehement' and 'violent' (the Venetian tribunal seems to have retained a distinction between formal heresy and violent suspicion of it, even when Rome itself had abandoned this).[17]

Most people in these categories were of very modest social standing, Italians or Levantines whose occupations ranged from the tailor's journeyman and the 'Turkish merchants' broker to the wandering pedlar and the professional rogue. To some of them baptism had been a device to tide them over temporary difficulties, and they had sometimes, by the same token, reverted to Judaism to suit their own convenience, perhaps to seek hospitality or jobs through their old Ghetto connexions. Inconstancy, rather than a determined attachment to Judaism, was their besetting fault; ill-educated, they were far better placed than the Portuguese merchants to plead ignorance of the law. In the late 1620s and the 1630s, such people incurred sentences varying from mere public penance outside the portals of St Mark's to public penance followed by a spell of seven years in the penal galleys. One or two had higher social pretentions, but these were not substantiated. Felice Magalotti, a raffish character born in Salonica but probably of Spanish descent, described himself as 'on the business of a merchant', but there was no evidence of his actually engaging in trade. Andrea Nunciata likewise claimed to be a merchant and to have rich relatives – the uncle who denounced him, the Jew Joseph Teseo, was minter to the Duke of Modena. But Andrea's preoccupation was claiming an inheritance, and in Venice he was accused before lay courts of theft or receiving stolen goods a crime which seemed to remove him from the ranks of the respectable.[18]

Understandably, within this category also, the heaviest penalties were imposed on those with the firmest intentions – on whose who were guilty of something worse than merely resuming Jewish dress and associations, guilty, indeed, of systematically exploiting the sacrament of baptism in order to obtain the alms and patronage briefly bestowed on new converts

[17] Note the sentence on Iseppo Bon, S.U., b. 94, 22 Jan. 1637; cf. Masini, *Sacro Arsenale*, pp. 219–26.

[18] See S.U., b. 87, proc. Felice Magalotti, 17 Aug. 1629 to 7 May 1630; b. 89, proc. Pier Vincenzo Maria Sandoval, 26 Aug. to 5 Oct. 1632; proc. Giovanni Battista Bonaventura, 1 July to 9 Dec. 1632; b. 91, proc. Andrea Nunciata, 26 April 1633 to 24 Jan. 1636; b. 94, proc. Iseppo Bon, 9 Jan. 1636 to 29 Jan. 1637.

to Christianity. Ignorance or weakness was much harder to plead on these occasions, and the prisoners came dangerously close to being members of the professional, deceiving poor. As poor persons, however, they lacked the dignity of the true heretic. Hence the heavy but degrading sentence of public penance and of seven years' galley service passed in 1637 upon Iseppo Bon, alias Francesco Maria Leoncini, born the Jew Moses, son of David Israel of Salonica. It was a distant echo of the sentence of twenty years' service passed in 1548 on Aaron, afterwards Giacomo, Francoso of Sarzana, who had been rebaptized on three occasions after his initial conversion to Christianity in Venice. This exceptional severity had been justified by the tribunal on the grounds that the prisoner had known very well what he was at – he had been 'warned that he was committing errors and doing evil deeds'.[19]

Since intention and motive played so prominent a role in the determination of crime and punishment, penalties could be substantially reduced, though not removed altogether, by a convincing plea of insanity. Elena de' Freschi Olivi, mother of a zealous convert, caused public scandal by abusive words spoken openly in a Venetian parish church in 1555. Here the tribunal accepted the arguments urged by her son to the effect that she was a lunatic with lucid intervals, and proceeded to offer her a choice: she was either to accept imprisonment for two years in the women's prison in the ducal palace, followed by perpetual confinement in a room in her son's house; or she could choose perpetual confinement in the great hospital at Treviso, which – unlike the Venetian hospitals – had accommodation for the insane. The avowed purpose of the sentence was not to punish here or deter potential evildoers, but to protect Christian society: to preserve the minds of the Christian faithful from her 'scandalous ravings', 'especially in matters which concern the sacraments of the Church and the Christian faith'. However, the allusion to the women's prison, the choice she was offered and the threat of perpetual banishment for failure to comply with the conditions presented to her all suggest that she had not been totally absolved of responsibility for her acts: merely that this was regarded as diminished. Determined to show disapproval of the offence, the tribunal could not totally discard all suggestion of punishment.[20]

Lighter punishment could be earned by active collaboration with the tribunal, which was the most effective proof of repentance, and could wholly alter the surface meaning of a sentence of perpetual imprisonment.

[19] I.Z., pp. 75–7, proc. Giacomo Francoso, 10 April 1548.

[20] As it happened, the hospital at Treviso was unable to accept her. On the petition of her son she was released immediately into his custody, to live perpetually confined in one room of his house. See I.Z., pp. 218–24, proc. Elena de' Freschi Olivi, 12 Sept. to 16 Nov. 1555.

For Filipe de Nis, sentenced in 1586, this actually amounted to nothing worse than enforced residence under surveillance and curtailment of his right to depart from Venice. He had one bargaining counter, in the form of a promise to persuade his wife and children to return to Venice from the Levant and to abjure Judaism; his wife and her maidservant actually did this some two years after his sentence, and within a further seven months he was seeking – though with what success is not known – release even from the obligation to provide the Inquisition with guarantors.[21] And the exceptionally mild sentence of one year's imprisonment with public penance passed on the 'vehemently suspect' Andrea Nunciata in 1636 must surely be explained by his readiness to denounce a fellow-offender, the professional rebaptizer Iseppo Bon. Such leniency disgusted the Cardinal Patriarch Federico Cornaro, who thought the prisoner ought to be sentenced to five years at the oar. This was, perhaps, a fair indication of the absolute value in the normal currency of punishment of the crimes committed by Nunciata. But the Patriarch was overruled.[22]

To outward appearances, less rich, prominent and responsible persons were accused of less heinous offences – suspicion of heresy rather than formal heresy – and suffered penalties which were more degrading but more finite. In reality the situation was more complex, not only because discretion was extensively used in cases of perpetual imprisonment, but also because galley service could well prove to be a concealed sentence of death or perpetual slavery.

There were three elements in sentences: first, that of abjuration of the crime or error and conciliation with the Church; second, the spiritual penance; third, the physical or corporal penalty. As time passed, there was an increasing emphasis on formalizing the first two components, and on purging error and redeeming the soul, rather than simply inflicting punishment. In the sentences passed on Francoso in 1548 and on Pietro of Naxos in 1553, the prisoner had already begged pardon, and there was no mention of imposing spiritual exercises upon him during his time in the galleys. But in 1588 Giovanni Battista Capponi was required to make a formal abjuration and to sign it, and it was further stipulated that during his five-year sentence he should recite five Paternosters and five Ave Marias every day, and that every week he should say the seven penitential psalms with the litanies.[23] In the intervening years, the nuncios Facchinetti and Bolognetti had pressed for penance and abjuration to be made more public, in the face of resistance from a government none too anxious to advertise the presence of the Inquisition in the city. Conscious

---

[21] S.U., b. 54, proc. Filippi, 17 Oct. 1586, 31 Dec. 1588 to 3 Jan. 1589, Summer 1589.
[22] S.U., b. 91, proc. Andrea Nunciata, 12 Jan 1636.
[23] S.U., b. 61, proc. Giovanni Battista Capponi, 22 Nov. 1588.

of the deterrent powers of open and exemplary punishment, Facchinetti would have liked the death penalty to be publicly inflicted.[24] By 1581, it was already the custom for solemn abjurations to be made in public, but only in obscure places where no one ever went; Bolognetti scored a triumph in arranging that the solemn abjuration of certain necromancers should be pronounced in St Mark's itself, where it attracted a huge crowd and brought Venetian proceedings more nearly into line with those of the supreme court in Rome and its public ceremonies in Santa Maria della Minerva.[25] In the late 1620s and 1630s, public penances, if not public abjurations, were demanded of those convicted of suspicion of heresy; they were to be paraded in garments shamefully coloured yellow, the equivalent of the Spanish *sambenito*, outside the great doors of St Mark's for a spell of one hour, bearing on their chests papers which baldly described their offences. Humiliation of this kind was at once an element in the punishment and a means of communicating it, by a face-to-face demonstration, to the society which the Inquisition was seeking to discipline and guide.

The physical penalty of galley service was imposed on Francoso in 1548 'that he may not escape punishment for the faults and errors he has committed against the sacrament of baptism and the Christian faith, and that his punishment may be an example to others.' The formula of 1588, at the trial of Capponi, laid a quite different emphasis on the spiritual rehabilitation of the prisoner – 'that you may the more easily seek from the Lord God who is father of mercy the forgiveness of your sins and the grace that in future you may be preserved not only from lapsing into heresy but even from the slightest suspicion of it.' It was the florid language of the Catholic Reformation which laid the heaviest stress on the conquest or reclamation of souls; the sentence on Felice Magalotti in 1630 struck a more sober, less evangelical, note, but brought together tersely enough the notions of deterrence and rehabilitation. The sentence to a penal term was imposed 'that these your errors may not go entirely unpunished and that you may show greater caution in the future and that you may serve as an example to others that they may abstain from such numerous and grave excesses. . . .'[26]

Galley service was the most widely used punishment for prisoners convicted of judaizing. It was a selective punishment suitable for the lowly born, deemed in Venetian secular law appropriate to the idle and feckless,

[24] See letters of Facchinetti, 31 Aug., 5, 12 Oct. 1566, 1 Feb., 17 May 1567, 20 March 1568, in N.V., VIII, pp. 99, 115, 119, 166, 217, 363–4. It seems the Venetians held that 'the pertinacity of some of those who die inspires more compassion in simple souls than terror in evildoers.'

[25] Stella–Bolognetti, p. 288.

[26] S.U., b. 87, proc. Felice Magalotti, 7 May 1630.

to vagabonds, thieves, blasphemers and roughs; patricians could generally expect fines, imprisonment or banishment, and not until 1633 was
such social discrimination legally abolished in an important series of laws
directed against the unauthorized carrying of firearms.[27] Inquisitorial
practice was in this respect very much in harmony with that of the state,
though there was a period – starting some years after the revival of the
Inquisition – in which, for reasons unknown, the state itself opposed
condemnations to the galleys for religious offences. The practice was restored on Facchinetti's instigation in 1568.[28] Its deterrent value (this was
what generally interested him) could well have seemed considerable, and
the Venetian admiral Cristoforo da Canal had advocated galley service
for felons partially on pious and humanitarian grounds, for he professed
to see the rigorous discipline of the galleys, where blasphemy, gambling
and vice were strictly forbidden, as a means of reclaiming souls for Christ.
In state legislation galley service was upheld on the grounds of utility: it
helped to clear overcrowded prisons, thus reducing the risk of disease, it
saved prisoners from lying 'unfruitful' in the gaols, and the state, faced
with severe difficulties in recruiting free labour, allowed itself to become
heavily dependent on the muscle-power of convicts to man its regular
fleet.[29] Galley service relieved judges, both clerical and lay, of the unwelcome responsibility of imposing sentences of death and mutilation.[30]

Nevertheless, the harsh conditions of galley service in the late sixteenth
and early seventeenth centuries were such that at least half the condemned oarsmen died or became unfit to serve before the expiry of their
sentences. Prompt release after completion of the official sentence became
exceptional, since most prisoners rapidly fell into debt to the state, if only
for clothing and medical care, and some of them started their terms
already encumbered with the costs of their arrests and trial. Such debts
had to be worked off by further arduous service at a standard monthly
rate of pay. Hence, apparently limited sentences of eighteen months or
three years at the oar could well imply a slow death from disease or
exhaustion or an unending loss of liberty.[31] In the 1630s galley sentences

[27] See A. Viaro, 'La pena della galera: la condizione dei condannati a bordo delle galere
veneziane', in G. Cozzi, ed., *Stato, società e giustizia nella Repubblica Veneta (sec. XV–XVIII)*
(Rome, 1980), pp. 398–401.

[28] N.V., VIII, p. 455, 6 Nov. 1568.

[29] See Cristoforo Canale, *Della milizia marittima libri quattro*, ed. M. Nani Mocenigo
(Venice, 1930), pp. 174–5; A. Tenenti, *Cristoforo Da Canal: la marine vénitienne avant Lépante*
(Paris, 1962), pp. 17–19, 81 ff.; G. Scarabello, *Carcerati e carceri a Venezia nell' età moderna*
(Rome, 1979), p. 49.

[30] Viaro, 'La pena . . .', pp. 397–8; on death sentences, see Grendler, *Roman Inquisition . . .*,
pp. 57–60.

[31] Viaro, 'La pena . . .', pp. 403–19, 422–4; also A. Tenenti, *Piracy and the decline of Venice,
1580–1615*, transl. J. and B. Pullan (London, 1967), p. 114.

pronounced by the Inquisition were often deemed the equivalent of far longer spells in a close prison: eighteen months in the galleys would be replaced, if the prisoner were found unfit to serve, by three years' close imprisonment and a spell in the pillory, seven years in the galleys by twelve years' imprisonment and a spell in the pillory.[32] Francoso seems to have survived the twenty-year sentence imposed upon him in 1548 and to have been promptly released.[33] But 'Franciscus Hispanus', who in January 1581 had already served thirty months in the galleys after being sentenced to a mere eighteen, and Pier Vincenzo Maria Sandoval, who in 1633 died on the Pasqualigo galley within five months of his condemnation by the Inquisition to a three-year term, were typical casualties of a judicial punishment imposed by both clerical and lay courts in Venice.[34] The modest trial expenses of Marco di Francesco of Padua, condemned in 1587 to two years in the galleys, and those of Felice Magalotti, condemned to eighteen months in 1630, may well have laid the foundations for years of debt slavery.[35]

In general a Jew could be charged with heresy or suspicion of heresy only if he had entered Christianity through baptism, though Jews who had entered the house of converts or made a solemn promise before witnesses to turn Christian could incur similar charges if they reneged before baptism.[36] The Inquisition was sometimes faced with the task of determining the factual issue, whether baptism had or had not taken place. With Portuguese New Christians the practical difficulties of proving baptism from so great a distance might be considerable; the very fact that crypto-Judaism was thought to be rife in Portugal increased the probability that parents would have avoided baptizing their children.[37] Pope Paul IV attempted to overcome these complications by his decree of 1556, to the effect that since it was against the law of the land for a Jew to live in Portugal, all persons who had been born or even residded there must be treated as baptized Christians.[38] The Venetian Inquisition hesi-

---

[32] S.U., b. 87, proc. Felice Magalotti, 7 May 1630; S.U., b. 94, proc. Iseppo Bon, 22 Jan. 1637.

[33] I.Z., pp. 77–8, proc. Giacomo Francoso, 26 Feb. 1568.

[34] S.U., b. 45, proc. Gaspar Ribeiro, test. 'Franciscus Hispanus', 26–28 Jan. 1581; b. 89, proc. Sandoval, inquiry into his death, 10–21 Feb. 1633.

[35] S.U., b. 59, proc. Marco di Francesco of Padua, a bill from the constable of the governor of Belluno for 32 lire and 11 soldi; b. 153, a list of expenses in Magalotti's case amounting to 64 lire and 6 soldi.

[36] Cf. the cases of Aaron and Asher, and of Alessandro Ferro, described below, pp. 276–7, 296–7.

[37] Pullan, ' "A ship ..." ', pp. 33, 49–50.

[38] For the text see Albizzi, *Risposta*, p. 217; Pastor, 'Allgemeine Dekrete ...', p. 496; M. Stern, *Urkundliche Beiträge über die Stellung der Päpste zu den Juden* (2 vols., Kiel, 1893–95), I, pp. 116–17.

tated to apply this rule without question in the case of Righetto, although
– fortified by advice from Rome – it invoked it to convict Filipe de Nis in
1586.[39]

Posing as a Christian created none of the same liabilities as did baptism
– so long, at least, as the sacraments were avoided. This principle was
argued with great vigour in his own defence by Righetto. Surface conformity, practised in a society which demanded universal loyalty to Catholic
Christianity, as in Spain, or Portugal, or the Spanish Low Countries,
should be interpreted as an act of mere expediency, a skin-deep disguise
assumed to preserve life and property. To convict him,

> It would be necessary to prove I had been baptized, since the fact of
> living among Christians bearing the name of Christian proves no-
> thing of the sort. Time and again we have seen Christians in the
> Levant call themselves by Turkish names and live among the Turks
> for reasons of their own, but without being circumcised or commit-
> ting those acts by which one accepts the faith of Islam. Such people
> return to Christianity when they come home.

The fact that the Inquisition took some trouble to establish baptism
beyond doubt – only to find that the relevant parish registers had disappeared beneath a Lisbon landslide – suggests that his arguments caused
his judges disquiet.[40] Venetian patricians themselves began to urge a
similar argument when debating the case of Nemias of Ferrara, who was
said to be a native of Salonica but to have lived as a Christian in the Low
Countries. If Jews dwelt there as Christians, they surely did so out of mere
necessity, for otherwise they could not trade or be tolerated at all in those
lands.[41] True, acceptance of baptism was generally an involuntary act,
and dissimulation by a merchant or traveller a deliberate one. But only
the mystical power inherent in the sacrament, effective without the faith
or express consent of the subject, could impose on him the binding allegiance that rendered him capable of Christian heresy, or treason to the
Church and to God.

Non-baptism was most commonly urged in their defence by Portuguese
Jews. But the question could sometimes arise in connexion with those of
other nationalities, as in the strange case of Mariana the Pole. At the time
of her arrest in 1624, she was a poor Jewess aged about forty, living in the
Ghetto by doing odd jobs. Her story was that in 1606 she and her first
husband, a Jew named Aaron, had been shipwrecked on travels in the

[39] Pullan, ' "A ship ..." ', pp. 50–1; S.U., b. 54, proc. Filippi, 24 Oct. 1585, 1 Feb., 27
March 1586.
[40] Pullan, ' "A ship ..." ', pp. 46–7.
[41] C.E.R., reg. 4, fol. 5r.–v., 26 March 1588.

Mediterranean and had then separated. She was taken first to Sardinia and then to Palermo, and in these dominions of the Crown of Aragon she dared not reveal herself as a Jew. She admitted to having married a Christian in Naples about 1616 – not in church, but in accordance with the local custom which caused widows to wed in their own homes – and to having lived with him for six years. She could hardly avoid telling her devout husband that she had gone to Communion and confession, but she never in fact did so. By her own account she took a rosary with her to church and enjoyed listening to sermons, but never so much as made the sign of the cross. On Fridays and Saturdays she observed the Christian dietary laws, but during Lent obtained from a physician a licence to eat meat on account of a liver complaint. The sacraments could be avoided with impunity because checks were not made by the parish priests in Naples. They undoubtedly would have been in Rome, and when her husband decided to move to that city she thought it prudent to return to Poland. Seemingly acquiescent, her husband 'guided her towards Germany' and perhaps even took her as far as Venice, where she ended by making her way to the Ghetto. She told her judges, 'I have been among Christians because I was forced to be, and had I intended to become a Christian I would have done so on the first day. I was made a slave.' 'My husband was fond of me and I liked him, but I lived with him as a slave and always with the intention of rejoining the Jews as soon as I was permitted to depart.'[42]

There was nothing to corroborate Mariana's story, but no one to contradict it either; she may well have known how to frame it in order to avoid serious consequences for herself, and it is quite possible that she changed her story and admitted to baptism after being sent to Rome. For the purposes of this chapter, however, its truth or falsehood does not matter: the case demonstrates that, where serious doubts arose concerning a person's baptism, the Inquisition would hesitate to punish, especially where conformity could be represented as the product of *force majeure*. It was more interested in claiming Mariana for Christianity than in punishing her, and having agreed to be baptized and return to her second husband, she was sent to rejoin him.[43]

Mariana's case naturally raises the question of what action could be taken by the Holy Office against a Jew who, though never baptized, had some sacramental contact with the Catholic Church, and had made this in Venice itself, where Jews could declare themselves. Where a Portuguese

---

[42] S.U., b. 79, proc. Mariana Polacca, test. the prisoner, 18 April 1624.
[43] Ibid., 1, 13 June, 6 July 1624; see also B.A.V., MS Barberino–Latino 5195, fol. 79v.–80. Compare the denunciation of Giacomo Periti by Costantino da Smirna, S.U., b. 92, 8 April 1636.

Jew behaved ambiguously, and there was genuine doubt among the witnesses concerning his real allegiance, he could be treated as a Jew performing the acts of a Christian – at least in the early years, before Paul IV attempted to claim all Portuguese as Christians. In 1549 this fate overtook Francisco Olivier, who was condemned to four years' galley service for having intercourse with a Christian woman and for irreverently following up the acts of a Christian with those of a Jew.[44]

In principle, no unbaptized Jew could be charged with heresy or suspicion of it. But the Inquisition claimed the right to judge crimes other than heresy. For the Church must defend itself against open or secret attack from without as from within. However, the need for an inquisitor's expertise was reduced where Jews or infidels were being accused of simple disrespect for Christianity. Delicate theological questions were not likely to arise in trials involving simple blasphemous oaths or physical attacks on sacred images, and the Church's penances and spiritual sanctions meant nothing to non-Christians. Hence, there would always be an argument for leaving such matters to the lay magistrate, as defender of the Church.

[44] I.Z., pp. 79–91, proc. Francesco Olivier, 20 July to 8 Aug. 1549.

6

Jurisdiction, Crime and Punishment: Attacks upon Christianity

In the sixteenth and seventeenth centuries, clerics and others who used the official language of the Church were accustomed to portray the Jews as treacherous domestic enemies of the Christian societies which sheltered them. The *perfidia* of the Jewish 'sect' (*'perfidia'* being a term inherited from conciliar decrees and papal letters of the thirteenth century) suggested not only a perverse rejection of the Christian faith but also a determination to undermine and corrupt it.[1] In a decree of the Patriarch Trevisan in 1560 Jews were described as 'most bitter enemies of Christ and his flock',[2] and his successor, Cardinal Priuli, declared in a memorandum submitted to the Senate that 'The fraudulent treachery of the Jews must be feared all the more because these are domestic enemies who can have dealings with every simple and unwary person.'[3]

How would the Church repel these attacks? Thomas Aquinas had opined that whilst the Church could not lay spiritual penalties on infidels or Jews it should none the less be entitled to inflict temporal punishments upon them, and to use its authority over its own flock to discomfit offend-

---

[1] For instances of its use, see Friedberg, ed., *Corpus Juris Canonici, Pars Secunda*, col. 773–4, 775–6, 816, 1290; F. Peña, ed., *Literae apostolicae diversorum romanorum pontificum, pro officio sanctissimae Inquisitionis, ab Innocentio III Pontifice Maximo usque ad haec tempora* (Rome, 1579), pp. 5, 36–7; and, among many examples found in the Inquisition papers, I.Z., p. 317, proc. Giuseppe Margaran, test. Francesco Marcolini, 11 April 1559; I.Z. II, p. 126, abjuration of Marcantonio degli Eletti of Vigevano, 11 May 1570; S.U., b. 92, proc. Carlo Antonio Barberini, test. Fra Girolamo Bonezzi of Reggio, ca. 27 Aug. 1636.

[2] U.C., b. 2, reg. 4, fol. 152v.

[3] S.T., filza 141, 31 Jan. 1596 Venetian style; B. Pullan, *Rich and poor in Renaissance Venice: the social institutions of a Catholic state, to 1620* (Oxford, and Cambridge, Mass., 1971), p. 557.

ing Jews – for example by ordering Christians to boycott them.[4] His authority was reinforced by the Inquisitor Eymeric, who declared that Jews might be judged by the Inquisition if they denied beliefs common to Christianity and Judaism. Should a Jew deny that God was one, and the creator of all things, his temerity would subject him to the authority of the Christian Holy Office, for he would become a heretic directly against his own law, and indirectly against Christian law. Should a Jew engage in any form of witchcraft or sorcery which involved sacrificing to demons, he would become subject to the Inquisition, especially if he did so in the presence of Christians. For he would in effect be withdrawing his allegiance from God to the Devil, and be liable to seduce Christians by this act of apostasy, of which he would be no less guilty than any Christian witch or conjuror. In any case, Jews could become supporters, receivers and defenders of heretics, even where they could not be heretics themselves. As such, they could be subject to the Inquisition. Passing from details to generalities, Eymeric argued boldly that the Pope, as vicar of Christ and heir to St Peter, had power over all infidels because Christ had power over them, and because the injunction to Peter, 'Feed my sheep', made no exceptions.[5] As a delegate of the Papacy, an inquisitor could presumably claim an equally comprehensive authority.

Both in Peña's commentary on Eymeric, published in 1578, and in the edition of the Inquisitor's *Repertorium* sponsored by the nuncio Castagna in the 1570s, the stress fell on punishing Jewish malpractices in so far as they were committed in the presence of Christians and threatened to lead them into religious error. If they were merely shocking but not seductive, or (like usurious lending) damaged Christians materially but not spiritually, they would be more appropriately punished by other judges, episcopal or lay.[6] Eymeric's principles were revived in Gregory XIII's Bull *Antiqua iudaeorum improbitas* of 1 July 1581. This was one of several papal measures with a common purpose – to increase the number of Christian souls by preventing defections and by winning converts. Professing Jews must be stopped from sheltering apostates, especially New Christians, and converts must be protected from insult and discouragement. The Bull authorized inquisitions to judge Jews in ten cases, including offences against common beliefs, sacrifices to demons, encouraging Christians to embrace Judaism, and aiding and comforting heretics. Its remaining clauses were all elaborations on the theme of blasphemy, ranging from the possession of blasphemous books in the shape of the unexpurgated Talmud to the utterance of words or the performance of rituals abusing Christ, the Church or the

---

[4] Aquinas, *Summa Theologica*, 2.2 q.10 art. 8 and 9, pp. 89–90; Friedberg, ed., *Corpus Juris Canonici, Pars Secunda*, col. 775–6.
[5] Eymeric, pp. 244–51.
[6] Peña, p. 95; *Repertorium Inquisitorum* ..., pp. 491–2.

sacraments.[7] Subsequent legislation of Clement VIII, in 1593, strove to extend the Holy Office's jurisdiction still further, by empowering it to judge Jews who kept, concealed or circulated not only Talmuds and condemned Jewish books but any works, in print or manuscript, which were forbidden to Christians on grounds of heterodoxy, scandal or obscenity. In the spirit of the earlier legislation of Gregory XIII, special mention was made of books attacking neophytes who had completed the transition from Judaism to Christianity.[8]

Reasonably enough, it would be claimed in later years by Albizzi that the Bull of Gregory XIII was no more than a move to codify long-standing papal and conciliar laws against the Jews and to revive the judgments of such respected authorities as Eymeric and Baldus.[9] But so explicit a statement might well alarm a government which, having seriously considered expelling the Jews ten years before, was now coming to terms with them again. It did not merely affect the Jews, but raised the general principle of the Inquisition's entitlement to extend its jurisdiction beyond cases of heresy. In mid-September 1581, the Cardinal Inquisitors-General decreed that where the Bull could not otherwise be promulgated it should be published in churches and affixed to their doors.[10] By the end of that month Campeggio, the nuncio in Venice, had received an official complaint from the Doge, who said he was not the first prince to express misgivings; and Campeggio was trying to reassure the Doge that the Bull contained nothing that could infringe the jurisdiction of any lay ruler.[11] Their exchange was inconclusive, and over the next few years it did in fact prove possible for the Inquisition, on several occasions, to assert its authority over professing and unbaptized Jews, and to adopt a fairly broad view of the kind of conduct which could expose such people to the intervention of the Inquisition.

Since its early days the renewed Inquisition had received denunciations of Jews alleged to have tried to reclaim Jewish converts to Christianity. But in 1579 it developed a new concern when a Spanish visitor from Cordova noticed a young Negro of about fourteen wearing the yellow cap of the Jews in the Ghetto, and rebuked him for turning Jew when he was surely no Jew by race. A Ghetto broker alarmed the Spaniard with the story that the Jews bought slaves in the markets of Constantinople and then circumcised them, made them 'of their own law', and brought them to the West. When the Spaniard reported to the Inquisition, at least one

---

[7] B.R., VIII, pp. 378–80, and the extensive discussion of the Bull in Albizzi, *Risposta* . . . , pp. 190–230.

[8] 'Cum Haebraeorum malitia', 27 Feb. 1593, B.R., X, pp. 25–8.

[9] Albizzi, *Risposta* . . . , pp. 191, 192, 194–5, 228, 230.

[10] Pastor, 'Allgemeine Dekrete . . .', p. 515.

[11] C.E.R., reg. 2, fol. 84r.-v., 28 Sept. 1581.

and perhaps two people were arrested for interrogation. They were actually brought in, no doubt for political reasons, by the Heads of the Ten, although the Inquisition was subsequently allowed to question them. Any attempts to punish the purchasers and proselytizers of slaves were, however, frustrated by the failure of the arresting officers to find the youth with whom Don Ferdinando de las Infantes had held his avuncular conversation. The dark-skinned Samuel Maestro, whom they did detain, appeared to be the child of a well-to-do Jew by a middle-aged servant of Ferrara who was 'neither white nor black', and was said to be Jewish herself.

Despite much confusion over the origins of the Negroes in the Ghetto, the preoccupations both of the informants and of the Inquisition emerged quite clearly. Jews should not own slaves; any sign of dominion on their part, even at a domestic level, was profoundly distrusted. No evidence of conversions to Judaism, of expansion on the part of what ought to be an inert and shrinking religion, could be tolerated. True, they were not recruiting Christians; but in a time of missionary fervour every heathen was potentially a Christian, and conversionists resented competition. 'Are you not ashamed,' the pious Spaniard remonstrated, 'you were born black, you have this grace given you by God to be able to turn Christian, and you have become a Jew?'[12] Later the nuncio Bolognetti declared that the Turks would never have allowed these conversions, and so the Christian religion should likewise refuse to permit conversion to any faith other than the ruling faith. He could only deplore the lack of hard evidence about the practice.[13]

This was no solitary example of the Inquisition's growing concern with unbaptized Jews. During the 1580s two such persons were fined for insulting behaviour towards Christians, and charged in hyperbolic language with the intention of attacking, through these victims, both the Church and the faith. The more prominent was Mendlin, who was in a modest way a public figure, for he served as banker to the small seaside settlement of Muggia near Trieste, one of several Venetian townships which

[12] S.U., b. 44, proc. Samuel Maestro, 30 April to 6 Aug. 1579; cf. also ibid., proc. 'Negromanti', test. Antonio Saldanha, 15 Sept. 1579, who says that about three years earlier the Jew David Pas had told him that Portuguese New Christians, both in Portugal itself and in Venice, habitually judaized the slaves in their own households and gave them gentle and loving treatment. Jews' headgear might be either yellow or – cf. the case of Felice Magalotti, above, p. 54 – red.

[13] Stella–Bolognetti, p. 289. The only well-authenticated case of a servant being converted to Judaism, that of Luna Maura, servant to the Filippi, occurred after Filipe de Nis had bought her as a slave on the island of São Tomé ca. 1566–67 and had her baptized; she admitted to having lived with the family as a Jewess in Venice when they subsequently judaized outside the Ghetto, but not to having attended any synagogue there. The Filippi and their household were treated as apostates – S.U., b. 54, proc. Filippi, 14 June 1586, 31 Dec. 1588, 3 Jan. 1589.

chose to depend for small loans on a Jewish rather than a Christian pawnshop.[14] Hence its citizens were a suitable target for sermons designed to warn them of the dangers of the Jewish presence. One of these was Mendlin's undoing, for he was accused of complaining to Fra Cornelio Rosa, the commune's Lenten preacher, 'that he had made so bold to speak out against the Jews; and Mendlin uttered threats, and said that he had such power in the place that the preacher would now receive less alms than was the custom.' The Bishop of Trieste moved strongly for the case to be tried by the *Podestà*, the Venetian governor.[15] Mendlin had previously been tried in the *Podestà*'s court for blasphemy, but had been acquitted on appeal to the *Esecutori contro la Bestemmia* in Venice.[16] On this second occasion the *Podestà* dismissed the case, but the banker's opponents adopted a new tactic and referred it instead to the Holy Office in Venice. Surprisingly, the lay attachés and the Collegio allowed the case to be heard and the Jew to be imprisoned during investigation for two and a half months and eventually fined 25 ducats. Both the facts in the case and the jurisdiction of the court were contested by the defence, Mendlin's three advocates stating the conservative position that Jews were outside the Church, incapable of heresy, and therefore not subject to its judgment – 'in accordance with the general rule that "The enemy of the Church is neither saved nor judged by the Church".'[17] Mendlin's conviction was a serious blow to this principle, which was already under open attack from the recent papal Bull.

Soon afterwards the tribunal showed equal zeal in protecting one of the Church's recent converts from Judaism. Neophytes were almost as sacrosanct as clergymen, and could be expected to show less fortitude under attack. Benedetto, otherwise Baruch, a tailor in the Ghetto, was fined 20 ducats and sentenced to make a public apology for that

> with brazen temerity and in contempt of the Christian faith, striking terror into other Jews who incline to receive holy baptism, he said to Giovanni Francesco Cagli, formerly a Jew but now a Christian, that he had done evil to convert, that he was a renegade dog, and other things, as the indictment will show.[18]

For a poor artisan, the penalty was a heavy one – equivalent to fifty or

---

[14] Cf. Pullan, *Rich and poor* . . . , pp. 540–5.

[15] S.U., b. 52, proc. Mandolino da Muggia.

[16] E.B., filza 56, Not. 2, fol. 150, 11 July 1579.

[17] S.U., b. 52, proc. Mandolino da Muggia, sentence dated 14 Aug. 1584, and plea by the advocates Calidonio, Mascharini and Trevisan. Mendlin claimed to have done no more than suggest 'that his reverence be pleased to reprove neither the Jews nor dealings with them, for he, Mendlin, is a public functionary. And so he must perforce do business with Christians, and this is done for their benefit.'

[18] Ibid., proc. Benedetto da Roma, 14 July 1584 to 8 Feb. 1585; citation issued on 27 Sept. 1584.

sixty days' wages of a master mason at this time, and to perhaps ninety days of a journeyman's earnings.[19] And the Inquisition could perhaps have been moved by Peña's ill-natured comment that a fine was doubly painful for a Jew because he came of an avaricious people.[20]

Any Jew who tinkered with the supernatural in the presence of Christians could now attract the attention of the Inquisition, even if he escaped its punishment. The Holy Office inquired, albeit inconclusively, into the activities of two Jews who performed rites of exorcism on a Christian child 'possessed by spirits', goddaughter of a silk-spinner in the neighbourhood of the Ghetto. In the course of these they used Christian properties and formulae, though it could hardly be said that they were worshipping the spirits in the child or doing anything other than commanding them in the name of God: 'I conjure you by the God of the Christians and by the God of the Jews, and by the saints of the Christians and by the saints of the Jews, to come forth from this body.' And the exorcist had made the spirit swear on the Christian Gospel to emerge by the child's foot, which caused her to suffer violent convulsions and left her exhausted and stunned. The Christian witnesses of the scene were unimpressed, distrustful, even frightened when 'that same day the child excreted certain matter, and when I saw it I did not want that Jew to come again.' Hence their remorseful complaint to the Inquisition. It might well have been argued that the Jews were usurping the powers of Christian priests, who had for various reasons refused to exorcize the spirits, and the *Repertorium* for inquisitors took the view that any Jew who used Christian words or symbols, for example by making use of a cross or invoking the name of Jesus, would risk being taxed with contempt for Christianity. Since the case petered out and the exorcists were never arrested, the records lead only to the bald conclusion that the Inquisition showed enough interest to conduct a preliminary investigation into the case.[21]

More menacing action was taken against supposed attempts by Jews to proselytize and recruit Christians to their own ranks. Despite the cases of Pietro of Naxos, Capponi and Moretto, there was little clear evidence of the power of Judaism to corrupt Christians who had no Jewish ancestry. Spanish or Portuguese New Christians were more clearly at risk, and more likely to seek aid and shelter from collaborators within orthodox Jewry. Some described how, as youths or adults, they had been approached or even converted by persons who reminded them of their

---

[19] See B. Pullan, 'Wage-earners and the Venetian economy, 1550–1630', *Economic History Review*, second series, 16 (1964), p. 426.

[20] Peña, p. 95.

[21] S.U., b. 54, proc. Jewish exorcists, 11–13 Sept. 1584; *Repertorium Inquisitorum* ..., p. 492.

heritage. Usually this appeared to have happened long before their arrival in Venice: their tempters had done their work in Salamanca or in Antwerp, and were beyond the reach of the Venetian Inquisition.[22] But in the case of the Filippi in 1586 the tribunal seemed to be unearthing evidence against Jews who had, within Venice, collaborated in the process of transforming baptized Christians into Jews. They interrogated Valentin, son of Jacob, of Salonica, suspected of acting as middleman when the young Francisco Dies was handed over by his father to be servant to the apostatizing Filipe de Nis. Suspicion proved deep enough for him to be sworn not to depart from Venice and compelled to give a security of 200 ducats; prudently, he fled the city.[23] Filipe de Nis himself eventually confessed that when he fell sick in his house at San Leonardo in Venice he had sent for a certain Dr Benarogios to circumcise him, and had later retained one 'Josenaar' to circumcise his nephew.[24] After the two circumcisors had failed to respond to the Inquisition's summons, it issued a decree of banishment against them, with the proviso that should they break the ban they must be relaxed to the secular arm to be punished as 'apostates and accessories of apostates, who may be publicly burned, or else drowned in the depths of the sea'.[25] And in 1588 the testimony of Miguel Ferrante, a Portuguese child aged eleven, threatened to implicate the Jews Galindo and Macchioro, who had sought to inveigle him into Judaism.[26]

At no time, between 1579 and 1588, had professing and unbaptized Jews actually suffered penalties which compared with those inflicted on baptized Christians found guilty of judaizing. But the potential of the Inquisition had been demonstrated and the evangelical interests of the Church in some degree secured. The events of the 1580s cast doubt on Sarpi's later contention that the Bull of Gregory XIII could never have been observed, because of the elastic powers it awarded the Holy Office.[27] On the other hand, it was true that the papal Bull was not expressly invoked as justification for the Inquisition's actions, and true, too, that by 1589–91 (as will appear later) the state had become anxious to claim as its own not only unbaptized Jews but all immigrants who – whatever their past – presented themselves in Jewish dress and lived in the Ghetto.

At all times the scope of the Inquisition was limited, not only by the discretion exercised by the lay attachés and the Collegio, but also by the existence of two lay magistracies dedicated to suppressing blasphemy, as

[22] E.g., S.U., b. 54, proc. Filippi, test. Filipe de Nis, 14 June, 29 July 1586; test. Filippa, 31 Dec. 1588.

[23] Ibid., 13 Nov. 1585, 9 Jan. 1586.

[24] Ibid., 21, 31 Oct., 10 Dec. 1585; 14 June, 29 July 1586.

[25] Ibid., 20 Aug., 21 Oct., 14 Nov. 1586.

[26] S.U., b. 61, proc. Miguel Ferrante, 15–22 March 1588.

[27] Sarpi, 'Inquisizione', pp. 173–5.

distinct from heresy, and to preventing the corruption of Christians through intimacy with Jews. These were the *Esecutori contro la Bestemmia* and the *Ufficiali al Cattaver*. The *Esecutori* were an eminent magistracy, a subcommission of the Council of Ten created in 1537. For the suppression of blasphemy, a sin which would surely bring the wrath of God upon any community which connived at it, was a matter highly relevant to that public safety which the Ten existed to guarantee. With time, the brief of the *Esecutori* began to range far wider than that of the Inquisition, since their jurisdiction extended to all forms of evil living and public disorder, in taverns and gaming houses as well as in churches and sacred places. This magistracy became the versatile instrument of a puritanical regime determined to keep a strict watch on immigrants and to control undesirables. Blasphemy and gaming, at cards or dice, were two specific signs of a general tendency towards loose and antisocial behaviour which a court could seize upon and punish. There was no doubt of the technical ability of professing Jews to commit blasphemy against the Christian religion, and the *Esecutori* met fewer obstacles to judging Jews than did the Inquisition.[28]

Their colleagues, the *Ufficiali al Cattaver*, formed a more menial board of magistrates. It was their task to maintain social distance between Christians and Jews, by supervising the Ghetto Nuovo, enforcing the wearing of distinctive headgear, and keeping a careful watch both on Christians who entered the Ghetto to perform domestic services for Jews and on the entry of Jews – physicians, musicians, old-clothes dealers – into Christian homes.[29] There was a distinction in principle between Jews who merely violated regulations governing dress and residence, for they as simple offenders against state laws would be subject to the *Cattaveri*; and Jews whose offences against these laws were such as to arouse suspicion of heresy, their appearances in the guise of both Jews and Christians suggesting that they had an allegiance to Christianity and were treating it lightly. In such cases, the *Cattaveri* – if they had happened upon the offender first – might prove willing to surrender him to the Inquisition and provide a transcript of his trial.[30] Cases involving sexual relationships between Christians and Jews, so long as there was no abuse of the sacrament of marriage and no suggestion of the Christian involved being converted to Judaism, were probably regarded as the proper business of the *Cattaveri* or of the *Esecutori*. Denunciations of seducers or prostitutes are found in the Inquisition's files, but there is no trace of their developing into trials.[31] A

---

[28] See the excellent survey by R. Derosas, 'Moralità e giustizia a Venezia nel '500–'600: gli Esecutori contro la Bestemmia', in Cozzi, ed., *Stato, società e giustizia* ..., pp. 431–528.

[29] U.C., b. 2, reg. 4; Pullan, *Rich and poor* ..., pp. 550–8.

[30] As in the case of Felice Magalotti, S.U., b. 87, 17 Aug. to 4 Sept. 1629.

[31] E.g. the denunciation of David Pas by Andrea Nin in S.U., b. 49, 3 Feb. 1582, and that of La Ghitella, Ricca and Regina in S.U., b. 75, 20 Aug. 1620.

division of labour between the two lay magistracies was eventually established in 1641, by providing that the *Cattaveri* should handle cases of sexual intercourse between Jewish males and Christian women, and the *Esecutori* deal with similar affairs between Christian males and Jewish women.[32]

Although the Inquisition did not prosecute Jews for blasphemy, there are instances of its charging former Jews with heretical blasphemy. Outlined in inquisitors' manuals, the distinction between the two offences was accepted by the Church and applied in states other than the Venetian. Simple blasphemy was a mindless act of disrespect towards a celestial being, God, Virgin, saint or angel, whose nature and attributes were in no real sense being questioned.[33] Indeed, it gained much of its force from its power to shock rather than mislead, and from the very fact of being a momentary denial of reverence to a being that, in the eyes of the blasphemer and his audience, ought to command it. It might imply nothing worse than over-familiarity with the holy – the debasing use of the Madonna's name to lend force to a statement or a threat, *Per la Verzene Maria*. It often sprang from the excitement of gambling, itself an activity ruled by the supernatural powers of good and evil fortune; it could express frustration with an oppressively pious atmosphere, in home or institution. The fact that mutilation of the tongue was considered an appropriate penalty in serious cases suggests that the offence was located in an unruly part of the body rather than – as with heresy – in the soul. Alternatively, blasphemy could be an open and malicious attack on Christian beliefs, committed from outside the Church by one who had never professed to share them. Obscene and scandalous it might be, but it entailed no disloyalty, save possibly to the host state whose duty it was to protect the Christian religion.

Certain kinds of stereotyped blasphemy were commonly attributed to

[32] E.B., b. 54, Capitolare, fol. 91; cf. U.C., b. 2, reg. 4, fol. 183, 24 March 1670. Sexual relations between Christians and Jews had been forbidden by the Quarantia Criminal in accordance with the Church's legislation in 1424 – see D. Jacoby, 'Les juifs à Venise du XIVe au milieu du XVIe siècle', in H. G. Beck, M. Manoussacas and A. Pertusi, eds., *Venezia centro di mediazione tra oriente e occidente (secoli XV–XVI): aspetti e problemi* (2 vols., Florence, 1977), I, p. 172.

[33] Cf. the nuncio's account of a blasphemy case in 1596 – very likely that of Battista di Domenico dei Sempreboni, a lacemaker, and of Lelio, son of Giulio Dronati, a linen-weaver from the Bergamasco (E.B., b. 57, Not. 3, fol. 277v.). The Inquisition was satisfied that the accused, whom it thought innocent of heretical blasphemy, had spoken the words out of bravado, foolishness (*morbidezza*) or sheer craziness, but not without a sense of sin, and not with any intention of contravening the faith of the Church (D.N., filza 32, fol. 379v.–380, 385v.–386, 16, 30 Nov. 1596). Although in the Papal States Paul IV made the Inquisition responsible for blasphemy in general, in 1555–56, in 1590 the Inquisitor in Genoa was instructed to touch only cases of heretical blasphemy – Pastor, 'Allgemeine Dekrete . . .', pp. 494, 496, 525.

Jews, though the evidence that they actually spoke them is not convincing. They were supposed to slander not only Christ's divinity but also his birth and character, depicting him as magician and seducer, justly condemned as a criminal by the Jews; and they were said to call the Virgin a whore. Crucifixes and consecrated hosts would likewise be victims of their blasphemy: a former Jew was said to have refused the sacrament with the words 'that he did not wish to receive a hanged man.'[34] A convert charged Isaac Cohen, a Levantine Jew, with repeating the story that Christ performed his miracles by raiding the Holy of Holies and stealing certain 'names of God', and with saying that Christians could command respect for him, as the Turks did for the equally false Mahomet, solely by *diktat*, by virtue of their *de facto* supremacy.[35] A boy in the house of converts was alleged to have said 'that Christ was a bastard born of carnal sin when the Virgin Mary had the menstrual blood upon her'.[36]

Uttered by former Jews converted to Christianity, such as Elena de' Freschi Olivi or Salvatore da Caglione, such remarks would surely qualify as heretical blasphemy, if not as evidence of apostasy. The distinction between blasphemy and heretical blasphemy was sometimes a fine one; in general, blasphemy could qualify as heretical if it denied, even implicitly, some article of faith. It was generously defined in inquisitors' manuals, by learned men analysing the implications of disreputable clichés in a way which might have astonished the ordinary people who spoke them.[37] Giovanni Battista Bonaventura, a fairly recent convert, was convicted in 1632 for uttering the phrases *Al cospetto di Dio* and *putanazza di Dio*. The first was a euphemism for *al dispetto di Dio* or 'in defiance of God', and – though once claimed for the lay courts when the Ten legislated about it in 1548 – could be called heretical in that it denied God the attribute of almighty (it was commonly used in conjunction with such threats as 'I'll break your arms and tear out your heart').[38] The second phrase was defined in a textbook as heretical because it denied the goodness of God. Since these were commonplace phrases, and suggested that Bonaventura

---

[34] For examples, see S.U., b. 36, proc. Abraham detto Righetto, test. Giovanni Antonio Vicinio, 27 March 1571; b. 43, proc. 'Odoardo Dyes', denunciation by the broker Antonio Moretti, 12 April 1578; the remark 'che non vuole ricevere un' impiccato' attributed by the inquisitor in Vicenza to Salvatore da Caglione, S.U., b. 101, 21 Feb. 1645; testimony against the Pappi by Prudenza, daughter of Zaccaria Pasquale of Vicenza, S.U., b. 107, 19 May 1660.

[35] I.Z., p. 97, proc. Francesco Colonna, 28 Nov. 1553; for the story, cf. F. Secret, *Les kabbalistes chrétiens de la Renaissance* (Paris, 1964), pp. 11–12, 77, 241.

[36] I.Z. II, p. 33, 46, proc. Aaron and Asher, test. Samuel of Cairo and interrogation of Asher, 8, 25 May 1563.

[37] Eymeric, p. 232; Masini, *Sacro Arsenale*, p. 18.

[38] E.B., b. 54, Capitolare, fol. 5v.–6, 19 Oct. 1548. For the use of similar blasphemies in a Lombard city, cf. G. Politi, *Aristocrazia e potere politico nella Cremona di Filippo II* (Milan, 1976), pp. 261–9, 301, 385.

was adopting the improprieties of Christians rather than denying their beliefs, he escaped with a public penance and abjuration *de levi*.[39]

At long intervals, the *Esecutori* punished a number of Jews for blasphemy. Tullio Romano, in 1549, was to be publicly paraded on a high platform, crowned with the 'mitre of ignominy'; his tongue would be placed in a yoke or a clamp for one hour, and then be cut across; he would afterwards be returned to prison and given eight days to leave the country for a spell of ten years' banishment.[40] Moses, son of the late physician Joseph de Datolis, was sentenced in 1574 to banishment for 'blaspheming against the law' or 'the most holy name of God', but was reinstated the following year when his accusers were themselves convicted of perjury.[41] And in 1611 Simon Scocco escaped the penalty of public mutilation only because the Jewish community volunteered to pay a total of 100 ducats on his behalf to a number of hospitals, nunneries and other religious institutions. He was none the less sent to serve in the galleys.[42]

Much more sweeping action was taken against the blasphemy supposedly contained in Jewish literature, and against the printers, sponsors or importers of Hebrew texts, whether Jewish or Christian. Here the weapons were heavy fines, or the destruction of the editions, or commandments to the effect that they must be disposed of abroad – with heavy financial losses to everyone interested in their production. In the 1550s and 1560s the role of the *Esecutori* in the censorship of the Jewish press overshadowed that of the Inquisition. They were made responsible by the Council of Ten for the wholesale destruction of the Talmud ordained by the Cardinal Inquisitors-General in 1553, and in this affair the Inquisition did no more than list summaries of the Talmud and works closely derived from it, which were also destined for the flames.[43] When, in the later 1550s, Christian surveillance of Jewish literature was extended to include all other Hebrew works and designed to purge them of the attacks on the Christian religion they supposedly contained, it was the *Esecutori* who followed the Pope's example by appointing correctors said to be well versed in Hebrew.[44] And it was they who, as late as 1568, carried out a

---

[39] S.U., b. 89, test. 1, 8, 20 July 1632; on 3 August he himself said: 'I do not blaspheme. Sometimes, when the Devil tempts me, I say *"Al cospetto de Dio"*.'

[40] E.B., b. 56, Not. 1, fol. 107v.–108, 6 and 16 Sept. 1549.

[41] Ibid., b. 56, Not. 2, fol. 102v., 123–4, 30 July 1574, 15 Nov. 1575.

[42] Ibid., b. 57, Not. 4, fol. 224r.–v., 9 Feb. 1610 Venetian style; b. 58, Not. 5, fol. 27v.–28, 1 Dec. 1614.

[43] See Peña, *Literae apostolicae* ..., pp. 97–9; N.V., VI, pp. 258, 267, 274–5, 277, letters of the nuncio Beccadelli, 26 Aug. to 21 Oct. 1553; D. Kaufmann, 'Die Verbrennung der talmudischen Litteratur in der Republik Venedig', *Jewish Quarterly Review*, original series, vol. 13 (1901, reprint 1966), pp. 536–8; Paschini, *Venezia e l'Inquisizione romana* ..., pp. 108–12; Grendler, *Roman Inquisition* ..., pp. 92–3.

[44] E.B., b. 56, Not. 1, fol. 161v.–163v., 24 July 1559; Peña, *Literae apostolicae* ..., pp. 94–5.

second ruthless and costly attack on Jewish literature, which was justified on the grounds that the books involved were 'not corrected, and not purged of the malevolent and detestable words which they openly utter to the detriment of our faith'.[45]

Taxed with blasphemy, Jewish literature fell under a lay magistracy, and this was a serious constraint on the Inquisition's authority over it. But the Talmud was also said to violate the laws of Moses, nature and decency, and was held to distract the Jews from the Old Testament in such a way as to impede their chances of seeing the truth latent within it and recognizing Jesus as the Messiah.[46] In so far as it was guilty of such errors, Jewish literature could be said to offend against the common beliefs of Jews and Christians, and to become indirectly heretical against Christianity; the Cardinal Inquisitors-General had said of the Talmud that it contained 'virulent, heretical, and perverted dogmas'. In Cremona, another great centre of Jewish printing, the Inquisition was striving to assert its control over the Talmud in the years 1557 to 1559.[47] Arguably, it might be dangerous to rely on the judgment of laymen, who would be advised by correctors of books who were often neophytes; however well they knew their Hebrew, they would never equal an inquisitor's expertise in theology. Greater skill and sensitivity would surely be required for expurgating a new or little-known work than for destroying utterly one whose errors were already notorious. For all these reasons, the Inquisition had a necessary part in the day-to-day control of Jewish publications, and its responsibilities probably increased during the 1560s, when it was successfully absorbed into the state's machinery of censorship.[48] Its position now gave it some authority over all Christian presses; since 1548, they alone had been legally entitled to print Jewish works.

From the case of Samuel Ventura, tried by the Inquisition in 1565–66, it becomes clear that its jurisdiction now extended even to ephemeral, non-literary publications concerned with purely Jewish affairs. These must still be submitted to the corrector Vittorio Eliano, a convert from Judaism who had served in Cremona and now worked in Venice both for the Holy Office and for the *Esecutori*. Ventura was banished *in absentia* for violating this licensing law; he had managed to publish invective against another Jew, the physician Joseph de Datolis, by appending it to the text

---

[45] Grendler, *Roman Inquisition* ..., pp. 140–2; P. F. Grendler, 'The destruction of Hebrew books in Venice, 1568', *Proceedings of the American Academy for Jewish Research*, 45 (1978), pp. 111–19; E.B., b. 56, Not. 2, fol. 41 *bis*, 22 Sept. 1568.

[46] Cf. K. R. Stow, 'The burning of the Talmud in 1553, in the light of sixteenth-century Catholic attitudes toward the Talmud', *Bibliothèque d'humanisme et Renaissance: travaux et documents*, 34 (1972), pp. 435–59.

[47] Stern, *Urkundliche Beiträge* ..., I, docs. 112–25, pp. 117–35.

[48] Grendler, *Roman Inquisition* ..., pp. 151–4.

of a paper seen and approved by the corrector and slipping it into the hands of the compositors at the press of Marino Cavalli.[49]

For at least sixty years, consciousness of the evils latent in Jewish literature was fostered by the *Bibliotheca Sancta* of Fra Sisto da Siena, published in Venice in 1566,[50] and the Inquisition was not idle. In 1570, it heard evidence against Marc' Antonio Giustinian, the former publisher of the Talmud, which suggested that he had salvaged remnants from the holocaust of 1553 and was starting up in business again as a specialist in oriental printing when serving as governor of the island of Cefalonia, away from the strict controls exerted over the press in Venice itself.[51] Some censorship was carried out mechanically, according to instructions issued in Rome and intended to eliminate simple disrespect for Christ. These included, for example, a directive to eliminate a sentence which the Jews were believed to add to the Pentateuch: 'where it speaks of the throne of God,' explained the corrector, 'it says "Super sede mea non sedeat alienus," and they call Christ *alienus*.'[52] More discretion was required, and subtler issues were raised, in 1592 when Sebastiano Tagliapietra, lecturer in Hebrew at the Patriarchal Seminary, examined the *Mif'aloth Elohim* of Don Isaac Abravanel, about to be published for the first time under Jewish sponsorship by the distinguished Christian printer Giovanni di Gara. In his opinion, its false conclusions and things 'repugnant to our Catholic faith' included the theory that at the end of 50,000 years 'the souls of the just shall be united with God, and there will be no increase in the numbers of angels or of souls, and the souls of the impious which have not by that time been purged will be made as nothing, as if they were corruptible bodies.'[53]

---

[49] I.Z. II, pp. 49–66, proc. Samuel Ventura, 10 Dec. 1565 to 5 Feb. 1566; for Vittorio Eliano, see also Stern, *Urkundliche Beiträge* ..., I, doc. 124, p. 133, and E.B., b. 56, Not. 2, fol. 4v.–5, 25 Sept. 1561. For the official ban on printing by the Jews themselves, see B. Ravid, 'The prohibition against Jewish printing and publishing in Venice and the difficulties of Leone Modena', in *Studies in medieval Jewish history and literature*, ed. I. Twersky (Cambridge, Mass., 1979), pp. 136–41.

[50] C. E. Ancona, 'Attacchi contro il Talmud di Fra Sisto da Siena e la risposta, finora inedita, di Leon Modena, rabbino in Venezia', *Bollettino dell' Istituto di Storia della Società e dello Stato Veneziano*, 5–6 (1963–64), pp. 304–11.

[51] I.Z. II, pp. 139–53, proc. Marc' Antonio Giustinian, 8 April to 27 May 1570; Grendler, *Roman Inquisition* ..., pp. 143–4; Grendler, 'Destruction ...', pp. 120–30. On Giustinian, see also D. W. Amram, *The makers of Hebrew books in Italy, being chapters in the history of the Hebrew printing press* (Philadelphia, 1909), p. 252 ff.

[52] I.Z. II, p. 168, proc. Antonio di Marc' Antonio Giustinian, test. Don Marco da Brescia, 29 Jan. 1575.

[53] See P. C. Ioly Zorattini, 'Il "Mif'aloth Elohim" di Isaac Abravanel e il Sant' Uffizio di Venezia', in *Italia: studi e ricerche sulla cultura e sulla letteratura degli ebrei d'Italia*, 1 (1976), pp. 54–69. On Isaac Abravanel, see B. Netanyahu, *Don Isaac Abravanel, statesman and philosopher* (second edition, Philadelphia, 1968); on Giovanni di Gara, Amram, *Makers of Hebrew books*, pp. 342, 351 ff.

During the 1590s Rome seemed determined to insist to other Italian inquisitors, especially in the Duchy of Savoy, that it was the business of the Jews themselves to expurgate their books. It was not for the Inquisition to give such literature a clean bill of health, for this would have suggested active approval of the portions of the works not actually censored as blasphemous. But it would be its duty to exercise retrospective censorship, by punishing Jews caught in possession of works which might be construed as attacking true religion.[54] How this attitude affected Venice is not known. Well into the seventeenth century it still had official correctors who declared themselves to be at once agents of the Inquisition, of the Heads of the Ten and of the *Esecutori contro la Bestemmia*.[55] It was to the Inquisition that Leon Modena applied in 1637, on finding to his alarm that an acquaintance was about to publish abroad a manuscript expounding the rites and customs of the Jews which he, Leon, had written some twenty years earlier 'for the perusal of persons who are not of the papal religion'. Belatedly, he produced a version of the manuscript,

> submitting myself and my work to the censorship of this most holy tribunal, so that should it contain anything whatsoever either directly or indirectly contravening reverence for, or the interests of, the Christian religion, the Holy Office may think of a suitable remedy.

The remedy proposed by the Dominican censor was the destruction of the work; but as it happened the Rabbi had no difficulty in obtaining a licence to print a revised edition in Venice in 1638, omitting the offending passages which dealt with the thirteen articles of Maimonides and with the doctrine of transmigration of souls.[56]

Although the *Esecutori contro la Bestemmia* were as much concerned as the Inquisition with the defence of the Catholic faith, and although their special concern with blasphemy and morality was always a tacit limitation on the Inquisition's powers, none the less the Inquisitor's expertise might still be required to identify and condemn the subtler departures from religious truth.

Between 1589 and 1591 the Venetian Senate made its most decisive moves to restrict the authority of the Inquisition over Jews. It now insist-

---

[54] Stern, *Urkundliche Beiträge* ..., I, doc. 161, pp. 170–5.

[55] Ibid, doc. 160, pp. 168–9.

[56] See C. Roth, 'Léon de Modène, ses *Riti Ebraici* et le Saint-Office à Venise', *Revue des études juives*, 87 (1929), pp. 83–8; M. R. Cohen, 'Leone da Modena's Riti: a seventeenth century plea for social toleration of Jews', *Jewish Social Studies*, 34 (1972), pp. 290–2; cf. also C. Roth, 'Leone da Modena and England', *Transactions of the Jewish Historical Society of England*, 11 (1924–27), pp. 206–7. For the manuscript of his *Relatione de tutti riti, costumi e vita degl' Hebrei*, presented to the Holy Office on 28 April 1637, see S.U., b. 94.

ed that even Spanish or Portuguese Jews settling in Venice must be presumed to be Jews if they presented themselves as such by living in the Ghetto and wearing the distinctive cap; despite the strong likelihood of their having had a Christian past, they were not to be 'molested on account of religion by any magistracy'. Since the term 'magistracy' might not include the Inquisition, it was also necessary to insist that Jews be subject only to the jurisdiction of the state, and to resist the claims asserted by the Inquisition over the past few years to judge professing and unbaptized Jews. The concrete result of those measures was to end the prosecution of Portuguese Jews for apostasy, and they sprang from the Senate's increasing anxiety to reassure a much valued mercantile community. Its specific policy towards Portuguese Jews must be analyzed in a later chapter.[57] This one will discuss only the Venetian government's insistence, at the Inquisition's expense, on its own jurisdiction over Jews in general.

Open battles over the issue were fought in the subject provinces rather than in Venice itself. The first clear example of a case being transferred from a local inquisition to the court of a Venetian governor arose, significantly enough, in Verona, where the Inquisitor Alberto da Lugo fell conspicuously foul of the state – for reasons at first unconnected with the Jews, but rather with his supposed attempts to put the state itself on trial before his court.[58] Gregory XIII's Bull had been received in Verona, where there was a small, impoverished Jewish community, in August 1581, and the Bishop had warned the Jews of its content, while at the same time expressing in reasonably friendly terms his confidence that they would commit none of the offences it described.[59] None the less, a few professing Jews were charged by the Inquisition in Verona, over the next few years, with speaking ill of the faith or with possession of 'evil' Hebrew books.[60] Much more momentously, in November 1590, Rabbi Matthias Bassano, who thought himself a confidant of the Inquisitor, denounced several of his co-religionists and charged them with organizing the removal into Turkey of three Jews recently converted to Christianity. The converts themselves were missing, and the Inquisition proceeded against those who had allegedly engineered their disappearance: there were suggestions of escape lines being organized for neophytes who had regretted their decisions, one passing northwards through Bolzano towards Poland and thence by the route of travelling leather-merchants to Turkey, the other (less deviously but more dangerously) eastwards through Venice

[57] See below, pp. 168–98.
[58] See above, pp. 22–3.
[59] S.U., b. 153, in fasc. marked 'Consiglio dei Dieci. Rettori – lettere (Santo Ufficio di Verona). 1581. 20 agosto'.
[60] B.A.V., MS Barberino Latino 5195, fol. 77v.–78.

itself. Three Jews living in the Ghetto Nuovo of Venice were mentioned as possible accomplices in these crimes; conceivably, prosecutions might have spread to Venice itself. Reasonably enough, Fra Alberto released the suspects on bail since the evidence was inconclusive, but he kept the files open;[61] three months later, he was himself in serious trouble, arrested, summoned to Venice and disgraced. In the autumn of 1591, having examined various procedural irregularities and questionable jurisdictional claims made by the Veronese Inquisition – including the case of a big-amous bombardier from Legnago – the Senate resolved to claim the case of the Jews as one proper to the lay courts and to argue the point at Rome with Cardinal Santa Severina. The nuncio should be informed that

> it is well known to all that Jews are subject only to the lay courts, since on account of their infidelity they are not subject to the cen-sures of any Inquisition of the Church. Hence they have always been judged by our own representatives, and they have that privi-lege, which we have always observed.

It was no watertight claim, but the nuncio, not knowing his precedents, failed to return a forceful reply. In December, the local Inquisition, perhaps intimidated by the experiences of Fra Alberto, gave way and released the trial records to the lay governors of Verona. Eager to demon-strate their piety, the authorities banished two of the accused and fined another four.[62]

Henceforth the Venetians and their governors were to maintain much more self-consciously the principle of lay jurisdiction over Jews, though they never suggested that Jews be immune from penalties for grave offences against Christianity. Indeed, it was important to argue that the justice of the state would actually be harsher than that of the Church – as did the Doge Grimani and the Senate in 1602, when the *Podestà* of Pirano in Istria was warmly encouraged to remove from the jurisdiction of the local Inquisitor the case of the Jewess Armellina, wife of Riviano, who was accused of reviling the Eucharist, performing acts of sorcery together with her husband's mother Sara, and thereby committing 'treason against God' or *lesa maestà divina*.[63] Any show of independence by the state against Rome was commonly accompanied by protests of its own ardent

---

[61] Q.C., filza 109, proc. 113 – copy of proceedings against Rabbi Marco de' Bassani, his son Grassini, Donato and Vivian Sanguineti, Abraham, son of Lazarus, and Rabbi Jacob Rapi, 8 Nov. 1590 to 7 April 1592.

[62] S.D.R.O., reg. 8, fol. 107v.–108v., 120v.–121, 125v.–126, 147v., 153r.–v., 154v., 156v., 160, 167v., 168, 8 June to 18 Jan. 1591 Venetian style – for the quotation, see fol. 154v., 3 Oct. 1591; C.E.R., reg. 4, fol. 195, 197v., 202r.–v., 13 Sept. to 11 Oct. 1591.

[63] S.D.R.O., reg. 13, fol. 178v., 187, 30 Nov., 1 Feb. 1602 Venetian style; C.E.R., reg. 11, fol. 27v.–28, 14 Dec. 1602.

Catholicism and by boasts of its own record as protector of the Church. Moses Belgrado, banker at San Vita al Tagliamento in Friuli, was clearly at risk when he was accused on vague evidence of converting a local cobbler's son who had no Jewish antecedents, but had emigrated through Venice to Salonica and had sent home two remarkable letters describing his new-found faith in Judaism. But the banker was imprisoned and arrested only after his departure from the Venetian dominions to keep a bank at Cento in the Papal States.[64] It was vital, not that Jews should escape punishment, but that the state secure discretion in dealing with them, since so many performed specialized economic functions which complemented those proper to Christians. True, the services of the Veronese community were comparable neither with those of the money-lenders of Friuli, nor with those of the oriental traders of Venice, nor with those of the Jewish cut-price mercers of Padua.[65] But their case, so nearly coinciding with the scandal of the Inquisitor of Verona himself, had focused senatorial attention on a major principle.

In Venice itself the mechanisms for avoiding open jurisdictional conflict were more highly developed than in the provinces. Sarpi urged on the representatives of the Venetian Republic the argument that the Church, offended by a Jew, was placed like a private individual: it must neither resort to self-help nor act as judge in its own case, but should rather complain to the state.[66] After the 1580s the Inquisition seldom invaded the Ghetto, and indeed it did so only in cases where there was at least a presumption of Christian baptism, as in that of Mariana. In those involving Portuguese or Spanish Jews, it intervened only when – as with Feliciana Diaz in 1635 – help had been requested by a young woman wishing to return to Christianity. No action seems to have been taken against Joseph Senior, her Jewish uncle, in whose house in the Ghetto she was found.[67] Cases involving difficulties over the baptism of converts' children, which might otherwise have drawn the attention of the Inquisition, were expressly delegated by the Senate in 1618 to the public prosecutors, the *Avogadori di Commun*;[68] and in 1637–8 it was the *Avogadori* who prosecuted before the Quarantia Criminal the Heads of the Ghetto, who

[64] See P. C. Ioly Zorattini, 'Note e documenti per la storia dei Marrani e giudaizzanti nel Veneto del Seicento', in *Michael: on the history of the Jews of the Diaspora*, ed. S. Simonsohn, I (Tel-Aviv, 1972), pp. 326–8, 332–4; P. C. Ioly Zorattini, 'Processi contro ebrei e giudaizzanti nell' archivio del S. Uffizio di Aquileia e Concordia', *Memorie storiche forogiuliesi*, 58 (1978), pp. 135–9.

[65] Cf. Pullan, *Rich and poor* ..., pp. 547, 554–5; D. Carpi, ed., *Minutes book of the Council of the Jewish community of Padua, 1577–1603* (Jerusalem, 1973), p. 476 ff.

[66] Sarpi, 'Inquisizione', pp. 174–5.

[67] S.U., b. 92, proc. Feliciana Diaz, 5 to 19 April 1635.

[68] See B. Ravid, *Economics and toleration in seventeenth-century Venice: the background and context of the Discorso of Simone Luzzatto* (Jerusalem, 1978), doc. B, p. 123.

were accused of complicity in smuggling out of Venice to the Levant the wife and children of Leon Luzzatto. He had declared his wish to convert to Christianity, and the children, too, would certainly have been converted by his paternal decree.[69] Fifty years earlier, the Jews might well have been charged by the Inquisition with impeding the process of conversion.

Denunciations continued to be received, for example in cases of dabbling in magic, but neither the soothsayer Benjamin Abendana, reported in 1634, nor the banker's nephew Moses Naso, denounced in 1650 for offences against both the Mosaic and Christian law, seem to have attracted serious attention from the Holy Office.[70] It was only in 1658–61 that the principles of Eymeric and of Gregory XIII seemed demonstrably to have been revived, in an inquiry into the conduct of Isaac Levi. As Rabbi and preacher at the Italian synagogue he was a man of some prominence, but appeared at the same time to be one of varied and dubious interests. He had some knowledge of the occult and probably of alchemy, and his reputation as a diviner spread outside the Ghetto, by word of mouth, to Christian clients. He attracted the attention of the Holy Office because his performances suggested not merely divination – which was in any case reprehensible in Christians in that it sought to discover by superstitious rituals knowledge that should only be imparted by God – but also the worship of demons (which violated the law both of Christians and of Jews).

The ritual concerned, the *esperimento dell' inghistera*, had been practised among the Venetian people for many years, and had been noticed with disapproval by the Inquisition since the 1580s. It commonly called for a glass bowl filled with water; for the presence of innocent children, virgins, or even pregnant women with innocence alive in their wombs; and for the use of mildly sacred properties such as candles or holy water.[71] The innocence or virginity of those present became the virtuous power by which to command a figure, such as a white angel, which would appear in the water and give true answers to questions. For the experiment seemed to echo the ancient theory that only a conjuror in a state of virtue could command the powers of darkness – an argument rejected by Aquinas, who had condemned as delusive the belief that any unauthorized

[69] I.R.E.C., Carte Diverse, fasc. labelled 'Pie Case de Cattecumeni contro Università degli Hebrei', 30 July 1637 to 24 March 1638. The Heads of the Ghetto were released, but sentences of banishment were passed on two Jews more immediately implicated – Isaac, son of Vital Israel dal Ben, and Joseph Senior (see fol. 115–18).

[70] S.U., b. 90, denunciation of Benjamin Abendana by Emanuel Papo, 12 Dec. 1634; b. 105, anonymous delations of 15 Feb. and 31 May 1650.

[71] See R. Martin, 'Witchcraft and the Inquisition in Venice, 1551–1650', seminar paper delivered at the University of Kent, May 1981; and, e.g., the case of Valeria Brugnalesco and Splandiana Mariano, S.U., b. 59, 30 May to 31 July 1587.

person could actually command the spirits.[72] As did Venetian Christians, Isaac Levi used the *esperimento* to detect thieves; in his efforts to discover who had stolen a girdle from Ser Francesco Basilio of San Samuele, he placed the bowl of water on a tripod which also carried a round piece of paper inscribed with Hebrew letters and had three candles burning at the three points of the stand. Subsequent ritual was more disquieting than the properties used, for two young boys professed to see in the water the image of a crowned and enthroned king dressed in black and holding a book. On the Rabbi's instructions, they used the words: ' "Sacred Majesty, our master [by which they meant the Rabbi] does you reverence, and we conjure you by our virginity to give the answers to our questions." ' When, subsequently, they persuaded the king to show that the girdle had in fact been stolen, to show them an image of the thief and identify him as a tailor, and finally to give them the initial letters of his names, they again 'begged and conjured' him to do so, thus destroying the classic distinction between the conjuror who commanded and the witch who deferred. When, three years later, further evidence suggested that Isaac Levi kept in his garret a number of manuscripts concerning the occult, and that he was circumventing the press laws by copying and selling them to bookshops, the Holy Office was permitted to take action against him to the extent of seizing and examining thirteen books and manuscripts, all but two in Hebrew, found on his premises. Since there was no clear evidence of his possessing the works mentioned, and since there were serious discrepancies between the statements of the two Christian clients involved in the thief-catching experiment, the case failed to develop. The witness who denounced Levi had probably known all too well how to phrase his report, in such a way as to arouse suspicion of apostasy in the form of demon-worship and thereby attract the attention of the Inquisition. But the unclosed file of Isaac Levi serves as evidence that, despite the Republic's general hostility to the Inquisition's dealings with Jews, the principles outlined in the 1580s had not been totally forgotten.[73]

In cases involving Jews, as perhaps in most Inquisition trials, the mentality behind the offence and the degree of public scandal it caused were both of crucial importance. In their distinguishable ways, the clerical inquisitors and the host state were interested in the type of person behind

[72] See N. Cohn, *Europe's inner demons: an enquiry inspired by the great witch-hunt* (London, 1975), pp. 175-6.

[73] S.U., b. 108, proc. Isaac Levi, 17 May 1658 to 20 March 1659 and 5 Feb. to 10 March 1661. For the quotations, see test. Giovanni Giacomo Moro, 17 May 1658; Ser Francesco Basilio denied having witnesssed the *esperimento* which Giovanni Giacomo described (10 March 1661).

the offence and in his social standing. His status, intelligence and education reflected the responsibility with which he could be taxed, and also his
power to mislead others; these things helped to determine his punishment.
The state was interested in the social utility of potential prisoners of the
Inquisition, in the value of the services which might be rendered to the
community and the economy not only by themselves but also by the
group to which they belonged and which might be affected by their fate.
Solitary and insignificant individuals, or social undesirables, would never
earn its protection. For these reasons, and from a general anxiety to
control the expansion of clerical authority, the state showed some sensitivity concerning its jurisdiction over Jews. A professing Jew who knew his
place, who dressed and lived as he should, was one who accepted the
state's conception of right order and had the right to be judged by its
criteria. Its authority to judge him for religious scandal was founded on
its claims as protector of the Catholic Church and on its desire to placate
the wrath of God.

Arguably, the quality of evidence transmitted by the Venetian Inquisition is the higher because it had to consider carefully the precise grounds
on which it would proceed. Before an arrest could be made, the clerical
members had to justify these to the *Assistenti* who were concerned to
protect the state's jurisdiction and take account of its economic interests.
To be able to involve prisoners in its proceedings, it had to start from a
reasonably strong *prima facie* case: it could not simply arrest them and
apply pressures which would make them convict themselves. Because
opportunities for judging Jews or former Jews were thereby restricted, and
the number of serious cases relatively small, the inquisitors in Venice had
comparatively few chances to build up stereotypes in their own minds and
to force individual cases into a recognized mould.

7

Denunciation and Defence

Clearly, the Venetian Inquisition prosecuted only a small proportion of those persons whom the canon law entitled it to pursue. Time and manpower were limited, jurisdictional disputes could well arise, and the state might either recognize no public interest in a prosecution or regard it as actively harmful to the common welfare. At most times, save possibly in the 1580s and the 1620s, unpursued denunciations and abortive inquiries about Jews or Judaism outnumber proceedings which actually resulted in arrests and sentences, or were otherwise brought to some firm conclusion. Loss of records makes some processes seem truncated, and others came to nothing because the suspects could not be found. These considerations apart, what distinguished the case which developed from the case which was brushed aside or allowed to peter out?

According to Eymeric, proceedings in matters of the faith could be started by three methods. A private accuser could launch the equivalent of a private prosecution. He could charge another person with an offence and inscribe himself *ad poenam talionis* if he should fail to prove his case: in other words, he would take upon himself the punishment which would have descended on the accused. Even in Eymeric's day – his treatise was written in 1376 – it was unusual to resort to this device, and an inquisitor would be expected to dissuade an accuser from employing it. Eymeric's commentator Peña remarked that had the *poena talionis* been essential to prosecutions the Inquisition would have found no one to risk laying information in matters of faith. More common was the method of delation or denunciation. A delator, in the strict sense of the term, did not undertake to prove his case. In principle he might be doing no more than reporting rumours of suspicious behaviour, leaving it to the Inquisition to make the inquiries and eventually decide what charge, if any, to level against the named person. No delator could guarantee that the Inquisition would act on his information; the Inquisitor would be proceeding *ex officio*, using his official discretion, and not at the instance of a party. Should the Inquisitor's inquiries turn up enough damning evidence, an accuser would eventually appear on the scene in the shape of the Procurator-Fiscal, the officer of the court who drew up the formal indictment; it was his intervention that virtually eliminated the private prosecutor. Finally, a third method could be contemplated, in that an Inquisition could proceed without a particular delator or accuser, but on the strength of local rumour or 'clamor', especially if it reached the Inquisitor's ears through reputable and zealous persons. And apart from these three processes, it was always possible for a person to confess his own crimes to the Inquisition and seek absolution and reconciliation with the Church.[1]

In Venice in the late sixteenth century the memory of the *talio* survived among some of those involved in the Jewish trials. It was of little practical importance, though as late as 1570 Angelo Fasuol presented himself as the accuser of Marc' Antonio Giustinian, Governor of Cefalonia, and was duly warned of the consequences of failure to prove his case.[2] In Venice, as elsewhere, the Fiscal had become the formal accuser of the prisoner, where the Inquisitor directed the inquiry and the tribunal as a whole gave judgment between the two adversaries, the Fiscal and the accused. Before sentence, the Fiscal would move for the resolution of the case; in the text of sentences, he might be described as bringing or 'introducing' the case before the court.[3] It was probably the Fiscal who extracted from the transcripts of evidence the lists of specific accusations or *libelli accusatorii* with which the accused was eventually faced.

Denunciation was the commonest method by which trials or inquiries were set in motion, although some serious cases were referred to the Inquisition by secular magistracies which, in the course of their own investigations of other crimes, had happened on evidence which might interest the Holy Office. Denunciations fell into four broad categories. They might arrive in writing, in the form of anonymous, or at any rate unsigned, delations. Or they might be signed and presented by persons who had a close acquaintance, or business dealings, or a relationship as debtor or creditor, or even some tie of blood with the person they named. Or, again, a report might be put in by a person not closely acquainted with the offender, perhaps not himself a witness to the alleged misdeeds, but reporting a general scandal which had been caused in a neighbour-

[1] Eymeric, pp. 283–4; Peña, pp. 124–6; Masini, *Sacro Arsenale*, pp. 21–4, 26–7.

[2] I.Z. II, pp. 139–43, proc. Marc' Antonio Giustinian, 8 April 1570; cf. also b. 44, proc. 'Negromanti', test. Antonio Saldanha, 12 Sept. 1579.

[3] E.g., I.Z., pp. 75, 90, 141, 218–19, 245.

hood or parish, in a church, or in some public place such as a prison; where, for example, a priest reported some blatant religious offence in his parish, there was a kind of fusion between denunciation and 'clamor'. Finally, a person might report himself for some grave offence, appearing 'spontaneously' before the tribunal to tell his story.

Generally, results would most likely be produced by clearly identified persons naming other clearly identified persons who had before witnesses committed specific actions or spoken scandalous words which could be clearly described – particularly where some tangible evidence was available, in the form of incriminating documents, letters or prohibited books. Accounts of generally suspicious behaviour, in the form of associations with Jews for business purposes or a lack of conspicuous piety, might be useful supplementary evidence. But they were not a sufficient foundation for an effective prosecution. Clerics would occasionally draw the tribunal's attention to general abuses, as a Dominican from Lisbon reported in 1579 the remark of an aged Portuguese merchant that 'in the Ghetto there were over a hundred Portuguese whom he knew for certain to have been baptized in Portugal.'[4] But there is no record of the Inquisition descending on the Ghetto to ferret out offenders who had not been named to it. The more 'impersonal' the testimony appeared to be, the less close the relationship between delators, witnesses and the accused, the more public the offence and the greater the authority of the person laying the information, the greater the chances became of a successful prosecution.

In principle it was possible to start proceedings, even to make an arrest, on the strength of a single witness's testimony. This, by itself, would not have sufficed to convict of heresy, though it might have been enough to justify torture. Having heard at second or third hand an account of the scandalous remarks of Elena de' Freschi Olivi in a parish church, the tribunal stipulated that if 'the aforesaid denunciation be upheld by even one single witness', she should be cast into prison. As it happened, there was no difficulty in at once obtaining the evidence of two respectable witnesses to the incident.[5] To arrest on the word of a solitary witness was in practice exceptional, though it was justifiable in law. The practice was challenged by the state itself after the unwelcome arrest of Nemias in 1588, but it was then firmly defended by the nuncio, who said

It was laid down by the sacred laws that in the matter of offences against Christianity (*in materia di lesa dignità di religione*) the word of one person was sufficient not only to making inquiries about the person denounced but also to casting him into prison, and that

---

[4] S.U., b. 45, proc. Ribeiro, test. 'Fra Domenico de Pace', 28 Jan., 23 April 1580.
[5] I.Z., p. 152, proc. Freschi Olivi, 19 March 1555.

nothing could be argued against it, save enmity on the part of the delator or of the witness examined.

He would not surrender this principle. Nor would he concede that the delator had been inspired by malice.[6]

At intervals people would appear before the Holy Office to denounce themselves for judaizing. Some had tired of their experiments with the faith. Others, whose birth had poised them ambivalently between Christianity and Judaism, were seeking to escape from Jewish relatives whose hold upon them had become oppressive.[7] Self-denunciation was sometimes a means of anticipating trouble and of deflecting it on to persons more guilty than he who confessed. When the convert Francesco Colonna was recognized by a Dominican friar in an attempt to escape to the East, he hastened to confess his own sin to the Holy Office and to blame it on two seductive and blasphemous Levantine Jews, hoping to 'obtain absolution without danger to himself and have the Jews punished for their evil acts, so that never again will they dare to lead an innocent astray.'[8] Self-delators, who had given proofs of repentance, were usually treated leniently and could expect only to have to abjure and to perform spiritual penances.[9] Having heard they were the subject of the Holy Office's inquiries in 1555, Duarte Gomes and Agostinho Enriques were well advised to recover the initiative by presenting themselves to it and offering evidence to clear their names.[10]

Unsigned delations could sometimes spark off inquiries, although – where the delator's identity was genuinely unknown to the court – they might fail to arouse interest. About 1588, several inmates of the debtor's prison at Rialto declared themselves scandalized by the irreligious conduct of one of their number and sent in an unsigned paper begging for his removal. A month later, disappointed at the lack of response, they tried again, now listing eight witnesses to Capponi's crimes. But still they did not sign it. Only when one of them was told by his confessor that the informant must declare his identity did they send in a third note, on which the Inquisition began to act.[11] In practice the rule was not so firm, since persons who had duly signed their delations might become equally

[6] C.E.R., reg. 4, fol. 20v.–21, 28 June 1588; D.N., filza 26, fol. 268v., 2 July 1588.

[7] S.U., b. 77, proc. Fernão de Martin de Almeda Pereira, 28 July to 3 Aug. 1623; b. 92, proc. Feliciana Diaz, 5 to 19 April 1635.

[8] I.Z., pp. 95–100, proc. Francesco Colonna, 28 Nov. 1553. Cf. also the much later case of Prudenza Pasquale, S.U., b. 107, 19–20 May 1660.

[9] But cf. S.U., b. 32, proc. 'Giovanni Battista' of Lisbon, 18 Dec. 1582 to 8 Feb. 1583, and below pp. 221–2.

[10] S.U., b. 24, delation of Gomes and Enriques, 9 March 1555; I.Z., pp. 228–9, 246, proc. 'Odoardo Gomez', 15 July, 19 Sept. 1555.

[11] S.U., b. 61, proc. Capponi, delations and test. Giovanni Alvise Zaffardo, 12 July 1588.

impatient at the seeming lethargy of the tribunal, and since an unsigned delation could sometimes attract attention if it named witnesses. Those listed in papers concerning Filipa Jorge in 1575 and the Bottoni sisters in 1591 were examined without producing results, but the unnamed delator of Giorgio Moretto set in motion a train of events which resulted in Giorgio's condemnation to three years in the galleys.[12]

Between the mid-sixteenth century and the 1630s, cases which had grave consequences for the accused – prolonged confinement under arrest, custodial sentences, heavy fines – generally met at least one of three conditions. They might arise from denunciations by persons of standing who were not closely acquainted with the accused, but were carrying out some kind of public function. Or they might have been referred to the Holy Office by a Venetian magistracy. Or they might involve misconduct in a public place, witnessed by a large number of 'scandalized' persons. Aaron Francoso, a rebaptizer, suffered in 1548 in consequence of information laid against him by the churchmen he had most recently tricked – by the Abbot of Santa Maria di Vangadizza in the Polesine di Rovigo and by the archpriest of the church.[13] In Cyprus, four years later, an official of the Bishop of Paphos reported to the deputy vicar that he had heard from 'many persons' of the arrival on the latest boat from Egypt of a Christian friar who had once denied the faith and become a Jew;[14] some months later, Pietro of Naxos received his heavy sentence in Venice. Elena de' Freschi Olivi was reported by a parish priest, and the three witnesses to her scandalous words were women in the congregation at a Sunday evening Mass. Two of them, Paola Marcello and Laura Diedo, were the wives of noblemen and plainly outranked Elena, who was the mother of a Jewish physician turned Christian; their status suggested integrity, and they were most unlikely to have been closely acquainted with her.[15] And in 1585 the parish priests of San Geremia and San Leonardo, together with three of their parishioners, denounced a Jewish household, thinly disguised as Christians, living outside the Ghetto: thus they initiated the charges against the Filippi.[16] In the trials of Capponi and Moretto, which followed three or four years later, the number of witnesses to their openly unorthodox behaviour in the Rialto prison or in the Ghetto was so large that only a small proportion could plausibly have been taxed with malice against the prisoner.[17]

In these six affairs, prosecution did not arise from deep-seated personal

[12] S.U., b. 39, proc. Jorge, July 1575; b. 67, proc. Bottoni, 14–16 May 1591; b. 64, proc. Giorgio Moretto, 8 April to 10 June 1589.
[13] I.Z., pp. 67–8.   [14] Ibid., pp. 128–9.   [15] Ibid., pp. 152–5.
[16] S.U., b. 54, proc. Filippi, 28 Sept. to 8 Oct. 1585.
[17] S.U., b. 61, proc. Capponi; b. 64, proc. Moretto. There were eleven witnesses actually called to testify to Capponi's misconduct in the prison; the case against Moretto was established by ten Jewish witnesses and eight Christians, mostly Ghetto functionaries.

enmities which had long been festering in communities or families. Two rather different situations can be discerned. In one of them, an established community closes ranks against newcomers or intruders, as the Jews of the Ghetto testify against the Christian, Giorgio Moretto, who has tried to be intimate with them. In the other, an artificial and temporary community of persons thrown together by circumstance, as are the prisoners at Rialto, express, through literate members who draw up delations, their distrust of a brash nonconformist from whose excesses they cannot escape.

In a small, close-knit community such as that of Muggia, the official positions held by hostile witnesses were of course no guarantee of their impartiality or public spirit. Those who accused the banker Mendlin in 1584 were the local physician, two judges of the commune, and its Procurator and syndic. But he claimed them as personal enemies, saying that they owed him money and were calling as witnesses either their own relatives or banished criminals. None the less, their standing and authority doubtless contributed to getting their suit a hearing and the banker a fine.[18]

For several persons brushes with police magistracies or – more spectacularly – with the Council of Ten were the prelude to Inquisition proceedings. The state was seldom reluctant to see undesirables further investigated from a different standpoint, even if its own magistrates had not convicted them. An evil-liver might easily be a heretic, and where a man was already in the cells (or even, for that matter, confined in a debtor's prison) the problem of capturing or obtaining permission to arrest him did not arise. Francisco Olivier, in 1549, had been in an affray at Santo Stefano; at the time of his trial he was in the cells of the *Signori di Notte*.[19] Samuel Ventura had not confined himself to written abuse of Joseph de Datolis, but had tried to hire the services of a Christian painter who lived just outside the Ghetto to disfigure Joseph and cut off his nose. His intended victim complained both to the *Signori di Notte* and to the *Avogadori di Commun*, who referred one of the complaints – about the unlicensed libel – to the Holy Office.[20] Andrea Nunciata, seventy years later, was first accused of purchasing stolen goods, and at the time of his opening encounter with the Inquisition had spent perhaps a year in the 'dark cells' of the *Signori di Notte*.[21] A similar fate had overtaken Iseppo Bon, the former servant whom he denounced, who had already been sentenced to six months in the same gaol.[22] Prosecutions would also

[18] S.U., b. 52, proc. Mandolino da Muggia, 1584.

[19] I.Z., pp. 79–80, 83, 20, 23 July 1549.

[20] I.Z. II, pp. 54–5, 56–7, proc. Ventura, petition of Joseph de Datolis to the *Signori di Notte*; test. 'Licinio depentore', 12 Dec. 1565.

[21] S.U., b. 91, proc. Nunciata, 4 April 1634.

[22] S.U., b. 94, proc. Bon, test. Giovanni di Ercole dalla Peota, Vicecapitano Grande, 9 Jan. 1636; test. Giacomo di Rolando Nate, 15 Jan. 1636.

gather momentum if endorsed, as was that of Felice Magalotti in 1629, by the *Ufficiali al Cattaver*;[23] when in 1632 a neophyte tailor denounced Pier Vincenzo Maria Sandoval to the Inquisitor at San Domenico di Castello he had by his side the constable of the *Cattaveri*, who offered evidence in corroboration.[24] Perhaps delators, learning the Inquisition's ways, realized that success was more likely if they could represent the culprit as generally irreverent, loose and immoral. A miscellaneous and imaginative list of charges was levelled at Bonaventura in 1632, and in 1644 Francesca della Fonte of San Giovanni in Bragora said of Stefano Valetta that she had heard him

> boasting, and saying that he had no fear, and that with money and friendship justice could be smothered, and that if he gave a pair of silken hose to a constable he could keep everybody quiet, and so forth.[25]

Should a man present a threat to security as well as to public order and decency, the state would surely be happy with his prosecution by the Holy Office. The long imprisonment of Righetto, believed to be a relative of the Duke of Naxos, coincided with the war of Cyprus and Lepanto and ended with his escape from prison conditions of astonishing laxity when the war ended.[26] As one commission of public safety recognizing another, the Ten in 1582 handed over to the Inquisition Giovanni Valetta, who was a convert to Christianity – probably a former Turk, but possibly a former Jew. He had been investigated by the Ten on charges of spying for the Turks; the Inquisition was content to ask whether at any time since his conversion he had worn the habit of Turk or Jew, and to release him when he denied the offence.[27]

It was quite probable that some of these prosecutions had sprung from personal quarrels, originating in the vindictiveness of disgruntled creditors or in efforts by evasive debtors to free themselves of their obligations.[28] In other circumstances the case might, for these reasons, have seemed unsound; but the emergence of a public interest in the accused man's detention compensated in part for the flaw.

[23] S.U., b. 87, proc. Magalotti, 17 Aug. to 4 Sept. 1629.
[24] S.U., b. 89, proc. Sandoval, 26, 31 Aug. 1632.
[25] S.U., b. 101, proc. Stefano Valetta, 17 March 1644; below, pp. 106–8.
[26] Pullan, ' "A ship ..." ', p. 45.
[27] S.U., b. 49, proc. Giovanni Valetta, 16 Jan. 1582.
[28] The denunciation of Righetto seems to have come from Don Diego Ortiz de Vera, formerly servant to the Duchess of Florence, who claimed to be his creditor for sums of 60 crowns and 10 crowns (S.U., b. 36, proc. Righetto, test. Don Diego, 7 Oct. 1570, 9 May 1571; petition of Righetto, late May or June 1571). Iseppo Bon claimed that Andrea Nunciata owed him 46 reali and 'had brought all these misfortunes upon me in order to demand my goods' (S.U., b. 94, proc. Bon, 3 April 1636).

Because of their supposed connections with Ottoman Turkey, prosecutions of Portuguese Jews were especially likely to become political events. In wartime, the Republic would agree to the Holy Office prosecuting a potential adherent of the Turk, but it was itself capable of obliging the Turk in time of peace, or of allowing the Holy Office to do so on its behalf. Gaspar and João Ribeiro, merchants, had fallen foul of Venetian secular law on at least two occasions. In 1567–68 they were fined for making usurious loans, and about 1571–72 – during the Turkish war, as it happened – they were confined in the Ducal Palace on charges of burning a slave-girl with a lighted torch.[29] But neither of these offences threw serious doubt on the Ribeiros' utility to the economy. Despite being denounced to the Roman Inquisition not only in Venice itself but also in Rome, Parma and Ferrara at intervals from 1569 onwards, neither was arrested until Gaspar was prosecuted after his son's death in November 1579. There was an intriguing but uncorroborated suggestion that the Ribeiros had boasted of paying a large sum of money for a *cucun*, a privilege or safe-conduct from the Turk which was guaranteed to protect those willing to be called his subjects or tributaries against molestation – even by the Inquisition.[30] More likely they owed their immunity to Venetian regard for those who claimed to have enjoyed the Portuguese King's trust and favour, as João pointedly did on more than one occasion. But there seemed little doubt that they were also ingratiating themselves with the Duke of Naxos through the clandestine marriage of João Ribeiro with a poor relative of the Duke's, the Jewess Alumbra. When, after João's death, the aged Gaspar was unwise enough to dispute about the repayment of her dowry, he not only allowed the affair to come to light through a remarkably specific piece of evidence – a marriage contract bearing his signature and exposing him to charges of crypto-Judaism – but also provoked the Turks into pressing the Venetians to deal with him. At first the Venetian government had wished to claim the matter as a 'civil and pecuniary action', as the concern of the *Avogadori di Commun*, who had jurisdiction over marriage contracts. But, as the nuncio Bolognetti maliciously put it, the Signory then

> recommended that it be despatched with an insistence which demonstrated how it feared to give the Turk the smallest suspicion of displeasure.[31]

[29] A.S.V., Giudici del Piovego, b. 1, Capitolare 1254–1568, second foliation, fol. 61v.–74v., 14 July 1567 to 6 April 1568; C.D., Criminali, filza 16, 12 Jan. 1571 Venetian style; S.U., b. 45, proc. Ribeiro, test. Benetto Locatelli, 18 Feb. 1581.

[30] S.U., b. 45, proc. Ribeiro, test. Samuel Abudent (otherwise João Lopez) in Rome, 27 April 1582.

[31] Stella–Bolognetti, pp. 136–7, 240–1. On the case in general, see Pullan, 'The Inquisition . . .', and below, pp. 230–41.

The public interest now demanded Gaspar's prosecution for heresy; expediency was a fickle protector, which could swiftly become a foe.

Men with some reputation for theft, violence, dishonesty or moral laxity, and men with a streak of political unreliability were prominent among those deeply entangled with the Inquisition. Women were not. Only one, Elena de' Freschi Olivi, suffered anything worse than spiritual penalties; others, once in the hands of the Inquisition, proved pliable and escaped with abjurations and penances. But women were seldom arrested, the blame generally falling on the men deemed to have misled them. There was no reason in principle why women should not be charged with grave religious offences; the Inquisition would have liked to prosecute Armellina of Pirano; and women had been prominent among the victims of the trials for judaizing which began to be held in the Viceroyalty of Naples and in Rome in 1569.[32] It may be that, like Isabella Medina, first wife of Gaspar Ribeiro, matriarchs were the members of Portuguese families most likely to perpetuate the memory of Judaism within the household; the wives of Italian Jews were often remarkably determined in resisting pressure to convert, even where resistance could mean the loss of their children.[33] But perhaps it was the very constancy of women which saved them – their more decisive attachment either to Catholicism or Judaism, for a number of reasons to be discussed in a later chapter.[34] It was the ambivalent and undecided, those who tried to be men of two worlds, who were most likely to attract the attention of the Holy Office.

A public interest was involved in the cases discussed above, and some of the delators who started them could claim to be serving it. Apart from parish priests, there were a few groups of people who might feel a special obligation to denounce crypto-Judaizers out of a sense of duty to the faith. True, the Venetian Inquisition lacked the kind of lay auxiliary force that Dominican inquisitors had been able to muster in other Italian cities. In Milan or Bologna, just as Christians might (by joining a brotherhood) profess a special devotion to a particular saint, some zealots could declare themselves 'crusaders', join a company of St Peter Martyr, and assume a special responsibility for denouncing suspicious behaviour to the Holy Office – though all Christians had this obligation in some degree.[35] Among its numerous confraternities, Venice had no such organization: always sensitive to undue clerical influence, it could never have allowed

[32] See Amabile, *Il Santo Officio ... in Napoli*, I, pp. 306–8, 315–16, 319; II, doc. 1, pp. 1–2, 5; doc. 2, pp. 6–12; doc. 10, p. 74.

[33] See below, pp. 233–4, 277–8.

[34] See below, pp. 225–8.

[35] G. Meersseman, 'Études sur les anciennes confréries dominicaines, II: Les confréries de Saint-Pierre Martyr', *Archivum Fratrum Predicatorum*, 21 (1951), docs. 27, 50 (misprint for 40), pp. 185–6, 192.

laymen to acquire a special obedience to an inquisitor. To remind Christians of their duty, its Inquisition depended on generalized edicts of faith; how frequently and effectively they were published is not known. That of 1622 included a reference to those who 'have adhered, or are adhering to, the rites of Jews, Muslims, Saracens or heathens, or have apostatized from the holy Christian faith'. But, unlike Portuguese edicts of faith, it did not contain detailed information as to how to recognize a judaizer.[36]

Confessors could remind penitents of their duty to lodge information with the Holy Office. When the notary Zaffardo told his confessor there was a heretic in the Rialto prison the priest urged him to inform the Inquisition and told him how to do it correctly.[37] Former Jews, or prospective converts, made some delations; it was a way of proving their sincerity, and they had an unusual knowledge of Jewish practices. So too, for rather different reasons, did governors or officers of the house of converts, the Pia Casa dei Catecumeni: they had a strong interest in preventing their former pupils from lapsing, and in tracking down the failures of conversionists in other cities.

In certain regions of Venice there was sensitivity to the outward signs of judaizing, the word 'Marrano' was known, and it seemed to mean something more than just a Portuguese or Spaniard. In the second half of the sixteenth century this was certainly true both of the parishes closest to the Ghetto itself and of the region of Santa Maria Formosa, which was the parish of Enriques and Gomes in the 1550s and of the Ribeiros in the 1570s, and attracted numbers of Jews who openly visited these merchants in their houses.[38] It may also have been true of the Frari quarter. For the Ghetto region, there is some evidence of popular hostility deep enough to result in denunciation – not, perhaps, of enmity towards Judaism as such, but of dislike and fear of Judaism being practised in the wrong place, outside the Ghetto's walls. When, in 1570, a Ghetto boatman denounced three families for crypto-Judaism he was able to include in his list of ten witnesses not only three Ghetto boatmen like himself but a number of others from quite widely scattered parishes. But his was the initiative, and he must have travelled quite widely within the city to gather evidence; it

[36] S.U., b. 153, 19 Jan. 1622; cf. I.S. Révah, 'La religion d'Uriel da Costa, marrane de Porto (d'après des documents inédits)', Revue de l'histoire des religions, 166 (1962), p. 61; I. S. Révah, 'Les marranes portugais et l'Inquisition au XVIe siècle', in The Sefardi Heritage, I, ed. R. D. Barnett (London, 1971), pp. 499–501.

[37] S.U., b. 61, proc. Capponi, test. Giovanni Alvise Zaffardo, 12 July 1588; cf. also ibid., test. Flaminio Pagan, 28 April 1588; S.U., b. 43, proc. Odoardo Dyes, test. Antonio Moretti, delator, 12 April 1578; b. 44, proc. 'Negromanti', test. Antonio Saldanha, 4 June 1579.

[38] I.Z., pp. 225–6, proc. Gomez, test. Donna Giulia, 26 March 1555.

was noticeable that the two witnesses examined from the parish of San
Tomà, near the Frari, themselves thought of the suspects merely as 'foreigners' and had heard the phrase *mezi marani* from 'certain young sailors'
who had come looking for them.[39] In 1585 a parish priest described a
conversation of the boatmen at the *traghetto* of San Geremia, the Ghetto's
parish, on the day the Filippi were arrested: 'Thank God,' said one, 'that
they will now rid this city of the Marranos,' but another replied: 'They
have left us the worst of the lot – the one who lives near the priest of San
Marcilian.' That priest, Don Bernardo Giordano, seemed less alert than
the girl of six who pointed out 'the Marranos' house' to his suspicious
colleague from San Geremia.[40] Away from these quarters the ability to
recognize a secret Jew was probably rare. Certainly the attempt to
denounce the Bottoni sisters, who lived in San Trovaso by the Giudecca
canal, ended in a fiasco.[41]

Spaniards and Portuguese in Venice made zealous delators. They
seemed far more conscious of secret Judaism than were most Venetians.
They alone boasted of laying traps for secret Jews, and they alone could
claim the knowledge to say, of Isaac or Jacob now living in the Ghetto,
that he had once been a Christian in Lisbon or had posed as one in the
Low Countries. Some Portuguese were clearly prone to using the Inquisition as a weapon in their personal quarrels, and were themselves more
vulnerable than most Christians to counter-charges of secretly practising
Jewish rites.

Inevitably, there was a danger that much of the Inquisition's information would be supplied by persons using it for ends of their own: that
the tribunal might become useful not only to a state which saw it as an
instrument of order, but also to private individuals who saw it as one of
vendetta, their denunciations becoming a sly substitute for personal violence. It can hardly have been difficult for informers to learn how to
present information in a way likely to interest the Holy Office. In facing
this risk, the Inquisition was not unique, and there is no reason to think it
more gullible than the secular magistracies of Venice. Indeed, it was
sometimes claimed by culprits that the information laid against them
before the Holy Office was only part of a general campaign of persecution
launched against them by their enemies through a succession of law
courts. In 1560, Giovanni Giacomo de' Fedeli claimed that Andrea
Pasqualigo had tried with his allies to prosecute him both before the
Signori di Notte and before the *Provveditori alla Sanità*, the office of public
health which had drastic powers of punishment, especially in time of

[39] I.Z. II, pp. 133–6, 'Contra Maranos', 10–21 Jan. 1570.
[40] S.U. b. 56, proc. Silva, test. Guato and Giordano, 13–14 Nov. 1585.
[41] S.U., b. 67, proc. Bottoni, 14–16 May 1591.

plague: 'realizing that these designs have not succeeded, they have con-
cocted further complaints in order to present them to the office of your
most excellent lordships'.[42] Similar assertions were made in 1589 by
Giorgio Moretto and again in the 1630s by Andrea Nunciata. In these
cases, the *Avogadori di Commun*, the *Signori di Notte* and the Heads of the
Ten had all (or so the prisoners said) been made the instruments of
cunning persecutors bent on exacting revenge by twisting the law.[43]
Sometimes, it seemed, information was laid in the Holy Office as retaliation for proceedings started by the subject of it in other courts. In 1570
the Governor of Cefalonia was proceeding against the chancellor and the
accountant-advocate-fiscal of the island; their brother laid information
against him before the Venetian Inquisition.[44] At a humbler level,
Francesca della Fonte in 1644 denounced for judaizing the man who had
reported her own husband to secular magistrates for begging in the false
guise of a cripple and for keeping an unlicensed lodging house.[45]

Since prisoners commonly defended themselves by alleging malicious
prosecution, it is easy to form a powerful, perhaps exaggerated, impression of the extent to which the Inquisition was exploited in this way,
and so came to serve a social purpose which, though genuine enough, was
not the one intended by its founders. But it is only fair to emphasize the
low rate of success where the prosecution obviously arose out of tensions
within a family or enmities within a foreign community; where the
accused had no prior record of undesirable behaviour; and where misdeeds were supposed to have been perpetrated in private rather than in
public. The secrecy usually promised to informers and hostile witnesses
was no infallible protection against retaliation, and where personal
enmities were involved there was a greater likelihood of the victim
identifying his adversaries. Denunciations could occasionally recoil in
unexpected ways on those who laid them.

It is possible to reconstruct three examples of tortuous attempts to enlist
the Inquisition's aid in personal conflicts. One occurred within the tense
and uneasy Portuguese community in Venice in the late 1570s. The
others arose within the immediate families of two converts whose wives
seemingly rebelled against them with the encouragement of allies and
perhaps lovers, playing on their former Judaism in order to remove them
from the scene: in the household of Odoardo Dyes in 1578, and in that of
Giovanni Battista Bonaventura in 1632.

About 1577, the Portuguese community in Venice, recently swelled by

---

[42] I.Z., pp. 312–13.
[43] S.U., b. 64, proc. Moretto, 13 April 1589; S.U., b. 91, proc. Nunciata, 12 Jan. 1636.
[44] I.Z. II, pp. 148–9, proc. Marc' Antonio Giustinian, paper presented 27 April 1570.
[45] S.U., b. 101, proc. Stefano Valetta, 17 March 1644.

immigrants from the Spanish Low Countries, was riven by a savage quarrel which focused on the impoverished family of País, who lived in the parish of Santa Maria Maddalena. João Ribeiro, who in his time kept several mistresses, made some ungentlemanly proposal concerning the eldest País girl to her father, and may even have got her pregnant. Violence broke out, João Ribeiro was scarred on the face by the girl's brother, the País scattered, and the father died in prison in Mantua, while the wife and daughters left for Ferrara and were reported to be living there as Jews.[46] Despite their departure, their influence seemed to linger on in Venice, with baneful consequences for a former lodger in the household. This was Antonio Saldanha, later described by one of his employers as 'a splendid writer and a most learned humanist'.[47] He was a recent arrival, who earned his living as an independent schoolmaster, as a private tutor to patrician and citizen families, and for a time as instructor to novices at the abbey of the Carità. He had been wounded in the País affray, and was soon suffering from an acute sense of isolation in his sickness which he blamed on the loyalty of the close-knit Portuguese Jewish fraternity to 'those accursed women', who apparently blamed him for their father's death. He saw himself as 'a poor wretch suffering for others' (by which he could well have meant the guilty Ribeiro), 'like asparagus among thorns' (come sparrago fra le spine).[48] Saldanha had never avoided Jewish company himself; he was once a regular guest in the house of David Pas, a professing Jew with courtly connexions living in the Ghetto and keeping (some said) a gambling house. In his present mood, however, Judaism presented itself as a bitter foe, and, as he later wrote to a colleague, 'his conscience troubled him for failing to unmask those Portuguese who did not live according to Christianity.'[49]

For the time being, however, he was probably too apathetic to do more than nurse resentment. To spur the outsider into action came the figure of Estevão Nogueira, a young soldier based at Milan, who called himself the son of Alvaro Anes Nogueira, Inquisitor and diocesan Vicar-General of Coimbra. Claiming to have from his father an extensive knowledge of the families of Portuguese emigrés to Venice, he used it to approach Miguel

[46] S.U., b. 44, proc. 'Negromanti', den. Antonio Saldanha, 11 Jan. 1579; test. João Ribeiro, 23 July 1579; test. Antonio Saldanha, 12 Sept. 1579; S.U., b. 45, proc. Ribeiro, den. Enrique de Mello, 16 Nov. 1575; test. Gaspar Ribeiro, 8 March 1580; test. Madonna Elena, 9 April 1580; test. Lorenzo Ottolin, 2 March 1581; test. 'Fra Domenico de Pace', 17 May 1581.

[47] S.U., b. 44, proc. 'Negromanti', test. Don Gabriele and Don Ferrandino Fiamma, 10 Sept. 1579.

[48] S.U., b. 45, proc. Ribeiro, letter of Saldanha to Vincenzo Scrova, 22 July 1577.

[49] S.U., b. 44, proc. 'Negromanti', test. Giovanni Antonio Rodeglia of Bologna, 4 June 1579.

Vaz, Jorge Lopez and their households. He won their confidence by the spurious claim to be a relative of theirs who had once been a Jesuit but had left the order. By these tactics, he supposedly tricked them into trying to reclaim him for the Jewish faith. Saldanha was persuaded to join him in denouncing Lopez and Vaz to the Inquisition of Venice, and he added further testimony implicating the Ribeiros, most of it ultimately traceable to the País girls.[50] Nogueira then went about his military duties, leaving Saldanha to face the repercussions of their joint action.

In the early months of 1579, the Inquisition proved disappointingly slow to act, whilst news of the denunciation leaked out and Saldanha – by his own account – found himself negotiating through a friend with the incriminated Portuguese, who threatened retaliation if he failed to undo what he had begun. It was agreed that he should forge a letter which purported to come from the absent Nogueira, grievously sick in Barcelona and troubled in his conscience, admitting that the denunciation was part of a plot which stemmed from a trivial personal grudge. Unfortunately, he underestimated the devious ingenuity of João Ribeiro, who proceeded to demonstrate to the Inquisition that the letter was indeed a forgery and to use it to discredit, not Nogueira, but Saldanha.[51] To contribute further to his downfall, Saldanha's enemies had sown counter-rumours about him with his employers in the hope that they would pass them on to the Holy Office. These suggested that he had taken up the Jewish faith in Ferrara.[52] It was not they, however, that ruined him and completed the process whereby the denunciation recoiled upon its maker; having found him uncircumcised,[53] the Inquisition pursued the judaizing charges no further, and probably dismissed them as mere weapons in the internecine warfare of the Portuguese. He was found to be a renegade Franciscan Observant, formerly a preacher in Lisbon, who had cast off his habit in Rome on failing to obtain a dispensation to leave the order. After arrest he suffered questioning about the books and other possessions seized in his house, and the suspicion grew that he had been implicated in a circle of necromancers bent on the acquisition of buried treasure with the aid of spirits, a clique to which the egregious Nogueira also belonged. For these offences Saldanha and certain members of his circle were tried and eventually sentenced to life imprisonment. There is no trace of action

---

[50] S.U., b. 44, proc. 'Negromanti', den. Nogueira and Saldanha, 11, 20 Jan. 1579; test. Saldanha, 4 June 1579.

[51] S.U., b. 44, proc. 'Negromanti', test. João Ribeiro and Antonio Saldanha, 11 Aug., 1 Sept. 1579; the forged letter appears in b. 45, proc. Ribeiro, and is dated 9 July 1579.

[52] S.U., b. 44, proc. 'Negromanti', test. João Ribeiro and Ruy Lopez, 23 July 1579; test. Francisco Oglies and Bernardo Rodriguez, 2, 3 Sept. 1579; test. Don Gabriele and Don Ferrandino Fiamma, 10 Sept. 1579; test. Antonio Saldanha, 12 Sept. 1579.

[53] Ibid., 15 Sept. 1579.

against Vaz and Lopez; João Ribeiro died in his bed a few months later, and the subsequent prosecution of his aged father was initiated by different pressures and based on different evidence from that presented by Saldanha.

Accusations of judaizing could plainly be used as expressions of conflict between the Portuguese, for both parties to the quarrel had invoked them. Denunciations might be made out of grievances such as Saldanha's or out of the officious mischief-making of Nogueira, who came close to that familiar figure of Inquisition literature, the spy from Spain or Portugal who pursues refugees abroad.[54] Though made from questionable motives, they were not necessary quite untrue. But the Inquisition, perhaps noting that Venetians had not been scandalized, and itself despairing of disentangling Portuguese rivalries, reacted with great caution.

Although the trials of Dyes and Bonaventura were separated by half a century, they presented to the Inquisition three common features: a strict or even tyrannical husband who had once been a Jew, a flighty wife, and a caucus of friends or relations who seemed to be abetting the wife's attempt to break away.[55] Odoardo Dyes had once been the Jew Isaac Salvarico, baptized in the church of San Zulian in Venice about 1562; his name was probably an Italian version of that of some Spanish or Portuguese benefactor who had stood godfather to him. Giovanni Battista Bonaventura was a Levantine Jew, baptized in the Venetian church of Santa Sofia, about 1626–28. Both had divorced their Jewish wives and taken others who were native Christians. The household of Dyes contained, according to his second wife, one book – a ledger, which she burned because it was his custom, every evening, to beat her over the head with it. Bonaventura enforced his will with a knife, and his parish priest, no hostile witness, called him 'governed by jealousy and fury, and replete with suspicion'.

Each husband cast aspersions on his Christian wife's morals. After conversion, Dyes had departed to the Low Countries, had lived out of wedlock with Susanna van der Blun, and had then married her in Antwerp about 1565 or 1566. Later he told the tribunal,

> When I took her to wife, low be it spoken, she was a common prostitute, as I undertake to prove, and I (being young) made friends with her and gave her board for two years.

Certainly, after their journey southwards to Venice towards 1578 to

[54] Cf., for example, G. Laras, 'Diego Lorenzo Picciotto: un delatore di Marrani nella Livorno del Seicento', in *Scritti in memoria di U. Nahon* (Jerusalem, 1978), pp. 65–104.

[55] S.U., b. 43, proc. Odoardo Dyes, 12 April to 6 Dec. 1578; b. 89, proc. Giovanni Battista Bonaventura, 1 July to 9 Dec. 1632.

escape the wars and 'the Lutherans', she had a number of male friends who suddenly replaced her husband in her affections, as two successive versions of her last will and testament suggest. In a modest way, Susanna was a woman of property, for she had a house in Ghent, some lands and possessions at Watervliet, and eight boats or barges at Biervliet – not to mention a claim to some bales of kersey which were being sent from Flanders to Venice. At first her entire estate was left in affectionate terms to her husband, but within three weeks she changed her dispositions drastically, left her possessions in the Low Countries to her brother and sisters, and bestowed her goods and stock in Turin and Venice on four persons described as her 'very good friends'.[56] They included the broker who was shortly to denounce her husband to the Inquisition, and a person later said by Dyes to be a Spanish soldier from Flanders with designs on Susanna.

Bonaventura and his witnesses maintained that his notorious jealousy had firm foundations, for his wife Meneghina, a Venetian mirror-maker's daughter, was receiving presents which varied from the pious to the lewd (from a valuable rosary to a man's member modelled in sugar) at the hands of the Flemish agent of the Pellicorni, merchants in the parish of Santa Sofia. Meneghina's determination to parade her charms in public was notorious: she had left the house 'splendidly bedecked'; she had walked the street in the fashionable high-heeled clogs and smelling of musk; she had been seen on the balcony of her husband's house in the Calle de' Preti. After Bonaventura's arrest, his wife, her mother and two friends lost no time in asserting their freedom by setting up house together, and the parish priest took the former Jew's son into his care to save him from corruption.

In neither case did the wife actually lay the information which sparked off the inquiry, but in both cases the evidence depended heavily on assertions made by the wife or her friends, and on incidents supposed to have taken place within the household. In both cases the husband was supposed to have deterred his wife from her Christian devotions – Odoardo Dyes had prevented Susanna from taking Communion and making her confession even in grievous sickness, Giovanni Battista had tried to stop his wife from going to Mass or 'taking the Jubilee'. For Odoardo, much depended on words he was said to have spoken to Susanna on her sickbed: 'Susanna, for your soul's sake take heed of what you do, and do not believe in Christ, for he is not the Messiah!' With greater variety it was said of Giovanni Battista by his detractors that he blasphemed, that

---

[56] W. Brulez, *Marchands flamands à Venise, I: 1568–1605* (Brussels–Rome, 1965), pp. 8–9, gives particulars of Susanna's wills and of other business transactions, taken from the books of the notary Giovanni Andrea Catti.

he ate meat or eggs at improper times and responded rudely to rebukes, that he had threatened to depart for the Levant and bear away wife and children with him; and, finally, that he had committed acts of sexual corruption, involving incest, sodomy and child prostitution – especially in the form of procuring for the Turks, to whom he was a broker.

Had the broker Moretti, one of Susanna's friends, really said to Odoardo Dyes that he would see him die in prison, or else at the hands of the Inquisition, and that he would steal away his wife? Was his motive, as the defendant suggested, merely to lay hands on bales of cloth from Antwerp? Whatever the truth behind these two cases – and informers surely had no monopoly of the art of lying – there was a smell of intrigue and adultery about each of them strong enough to cast doubt on the accusations and strengthen the defence's hand. Any former Jew was vulnerable to charges of lapsing, the convert of Italy no less than the *converso* of Spain. But the Inquisition was not blind to the dangers of malicious prosecution, and perhaps not eager to admit that the Church's campaigns for conversion had failed to produce good Christians. The Inquisition dropped its proceedings against Odoardo Dyes, and Bonaventura was convicted only of heretical blasphemy, which he had partially admitted; his women, if this was really their object, got him out of the way – but only for the six months for which the case was investigated. Matters of this kind had to be taken up; otherwise the Inquisition might have denied protection to a wife against the evil influence of her husband. But, depending as they did on the testimony of relatives, neighbours, servants and other persons easily caught up in domestic feuds, the risk of false information was too glaring to be ignored, and these prosecutions – lacking an element of the impersonal, lacking in open scandal and lacking in a clear public interest – were the least likely to succeed.

Skilful defences could give the tribunal pause and moderate its sentences, though absolutions were rare when the Inquisition had made an arrest. Once it had committed itself to this step, the central issues were the precise character and gravity of the offence and the extent of the penalty, rather than the absolute guilt or innocence of the prisoner.

Formal defences could be conducted wholly or partially by the accused person himself, and in this the Portuguese – whose relatives and friends sometimes had experience of campaigning to resist a different Inquisition – showed especial resourcefulness.[57] Duarte Gomes claimed to have studied arts, humanities, philosophy, medicine and to some extent theology, and to have been a public lecturer in Lisbon; after turning his hand to making money as a merchant and commission agent in Venice, he put both his broad education and his commercial connexions to good use

[57] Cf. Pullan, ' "A ship ..." ', pp. 47–8.

when he cleared himself of the suspicion of judaizing heresy in 1555, calling on his merchant acquaintances to vouch for his Christianity.[58] Elderly and dependent suspects were sometimes defended, formally or informally, by relatives who saw their personal honour or material interests caught up with the fate of the Inquisition's prisoner. Gaspar Ribeiro's most zealous champion was not among his lawyers – his impulsive, quarrelsome son-in-law, the Vicentine gentleman Vincenzo Scrova, was heavily fined for interfering with witnesses.[59] Since the Inquisition made no serious attempt in these cases to isolate the defendants from family or friends, they received much active assistance over and above mere legal advice.

Advocates, doctors in canon law entitled to plead in the ecclesiastical courts of Venice, could be empanelled to assist the defendant. Unlike the secular courts, which were manned by lay patrician judges of limited tenure addressing themselves to factual issues, the inquiries of the Holy Office were directed by a highly experienced professional judge applying an elaborate system of written law, and justice demanded that the defendant be advised on procedures and legal technicalities. And defences could be conducted not only on legal grounds, but also on historical, medical or theological. Righetto's defence was based not only on his advocate's pleas, but also on his own citation of chronicles which described the history of Portuguese Jewry in a way calculated to shake the assumption that all Jews born in his time in that country must have undergone legitimate baptism. And he exposed the deadly legislation of Paul IV to historical criticism, by showing it to be out of key with the more enlightened attitudes of that Pope's predecessors, and therefore to be dismissed as a temporary flaw in papal policy.[60] Dr Freschi Olivi's defence of his aged mother was a learned, at times pompous and didactic, synthesis of his medical and theological knowledge.

Despite appearances of a genuine legal contest between the Procurator-Fiscal and the advocate for the defence, the prisoner's side was handicapped in at least two respects. Procedures were weighted towards securing the interests of the Church and protecting its informers, rather than towards safeguarding the innocent, whose main protection would theoretically lie in the benevolence and pastoral care of the court itself.[61] As the *processo* unfolded, the inquiry was transmuted into the trial, and the defendant would be interrogated on oath without the presence or advice of a defence advocate: professional services were offered to the defendant only when the case against him appeared to be complete.

---

[58] I.Z., pp. 230, 232, proc. Gomez, 3 Aug. 1555; pp. 237–44, 3–5 Sept. 1555.
[59] See below, p. 233.
[60] Pullan, ' "A Ship ..." ', pp. 49–51.
[61] See Peña, pp. 132–3.

Furthermore, the dock and witness stand were seldom occupied at the same moment, and the names of delators and hostile witnesses were generally concealed from the prisoner. Always a delicate subject, the appointment of advocates and the suppression of witnesses' names had caused bitter controversy abroad in the first half of the sixteenth century, when the procedures of the Spanish Inquisition were heavily criticized by Portuguese and Neapolitans, fearful of its introduction into their own countries.

Advocates, so critics of the Spanish Inquisition declared, were hacks, false friends, sycophants, employees of the court charged with winning the prisoner's confidence only to betray him. They might, by persuading him of his own guilt and withdrawing their protection at a psychological moment, increase the sense of isolation to which the prisoner's separation from the world had already brought him, thereby hastening the collapse of his resistance. The right to appoint one's own advocate, instead of accepting a nominee of the court, was of especial concern in Portugal in the 1530s. Conscientious advocates in Spain were not always protected from disciplinary action by the court. And Henry Charles Lea, the great historian of the Spanish Inquisition, argued forcefully that although the presence of advocates on both sides created the semblance of an adversarial system, it was really no more than a sham.[62]

It is true that in Venice the performance of advocates was variable, and some prisoners such as Capponi made only a token use of them, preferring to throw themselves upon the court's mercy.[63] But only one, Tommaso Trevisan in the case of Filipe de Nis, actually declared a case indefensible.[64] Most advocates were probably appointed by the court, especially for foreigners who did not know the Venetian scene; Venetian residents had some genuine choice and the tribunal would urge them to exercise it, though they were unlikely, in a Church court, to be able to employ the lawyers who regularly served them in everyday business.[65] When first

[62] See Lea, *Inquisition of Spain*, II, pp. 478–81, III, pp. 38–52; Hercolano, *Inquisition in Portugal*, pp. 377–8, 380–1, 417.

[63] S.U., b. 61, proc. Capponi, 28 June 1588: the advocate Bulgarutius says on Capponi's behalf: 'he wishes to make no other defence, but trusts to the charity of the Holy Office; none the less he would remind you that this is a conspiracy on the part of a person from Treviso.'

[64] S.U., b. 54, proc. Filippi, 6 May, 3 June 1586.

[65] The advocate Giovanni de Rubeis was assigned to Felice Magalotti after he had said that he knew no advocates or procurators (entries of 15 and 27 Nov. 1629 in his *processo* in S.U., b. 87); Giovanni Battista Bonaventura, who lived in Venice, nominated Dr Pietro Abbetini to defend him – proc. in S.U., b. 89, 12 Aug. 1632. The Ribeiros had a regular lawyer, Don Francesco Vitale, to whom they paid a retainer of 50 crowns a year; he took part in the negotiations for the transfer of the case from the *Avogadori di Commun* to the Holy Office, but they were unable to use him in the Holy Office itself – S.U., b. 45, proc. Ribeiro, 9 Feb. 1581.

told by the Inquisition to make his defence, Gaspar Ribeiro was sunk in apathy and left the tribunal to name two advocates for him, though the court still pressed him 'more for satisfaction than need' to call on the assistance of 'any other doctor and advocate of the ecclesiastical courts of the city of Venice'. A third advocate was eventually enlisted, and the defence proceeded. True, the advocate was never freed of the obligation to act as a kind of judge himself, for his oath bound him to form some impression of the prisoner's guilt or innocence, and if need be to persuade him to confess 'and thus avoid greater evil and the sin of impenitence'.[66] But when Benedetto Bariselli was told in 1572 that 'he may without fear of incurring censures or other penalties extend his protection to Righetto,' the assurance seemed genuine enough.[67] And Righetto, Gaspar Ribeiro and Mendlin of Muggia were all vigorously defended with *bona fide* assistance from professional advocates.

It was the task of the defence advocates to compile lists of witnesses who could be summoned to testify for the prisoner, and to prepare lists of questions to be put by the court to both hostile and friendly witnesses. Their chances of practising the art of cross-examination were restricted, since – not coming face to face with the witnesses – they could not modify or develop their questioning in accordance with the replies received. Nor could they indulge in rhetoric, for their submissions or *allegationes* on behalf of the prisoner were made in the dry phraseology of a Latin document. And the *processo ripetitivo*, the elaborate device used in the prolonged trial of Gaspar Ribeiro, undoubtedly had special pitfalls for the defendant. By this mechanism, certain witnesses who had given information in the early stages of the trial were resummoned and re-examined by both sides – in this case about five months after their first appearances. The disadvantage for the defendant was that witnesses could be examined by the court not only on their own previous testimony but on the whole case previously built up against the accused, including evidence which had come to light since the witness's first examination.[68] None the less, it was sometimes possible for the defence to construct through witnesses a very extensive account of a prisoner's character, which ensured that it should not be depicted entirely by his foes or by his intimates. In the course of the Ribeiro trial, the tribunal summoned thirty-two witnesses, of whom thirteen were 'repeated'. Four of these thirty-two witnesses were summoned at a later date to add fresh testimony for the defence. Hostile testimony was balanced by as many as twenty-seven witnesses who spoke for the defence alone. Intimates of the prisoner tended to be summoned

---

[66] Ibid., 23 June, 20, 25 Aug., 15 Sept. 1580.
[67] S.U., b. 36, proc. Righetto, 6 June 1572.
[68] Cf. Firpo, *Il processo di Giordano Bruno*, pp. 61–3; Masini, *Sacro Arsenale*, pp. 95–107.

by the court, for the thirty-two such witnesses (not all classifiable) included eight Jews, six relatives of the Ribeiros by blood or marriage, five
servants or book-keeper clerks who had lived within the household, four
clerics, and three Portuguese acquaintances. The defence offered a different kind of testimony, which depended heavily upon casual or business
acquaintances from Rialto, the Ghetto, or the immediate neighbourhood
of Santa Maria Formosa, where the prisoner had lived and done business
from his house.

Inquisitorial practice in the second half of the sixteenth century inclined towards concealing the names of witnesses from the prisoner.
Eymeric had advised that they be suppressed if the 'power' of the prisoner
was such as to expose them to retaliation; in his opinion such 'power' was
not wielded only by persons of rank and influence, for a criminal with
neither property nor reputation to lose could prove more dangerous and
less scrupulous than a knight, a nobleman or a rich merchant.[69] Paul III,
in 1549, had responded to New Christian pressures from Portugal and
had attempted to restrict the use of the term 'powerful', at least in that
country, in such a way as to guarantee the survival of more open procedures; but he had been opposed by the King of Portugal, and Pius IV
was persuaded to cancel the brief in 1560.[70] Six years later, a decree of
the Cardinal Inquisitors-General implied that in the revived Roman Inquisition no special justification would now be needed for concealing
witnesses' names.[71] Although this procedure was applied in Venice, prisoners often knew who had spoken against them – particularly where they
had been questioned about offences committed in private, which could
have been witnessed only by a few people. Intelligent guesswork, the
memory of quarrels, and improper revelations by officials of the tribunal
help to account for such knowledge. Righetto's is a case in point, for his
advocate, Bariselli, argued in 1572 that the names of witnesses examined
in Lisbon should be revealed to the defence, and that he should be
allowed to discuss them with the prisoner, to establish or challenge their
credibility (distance from Venice would surely afford them protection).
Legitimately or not, the prisoner seems to have become acquainted with
the entire contents of the *processo*, though a corrupt relationship with
gaolers and officials could have been responsible for his knowledge. He
had boasted, said one witness, of being well placed to ruin the notary of
the Holy Office, 'who had read him all the *processo* and told him the

[69] Eymeric, pp. 295–6.
[70] Lea, *Inquisition of Spain*, III, pp. 257–9; cf. ibid., II, pp. 548–52, which shows that in
the early days of the Spanish Inquisition the suppression of witnesses' names was permissive
and not mandatory. Cf. also Hercolano, *Inquisition in Portugal*, pp. 444–6, for an earlier
attempt by Paul III to tackle the issue of concealment of witnesses' names.
[71] Pastor, 'Allgemeine Dekrete ...', p. 507.

witnesses, and everything. I said, 'Perhaps their lordships gave him permission.'"[72]

The clearest evidence that the tribunal strove for concealment comes from the few surviving copies of the transcripts of evidence handed to the prisoner when the case against him seemed complete. Those employed in the trials of Magalotti and Bonaventura, about 1630, closely follow the rules stated in the inquisitors' manuals: they were carefully edited so as to exclude the names and descriptions of those who gave incriminating testimony, and to remove any remarks particularly likely to identify them to the defendant. In the document designed for Magalotti, only one witness was named – Lieberman the innkeeper, who had openly identified Magalotti before the *Ufficiali al Cattaver*.[73] Witnesses could be brought in to look at a prisoner, on occasions when identification was crucial, as Moses, son of Leon Luzzatto, and David Grassini of Mantua were brought in to identify the young man who had lodged for a night in the Fraternity of the German Jews.[74] And the rules allowed confrontation between witnesses who were telling flatly contradictory stories, especially, perhaps, where the witness was himself being incriminated. It seemed appropriate, for example, to bring Capponi face to face with the bookseller from the Santi Apostoli who had sold him prohibited books: had the bookseller pressed this merchandise upon him, calling them rare books which could be sold at a profit, and had Capponi (knowing no Latin) innocently believed him? Or – as the bookseller said – had Capponi chosen the books spontaneously? Wherever the truth lay, the bookseller had awkward questions to answer, and had not earned the protection of anonymity.[75]

Concealment of witnesses tended to handicap the commonest form of defence – which lay in the allegation that hostile witnesses were inspired by malice, and might even be conspiring to frame the prisoner. Even before being called upon formally to make his defence, the prisoner could be invited by the court to name all persons who might bear him a deep-seated grudge. 'Capital enmity' would cancel testimony altogether; a lesser degree of odium would serve to weaken it. Inevitably, the process turned into a grim guessing-game, in which the prisoner was really trying to solve the rather different problem of identifying those who had testified against him, and giving reasons for disbelieving them. Had he known their names, there would have been an obvious incentive to invent personal quarrels in the hope of discrediting all hostile evidence. As the list of enemies lengthened, especially if the prisoner added to it over several

[72] S.U., b. 36, proc. Righetto, 31 July 1572, and test. Nicolò Tagliapietra, 1 Sept. 1573.
[73] S.U., b. 87, 89.
[74] S.U., b. 89, proc. Sandoval, 16, 23 Sept. 1632.
[75] S.U., b. 61, proc. Capponi, 18 June 1588.

sessions and a long stretch of time, the suspicion would grow that he had simply deduced or discovered who was responsible for the case against him.

The game was played to the full by Giovanni Battista Capponi, who had some prior experience of trial and imprisonment in Padua. Eleven witnesses gave hostile testimony concerning his conduct in the Rialto prison. Three were named by Capponi in his first list of personal enemies on 21 May 1588; two others were added a week later. He eventually added the other six names, but only on 19 July and 22 September – when he had apparently guessed or even actually read them from his copy of the *processo* (how thoroughly was it edited?). In addition, he named seven or eight persons who had nothing to do with the present case against him. He was hot-tempered and quick with his fists; he had been constantly involved in arguments and petty lawsuits; he had been suspected of involvement in sordid conspiracies to lure away the wife of a fellow prisoner; he was known to have informed on an adversary before another Venetian magistracy, accusing Giovanni Battista Milledonne of sacrilege to the *Provveditori sopra i Monasterii*. Faced with this unappetizing information, the court grew restive and told him:

> From the things you have said, even though you think by these means to discredit the witnesses against you, you only reveal yourself to be an evil man, in confessing that everyone hates you – a thing which can only arise from your evil and criminal ways; and so general an objection to the witnesses is unworthy to be considered.

To name categories of enemies was not acceptable – the Inquisition resisted the argument that the whole prison population bore him a grudge for betraying their plans to escape.[76] In other cases, it proved equally unimpressed by delinquent converts who asserted that all Jews hated them as defectors from their faith, and would stop at nothing to entangle them with the Inquisition.[77] Circles of close acquaintances could sometimes be discredited, but deadly hatreds were harder to attribute to more impersonal crowds.

Apart from attempts to provide innocent explanations of damning facts, or to dismiss incriminating documents as forgeries, a few standard defences emerged. A Jew might argue that, having never been baptized or formed any sacramental ties with the Catholic Church, he was incapable

---

[76] S.U., b. 61, proc. Capponi, 21, 28 May, 19 July, 22 Sept. 1588. On 30 June 1588 Don Gasparo Bonadio, clerk to the Rialto prison, said that Capponi had indeed warned him that Flaminio and others were smuggling in tools for a gaol break.

[77] E.g. in Magalotti's articles of defence, March–April 1630, S.U., b. 87.

of heresy and free of its jurisdiction. Conversely, he might adduce proofs of his exemplary piety and devotion to the Christian faith. Very occasionally, central facts might be at least partially admitted, and the argument focus on the interpretation of the prisoner's behaviour and the degree of his or her responsibility.

There was little doubt that Elena de' Freschi Olivi had in fact blasphemed against the Host or the celebrant at Mass in the church of San Marcilian. But were her shocking words a sign of madness or demonic possession, or was the old woman merely eccentric and (despite her recent conversion) still at heart a Jewess? Her son, Giovanni Battista, had some standing with the Holy Office as an expert, since he had collaborated in the destruction of the Talmud and could be called upon to inspect circumcisions.[78] The tribunal received from him statements in which he combined theological arguments that his mother was possessed by evil spirits and medical arguments that she was a lunatic or melancholic. She suffered 'alienation and weakness of the brain, to a greater or lesser extent according to the waxing and waning of the moon' – but the explanation, designed to impress the Holy Office, could not be purely medical or rely on natural phenomena alone. Lunatics, declared the doctor, were subject to possession not continuously but at certain specific times, the Devil taking advantage of the weakness of the body, its dryness and the increase of the melancholic humour as the moon declined or as warm weather came. He vexed the lunatic as an act of revenge upon good Christians, using demons to 'defame the creatures of God, by making them blaspheme and condemn our blessed God, as they have done to my poor mother' – what better than to attack the pious, even to single out the mother of a fearless persecutor of Jewish blasphemy, returning fresh curses for curses suppressed? 'If it was simple madness, without vexation by spirits, she would never have spoken those dreadful words in church, for it is not her habit to speak them at home'; 'it is not the custom of the insane to utter such blasphemies, but rather of those who are plagued by demons.'[79] The Inquisition considered seriously both the explanation that Elena was intermittently possessed and the possibility that she was merely deranged without supernatural causes. A service of exorcism failed to produce evidence of possession.[80] But the tribunal was prepared to concede something to the medical argument and to regard her as a case for hospital charity as well as mere confinement, though they did not accede to the doctor's plea that as one possessed she should be allowed entry to churches and that her outbursts should be tolerated.

---

[78] See below, pp. 282–3.
[79] I.Z., pp. 161–89, proc. Freschi Olivi.
[80] Ibid., pp. 210–11, 8 July 1555.

The Venetian Inquisition was neither credulous nor inflexible. It undoubtedly risked being used as an instrument of private conflict, but did not in this differ from the secular law courts of Venice, and was certainly not eager to be exploited by the vengeful. The evidence required to convict of heresy had to be concrete and specific, and publicly notorious offences, witnessed by crowds, were more likely to carry drastic penalties. Where no public interest was threatened, where no political issues were raised, where no Venetians had been scandalized, proof and punishment were harder to secure. Venetian society was not permeated with secret Judaism or with the fear of it in such a way as to produce a flow of delations based on trivial evidence; some Portuguese immigrants or visitors were preoccupied with these matters, but were suspected of dumping personal quarrels in the Inquisition's lap. The discretion of delators was not so tight, and the efficiency of the Inquisition was not so great, as to shroud the proceedings in impenetrable mystery or to allow the accused no chance of defence or retaliation. And it compared favourably with its nearest secular equivalent, the Council of Ten – if, that is, there was any truth in the invective of Renier Zeno against the Council's

> fearful procedure which is contrary to common law, and gives no copies of the evidence against a man, allows no objections to witnesses, decrees that the defence be made in dark cells, and allows no defence by either relatives or advocates; and that rigour from which the condemnation of innocents so often arises, as happened most recently to the Cavalier Foscarini.[81]

---

[81] Quoted in Derosas, 'Moralità e giustizia ...', pp. 525–6.

8

The Testimony of the Inquisition

Inquisition records are plainly of some value as a guide to the activities of the court which created them and to the mentality of its judges. But how great is their power to transmit information, not about the dominant culture which instituted, tolerated and manned the Holy Office, but about those people who became the subjects of its inquiries?

These records are especially tantalizing. To historians in pursuit of obscure, illiterate and unlearned people, they offer exciting prospects. Inquisitors seem genuinely interested in probing the intellect and the will, in discovering not only the facts about crimes committed against the faith, but also the motives and intentions behind them. They reconstruct both biographies and family histories. They show a generous sense of relevance and are not constrained by narrow rules of evidence. Those who study them seem to be offered the chance to practise on remote centuries a kind of oral history, though the historian is not the interviewer and the interrogators seldom ask the questions he most wants answered. The Inquisition offers to do what notarial documents, committee minutes-books and land registers cannot; it may become the key which unlocks the mind of the people, rather than merely revealing their public acts and their material transactions.

But there is, too, the disquieting reflexion that inquisitions may have been all too well equipped to enable churchmen and their lay colleagues to manoeuvre their prisoners and witnesses into an intellectual framework established by the learned and powerful, and even to make them serve their myths. The Inquisition may have been fated, not to discover truth, but merely to hear what it wanted to hear from those who came to know its interests and fed it with suitably slanted information; we have to reckon, not only with the preoccupations of the tribunal itself, but also with the disingenuousness of its witnesses. Were inquisitors really eager to discover the truth about a person, or were they merely concerned to use him, to find deviants to punish the better to define the frontiers of their own faith?

Historians dealing with witchcraft accusations throughout Europe and with trials for crypto-Judaism in Spain and Portugal have warned of the pitfalls of the trial records. Churchmen and their courts were liable to synthesize and rationalize evidence of popular belief and practice until it fitted their own system, folk magic and sorcery being transmuted by the learned into satanism and heresy.[1] Envisaging the encounter between inquisitor and prisoner, Mr Peter Burke writes:

> The interrogator had been through the whole business many times before and knew all too well what he was trying to find. The accused did not know what was happening and may well have been searching frantically for cues and clues as to what was wanted. The situation was like a parody of the interviews between modern anthropologists and their informants in the field – anthropologists are much concerned about the possibility that the answers they receive may be little more than what they have suggested, unconsciously, to the informant.[2]

False confessions obtained under torture are tragic clichés of this kind of history; hard by the borders of the Venetian state, in 1475, Jews were tortured into providing the Prince-Bishop of Trent with evidence to support his belief in their ritual murder of Christian children at Passiontide.[3] From distortion to fabrication; radical writers have suggested that crypto-Judaism in Spain and Portugal was essentially the creature of the Inquisition itself. Here the tribunal is portrayed as a social device, as the expression of an anti-semitism not related to the actual extent of Judaism, but originating in the problems and conflicts of the society which maintained the Inquisition. The Inquisition was designed, according to these theories, to prevent the natural assimilation of Jewish converts to Christianity; it may even have become the tool of the landed aristocracy and the Church, bent on resisting the advance of the New Christian

---

[1] See, for example, R. Kieckhefer, *European witch trials: their foundations in popular and learned culture, 1300–1500* (London, 1976), p. 28 ff.; E. W. Monter, *Witchcraft in France and Switzerland: the borderlands during the Reformation* (London, 1976), p. 144 ff.

[2] P. Burke, *Popular culture in early modern Europe* (London, 1978), pp. 74–5; note also the very similar remarks in his 'Witchcraft and magic in Renaissance Italy: Gianfrancesco Pico and his *Strix*', in *The damned art: essays in the literature of witchcraft*, ed. S. Anglo (London, 1977), p. 45.

[3] See E. Tessadri, *L'Arpa di David: storia di Simone e del processo di Trento contro gli ebrei accusati di omicidio rituale, 1475–1476* (Milan, 1974).

bourgeoisie, and using their Jewish origins to discredit them by inventing the spurious problem of a clandestine religion.[4] Mr Ellis Rivkin has argued that 'the documents of the Inquisition cannot be used as evidence of the religious life of the Conversos, but are a source only for what the Inquisition wanted the people to believe about the Conversos.' Hence, these records have value only in answering such questions as: 'How is a population made to believe the absurd?'[5]

The testimony of the Spanish and Portuguese Inquisitions has been stoutly defended.[6] What of the Venetian? To assess the value of Venetian evidence it is sensible to ask a number of standard questions concerning the nature of the records, the kind of evidence offered and accepted as proof of judaizing, the tactics employed in order to obtain confessions, and the extent of the tribunal's financial interest in condemnations and confiscations.

In general, inquisitorial procedures were a system of rational inquiry conducted by officials constantly committing their findings to a written dossier; as part of a network of tribunals responsible in some degree to Rome, they had to be prepared, at least in the more important cases of the late sixteenth century, to submit the full record to the examination of a higher court.[7] Venetian trial records were designed to capture every word spoken in the court itself, and to preserve or copy all written denunciations, affidavits, petitions, articles of defence, submissions by advocates or relatives, or other documents presented to it. The record shows who answered the questions, but not who asked them; the Inquisitor and his colleagues disappear behind the impersonal bureaucratic passive, 'He was asked,' although it seems likely that the Inquisitor himself put most of the questions. The nuncio Bolognetti chafed at time wasted in recording trivia, and was exasperated by the government's insistence that patricians as dignified as the *Assistenti* must always be present throughout these tedious proceedings.[8] It is reasonably certain, then, that the record – apart from the copies of the process handed to prisoners and their advocates – was unedited, and was subject to scrutiny by persons of high

[4] As is argued in A. J. Saraiva, *Inquisição e cristãos-novos* (second edition, Oporto, 1969).

[5] See E. Rivkin, 'The utilization of non-Jewish sources for the reconstruction of Jewish history', *Jewish Quarterly Review*, 48 (1957–58), pp. 193, 202.

[6] E.g. by Y. H. Yerushalmi, *From Spanish court to Italian ghetto. Isaac Cardoso: a study in seventeenth-century Marranism and Jewish apologetics* (New York–London, 1971), pp. 21–4; Révah, 'Les marranes portugais ...', pp. 503–4, 516–18; Révah, 'La religion d'Uriel da Costa ...', p. 62 ff.; G. Nahon, 'Les Sephardim, les marranes, les Inquisitions péninsulaires et leurs archives dans les travaux récents de I.S. Révah', *Revue des études juives*, fourth series, vol. 132 (1973), p. 33 ff.

[7] Cf. J. H. Langbein, *Prosecuting crime in the Renaissance: England, Germany, France* (Cambridge, Mass., 1974), pp. 21–2, 33, 129 ff., 221–2, 250–1; see also above, pp. 45–6.

[8] Stella–Bolognetti, p. 290.

standing, both lay and clerical, likely to approach it from different angles. Where cases were brought to a conclusion, abjuration and sentence are usually preserved, though there is no record of the debates of the Congregation of the Inquisition on the advisability of arrests or the sentences to be imposed.[9]

Stage directions were generally given in Latin. They described in formal language the particulars of the defendant or witness, and at their most complete would record his appearance, age, profession and place of residence. They recorded the taking of oaths. There was generally a clear distinction between statements volunteered by witnesses (introduced by the phrase *subdens ex se*) and statements made in response to questions. Transcripts distinguished between statements made in the first round of interrogation, and additions or corrections made by a witness when his testimony was read over to him. Demeanour was recorded when it might throw light on a witness's state of mind; in June 1580, a young book-keeper from Savona, testifying in the case of Gaspar Ribeiro, was described as wiping his face with a handkerchief, twisting himself about and sweating under the strain.[10]

Little discretion was allowed the notary in recording the words he heard; these he registered in the vernacular, and often in the dialect in which they were spoken. At least in the later sixteenth century, he wasted no time in touching up his notes, although in the seventeenth there was perhaps more tendency to present the dialogue in standard Italian. Such transcripts reproduce the exasperated rejoinder of a Rialto broker on being approached in his crowded box during business hours by officers of the Inquisition one day in 1575 ('What do you mean, you didn't know where to find me, here I am!').[11] The notaries reproduced the vocabularies of greeting, blasphemy and insult. They recorded the unceremonious attempts of prisoner or witnesses to fend off insistent questions, including Gaspar Ribeiro's 'I'm not telling you anything. Do you want me to tell you things I don't know? I can't guess. I'm not a wizard!' and his servant Mattea's 'I'll tell you everything bit by bit, don't go on at such a speed!' Attempts by witnesses to imitate Gaspar's eccentric mixture of Italian and Portuguese duly found their way on to paper.[12] If false or distorted in any way, such records could only have been fabricated by persons with a talent for composing dialogue which was often far removed

---

[9] Very occasionally, something of these debates can be discovered from other records – e.g. the case of Don Fulgenzio Camaldolese, C.E.R., reg. 20, fol. 21v.–40, 1 July to 26 Aug. 1622.

[10] S.U., b. 45, proc. Ribeiro, test. Nicolò da Ponte, 14 June 1580.

[11] S.U., b. 39, proc. Gomes, test. Giacomo Pera, 10 Sept. 1575.

[12] S.U., b. 45, proc. Ribeiro, 15 March 1580; test. Mattea da Rippa Sicca, 7–8 April 1580; test. Lauro de' Cremonesi, 18 Feb. 1581.

from the language of officialdom. It is certainly true that abjurations and sentences attempted to iron out the confusions arising from the record; but their tone and structure, which can savour of the well-trimmed statement to or by the police, are quite different from those of the raw material which precedes them.

Inquisitors' manuals contained warnings against the use of leading questions by the court. Their motive was not to protect the cowed witness from the bullying of the bench. Rather, the canonist Peña argued, it was to prevent an accused person from deceiving an inquisitor who showed too clearly what he expected of him.[13] Masini's compact textbook, popular in the seventeenth century, defined the improper *interrogatorii suggestivi* as those clearly inviting the answer 'Yes' or 'No'. 'An example would be: "Is it not true that N. blasphemed? I know you know that he swore blasphemously on two occasions, and said 'In defiance of God.'"'.[14] Venetian inquisitors followed the principle carefully, putting their initial questions in a neutral fashion, and closing in gradually from the general to the specific. In the later stages of a trial, when the facts appeared to have been established, they might begin to argue forcefully with an accused person or a witness, pointing out contradictions and inconsistencies in his statements or behaviour. A fair specimen of such dialogue can be taken from the trial of Iseppo Bon in 1636, in which he was charged with systematically repeating baptism in order to get the charitable benefits which were bestowed on Jewish converts – or as his delator put it, with 'trafficking in the holy religion, with great scandal to the holy faith'.[15] At his fourth interrogation, about seven weeks after his first interview, the Inquisitor asked:

Whether, when you were baptized in Rome, you were first catechized and instructed that baptism may not be received on more than one occasion, and that once baptized a man may not return to the Jewish faith?

He answered: They taught me the necessary things, such as the Creed, Our Father, the Ten Commandments, and other such matters; and I was told that I must not again return to Judaism. But I do not recall being told that I must never take baptism again.

It was then said to him: That is no answer, but a deliberate evasion. If you were told in Rome that once baptized you could not return to Judaism, then surely you were also told that you could not be

[13] Peña, p. 127.
[14] Masini, *Sacro Arsenale*, p. 27 ff.
[15] S.U., b. 94, proc. Bon, den. Andrea Nunciata, Jan. 1636.

rebaptized. Furthermore, you did say that you confessed to having been baptized a second time. Hence, we can only believe that you must have had grave qualms of conscience about it. You quite rightly told your confessor about that second baptism. But it should also have been mentioned in Vicenza, before you were baptized by the bishop or his vicar or any other persons, and you should not have committed the terrible sacrilege of taking baptism a second time.

In this and the subsequent dialogue, the Inquisitor was pressing the accused very hard. But he was always arguing from information which Iseppo Bon had himself supplied, and not from material he had himself suggested to him. He also met with resistance; the prisoner was eager not to give the Inquisitor what he wanted. 'I am ignorant,' said Bon. 'Are there not many who would like to know more than they do?'[16] In that sense the dialogue was genuinely two-sided, and the Inquisitor was not merely pouring the testimony into the mould of his own mind.

These detailed records are reassuring, in that they present a full account of the methods by which the Inquisition obtained its evidence. What was the nature of this evidence? In 1571 Matteo Priuli, Bishop of Vicenza, remembering his spell of four or five years attached to the office of the papal nuncio in Portugal, wrote: 'Your most reverend lordship will find that no Jews can live on any terms in that kingdom; indeed, if they so much as abstained from eating pork they would as suspects be denounced to the Holy Office.'[17] We need to know how far the Venetian Inquisition was prepared to convict of judaizing by building large assumptions on trivial evidence, and particularly on merely negative evidence of failure to observe normal Christian routines. And in view of the suggestion that at least one inquisition attempted to make a people believe the absurd, and in view of the catalogue of blasphemous Jewish rituals contained in Gregory XIII's Bull of 1581, it is necessary to ask whether the Venetian tribunal ever received, or credulously acted upon, evidence of a fantastic or inherently improbable character about the conduct of the Jews.

In general, the Venetian Inquisition was concerned with three kinds of judaizers who were actually Jews by birth or descent. They tended to create three different kinds of evidential problem. In practice the Inquisition was little interested in Spaniards or Portuguese who went straight to the Ghetto and presented themselves as Jews from the moment they arrived in Venice. It could expect to receive papers denouncing them, but

[16] Ibid., 8 April 1636.
[17] S.U., b. 36, proc. Righetto, written deposition, 26 April 1571.

– save in the case of Righetto – it would not prosecute solely or mainly on the evidence of a person's life outside Venice. Far more at risk were New Christians believed to be dissembling – to be combining the public persona of a Christian with the secret beliefs and rituals of a Jew, and so bringing together two incompatible ways of life. It was they who generally attracted nebulous evidence which suggested a bad Christian. Finally the Inquisition dealt with former Jews baptized in Italy, who had been solemnly warned on conversion of the dangers of associating with their former co-religionists. They would most likely be damned by evidence of frequenting the Ghetto or wearing Jewish dress. Unlike Portuguese Jews, they could not leave their past behind them at the frontiers of the Venetian state.

Judaism itself could be seen by the Inquisition's witnesses and informers as a perverse doctrine, a kind of standing insult to Christianity; as a rival system of devotional acts, festivals and dietary laws; or as an inferior culture insulated from the dominant Christian society. A man might be accused of blasphemous reflexions on Christ's divinity, or disputing the identity of the Messiah. It might be said that he attended synagogues, ate specifically Jewish foods such as matzos, ignored the austerities of Lent, prayed on his feet or abstained from work on a Saturday. Or he might be taxed with cultivating the society of Jews beyond the call of business dealings, or otherwise violating the social barriers set up between Christian and Jew by the state as well as the Church, particularly by eating at a Jew's table or sleeping in his house.

Bad Catholicism was hard to conceal in Venice, and the Inquisition could expect to hear much evidence about it. Though sheltering several creeds, the city did not grant them equality: the assertive symbols and ceremonies of the supreme religion, Catholic Christianity, spread far beyond the churches into alleys, squares and houses. Its processions, its images and certain of its rituals must be respected, if not believed in. Though one of the largest cities in Europe, Venice was not vast enough to guarantee anonymity; each of some seventy parishes was an intimate village, alert to newcomers, and the business community had a very precise focus, at Rialto. Public worship in open spaces brought transactions to a standstill; it was most edifying, said the Doge in 1580, 'to see, at San Marco or Rialto, at the sound of the Ave Maria, so numerous a people fall at once upon their knees . . .'.[18] Crypto-Jewish merchants, said Antonio Saldanha, would take flight shortly before the sounding of the bell, to avoid kneeling at its summmons. A servant of the Spanish ambassador swore however that the crucial test was not the kneeling but

[18] Tramontin, 'La visita apostolica . . .', p. 464.

what was actually said in prayer.[19] Images were ubiquitous, thrusting themselves upon the iconoclast, whether Protestant or Jew.

If ever there were any Citty [wrote the evangelical English chaplain, William Bedell] to which the Epithets would agree, which St Luke gives to Athens (which he calls *kateidolon*) this is it. Such a multitude of idolatrous statues, pictures, reliquies in every corner, not of their churches onely, but houses, chambers, shoppes, yea the very streets, and in the country the high wayes and hedges swarme with them. The sea it self is not free; they are in the shipps, boats, and watermarks. And as for their slavery and subjection to them, it is such, as that of paganisme came not to the half of it . . .[20]

Debtors in the Rialto prison ignored at their peril the figure of the Madonna of San Rocco, and even the sceptical Capponi contributed a few *soldi* when the inmates clubbed together to buy her candles for Holy Week.[21] The Eucharist was not merely kept in increasingly splendid tabernacles in the churches; it was borne abroad, ceremoniously, usually accompanied by members of the parish fraternity of the Blessed Sacrament, on its way to visit the sick, and it was paraded publicly on Good Fridays, its followers bearing torches or lighted candles.[22]

It was said in 1558 of the convert Gian Giacomo de' Fedeli, accused of continuing to live 'in the manner of the Jews', that he had failed to doff his hat when passing street altars, and had dodged the sacrament when it was carried through the streets.[23] Of the Filippi it was said in 1585 by neighbours and priests that they would not kneel for the Ave Maria, and would not remove their hats when passing the church. A boatman's wife asserted that one of their servants was unable to cross himself when local children challenged him to do so.[24] Failure to furnish a house with images and holy pictures would excite suspicion. When Agostinho Enriques sought to exculpate himself in 1555, he produced witnesses in Ferrara who swore that he kept in his house 'pictures of our saviour Jesus Christ,

[19] S.U., b. 44, proc. 'Negromanti', den. Saldanha, 11 Jan. 1579; test. 'Giovanni di Vichifo', 2 June 1579.

[20] William Bedell to Adam Newton, 1 Jan. 1608, printed as Letter V in E. S. Shuckburgh, ed., *Two biographies of William Bedell* . . . , p. 229.

[21] S.U., b. 61, proc. Capponi, test. Giovanni Maria Baroni and Giovanni Battista Antelmi, 28, 30 April 1588.

[22] Cf. G. Barbiero, *Le confraternite del Santissimo Sacramento prima del 1539* (Treviso, 1941); Pullan, *Rich and poor* . . . , p. 121; S.U., b. 45, proc. Ribeiro, test. Sebastiano di Francesco Barbarigo, 22 Nov. 1580.

[23] I.Z., p. 269.

[24] S.U., b. 54, proc. Filippi, test. Cecilia and Domenica, Don Antonio Bortolino and Don Giovanni Battista Guato, 3, 8 Oct. 1585.

our lady, the apostles, and other Christian paintings' and in particular
'one showing the judgment of our lord upon the adulterers'.[25] In the
house of his colleague, Duarte Gomes, a lamp was lit before the image of
the Madonna on saint's days and Saturdays.[26] Maria Lopes, deposing
against her father and stepmother, said that in their houses she had never
seen images, other than a wooden statue of the Madonna purchased for
12 crowns in Florence; her father had sold it, and had never bought
another.[27] Half a century later questions to a Jewish tailor and his land-
lady suggest that there ought to have been a holy picture (*quadro di
devotione*) and a pail of holy water even in the bedroom of a house kept by
a velvet-maker's wife.[28]

In some circumstances, mere respect was not enough. Former Jews,
whether Portuguese or Italian, would perhaps do well – as did the
Catholic Jewesses of Majorca – to engage in an almost ostentatious
piety.[29] Donna Giulia testified of Elena de' Freschi Olivi that 'when she
was in her right mind she was very devout at Mass, and said her rosary
and office, and beat her breast with vigour.'[30] A Spaniard said in 1579
that in seeking out judaizers the zealous Catholic should look, not merely
to the fact that a person attended church, but rather to conduct at the
elevation of the Host.[31] Mass could be a highly emotional occasion which
called for demonstrative behaviour, as witness the remarks attributed to
the impious Bonaventura by Lucrezia Mamacchio in 1632:

'My good woman, what does it mean when the priest raises that
thing on high and some beat their breasts, while others weep,
grimace, and do other tricks?' And I was shocked, for I thought he
was speaking of the sacred host, and so I turned my back. But then
I answered him, saying that people were begging pardon of the
most holy sacrament for their sins, and he, mocking me, said 'Leave
me be and go and chase yourself.'[32]

Communion could be expected to present special problems for secret
judaizers. There was some reason to believe that they would make their
confession, but would at all costs avoid taking the body of Christ. Tristão

---

[25] I.Z. II, pp. 84–9, 31 Aug. 1555.
[26] I.Z., p. 238, test. Agamenone Mongardini, 3 Sept. 1555.
[27] S.U., b. 49, proc. Diego Lopes and Catterina Mendes, den. Maria Lopes, 6 April 1582.
[28] S.U., b. 89, proc. Sandoval, test. Vendramina, 7 Sept. 1632.
[29] Cf. K. Moore, *Those of the street: the Catholic-Jews of Mallorca. A study in urban cultural
change* (Notre Dame–London, 1976), pp. 42–3.
[30] I.Z., pp. 160–1, 1 April 1555.
[31] S.U., b. 44, proc. 'Negromanti', test. 'Giovanni di Vichifo', 2 June 1579.
[32] S.U., b. 89, proc. Bonaventura, 20 July 1632.

da Costa, defending himself by declaring that he had always been a secret Jew and as such outside the Church's jurisdiction, said so in 1555; he had followed this tactic in Portugal.[33] Annual confession and Communion in a parish church, where the communicant stood some chance of being known and remembered, were the indispensable signs of adhesion to the Catholic faith. Hence the court was understandably suspicious of Duarte Gomes, who claimed to have communicated, not (as law and custom demanded) at Santa Maria Formosa where he lived, but only at vast and crowded churches such as St Mark's or the Frari: he had, he said, mistaken St Mark's for the cathedral, and in his country the cathedral was an acceptable alternative to the parish church. Fortunately for him, he found an ally in the Franciscan who had confessed him at the Frari and said roundly that 'had I not found him an excellent Christian I would never have given him absolution.'[34] Fabrizio Locatelli, parish priest of Santa Maria Formosa, testified that Gaspar Ribeiro had to his knowledge communicated twice in the last four years.[35] There were, however, unpleasant rumours – sometimes traced to a serving woman, sometimes to the País girls – that 'the said Gaspar, having at communion taken the most holy sacrament, went home and forced himself to spew it up, as poison he had taken to appease the idolators,' or, alternatively, that he and his wife and son came home from the service and spat out the sacrament behind the fire.[36]

Towards 1580, Spanish or Portuguese immigrants would excite suspicion if they failed to commission for their dead relatives funeral rites of suitable grandeur. Funerals in Venice seem to have been socially graded according to the number of clerics and lay fraternities following the coffin. A simple burial would be attended by the *capitolo* or 'chapter', which consisted of the parish clergy – the parish priest, at least two assistant priests, a deacon and a subdeacon, for most Venetian parishes had collegiate churches. More lavish funerals would demand the presence of one of the nine 'congregations' into which the Venetian clergy were divided.[37] It would be usual to hold a service in the parish church, and, if the body was to be buried at one of the outlying monasteries, another at the graveside. Gaspar Ribeiro caused suspicion by the meanness of the funeral he ordered for his son, for his rank and riches would normally have justified spending on the whole congregation of clergy; he wanted

[33] I.Z., pp. 261–2, 16 July 1555.

[34] I.Z., pp. 230–2, 234–6, 237, 3, 27 Aug., 3 Sept. 1555.

[35] S.U., b. 45, proc. Ribeiro, 15 Nov. 1580.

[36] Ibid., test. Mattea da Rippa Sicca and Nicolò da Ponte of Savona, 7 April, 14 June 1580; S.U., b. 44, proc. 'Negromanti', den. Antonio Saldanha, 11 Jan. 1579.

[37] Cf. Ad Limina Venezia, p. 1, fol. 15v., reports of the Patriarchs Matteo Zane (1604) and Francesco Vendramin (1612).

only the chapter of Santa Maria Formosa and its chaplains to turn out. 'Wishing to avoid expense', said his parish priest, 'he asked me to have three or four masses said in my church, and then to allow the body to be transported by boat to the church of Santa Maria della Grazia.'[38]

Similar misgivings were aroused a few years later by the family of Silva, living at San Marcilian. When a woman died in their house, having made her confession but received neither Communion nor extreme unction, the family wanted the corpse taken directly across the water to the Augustinian friary of San Cristoforo on the island of Murano, but the parish priest insisted they 'should follow the custom of the city and the faith'. Accordingly, a service was held in the parish church, and other parish priests, from San Geremia, San Marcuola and the Maddalena, came to join the local chapter and the parish fraternity of the Blessed Sacrament. One of them, however, recently involved in the case of the Filippi, was dissatisfied by the proceedings – by the speed of the service ('one could scarcely say a decent "Our Father"!'), the absence of mourners, and the perfunctory fashion in which the corpse was shipped off from the Scuola della Misericordia to be 'carried to the vault of Murano'. It transpired that the priest of San Marcilian had seen the body being prepared for the grave in a highly unorthodox fashion in the bereaved household – it was wrapped in a linen sheet and sprinkled with quicklime. Suspicions of judaizing were sufficiently aroused for officials of the Holy Office to visit the grave in the cloister at Murano forthwith, and exhume the body. The priest's statements about the burial were confirmed, and the former Jew Eusebio Renati pronounced that the corpse had been buried 'in the manner of Jews or Portuguese, or judaizing Portuguese, who are accustomed to wait until the corpses of their dead are demolished and reduced to dust, and afterwards they have the bones and dust exhumed and send them to Safed.' There had, none the less, been a counter-theory – to the effect that the dead woman was not Portuguese but a Florentine who had spoken good Italian at her last confession, and that the family did indeed intend to move her bones: but not to the Holy Land. The Holy Office seems eventually to have accepted that there was no proof of judaizing, since it eventually gave the deceased's brother permission to remove the remains to Florence.[39]

[38] S.U., b. 45, proc. Ribeiro, 26 Nov. 1579.
[39] S.U., b. 56, proc. Silva, 13 Nov. 1585 to 8 Feb. 1586. Cf. I.Z., pp. 145–50, for the wish to have the bones of 'domina Lumbria hebrea', who had died in Ferrara, transported to Jerusalem. On the growth of Safed as a Jewish settlement in the sixteenth century, see S. Schwarzfuchs, 'Les marchands juifs dans la Méditerranée orientale au XVIe siècle', *Annales: Économies, Sociétés, Civilisations*, 12 (1957), pp. 117–18. On the development of cabbalistic mysticism in Safed, G. Scholem, *Sabbatai Ṣevi, the mystical Messiah (1626–1676)* (Princeton–London, 1973), pp. 7–8, 18 ff.

Most Venetian observers would notice only signs of bad or neglectful Catholicism. If they involved breaches of the Church's dietary laws, they might well be ascribed vaguely to 'Lutheranism' and not to anything so precise as secret judaizing. Those living near the Ghetto, naturally the best informed, would know rudimentary things about the Jewish sabbath. Donna Cecilia and Donna Domenica, one a Friulian widow and the other a boatman's wife, noticed that the household of the Filippi would not give alms on Fridays or Saturdays, would not give fire to neighbours at the door, ate flesh on Fridays and Saturdays and brought in a large number of chickens on Fridays.[40]

Claims to a broader expertise on Jewish festivals and devotions, a readiness to see Judaism in terms of beliefs and arguments as well as rituals and routines, could be expected from Spanish or Portuguese residents in Venice. Some seem to have tested their acquaintances for crypto-Judaism out of curiosity and as a form of malicious recreation, but without immediate intentions of having the law upon them. In 1579 two Spaniards took a walk with two young men whose father had brought them from Flanders a year or two before, resolving to pray and take holy water in all the churches they passed on the way. Their suspected companions seemed reluctant to take holy water in more than one church, and later they made the excuse that they wanted to urinate and remained outside one of the churches altogether. The witness's friend then said to him: 'Look at those Marranos. They don't want to come into the church!' Questioned by the Holy Office, the self-appointed detective admitted that Spaniards, by and large, were prejudiced against all Portuguese living in the city.[41] He had not reported the matter of his own volition.

Estevão Nogueira and Antonio Saldanha, approaching the tribunal, were well primed, even didactic, and boastful of their achievements in arguing with learned Jews. Laying information against Miguel Vaz and Jorge Lopez, Saldanha asserted that they changed their shirts and other clothing on Saturdays; he could not resist the patronizing explanation that 'In Portugal this is a very characteristic sign of judaizers, and no sentence has ever been passed upon them save where this sign has been found . . .' And the families, he said, also celebrated Jewish festivals: Purim, coinciding with Lent and especially shocking because to the Christian it was a misplaced carnival, had been enjoyed in the house of Jorge Lopez in San Polo, and the families were also said to have observed Yom Kippur. As a schoolmaster, he knew that they failed to send their children to lessons at the time of the Passover. Where members of the

[40] See n. 24 above.
[41] See n. 31 above.

family had disappeared, it was hinted that they had been sent to Constantinople, the haven for those bent on shedding their Christian guise. There were suggestions, too, of an unhealthy acquaintance with the language of Jews, since one of Saldanha's targets had made a pun involving the fish called a Gò and the Jewish word *Goy*, meaning a Gentile.

Saldanha's principal achievement, however, was, so he said, to have been present at arguments about Scripture and to have spent eight days in coaching his accomplice Nogueira (himself 'very good at logic and philosophy') so effectively as to equip him to defeat a learned rabbi in the house of Jorge Lopez in September 1578:

> And the conclusion of it was, that he knew not how to answer my questions and was thrown into confusion, and said to me, 'Why do you want to believe in one who was hanged on a cross?', meaning our lord Jesus Christ, whom he also called by the name Manzel, which means 'son of an adulteress', and he said that he was rightly condemned, for what he did he did by magic.[42]

Other than neophytes such as Eusebio Renati, Venice had few experts on Judaism to compare with these Portuguese.

Inspection for circumcision became a normal feature of the trials of Portuguese Jews. Only evidence of a circumcision in adult life was really damning, since it could serve as conclusive proof of apostasy. One performed in childhood might be evidence against a prisoner's parents rather than himself, and could even help him by supporting the claim that he had always been a Jew, and was therefore beyond the Inquisition's jurisdiction. There were former Jews and surgeons in Venice who claimed to know the difference between childhood and adult circumcisions, and when one of them found that Filipe de Nis had a callous on his member he interpreted it as a sign of adult circumcision: the only possible defence was to claim it to be the result of a medical operation.[43] Unfortunately the absence of circumcision was no proof of Christian orthodoxy, for many immigrants in Italy might well have hesitated to take so irrevocable and painful a step; certainly this did not bar the prosecution of Gaspar Ribeiro, for all his confident invitation: 'see that I am a Christian! Send them to inspect my member!'[44]

Assumption of Jewish dress provided unusually damning evidence: it was hard to mistake, hard to excuse, and acceptable to the Inquisition as

---

[42] S.U., b. 44, proc. 'Negromanti', den. Saldanha and Nogueira, 11, 20 Jan. 1579.

[43] S.U., b. 54, proc. Filippi, 21 Oct. 1585; test. 'Bernardus Mille Janusii', 31 Oct. 1585; test. Filipe de Nis, 10 Dec. 1585, 14 June, 29 July 1586.

[44] S.U., b. 45, proc. Ribeiro, 8 March 1580.

proof of changed allegiance. Normally the victims were Italian or Levantine Jews, although the Portuguese Francisco Olivier suffered because he had worn both Christian and Jewish dress in rapid succession in Venice itself. He was described by Leonardo, a Friulian porter, as dressed in 'a long garment, and underneath that a blouse of yellow cloth. And he had a hat upon his head.'[45] The state itself had sanctioned a very elementary language of colour and dress – the black hat for Christians, the yellow or red hat or the yellow turban for Jews: a man wore his religious allegiance upon his head, and proclaimed it by the quarter in which he chose to live. Felice Magalotti, a baptized Christian, betrayed himself partly by hiring a red hat from a Jewish hatter in the Ghetto Vecchio for 4 soldi a day; there were two witnesses to testify that he had left his black hat in pledge, and had eventually restored the red one after about twelve days. There was no lack of testimony from Jews to the effect that he had not only stayed in the Ghetto, but had also bought meat and had it cooked on a Friday and even bound on the phylacteries.[46] Pier Vincenzo Maria Sandoval had not only changed hats indiscreetly, but had also slept in the Ghetto at the hostel for the poor maintained by the Fraternity of the German Jews.

There was a note to prove it in the records of the *Esecutori contro la Bestemmia,* whose duties had for some time included the issue of brief residence permits to visiting Jews. This described him by his Jewish name of 'Solomon of Cameo, a Roman, here to buy materials, lodging in the fraternity's house, fifteen days'.[47] Such well-attested adherence, however temporary, to the society of Jews gave the Inquisition the kind of evidence on which it would choose to convict.

Leon Modena, in the defence of the Talmud which he completed in 1627, regretted the appeal of extraordinary legends about the Jews to persons of education and rank.[48] Curious scraps of medieval gossip were revived with Eymeric's treatise; Gregory XIII's Bull of 1581 suggested *inter alia* that at Passiontide Jews might be capable of parodying Christ's death by nailing sheep or lambs to a cross; in 1588 Sixtus V at last recognized the cult of St Simon of Trent, the supposed victim of Jewish ritual murder committed over a century before; and a blood accusation

[45] I.Z., pp. 86–7, 27 July 1549.

[46] S.U., b. 87, proc. Felice Magalotti, test. Lieberman the innkeeper and Joshua Jesurum the hatter, 18 Aug. 1629; test. Magalotti himself, 8 Nov., 4 Dec. 1629; and much other testimony from Jews of the Ghetto.

[47] S.U., b. 89, proc. Sandoval, test. Giovanni Pio of Pirano, 31 Aug. 1632; Moses, son of Leon Luzzatto, same day; of the prisoner himself, 7 Sept. 1632; note from the *Esecutori contro la Bestemmia,* dated 17 Aug. 1632. On the registration of Jews arriving in the city, see E.B., b. 54, Capitolare, fol. 68r.–v., 18 July 1612; b. 57, Not. 4, fol. 266r.–267v., 12–13 Aug. 1612.

[48] Ancona, 'Attacchi ...', p. 322.

did arise in Verona in the early seventeenth century, although the case ended in acquittal by the *Podestà*.[49] For all this, there is very little sign that evidence of a fantastic nature was offered to the Venetian Inquisition, or that the inquisitors sought to extract it or act upon it: they showed no excessive interest in the suggestion that the Ribeiros had vomited forth the consecrated Host, which was in any case somewhat different in kind from suggestions that Jews stole Hosts or tortured them as if they were the living body of Christ. Blasphemous words following suspiciously stereotyped patterns, anti-Christian arguments, disrespect for images, evasion of Christian devotions – all these things might be attributed to Jews and crypto-Jews in Venice. Of bloodshed or murder, or of parody or inversion of Christian rituals and beliefs, few or no suggestions were made to the Venetian Inquisition. An unusual suggestion of ritualized blasphemy, performed symbolically against a powerful religious symbol, came – significantly – from a Castilian boy, not from a Venetian. He said of a family of Portuguese immigrants that they had flogged a marble crucifix in the yard below their house in Santa Croce for eight days on end soon after the Passover, and also that Alfonso, son of João Alvares (possibly the head of the family) had thrown into the fire a crucifix drawn on paper which the boy had kept pinned to the wall in his bedroom.[50] Unlike the case of El Cristo de la Paciencia in Toledo in 1630,[51] this did not develop into a *cause-célèbre*.

In general, the Venetian Inquisition could expect to be offered a good deal of rational but nebulous evidence calculated to excite suspicion by suggesting evasions of normal Catholic practices. It could be useful supplementary evidence, since any material bearing on the tenor of a man's religious life was of interest to the Inquisition. But seldom if ever did such evidence actually initiate a prosecution, and there was no attempt to build on such flimsy foundations alone. The Inquisition seems rightly to have distrusted evidence such as that of Saldanha and Nogueira, which savoured not only of the intriguer but also of the *agent provocateur*. Trials commonly focused on some crucial issue which ought to be established by rather more than the necessary two respectable witnesses. Had Righetto, or had he not, been born in Lisbon rather than Ferrara? Had Gaspar Ribeiro, or had he not, consented to his late son's marriage with the Jewess Alumbra? Without such a fulcrum, an inquiry based on suspicion would be likely to founder. Judaism was one among many preoccupations

[49] Eymeric, pp. 242–3; Peña, p. 94; B.R., VIII, pp. 378–80; Albizzi, *Risposta* ..., pp. 229–30; Tessadri, *L'arpa* ..., pp. 273–6; C. Roth, *The ritual murder libel and the Jew: the report by Cardinal Lorenzo Ganganelli (Pope Clement XIV)* (London, 1934), p. 44; Yerushalmi, *From Spanish court* ..., pp. 466–7.

[50] I.Z., pp. 93–4, deposition of Juan Aloncigaria, 11 June 1550.

[51] See Yerushalmi, *From Spanish court* ..., pp. 105–22.

of the Venetian Inquisition, and it had no obsessive desire to follow every trail which might conceivably lead to the secret Jew. The evidence which actually convinced the court is almost always concrete enough to command respect.

It is perfectly true that contact with the Inquisition or its officials could result in suggestions being made to a witness which might, in his mind, give his evidence a new twist, perhaps make him say things he would not previously have said. One example is provided by Margarita, a witness in the Ribeiro case. In April 1580 she described how, some years before, when she lived opposite the Ribeiros' house, 'I several times heard the cries of Giulia, servant to Gaspar, and she came out on the balcony and called him 'That Lutheran . . . he eats meat on Friday and Saturday.' And at that time I did not know what "Lutheran" meant.' She subsequently married a constable of the Holy Office and probably enlarged her knowledge of heresy; in the months which followed her first appearance before the court she must have had ample opportunity of discovering what the Ribeiros had been charged with. When summoned to repeat her testimony five months later, she gave a different version of Giulia's remarks, and reported her as saying ' "Dear sister, these treacherous Marrano dogs eat meat on Fridays and Saturdays." '[52] Certainly suggestions were also made to the parish priest of San Marcilian, who had apparently not understood the probable significance of the curious rituals of the Silva family, and was severely told: 'You should have realized that they were not good Christians, but rather Jews, and that they feigned these outward acts of a Christian in order to conceal their Judaism.'[53] However, the inquisitors would allow a person to tell his own story first, and add their interpretations later: it is generally possible to distinguish between the raw evidence offered and the layer of interpretation subsequently imposed.

Deep suspicion must of course attach to evidence obtained, not only by suggestion, but by a mixture of suggestion and duress. Especially dubious is the evidence contained in confessions made after the prisoner had seen the edited transcript of the witnesses' testimony against him. In Roman/canon law, confession was the 'queen of proofs'.[54] To the Inquisition, full confession and penitence were the goals at which the entire trial was aimed. To the historian, confessions made at some late stage in a trial must be the least satisfactory part of the Inquisition's testimony. In a very small proportion of the Jewish trials, physical torture played some part in the assembly of evidence, though it never did so at an early stage

[52] S.U., b. 45, proc. Ribeiro, 7 April, 7 Sept. 1580.
[53] S.U., b. 56, proc. Silva, test. Don Bernardo Giordano, 14 Nov. 1585.
[54] Cf. Langbein, *Prosecuting crime* . . . , p. 157.

in the proceedings, and it seldom added much to what was already known. More important, and more difficult to assess, was the influence of prolonged imprisonment and suspense, which could instil into the prisoner a desperate wish to have the case resolved – even against him.

Express rules governed the application of torture by the Holy Office. According to Eymeric it was justified where a case was half proved but not clinched. Defining half proof, he pronounced that where a person was accused of heresy by one witness, and also enjoyed an evil reputation, these facts became an 'indication' (*indicium*) sufficient to justify torture, though it was not enough to prove the heresy. Formulating the point rather differently, Peña argued that – as in criminal trials – one quite unexceptionable witness ought to be deemed sufficient to constitute semi-proof, so long as he had actually seen, heard or otherwise sensed the crime committed. It was also necessary that the prisoner should have made inconsistent or self-contradictory statements to the court.[55] Torture was not to be an opening move in a contest between the court and its prisoner, but rather a device used in the riper stages of a trial in order to resolve uncertainties. It must follow upon *indicia*, and not be used to create them.[56] A decree of the Cardinal Inquisitors-General in 1560 provided that prisoners who refused to answer, or failed to respond precisely and would not say 'yes' or 'no' when questioned about recent happenings, could be subjected to torture, so long as there were *indicia*, signposts pointing towards their guilt.[57] Nine years later, they also prescribed that persons convicted or confessed of heresy might be tortured for the purpose of discovering the 'final truth' and obtaining from them the names of accomplices.[58]

The use of torture was linked to the importance of confession as a judicial proof in the system of Roman/canon law. Very probably, resort to torture, on the part both of ecclesiastical and of lay courts, became less frequent during the sixteenth century in countries and under legal systems in which the judicial service came to consist of trained professionals, capable of reaching conclusions by less crude methods. Here there would be more room for judicial discretion, and less need to rely absolutely on the rule of thumb that where capital offences were being tried a case must be proved either by two eyewitnesses to the gravamen of the crime or by the confession of the accused. And the practice of convicting for suspicion of heresy, which was not a capital crime, could well reduce the rigorous

[55] Eymeric, pp. 313, 372–3; Peña, pp. 226–7.

[56] Masini, *Sacro Arsenale*, p. 131.

[57] Pastor, 'Allgemeine Dekrete . . .', p. 502.

[58] Ibid., p. 509. Cf. N.V., XI, pp. 318–19, 328–9, letters of Cardinal Scipione Rebiba on the case of Hieronimo Donzellino, a physician of Orze Nuove and a suspected heretic, 29 Jan., 12 Feb. 1575.

need for the conclusive proof of confession. Therefore, it would also reduce the need for torture.[59]

Significantly, the three examples of torture found among the trials for judaizing were all concentrated in the 1580s, the decade in which the Inquisition was most aggressive towards Jews, and all three concerned young men of low standing. On each occasion the torture was directed, not so much at establishing or disproving the guilt of the accused, as at eliciting the names of his accomplices and of the persons who had corrupted him. Readiness to divulge these would be a sign of repentance, and it would enable the Inquisition to extend its inquiries. On each occasion the prisoner had been guilty of contradictions or evasions. Francisco Dies had told, and subsequently withdrawn, a cover story that he had been born in Turin, and not in Spain or Portugal. Under torture he withdrew testimony implicating the Jew whom he had described as the middleman who handed him over to the judaizing Filippi to serve them while his father departed for the Levant.[60] At Belluno, Marco di Francesco of Padua, formerly a Jew, was accused of selling bogus indulgences, cards with the Ave Maria printed upon them falsely said to have been blessed by the Pope, and other fraudulent rubbish. In the governor's torture chamber he was exhorted to give all the names of other rogues and vagabonds caught up in the same racket, and to give the name of the printer involved; held to be telling lies and contradicting himself, he was hoisted on the rope but divulged no more names.[61] Giovanni Battista Capponi was tortured on instructions from Rome, two months after confessing to all the heretical speeches and irreligious actions attributed to him in the *processo*. His explanation of how he came by these strange notions was judged unconvincing, and as fire was applied to his feet he was sternly instructed: 'Tell the truth about your accomplices, and where and when you learnt the heresies and blasphemies which you have confessed and ratified.' He withstood the torture, crying 'What cruelty to try to extract from me thus a thing not in me to tell!'[62] In none of these cases did torture add substantially to the evidence against the prisoner himself.

In unusual circumstances, the papal nuncio in 1622 was forced to justify the practice of imprisoning during trial. He did not suggest that it would encourage confession. Its function was to help the prosecution form its case efficiently, and also to serve as a species of punishment in itself – presumably of someone who was to blame for having caused the suspicion which warranted his arrest. Of the case of Fulgenzio Camaldolese he said:

[59] Cf. Langbein, *Prosecuting crime* ..., pp. 155, 159–62, 241; Langbein, *Torture* ..., pp. 3–4, 6, 48, 51, 56.

[60] S.U., b. 54, proc. Filippi, 13 Nov. 1585.

[61] S.U., b. 59, proc. Marco di Francesco of Padua, 27 Oct. 1587.

[62] S.U., b. 61, proc. Capponi, 11 Oct. 1588.

Accused persons have always been imprisoned in cases of such gravity as this one, and the reasons are that they may purge the blame, that they may not suborn witnesses, and that all things may pass with due secrecy, especially while the *processo informativo* is in progress, after which we proceed to the defence and to the resolution of the case.

And he added that the Inquisition had comfortable cells.[63]

Its prisoners enjoyed one advantage in that – save for the very small number extradited – they were normally tried in the place of arrest and seldom completely isolated from family and friends. The imprisonment of those under investigation probably became more efficient, if not more harsh, about 1600 when the Inquisition acquired its own prisons and so came to enjoy the same facilities as the lay magistrates of Venice. In the early days its prisoners were usually confined in the district lock-up of San Giovanni in Bragora, one of the so-called *casoni* of the *sestieri* of Venice, which were used as debtors' prisons.[64] An unusual defendant, Righetto, whiled away months not only in that place but also in the state gaols at San Marco. These, though damp and insalubrious, were characterized by a kind of cheerful slackness, making it virtually impossible to isolate prisoners from the world in the style attributed to the Inquisitions of Spain and Portugal. Other prisoners in the same building were allowed to introduce members of their families, and Righetto, intimate with gaolers who became his gambling companions, was allowed out on escorted walks to shop, or see his advocate, or visit a nearby tavern. Donna Helysada, matron at San Giovanni in Bragora, had been shocked to hear of it: 'Can the prisoners of the Holy Inquisition really walk about in the corridors?' An official of the Inquisition assured her: 'There are three doors before you can get out.' Righetto broke the monotony of his long confinement once by escaping during a general gaol-break after Venice got wind of the victory over the Turks at Lepanto, though he was extradited from his refuge in Ferrara and returned to Venice early the following year. He escaped a second time, apparently for good, on a day in August 1573 when the gaol was mysteriously left quite unguarded.[65] Equally unusual were the conditions faced by the equally stubborn Gaspar Ribeiro: after his arrest in 1580, he was found to be suffering from depression or anxiety so severe as to bring him to the verge of suicide, and special arrangements were made for his confinement in his own house under the surveillance of two guards maintained at his reluctant expense.[66] Righetto and Ribeiro

[63] C.E.R., reg. 20, fol. 32, 23 July 1622.

[64] I.Z., pp. 74, 209, 256, 319; Pullan, *Rich and poor* ..., p. 395.

[65] Pullan, '"A ship ..."', pp. 34, 52–4; S.U., b. 36, proc. Righetto, test. Donna Helysada, 1 Sept. 1573.

[66] S.U., b. 45, proc. Ribeiro, 17 Feb. 1580.

were notably more resilient, perhaps in consequence of these unusual conditions of imprisonment, than was Filipe de Nis, who was treated in a more orthodox manner.

About 1580, the nuncio Bolognetti was writing of current plans to establish for the Inquisition headquarters of its own, including prison cells, on a site near San Marco. Costs were estimated at some 2,000 ducats and the building had been hopefully started, even though funds fell far short of that mark;[67] for some years past certain fines had been earmarked as contributions to the building.[68] It seems indeed that the Inquisition prisons, erected near the back of what subsequently became the new prisons and on the corner of the Calle degli Albanesi, came into use well before the determined move to build the new state gaols which began in 1589.[69] Certainly Capponi was removed in 1588 from the debtors' prison at Rialto to a special prison of the Holy Office.[70] On instructions from Rome the Inquisition in the 1590s tried to insist on its own right to nominate the gaoler – even if it could do no more than formally confirm the appointment of a constable already installed by the state. The prison was kept for the use, not only of the Inquisitor, but also of the nuncio and Patriarch.[71]

Petitions from Filipe de Nis suggest that by the mid-1580s the Inquisition was isolating its prisoners more effectively. A rich man might be able to purchase marginally better surroundings because the more comfortable cells tended to be less secure and pledges had to be given by those who occupied them. He might, on the other hand, suffer greater mental agonies for having left more property and business behind him. In 1585 Filipe asked to be moved from a cell called La Rubiera to a more comfortable one called La Piovana, and was required to find a guarantor to stand surety for him to the tune of 1,000 crowns. After forty days confinement he complained of the dampness and stench of the prison; it was impossible to sleep without opening up the balcony. He complained of total ruin, of having to depend for life itself on Jewish charity, but was authorized to appoint accountable agents to look after his affairs in the world outside. After fifty-five days, he called himself 'dead or buried alive, knowing nothing of the world, or of his affairs, or of his wife and child-

[67] Stella–Bolognetti, pp. 293–4.

[68] I.Z. II, p. 165, proc. Antonio di Marcantonio Giustinian – on 18 Jan. 1575 he was fined 100 ducats, the fine to be applied to the maintenance of the building assigned to the Holy Office and its prisons, and also to defraying the expenses of the *processo* against him.

[69] See Scarabello, *Carcerati e carceri* ..., pp. 90–1, 217, n. 39.

[70] S.U., b. 61, proc. Capponi, 2 June 1588 – paper marked 'Fiat translatio ad carceres Sancti Officii' and signed by the Inquisitor.

[71] B.A.V., MS Barberino Latino 5195, fol. 61v.–62; MS Vaticanus Latinus 10945, fol. 39v.

ren.'[72] No doubt this imprisonment – which lasted for nine months – played some part in his decision to surrender after being called upon to abjure.

In his manual the Inquisitor Masini condemned the use of hunger and thirst as weapons against the prisoners of the Holy Office.[73] By the prisoners' own accounts, the regime was harsh enough – in 1629, Felice Magalotti, on being returned to prison, protested to the court,

> I demand to be allowed to confess, I am in poor health, my whole body is covered in sores, I sleep on the ground, and I have no means to live but the bread of St Mark. I am dying of want of every kind.

Nearly five months later he was still begging for the despatch of his case, and he described himself as 'dying of the great sickness with which I am afflicted'. On this occasion his wish was granted and abjuration and sentence followed within a week or two.[74] Soon afterwards, Pier Vincenzo Maria Sandoval complained: 'They give me neither broth nor bedding; just bare boards.' He made no formal defence, and his case was resolved within six weeks;[75] the ordeal of Felice Magalotti, who had offered a defence, lasted eight months, although he escaped in the end with a lighter sentence. Whatever the prison, the danger of death from typhus must always have been present; resistance to the tribunal, prolonging the proceedings, might entail not only frustration and boredom, but a considerable physical risk.

None the less it is true that prolonged imprisonment and confession seldom actually extracted new information – the effect of this kind of duress was to produce on the prisoner's part an acknowledgement of the facts which told against him, and a formal declaration of repentance. Confessions are clearly no guide to the prisoner's true state of mind. Filipe de Nis conveys a powerful impression of one who, since his cover stories had failed to convince, had now determined to play to perfection the role of penitent designed for him by the Holy Office. He came to prostrate himself before an altar and adore Christ and the Virgin, saying: 'God has enlightened me and I beg you for mercy. I have done penance in prison, and I beg mercy of you, for love of the five wounds of Our Lord Jesus Christ.' Joy had burst upon him, he said, the previous morning at dinner time. 'And in future I no longer wish to eat the food of the Jews, but wish instead to eat with Hieronimo the gaoler.'[76] Giovanni Battista Capponi,

[72] S.U., b. 54, proc. Filippi, 23 Oct. 1585, Nov. 1585.
[73] Masini, *Sacro Arsenale*, p. 162.
[74] S.U., b. 87, proc. Magalotti, 4 Dec. 1629, 27 April, 7 May 1630.
[75] S.U., b. 89, proc. Sandoval, 23 Sept. 1632.
[76] S.U., b. 54, proc. Filippi, 9, 12 June 1586.

having strenuously denied the charges against him, suddenly decided to admit to them all, though in a way which satisfied neither the Holy Office nor himself, for he went on returning wistfully even after his first confession to the story of a conspiracy against him by his enemies.[77] For all this, confessions can be put to some cautious use where – as does that of Filipe de Nis – they contain autobiographical or other material not suggested to the prisoner and not clearly designed to give the Inquisition what it seemed to expect; incidental detail may be more convincing than general drift. Spontaneous confessions offered by self-delators are clearly in a rather different category from those offered after prolonged trial, although there is often no prospect of checking these against the testimony of witnesses. Witness testimony, untidy and confusing though it often is, remains the most informative source within the Inquisitor's records.

There is no evidence to suggest that either the Venetian Inquisition or its host state had any major financial interest in manufacturing evidence against rich Jews, or to suggest that informers were financially rewarded in such a way as to encourage the submission of false denunciations. From such denunciations they might make other gains, such as the discomfiture of an enemy; but financial profit was unlikely to be made. Prospective delators would sometimes try to strike bargains with the Holy Office, by promising to reveal their knowledge if they were guaranteed rewards from the confiscated estate of the heretic; but there is no trace of the Inquisitor and his colleagues actually acceding to these proposals.[78]

As stated by Eymeric, it was the general rule that by rights a heretic should forfeit his goods from the day he committed heresy. But should he repent before sentence was passed, he might have them restored. It was the duty of temporal princes and powers to confiscate the goods of an impenitent heretic, and of a relapsed one.[79] But the Venetian state was usually reluctant to interfere in this way with private property, and the ecclesiastical authorities came to acquiesce in what Bolognetti called the 'style of Venice'. In 1557, the governors of Bergamo were instructed by letter of the Doge that the goods of certain local heretics, the Belinchetti, were not to be confiscated, 'a thing which is done neither in our own city nor in any other'.[80] Better-known legislation, of a more general character, issued in 1568, became a precedent later cited by Sarpi and criticized with gusto by Albizzi. The Council of Ten then prescribed that although the goods of Venetian heretics should rightfully come to the fisc, provincial governors should allow them to be 'enjoyed and exploited' by 'those

[77] S.U., b. 61, proc. Capponi, 11 Aug., 22 Sept. 1588.
[78] E.g., S.U., b. 24, denunciation of Abraham Benveniste, alias Agostinho Enriques, 6 March 1568; b. 32, denunciation of Duarte Enriques, undated.
[79] Eymeric, p. 389; Peña, p. 270 ff.
[80] S.U., b. 153.

heirs of the condemned man who would succeed *ab intestato*', on condition that they gave no part in them to the condemned themselves.[81] No explicit distinction was made here between the treatment accorded to penitent and to impenitent heretics.

Certainly the Holy Office itself had a modest and not always adequate income which was independent of confiscations and fines. According to manuscript notes made in the eighteenth century and surviving among the miscellaneous papers of the Holy Office, up to 1561 the Inquisitor was paid 12 gold ducats a month by the state. But from that year onwards the regular income of the Holy Office came to depend on assignations of revenue from ecclesiastical sources – first from the diocese of Verona, then (in 1578–79) from that of Torcello and from the canonry of Cividale di Valcamonica. This income was spent on the payment of officials and the upkeep of buildings and prisons. The nuncio Bolognetti seemed to approve of these arrangements because they demonstrated the Inquisition's integrity and its lack of interest in financial gains from the conviction of heretics.[82]

It remained true, however, that the goods of a judaizing Christian – certainly those of an impenitent one – were still liable to confiscation even after 1568. The grounds for this exception are obscure. But it might well have been supposed that with rich Portuguese judaizers there was an exceptionally strong risk of the whole family participating in the crime, since Jewish belief might well be inherited with Jewish blood. Furthermore, there was reason to fear that New Christian or Marrano families had come to Venice with the intention of setting their affairs in order and then migrating to the Levant. Exported wealth might go to strengthen the enemies of Christendom.[83] The Marrano family was not really as naturally united as this might suggest, and not always so eager to depart from Christian territory. But the theory would have been a reasonable one. The dire possibility of confiscation was certainly present during the trial of Gaspar Ribeiro, who died without admitting his fault, and whose memory was condemned as that of a judaizing heretic. A cousin of his son-in-law was pointedly asked:

---

[81] Ibid.; Sarpi, 'Inquisizione', pp. 127, 182–3; Albizzi, *Risposta* ..., pp. 276–8; Battistella, *Il Santo Officio ... in Friuli*, p. 70; Grendler, *Roman Inquisition* ..., p. 50. Venetian policy was criticized on the grounds that it removed a major deterrent, in that the father who committed heresy need no longer fear depriving his children of their inheritance. Heresy would be treated more lightly than certain worldly crimes, for which confiscation of goods was a normal penalty, and treason to God would be more lightly punished than treason to the state.

[82] S.U., b. 153; N.V., XI, p. 105, Rebiba to Castagna, 5 Dec. 1573; Stella–Bolognetti, pp. 293–4. For revenues and expenditure in 1645, see B.A.V., MS Vaticanus 10945, fol. 162.

[83] See below, pp. 179, 186–7.

if he knew that in this case Vincenzo and his wife and children would suffer great prejudice if Gaspar were declared a judaizer, in that the result would be the confiscation of his goods, and hence the disinheritance of Gaspar's only daughter, the wife of Vincenzo, the witness's kinsman?

Whether confiscation was actually carried out, despite Violante's record of resistance to her father's wishes, and despite the efforts of her nominally Christian but far from pious husband, is not known.[84] For the Filippi, after the abjuration of Filipe de Nis, the question does not seem to have arisen; he was merely required to give a substantial pledge of 1,700 ducats against unauthorized departure from Venice.[85]

At least in the sixteenth century, the Venetians were not only a trading nation, but also one actually governed by patricians who either had direct mercantile experience and interests themselves, or else had relatives involved in trade. Venetian finances relied on a steady flow of revenue from customs duties and transit taxes which could only be maintained by preserving mercantile confidence.[86] It was not concerned to seek windfall profits from the confiscation of wealth, which could only undermine that confidence – at least on the part of foreign communities. The Venetians would have appreciated the words of a rich merchant, about to leave Portugal in the early 1540s, 'that he could not live in a land where, for a letter that the Cardinal Viseu had written him, he could be made to pay 33,000 ducats.'[87] Venice's cordiality towards foreign traders varied quite considerably through time, but even at times of hostility towards Portuguese merchants – as in 1550 – its policy was to expel or repel those who did not wish to live as Christians, rather than to seize their goods after arrival.[88] In one of his remarkable defence submissions, Righetto chose to contrast the policies of the Venetians and of the Emperor Charles V most favourably with those of Paul IV and the cardinal-nephews who abetted his attack on the Iberian Jews of Ancona in 1556: a move which had started as an attempt to blackmail the Jewish community into paying a massive fine of 50,000 ducats.[89] Certainly the Republic did not indulge

---

[84] S.U., b. 45, proc. Ribeiro, interrogation of Antonio Maria Aragona, 28 Feb. 1582; ibid., 7 to 11 Dec. 1582; Pullan, 'The Inquisition . . .', pp. 223–4, 229–30; below, p. 233.

[85] S.U., b. 54, proc. Filippi, 17 Oct. 1586.

[86] See R. T. Rapp, *Industry and economic decline in seventeenth-century Venice* (Cambridge, Mass., and London, 1976), p. 141, for the calculation that in 1587 trade taxes accounted for 36 per cent and in 1670 for 15 per cent of the revenue of the Venetian state.

[87] S.U., b. 36, proc. Righetto, test. Don Emanuel Rocha, 17 Sept. 1571; Pullan, ' "A ship . . ." ', p. 41.

[88] See below, pp. 174–6.

[89] Pullan, ' "A ship . . ." ', pp. 50–1.

in cat-and-mouse games like those of the Portuguese Crown, in which the threat of investigation by the Holy Office was held over a community of Jewish descent and temporarily withdrawn in return for a substantial payment.[90]

Apart from confiscations, fines could still be levied, but they were measured at most in hundreds rather than in thousands of ducats, and the largest fine recorded in these cases was one of 500 ducats imposed in 1580 on Vincenzo Scrova for interfering with witnesses.[91] Nor is there evidence of undue concentration on rich men, since the Inquisition was at least as much concerned to punish poor Jews conducting themselves like rogues and vagabonds. Indeed, the evidence concerning the Ribeiros suggests that the Inquisition – whether restrained by the *Assistenti* or not – had at first been a reluctant rather than an eager prosecutor. And Righetto, ruined by gambling, though sometimes said to be less derelict than he pretended,[92] was surely a security risk rather than a tempting prospect for a confiscator. It is true that only men of riches or of good family were likely to be convicted of formal heresy or apostasy, as distinct from suspicion of heresy: but this was surely a tribute to their education and their responsibility for their acts, rather than a device for seizing their money and merchandise.

Any recording institution will naturally impose its own distortions upon the material it preserves; the historian's task is surely not to claim impartiality for any particular source, but to identify and take account of the peculiar distortions to which it is especially prone. In the end, the records of the Inquisition are useful chiefly for demonstrating what kind of person was most likely to fall foul simultaneously of the Church and the state, by violating the canons of order which each held most dear. There is no reason to believe that the Inquisition deliberately manufactured evidence or, by brutality, carelessness, credulity or corruption, encouraged others to do so. Its records are detailed enough to be watched carefully for evidence of suggestion and stereotyping, and sometimes indeed they answer such questions as: 'What were the blasphemies most commonly attributed to Jews?' rather than such questions as: 'How did Jews habitually blaspheme?' But one commonsensical rule can be applied – that the earlier part of a trial, in which the questioning was most neutral, provides the best evidence of the belief and conduct of the accused and witnesses, and the later part provides the best evidence of the goals the tribunal itself was hoping to achieve. Very few trials depended merely on dialogue

[90] See Révah, 'Les marranes portugais ...', p. 514; Lea, *Inquisition of Spain*, III, pp. 259–60, 267–70.
[91] S.U., b. 45, proc. Ribeiro, 10–13 Sept. 1580.
[92] Pullan, ' "A ship ..." ', pp. 43, 44.

between the Inquisitor and his prisoner; those that did were generally the product of a spontaneous confession offered by a self-delator. The greater part of the trial records consist of an accumulation of witness testimony, much of it bearing on the performance of specific actions which implied heretical beliefs; and, since elaborate defences were sometimes mounted, it often happened that the prisoner was portrayed by friends as well as by enemies. Jews, former Jews and persons of Jewish descent came of a people well used to Christian hostility, and capable of showing both wariness and caution in resisting suggestions put to them by a Christian inquisitor. True, Inquisition trials, as distinct from the abjurations and penances which commonly followed them, were a secret kept from the public. But this fact must surely disarm the suspicion that the Holy Office was designing show trials to impress the people or doctoring its records for propaganda purposes. It had to expose its proceedings, not only in writing to Rome, but also at their first enactment to a representative of the Venetian state in person; and the Holy Office could not, like the Spanish Inquisition, develop into an *imperium in imperio*, accountable to none but itself.

PART II

Toleration and the Inquisition: the Place of the Jews in Venetian Society

9

Nations Set Apart:
Christian and Jew in Venice

Seldom did the Inquisition arrest and investigate Jews who had lived long in Venice or firmly aligned themselves with one of the Jewish communities recognized by the Senate. Most of the subjects of its inquiries were in some sense either transients or marginal men or both: persons guilty of ambiguous conduct and uneasily poised on the frontier between Christianity and Judaism. Some were adventurers; some were vagabonds; some could not meet the demands of society and the Church that they adhere firmly to one allegiance or the other. Some had misunderstood the nature of the liberty of Venice, mistakenly believing that almost any form of indiscreet behaviour would be tolerated. A Portuguese priest ascribed to João Ribeiro the insolent declaration

> that he lived in a free city, that God had given him great wealth, and so to hell with the Pope and the Portuguese Inquisition, and that he held the Signory of Venice in the palm of his hand and was its master, and with a snap of his fingers could order the bigwigs and magistrates to do his bidding.[1]

If he really uttered these words, they were symptoms of a hubristic disposition that helped to provoke an investigation of his family's affairs. Guilty of similar excesses were the Filippi when they took a fine house outside the Ghetto, allowed their sabbath ceremonies to be seen from the street, and professed to believe that a Jew could live where he chose if only he paid enough in fees or fines to the *Cattaveri*.[2] The recipe for peace was to stay within the limits, both social and physical, assigned to Jews by

[1] S.U., b. 45, proc. Ribeiro, den. Enriquez de Mello in Rome, 16 Nov. 1575.
[2] S.U., b. 54, proc. Filippi, test. Solomon Marcos, 12 Oct. 1585.

society and the state; to provoke, within the confines of the city, no scandal offending God. Should such discretion be observed, the state might prove willing to protect from the Inquisition even those liable to its severest penalties. Depending as it did on the *Assistenti* for arrest and sanctions and on Venetians (as well as Portuguese and Spanish 'experts') for information, the mixed tribunal of the Inquisition could hardly fail to respond to the attitudes of its host state and society.

Venice's social structure is best described in terms of legally defined estates or orders endowed with specific privileges, and in terms of corporations with expressly declared rights and duties, specializing in particular fields of social and economic action. One corporation of specialists within this highly regulated society was the *Università degli Ebrei*, which comprised the several Jewish nations, and the Jews could also be said to form an estate of outcastes, lower in status than all the recognized Christian orders. For most purposes, the Christian social categories recognized by the Venetian state consisted of noblemen, of citizens and merchants, of artisans or guildsmen, and of clergy. The social framework was more rigid and formalized than that of the great commercial boom towns of the sixteenth and seventeenth centuries, such as Antwerp, Seville, Lyons or Amsterdam; in the ancient trading republic every man was expected to know his place. Venice had a legally defined patriciate which remained, till wartime admissions to its ranks began to be made in 1646, remarkably impervious to new wealth and parvenu dynasties.[3] It made grants of citizenship, *de intus et de extra*, conferring the right to trade between Venice and the East, in a cautious, not to say grudging, manner; and it maintained a strong guild system, although some of its retailing guilds were quite loosely built and were inwardly fluid.[4] But Venetian economic planners were prepared to allot determinate and circumscribed roles to foreigners and newcomers who could complement, rather than compete with, the activities of the long-established Venetian nobility and citizenry. Hence the Senate assigned specific privileges and obligations to the Jews, which were spelt out in minute detail in the contracts or *condotte* periodically concluded with the 'Germanic' and Sephardic communities within Venetian Jewry. So long as they met these obligations and caused no scandal, the Jews could rely on government protection – especially after

[3] On the Venetian patriciate, see J. C. Davis, *The decline of the Venetian nobility as a ruling class* (Baltimore, 1962); P. Burke, *Venice and Amsterdam: a study of seventeenth-century elites* (London, 1974); J. Georgelin, *Venise au siècle des lumières* (Paris–The Hague, 1978), p. 619 ff.; A. F. Cowan, 'The urban patriciate: Lübeck and Venice, 1580–1700' (University of London Ph.D. thesis, London School of Economics and Political Science, 1981).

[4] On the citizenry, see Pullan, *Rich and poor* ..., pp. 99–108; U. Tucci, 'The psychology of the Venetian merchant in the sixteenth century', in *Renaissance Venice*, ed. J. R. Hale (London, 1973), p. 360 ff.; Georgelin, *Venise* ..., p. 667 ff. On the guilds, see R. S. Mackenney, 'Trade guilds and devotional confraternities in the state and society of Venice to 1620' (University of Cambridge Ph.D. Thesis, 1982).

about 1580, when their position grew increasingly stable, save for a spell of grave uncertainty during the 1630s.[5]

Within the Venetian economy, the traditional function of the Jews was to provide cut-rate pawnbroking services – theoretically for the benefit of the poor, although well-to-do persons frequently tried to make use of them. From 1598 onwards these were financed by taxes levied on all the three resident Jewish communities, including those Sephardic Jews who were traditionally not moneylenders but rather traders.[6] Five per cent pawnbroking, as practised from 1573 onwards, could not be self-financing, if only for the reason that capital had to be borrowed to float the loan banks at rates of interest markedly higher than 5 per cent – i.e. at $8\frac{1}{2}$ per cent in 1607 and at 7 per cent in the late 1650s[7] The main sources of Jewish wealth, making it possible to raise and pay interest on this capital, were the trade in second-hand clothing, jewellery, furniture and other articles known as *strazzaria*, and – no doubt this was far more profitable – the extensive overseas trade conducted by Sephardic Jews, especially with their co-religionists in the Levant. In economic terms, the presence of the Jews could also be justified by their prowess as consumers who generated demand for goods produced or handled by Venetian artisans, without entering into competition with them. For Jews, although a select few won fame as physicians[8] and some were well known as dancers, musicians and music teachers, theoretically produced nothing of their own, with one or two rare and carefully specified exceptions. Among these were veils and coifs which would meet the demands of Jewish fashion and perhaps accord with the custom that a Jewish bride should cover her own hair, sometimes by means of a coif, at her wedding.[9] In Venice even Passover matzos were supplied to Jews by Christian bakers.[10] Rabbi Simon Luzzatto, the Jews' most famous apologist,

[5] On the Jewish economy in general, in addition to C. Roth, *The history of the Jews of Venice* (Philadelphia, 1930, reprint New York, 1975), see R. C. Mueller, 'Les prêteurs juifs de Venise au Moyen Âge', *Annales: Économies, Sociétés, Civilisations*, 30 (1975), pp. 1277–302; Jacoby, 'Les juifs ...'; E. Ashtor, 'Gli inizi della comunità ebraica a Venezia', *Rassegna mensile d'Israel* (Nov.–Dec. 1978), pp. 683–703; Pullan, *Rich and poor ...*, pp. 431–578; B. Ravid, *Economics and toleration ....*

[6] Pullan, *Rich and poor ...*, pp. 570, 573–4.

[7] S.T., filza 184, 5 Oct. 1607; filza 660, 12 Feb. 1658 Venetian style.

[8] See, now, N. E. Vanzan Marchini, 'Medici ebrei e assistenza cristiana nella Venezia del '500', *Rassegna mensile d'Israel* (April–May 1979), pp. 132–61.

[9] Pullan, *Rich and poor ...*, p. 506; Leon Modena, *Relatione*, in S.U., b. 94, I, ch. v; when Alumbra, cousin to the Duke of Naxos, called at the Ribeiro house in Santa Maria Formosa, she was wearing 'a coif and veils and other things as Jewish women do' – S.U., b. 45, proc. Ribeiro, test. Mattea da Rippa Sicca, 7–8 April 1580.

[10] C.S.M., b. 62, 9 Aug. 1594, 18 Dec. 1596; cf. S.U., b. 64, proc. Giorgio Moretto, 8 April 1589, where Alessandro di Innocenzo of Verona, a baker at Santa Maria Formosa, describes how he went into the Ghetto to cook *azimi* of unleavened bread on the oven owned by Jacob de' Cresci.

guessed in 1638, somewhat hyperbolically, that their presence in Venice was then sufficient to keep 4,000 artisans employed in serving their needs and in manufacturing the goods which Jews despatched to other parts of the world.[11]

Apart from performing these services, the Jews were liable to various forms of special taxation: formally owning no property, they could only be accommodated within a kind of alternative fiscal system geared to their activities. In the mid-sixteenth century, Jewish fiscal obligations consisted largely of the duty to maintain the banks and also to pay a special tax peculiar to the Jews, consisting of several thousand ducats per annum. Such a tax was later justified on the grounds that the second-hand trade did not contribute to customs revenue.[12] Between 1548 and 1573, interest rates were systematically depressed in successive *condotte*, and the regular tax seems to have been chiefly replaced after 1573 by the obligation to finance banks which clearly could not hope for profit and could no longer legally draw to any extent upon Christian capital.[13] However, with further settlements of Sephardic Jews in Venice in the last decade of the century, the obligations of all Jews to the state could be increased, and indeed they became both complex and varied. Outbreaks of war, and the need to fit out and man the reserve fleets of the Venetian navy, brought much extraordinary taxation. Contracts of the Germanic nation from 1624 onwards obliged them to perform a special service allied to their function as dealers in furniture, tapestries and hangings: this included the tasks of decorating the ducal palace with suitable objects when the Doge held public banquets, of adorning the ceremonial ship called the *Bucintoro*, and of festooning 'the place where our supreme lords [*Signoria Nostra*] go on Carnival Thursday [*Giobba Grasso*]'.[14] And the Jews were required to furnish the official lodgings assigned to princes or other high-ranking official visitors. By 1659 this duty was valued at approximately 5,000 ducats per annum, and it then accounted for about $8\frac{1}{2}$ per cent of the sum paid annually to the treasury by the Jews, while the obligation to maintain the banks stood for some 14 per cent. The most massive contributions of the Jews, however, then lay in the payment of special taxes and forced loans. Reviewing their position in 1659, the *Università degli Ebrei* claimed to have 'sacrificed' over 1.3 million ducats

[11] S. Luzzatto, *Discorso circa il stato de gl' Hebrei, et in particolar dimoranti nell' inclita Città di Venetia* (Venice, 1638), fol. 28 ff. He was using the suspiciously high estimate of 6,000 for the Jewish population of Venice – for other figures, see below, pp. 156–7.

[12] B. Ravid, 'The legal status of the Jewish merchants of Venice, 1541–1638' (Harvard University Ph.D. thesis, 1973), pp. 209–10 – remarks of Maffeo Michiel in 1611.

[13] Pullan, *Rich and poor* . . . , pp. 520–40.

[14] Ravid, *Economics and toleration* . . . , pp. 119–20; subsequent *condotte*, up to 1658, assembled in S.T., filza 649.

during the war of Crete, which had begun in 1644. It may be that at least a quarter of this sum consisted of large deposits made in the 7 per cent loan funds in the Mint. Annual contributions to the treasury amounted at this time of stress to nearly 60,000 ducats, of which about three-fifths proceeded from direct taxes.[15]

Generally, the Jews were treated as dispensers of cash holding large sums in liquid wealth, whose services could be called upon liberally in times of emergency and not only in war. They were said by Luzzatto to have advanced some 10,000 ducats to the government at the time of the great plague of 1630–31[16] – thus providing a Venetian parallel to the large public Christian banks or *monti di pietà* on the mainland, which were similarly used by their local governments for the purpose of financing relief.[17]

By 1600 the corporation of Jews settled in Venice comprised three recognized Jewish nations. Of these the oldest was that of the so-called Germanic Jews, which in practice contained Jews of Italian birth and family, as well as large clans of German descent such as the Luzzatti and a dwindling number of recent immigrants from Germany. With time many of the Germanic Jews came to regard themselves as more Italianate than Germanic, and more Venetian than anything else. An agreement of 1603 between the nations of Jews referred to 'those who are of the German or Italian nation and have not been Turkish subjects'.[18] Despite the official vocabulary which equated Italian and German Jews, Leon Modena distinguished clearly and repeatedly between the two, and sometimes identified differences of outlook and custom as well as of language.[19] Caliman, son of Abram Grassin, said in evidence in 1638, 'I am an old man of fifty-six years, born here in Venice, and I know these things by virtue of my knowledge and experience of the Ghetto.'[20] In a memorandum addressed to the Senate some twenty years later, his nation described themselves as 'we, the Venetian Jews, although we are called the Germans' ('noi hebrei venetti se bene chiamati tedeschi'), and the Senate itself was prepared to term them 'the Jews who are called Germans, although they were born here in this city.'[21] This sense of permanence, of identification with the only city they knew as a place of residence, was a measure of the Germanic Jews' capacity for discreetly and unobtrusively discharging the role assigned to them by the govern-

[15] See Appendix I, below, pp. 317–18.

[16] Luzzatto, *Discorso* . . . , fol. 29v.

[17] Pullan, *Rich and poor* . . . , pp. 606–9.

[18] C.S.M., b. 62, 14 April 1603.

[19] Leon Modena, *Relatione*, in S.U., b. 94, I, ch. i, ii; II, ch. vi, vii.

[20] I.R.E.C., Carte Diverse, 'Pie Case de Cattecumeni contro Università de gli Hebrei', fol. 13v.–14, 87v.

[21] S.T., filza 660, 12 Feb. 1658 Venetian style; reg. 156, fol. 51v., 22 March 1658.

ment. Even the rise, a few years later, of a Jewish Messiah in the Turkish Empire failed to shake the determination of the Venetian rabbis to restrain all outbreaks of enthusiasm that might provoke the disapproval of the Venetian state.[22]

Traditionally the Germanic-Italian Jews were bankers, pawnbrokers and dealers in used articles. From 1613 onwards, however, they were clearly contemplating breaking out of this sphere and were petitioning the Senate for the right to engage in international commerce; from 1634 it became legally possible for individuals to obtain licences entitling them to do so at the hands of the *Cinque Savii alla Mercanzia*, the Venetian board of trade.[23] Long before that, in the 1590s, Jews bearing the Germanic-Italianate names of Luzzatto and Callimani were apparently purchasing new textiles, some of them imported from Enghien in Flanders.[24]

Members of the settled Germanic-Italian community in Venice, as distinct from the many transient visitors who put up in its hostels, seldom fell foul of the Inquisition. Most of them knew their place too well. Although the Jews were seen by churchmen as a potential source of doctrinal contagion, the Inquisition was more concerned with those Christians who overstepped the mark and showed undue familiarity with them in such a way as to suggest a contempt for Christian beliefs and observance. Far more uncertainly placed were some of the Sephardim. These Jews were divided somewhat erratically – according to their origins and allegiances – into Levantines who were or had been subjects of the Ottoman Sultan, and Ponentines or Westerners who had migrated more directly from Spain, Portugal, the Low Countries or elsewhere in the western world (such as the ports of Ancona and Livorno). Until 1589, the only recognized legal category of Sephardim consisted of Turkish subjects who were all in theory transients or *viandanti*. But from that time onwards two other categories were created, and these consisted of resident Levantine and Ponentine Jews, entitled to settle in the city and engage in international commerce, especially trade with the Ottoman Empire.[25] Some of the Sephardim were descendants of firm Jewish believers expelled from Spain in the diaspora of 1492; the elderly Moses Cardiel, giving evidence to the Inquisition in 1580, said that his father was 'one of those expelled as Jews from Spain'.[26] Others had not been expelled as Jews. They, or their families, had been professing Christians at the time of their flight or emigration, and had returned to Judaism in a spirit of remorse, or faith, or nostalgia, or fear, or (as some said) sheer opportunism. Their

[22] Scholem, *Sabbatai sevi* ..., p. 496 ff.
[23] Ravid, *Economics and toleration* ..., pp. 37–8, 125–6.
[24] See Brulez, *Marchands flamands* ..., pp. 127, 317, 600–3.
[25] For details, see below, pp. 187, 195–6.
[26] S.U., b. 45, proc. Ribeiro, 25 Aug. 1580.

retreat from Christianity made them liable to the penalties of heresy or apostasy at the hands of the Inquisition. But their connexions with relatives and co-religionists in the Ottoman Empire, their capital and commercial know-how, made them a sought-after prize for governments bent on preserving or developing their economies, and the Venetian Senate eventually gave them express guarantees against molestation for religious offences. The special problems of the Sephardic Jews will be discussed in the next chapter.

Somewhat indeterminately placed on the spectrum were Jews who were subjects of Venetian colonies such as Corfu, Crete or Zante. Very likely they regarded themselves as transient Levantine Jews, although many found it easy to detach themselves from co-religionists through the privilege of wearing the black hat normally reserved for Christians, rather than the distinctive red or yellow headgear, the cap or turban, of a Jew. In the mid-seventeenth century it was said of Corfiot Jews that a few might come to Venice, but they would stay only to transact their business and then depart. Descendants of David Mavrogonato of Crete enjoyed the privilege of wearing the black hat: when one of them, the physician Jeremiah, arrived in Venice in the 1630s he claimed to be a Levantine and entitled to a room in the houses reserved to Levantines.[27] Colonial Jews presented no collective problem to the Venetian Inquisition, although one individual, the Cretan convert who took the name of Paolo Loredan, figured for a time in its records in the 1580s.[28]

Like other religious and professional corporations, such as the guilds and confraternities, the *Università degli Ebrei* enjoyed certain powers of self-government under strict surveillance from patrician magistracies. If anything the segregationist policies of Church and state in the sixteenth century accentuated the tendency towards greater autonomy.[29] Like the guilds, the corpus of Jews was united not only by a common social and economic purpose but also by religious bonds; the authority of the synagogue and its powers of exclusion from the civic-religious community were used for the maintenance of internal discipline. Of the supervisory magistrates, the *Ufficiali al Cattaver* were responsible for the Ghetto Nuovo and for regulating contacts between Christian and Jew; the *Cinque Savii*

[27] On the Mavrogonati, see Jacoby, 'Les juifs ...', pp. 176–7, 201; E.B., b. 58, Not. 5, fol. 200, 212, 31 Oct., 18 April 1635; b. 59, Not. 7, fol. 1, 8 July 1654; on Corfiot Jews, S.T., filza 660, filed under date 12 Feb. 1658 Venetian style – report of the *Savi di man propria*, 31 Jan. 1658 Venetian style. The Levantine Jews had Jeremiah Mavrogonato evicted on the grounds that he had obtained his lodgings 'by violence'. See also S. W. Baron, *A social and religious history of the Jews* (second edition, New York, 1962 onwards), XVII, p. 46 ff.

[28] See below, pp. 297–8.

[29] Cf. M. A. Shulvass, *The Jews in the world of the Renaissance*, transl. E. I. Kose (Leiden–Chicago, 1973), p. 50 ff.

alla Mercanzia dealt with the commercial activities of Jews and with the affairs of the Ghetto Vecchio; the *Sopraconsoli* oversaw the banks and conducted auctions of unredeemed pledges; the *Esecutori contro la Bestemmia* had, from 1612, the task of granting residence permits to newly arrived Jews, and, from 1618, that of punishing disorderly persons who tried to extort from the bankers sums in excess of the regulation 3 ducats per pawn-ticket.[30] Especially jealous of their own jurisdiction were the *Cattaveri*, who were suspicious of any attempts on the part of Jews to erect their own tribunals or aspire in other ways to improper authority. To force Jews to accept only Jewish justice, they declared in 1581, was 'contrary to the liberty of this most excellent dominion' and 'everlastingly oppressive of the Jews who desired the justice of the Venetian state'.[31] Almost sixty years later the leaders of the Jews, on trial before the Quarantia al Criminal, explained that even when they proposed to do something so innocuous as paying a wage to a servant who would extinguish the Ghetto fires on the sabbath, the *Cattaveri* had proceeded against them for 'arrogating undue authority'.[32]

In the 1630s, when the system was fully developed, there were seven Heads of the Ghetto, three Germans, three Ponentines and one Levantine. In their own words, they governed, within the limits allowed them, by means of 'conventions concluded between our three nations of Jews and approved by the Most Excellent Senate'. It was their duty to apportion, collect and administer the taxes specific to the Jews, to represent the Jews before 'any and every magistracy, council and college', and to 'defend and uphold the articles of our *condotta*'.[33] They might well have added that their powers included the scrutiny of immigrants and visitors, subject to the higher authority of the *Esecutori contro la Bestemmia*; should they refuse to license a visitor beyond the first fifteen days of his sojourn, they were obliged to give their reasons to those magistrates.[34] The venerable Heads of the Ghetto[35] – their electors seemed to share the Venetian government's respect for age and experi-

---

[30] For the last points, E.B., b. 54, Capitolare, fol. 68r.–v., 87v.; b. 57, Not. 4, fol. 266r.–267v.; b. 58, Not. 5, fol. 64r.–66v.; Ravid, *Economics and toleration . . .*, pp. 121–2.

[31] U.C., b. 2, reg. 4, fol. 41v.–42v., decree of 14 Feb. 1581.

[32] I.R.E.C., Carte Diverse, 'Pie Case . . .', fol. 88, 30 Jan. 1637 Venetian style.

[33] Ibid.; also fol. 26v., test. Isaac Senior, 19 Jan. 1637 Venetian style, and statement of the *Avogador di Commun*, fol. 42r.–v., 24 Jan. 1637 Venetian style.

[34] S.U., b. 87, proc. Felice Magalotti, test. Lieberman, 18 Aug. 1629, test. Isaac Zacuto, 14 March 1630; b. 91, proc. Andrea Nunciata, test. Vielmo dalla Baldosa and other Heads of the Ghetto, 22 June 1634.

[35] I.R.E.C., Carte Diverse, 'Pie Case . . .', fol. 43v., 25 Jan. 1637 Venetian style, where Joseph, son of Abram Sachi, Head of the Levantine nation, gives his age as seventy-four; also fol. 47, the same day, where Joseph, son of Moses Cividal, says he is eighty-six and broken with age.

ence – enjoyed enough authority to support Dr Cardoso's claim (in answer to Genesis 49: 10, as cited by conversionists) that the sceptre had not after all departed from Israel. Every community, he said, was 'like a Republic apart, governing itself by the Law which God gave it, and by its Sages who are its Ministers and Governors, God having desired to give us this consolation in the midst of the nations by means of the princes in whose hands we are'.[36]

In the eyes of churchmen, Jews could be accommodated in a Christian community so long as they were manifestly in it but not of it, and were segregated in such a way as to forestall the pollution of Christianity by Judaism, to discourage any form of undue intimacy between Christian and Jew, and to emphasize the hierarchical relationship between Christianity and Judaism. Business transactions between Christian and Jew could hardly be prevented, conversation could sometimes lead to conversions to Christianity, and – as the Capponi case suggests – segregation extended neither to ships nor to prisons.[37] But sharing meals, sleeping under the same roof, sexual relationships and any form of association implying equality, hospitality or mutual acceptance: all these things, if not specifically forbidden, were at least highly suspect. As the stubborn adherents of a defeated and superseded religion, Jews must be demonstrably inferior socially to Catholic Christians: Judaism must never seem to be a paying proposition, the Jews must be manifestly landless and powerless. Indeed, their standing must be so low that conversion would always bring promotion and the chance to escape from a cramped and squalid world directed towards financing a dishonourable occupation. There must be no confusion of things which ought to be kept apart, the more so as the Jews enjoyed the privilege of openly practising their own religion, of having meat prepared in accordance with their dietary laws and of maintaining their own cemetery on the Lido.

Prayer-meetings for the small Jewish community of fifteenth-century Venice were first permitted in 1464;[38] permanent synagogues were established some years after the institution of the Ghetto as an area of compulsory residence for the Jews.[39] By 1580 Jews themselves were saying that there were at least four and perhaps as many as six synagogues in Venice, for the different nations attended different places of worship.[40] Permission to open synagogues could be reconciled with ecclesiastical tradition, for – as the inquisitor Eymeric had once explained – 'The rites of the Jews are

---

[36] Quoted in Yerushalmi, *From Spanish court* . . . , p. 383 (cf. also pp. 350–1, 468–9).
[37] S.U., b. 61, proc. Capponi, test. Capponi, 20 Sept. 1588.
[38] See Ashtor, 'Gli inizi . . .', p. 700.
[39] Jacoby, 'Les juifs . . .', pp. 210–11.
[40] S.U., b. 45, proc. Ribeiro, test. Leon Luzzatto, 6 Dec. 1580, test. Moses Abenini, 29 Dec. 1580.

tolerated by the Church because in them we have testimony to the Christian faith, even from enemies and outsiders.' Jewish ceremonies always contained a degree of truth, since they celebrated things which had already happened and which the Christian knew to be of the past; the error of the Jews was to see them as things to come, but the things themselves were valid enough.[41] In this sense the Jews were more highly privileged than any other community of religious aliens, with the sole exception of Greeks adhering to the Union of Florence.[42] Protestants could expect only liberty of conscience, as distinct from freedom of public worship, or seize the chance to attend an embassy chapel; Turkish merchants had a fondouk but not a mosque. Synagogues could be viewed by Christians, and one of their more distinguished visitors was the Duke of Savoy, who came to the city to meet Henry III of France in 1574.[43] They were a cause of unease to the Patriarch Priuli, who wanted them closed to the Christian public, but nothing prevented the English traveller Thomas Coryat from seeing them on his Venetian trip in the early 1600s.[44]

The Ghetto in the *sestiere* of Cannaregio was an expression of a concept of order shared by the Catholic Church and by the Catholic state of Venice. It declared in physical terms their ambition to restrict Jews to a confined and circumvallated place in the economic, social and religious systems and to curtail any display of prosperity on the part of the more successful among them. On the other hand, repulsive though they might be to immigrants who had been part of a dominant culture in other states and societies, the Ghetto and the distinctive dress of a Jew offered protection of a kind, and they helped to preserve the distinctive culture of Judaism. Barriers to intercourse with Christians were also barriers to assimilation, although it was hoped that deprivation might lead to conversion. Officers of the Inquisition seldom violated the immunity which the Ghetto bestowed even upon ex-Christians who had gone to live in it, though they were known to enter it in pursuit of children thought to have been baptized – as, in 1586, they removed Jorge, a nine-year-old boy recently arrived from Seville, in the face of an angry chorus which called

---

[41] Eymeric, pp. 247–8; cf. Aquinas, *Summa Theologica*, 2.2 qu. 10 art. 11, in his *Opera omnia*, VIII, p. 93.

[42] Fedalto, *Ricerche storiche* . . . , especially p. 44 ff.

[43] S.U., b. 44, proc. 'Negromanti', test. Antonio Saldanha, 12 Sept. 1579, who says that David Pas encouraged him to look at 'the synagogue which the Duke of Savoy visited when he was in Venice'. Cf. N. Barozzi and G. Berchet, *Delle accoglienze ai Principi di Savoia fatte dai Veneziani, 1367–1722* ((Venice, 1868), pp. 8–9.

[44] See Priuli's memorandum in S.T., filza 141, 31 Jan. 1596 Venetian style, in which he suggests that 'The Jews must not admit Christians to their synagogues, nor must they distribute outside the Ghetto either matzos or other foods made according to their ceremonies'; T. Coryat, *Coryat's Crudities* (2 vols., Glasgow, 1905), I, pp. 371–3.

them 'Assassini!'[45] Most vulnerable were those who, though fully aware of their Jewishness, could not accept for themselves the squalor of the Ghetto and the badge, and who by trying to live as Christians sank into a dangerously ambiguous or anomalous situation, fitting into neither of the clear categories of Christian and Jew recognized by the state and society.

There were excellent reasons to be nervous of wearing the badges of a Jew. That they could bring humiliation, insult, and perhaps even violence is suggested by the provisions in the *condotte* or the licences of the *Cattaveri* exempting Jews from the obligation to wear them on journeys, by the anxiety of Jewish physicians to obtain the privilege of wearing the black hat, and by the readiness of leading Jewish merchants during the war of Crete to offer large sums of money in exchange for this among other advantages. Their proposals were then rejected, opponents saying it had always been

> the public intention that their badge [*contrasegno*] should serve as a bridle to ensure that they lived apart from the common run of men in the city, for this is the custom in all the states of the princes, even in countries where they enjoy greater freedom.[46]

The Ghetto had been imposed upon the Jews in 1516, in response to the need to segregate and house an exceptionally large population of Jews who had immigrated in time of war from the Venetian mainland state.[47] Up to a point, it can be compared with other ethnic quarters or concentrations of foreign traders in the city. Some had arisen naturally, as had the Greek quarter in Castello or the Albanian quarter whose original centre of gravity was in Santa Maria Formosa.[48] Others had been created by government fiscal policy: for it was easier to impose communal taxes or levy duties on merchandise at special rates if concentration were enforced. The Fondaco dei Tedeschi for German merchants was at Rialto, and German artisans, including bakers, goldsmiths, tailors and shoemakers, tended to live in the same area.[49] Places of worship, such as San

---

[45] S.U., b. 57, proc. 'Giorgio of Seville', test. Hieronimo, Minister of the Holy Office, 13 Aug. 1586.

[46] See, for example, Vanzan Marchini, 'Medici ...', pp. 136–8, 157–8; Ravid, *Economics and toleration* ..., p. 119; U.C., b. 7, reg. 3, fol. 108v.–119, 24 Jan. 1643 Venetian style to 14 May 1644; S.T., filza 660, 12 Feb. 1658 Venetian style.

[47] See Pullan, *Rich and poor* ..., pp. 478–88.

[48] See F. Thiriet, 'Sur les communautés grecque et albanaise à Venise', in Beck and others, eds., *Venezia centro* ..., I, pp. 219, 221.

[49] Jacoby, 'Les juifs ...', pp. 178–9; P. Braunstein, 'Remarques sur la population allemande de Venise à la fin du moyen âge', in Beck and others, eds., *Venezia centro* ..., I, pp. 237–8; Stella–Bolognetti, pp. 278–80; and, in general, Simonsfeld, *Fondaco dei Tedeschi* ....

Giorgio dei Greci in Castello or San Bartolomeo at Rialto, the site of confraternities for the German nation and the place for preaching in the German tongue, acted as natural foci for foreign communities.[50] When Turkish merchants agitated for better conditions in 1573, they wanted 'a place of their own, as the Jews have their Ghetto, to accommodate their merchandise'. Establishing a fondouk or exchange-house for them and their wares (an aim achieved satisfactorily only in 1621) was seen both as a means of protection and as one of imposing discipline and averting scandal.[51] In spirit, therefore, it was not altogether removed from the Ghetto.

However, the Ghetto differed from other concentrations in being an area of compulsory residence, and in being designed for all Jews and not only for merchants. It was hardly the region the Jews themselves would have chosen. Before legal segregation was imposed, the newly arrived Jews of the early sixteenth century had chosen to live in the parishes of San Cassiano, Sant'Agostino, San Polo and Santa Maria Mater Domini, not far from the central markets and the licensed shops of the second-hand dealers at Rialto. And the banker Chaim Meshullam had made so bold as to rent the splendid palace of the Ca Bernardo, near Campo San Polo. The forcible transfer of the Jewish population to the peripheral region of San Geremia, where the Ghetto was established, was a method of clamping it down to its proper level in the social hierarchy.[52] In Venice, as in other cities, a Jewry was one thing, a Ghetto another. Jewries could grow up in convenient places as the result of a natural desire to congregate in the vicinity of Jewish institutions. Ghettoes, in the strict sense of the word, were always imposed by legislation, and were generally established on remote and inconvenient sites.

Overcrowding in the Ghetto became increasingly severe as population expanded. The Jewish population probably grew at least as fast proportionately as that of the whole city during the sixteenth century, and between the late sixteenth and the mid-seventeenth century it rose quite steeply even though the city's population was at best stable and at worst declining. Credible figures for 1586, 1642 and 1649 suggest that, despite the great plague of 1630–31, the number of Jews increased by just over 60 per cent (from 1,694 in 1586 to 2,671 in 1642 and 2,629 in 1649). About 1660, a patrician of the Loredan family, in a defence of the Jews, alluded to a printed census which estimated the number of Jews in Venice at

[50] Fedalto, *Ricerche storiche* ..., p. 44 ff.; Tramontin, 'La visita apostolica ...', pp. 517–18; A. Niero, 'Ancora sull' origine del Rosario a Venezia e sulla sua iconografia', *Rivista di Storia della Chiesa in Italia*, 28 (1974), pp. 475–6.

[51] Preto, *Venezia e i Turchi*, pp. 130, 132–3, 136–7.

[52] Pullan, *Rich and poor* ..., pp. 486–8.

4,860; but with studious moderation he preferred not to suggest that there were actually more than 4,000 and chose to base all his precise calculations on the figure of 2,629 which had emerged in July 1649 from a survey by the *Provveditori alle Biave*, magistrates concerned with the victualling of the city.[53] Much of the increase recorded in these figures was surely a reflection of the government's policy of encouraging Levantine and Ponentine settlement. If there was any sudden rise in the Jewish population in the middle of the seventeenth century, it could have been the consequence of heavy southward migration from eastern Europe after the Chmielnicki pogroms[54] – although, up to 1670, this movement seems to have left no trace in the surviving records of immigration and settlement in the *Notatorii* of the *Esecutori contro la Bestemmia*.[55]

In response to this population growth, the Jewish quarter was allowed to expand on only two occasions – through the enclosure of the Ghetto Vecchio in 1541, and through that of the Ghetto Nuovissimo between 1633 and 1636.[56] On neither occasion was living-space dramatically increased, for neither operation annexed more than twenty houses, and these were no palaces. Of those added in 1541, some were on two floors, others on one floor only, and some had small yards or gardens. Unpromisingly, they were described as 'old, ruined, and in a bad state'.[57] Otherwise, accommodation could be improved only by filling in vacant spaces and taking up every square inch of vacant ground, or else by adding new storeys to existing buildings. Levantine Jews found the Ghetto Vecchio, which was supposed to be reserved for them, a restless, noisy and violent place. They complained in 1576 that it had 'become by day and night a den of thieves and harlots, troubled by rows, clashes of weapons, and threats'. And five years later they spoke of 'many bold creatures who give shelter in the Ghetto Vecchio to vagabond Jews, who have no business or occupation, but merely dwell in the Ghetto, committing many violent acts, and troubling the merchants of the Ghetto'.[58] Conditions which intensified competition for space had the predictable result of forcing rents to exorbitant levels. Simon Luzzatto explained that the rent-yield of the

---

[53] See D. Beltrami, *Storia della popolazione di Venezia dalla fine del secolo XVI alla caduta della Repubblica* (Padua, 1954), p. 79; Loredan's speech in C.S.M., b. 62, fasc. 165. Rapp, *Industry and economic decline* ..., pp. 176–7, thinks the figure of 4,870 'most reasonable' for 1655.

[54] Suggested by Rapp, *Industry and economic decline* ..., p. 177, with reference to A. Milano, *Storia degli ebrei in Italia* (Turin, 1963), p. 312.

[55] See below, Appendix II, p. 319.

[56] See B. Ravid, 'The establishment of the *Ghetto Vecchio* of Venice, 1541', *Proceedings of the Sixth World Congress of Jewish Studies*, II (Jerusalem, 1975), pp. 161–6; Ravid, 'Legal status ...', pp. 273–5, 280–1.

[57] C.S.M., b. 62, fasc. 165, paper dated 19 Aug. 1541.

[58] Ibid., 3 Jan. 1575 Venetian style, 8 Nov. 1581.

narrow houses in the Ghetto was three times as high as it would have been on similar cramped accommodation in the Christian city;[59] and the noble Loredan (who learned much from him) testified some twenty years later that 'four to eight Christians would take up the space occupied by twenty Jews.'[60] Confirmation comes from the calculations of a demographic historian, from which it seems that in 1586 there were 826 persons per hectare in the Ghetto Vecchio and 662 in the Ghetto Nuovo; in 1633 the density had apparently risen to 1127 in the Ghetto Vecchio and 903 in the Ghetto Nuovo. The latest addition, the Ghetto Nuovissimo, was soon teeming with people, but it appeared to have relieved the pressure on the Ghetto Vecchio. So much can be inferred for the figures for 1642, suggesting 568 per hectare for the Ghetto Vecchio, 1,023 for the Ghetto Nuovo and 1,100 for the Ghetto Nuovissimo. Density of population in the Ghettoes was two to four times as high as the average levels in the city of Venice as a whole in those years (351 persons per hectare in 1586, 236 in 1633 after the great plague and 278 in 1642).[61]

The Jews themselves did not own the Ghetto: or rather, they had no hope of acquiring the land on which it stood. Since 1423–24, Jews and Jewesses in Venice and the mainland dominions had been forbidden to purchase or otherwise acquire lands or houses, lease them, hold them in fee or receive them as pledges for loans. They were permitted only to rent them from year to year.[62] Such legislation was still being cited as authority in the early seventeenth century.[63] At that time *condotte* ordered Jews to enter into contracts only for houses occupied by themselves and their families.[64] For their part the Jews, so long as they remained uncertain of their future in Venice, had every incentive to keep their assets liquid, and the heavy taxes imposed on them would hardly in any case have allowed a large surplus for investment. The site of the Ghetto, and the original huddle of decrepit houses, were the property of a patrician family, the Minotti. It should be said that the regulations did not in fact prevent Jews from treating houses as if they were their own property and pledging them as security for loans, and that modest Jewish property-developers were not unknown. It seems that Caliman Belgrado bought his own house from Camilla Minotto in 1578, and also built and rented out seven houses in the garden or orchard of the Ghetto Vecchio. At the time of his death, about 1613, they were yielding him annual rent of 267

[59] Luzzatto, *Discorso* ..., fol. 30.
[60] C.S.M., b. 62, fasc. 165.
[61] Beltrami, *Storia* ..., pp. 38–43.
[62] U.C., b. 2, reg. 4, fol. 155.
[63] C.J., filza 13, fol. 185, 30 July 1618 (in the case of Israel of Ceneda).
[64] Ravid, *Economics and toleration* ..., p. 114.

ducats, and his heirs could apparently claim rights over them.[65] None the
less it was true that Jewish proprietorship could not extend outside the
Ghetto, and that even the richer Jews were denied that most essential
symbol of status – the right to an ample house and land.

If superior wealth were to find some outlet in the Ghetto, it could do so
only through the women's dress and personal splendour, or through ceremony and hospitality, at weddings, circumcisions or the festival of Purim.
In the galleries of synagogues, wrote Thomas Coryat,

> I saw many Jewish women, whereof some were as beautiful as ever I
> saw, and so gorgeous in their apparel, chaines of gold, and rings
> adorned with precious stones, that some of our English Countesses
> do scarce exceede them, having marvailous long traines like
> Princesses that are borne up by waiting women serving for the same
> purpose. An argument to prove that many of the Jewes are very
> rich.[66]

But space, greenery, perhaps even light and privacy, would be denied
even to the most rich or aristocratic of Jews in the conditions of the
Venetian Ghetto.

The Jews were set apart, but Venetians in general could not be relied
upon to despise or detest them, save perhaps at certain seasons of the year
such as carnival or Passiontide. Jews were one among several foreign
nations, and so circumscribed as to offer no unwelcome competition. In
an optimistic account of Judaeo-Christian relations in Venice, Rabbi
Simon Luzzatto said of Jews in other towns and countries that

> Usury makes them unpopular with all the orders of the city; engag-
> ing in crafts with the lesser people; the possession of property with
> nobles and great men. These are the reasons why the Jews do not
> dwell in many places. But these circumstances do not arise in
> Venice, where the rate of interest is only 5 per cent, and the banks
> are established for the benefit of the poor and not for the profit of
> the bankers. The Jews cannot engage in crafts or manufacture, nor
> can they own real property. Hence they do not seem burdensome or
> threatening to any estate or order within the city.[67]

---

[65] I.R.E.C., Atti Giudiziari, fasc. marked 'Pro Catecumenis contro Ebrei Ponentini',
fol. 22r.–23r. See Brulez, *Marchands flamands* ..., pp. 14–15, for an agreement of 1581 in
which Joseph Samega and his wife Regina used a house in the Ghetto Vecchio which they
were sub-letting to Abraham Sulan as security for a debt to two Flemish merchants for the
purchase of kerseys: should it prove necessary, the tenant would transfer the payment of
rent from the Jews to the merchants.

[66] Coryat, *Coryat's Crudities*, I, pp. 372–3.

[67] Luzzatto, *Discorso* ..., fol. 87.

And there are in fact few traces of real popular unpleasantness or violence towards the Jews; they may have been stronger among foreigners than among native Venetians. In 1572 Righetto, when a prisoner of the Inquisition, complained of being confined in the district lock-up of San Giovanni in Bragora, because it cut him off totally from his co-religionists:

> ... in this *sestiere* [of Castello] you will never find a Jew, because he would at once be stoned or beaten with sticks by Greeks and by other peoples that dwell in those parts.[68]

It was as though the imported enmities of the Balkans, perhaps originating in rivalries within the Ottoman Empire, were proving more virulent than those rooted in the settled society of Venice. Children's mockery seems to have been more of a problem than was adult resentment against the Jews, for a special Canal degli Ebrei had eventually to be dug in 1668 to allow Jewish corpses to be borne decently to the Lido: previously they had been forced to pass under the wooden bridge of San Pietro di Castello, where children awaited them with stones.[69]

For many Christians the Ghetto was not a place of darkness, fear or squalor. For them the Jews were a source of employment and entertainment, and some could be dicing companions; Noah the Jew was charged before the *Esecutori contro la Bestemmia* in 1576 with keeping a gaming-house for Jews and Christians in the Ghetto.[70] The Inquisition had misgivings about the familiarity and risqué conversations which might arise from relationships between employer and employed, though condemnation was inevitable only for those who actually ate and slept in the Ghetto. About 1566, Battista de' Leoni, a book-keeper and son of a schoolmaster, worked for Chaim Saruc in the Ghetto for six or seven months; it was thought that he might have been the source of certain shocking opinions put about by one of his father's former pupils. But he took care to deny anything beyond a purely business relationship with his employer and with any other Jews.[71] In 1580, Domenico, a goldsmith from San Moisè, reported that when he and a companion named Antonio were working in the house of David the Jew and making two 'pyramids' or *rimmonim* to adorn the Sefer Torah, the scroll containing the Five Books of Moses, he had piously said to their employer, ' "We don't know who is to be saved – the Jews, or we others," and he told the story of the father

[68] S.U., b. 36, proc. Righetto, petition of April–May 1572. The Greek population of San Giovanni in Bragora was said in 1581 to account for about half the 2,500 souls residing in the parish – see Tramontin, 'La visita apostolica ...', pp. 527–8.

[69] See Georgelin, *Venise ...*, p. 945, n. 66.

[70] E.B., b. 56, Not. 2, fol. 127v., 20 Feb. 1575 Venetian style.

[71] S.U., b. 33, proc. Alvise de' Leoni, Zacharia Pensabene and Francesco Guerra, 8, 10 May 1571.

who gave three rings to his sons, and each of them thought he had the true one.' It may be that Boccaccio's story, told by Melchizedek the Jew to Soldan Saladin, was as familiar to Antonio as to Domenico Scandella, the miller of Friuli who was to repeat it to the Inquisition in 1599.[72] Living on despite the censor, the story suggested a relationship between the three great faiths of Christianity, Judaism and Islam very different from the theory of toleration entertained by the government and Church in Venice – for that was based on a conviction of the perversity and imperfection of the Jews, combined, none the less, with a sense of their utility and some expectation of their eventual recognition of Christian truth.

There were other disquieting signs that intimate contact with the Ghetto might increase respect for the Jews and instil in Christians a taste for sceptical epigrams. Valeria Brugnaleschi, a physician's widow, frankly admitted in 1587 to having lived in the Ghetto about two years before, teaching and reading from the Old Testament to some seventy or eighty Jewish girls at a farthing a time, and eating and drinking food and wine which the Jews supplied to her. It seemed that the food included both fish and matzos, but never meat. She was reported to have said that the 'Jews observe their law better than we Christians do ours' and even that 'the Jewish faith is better than ours.' Like the errant goldsmith, Valeria had indulged in other sceptical remarks. He had questioned the immortality of the soul, saying: 'We are like cats; no need to look for the soul when the body's dead!' She had rashly said that all days were equal, meaning that there were no feast days or fast days on which a special diet had to be observed, and had even blasphemed against God's providence and said that she believed in him no longer, for he was not impartial. Had he not made some men rich and others poor? Having confessed her Ghetto connexions to the parish priests of the Maddalena and San Marcuola and been refused absolution, Valeria moved out of the Ghetto and went to live with her daughter Splandiana at San Polo, but she still invited a Jew to the house to perform certain magical rituals.[73] Valeria's admissions of familiarity with the Ghetto doubtless contributed to a general impression of a loose, undisciplined and sceptical person who was well worth prosecuting as an undesirable – although it was not for this, but for their experiments with magic, that she and her daughter Splandiana were condemned to a public whipping, to the pillory and to five years' banishment.[74]

[72] S.U., b. 46, proc. 'Antonio aurifex in Rialto', 18 Oct. 1580. Cf. C. Ginzburg, *The cheese and the worms: the cosmos of a sixteenth-century miller*, transl. J. and A. Tedeschi (Baltimore–London, 1980), pp. 49–50, 152. See the third story of the first day of the *Decameron*.

[73] S.U., b. 59, proc. Valeria Brugnaleschi and Splandiana Mariano, den. Lugrezio Cilla, 30 May 1587, test. Fulvia and Valeria Brugnaleschi, 10, 11 June 1587.

[74] Ibid., 31 July 1587.

Sometimes useful to skilled craftsmen and to people with at least a smattering of letters, the Ghetto was mostly an employer of casual labour and of domestic servants who performed menial tasks on the sabbath. A long list, compiled in 1620, of persons who might bear witness in a case involving three Jewish prostitutes shows how the Christian world and that of the Ghetto would intersect. It is packed with the names of Christian porters, brokers, street-sweepers, stall-holders, pedlars of food, 'Friulian women who carry water in the Ghetto', and attendants at the banks and the offices of the *Cattaveri* and the *Sopraconsoli*.[75] Christian cake-sellers had to be severely warned not to enter the houses or staircases of the Ghetto unless they were called, and on no account to go there at night.[76]

On occasion poverty seemed to induce people of no particular skills to take work in the Ghetto which allegedly exposed them to attempts at conversion to Judaism. Francesco Careton, who worked for a bookseller, left his employment at the sign of the Golden Book about 1655. Encouraged by a craftsman who made buckles and clips for books, he took work with the Jewish booksellers Salvatore and Samuel Lezzi. According to his story, he worked for them for two and a half years and they tried to convert him to Judaism and sent him to Amsterdam for the purpose. Francesco's brother Pietro, whom he introduced to his employers, was very much the low-grade worker forced to take whatever work he could get. He had once been a sorter and cleaner of wool, and was now employed by the brothers Lezzi in folding and smoothing the pages of Hebrew books. There was nothing to confirm Francesco's story of attempted proselytization, and Pietro was merely ordered 'To obtain other employment as swiftly as may be, and to inform the most reverend father inquisitor when he has done it.'[77] And a maidservant named Prudenza, daughter of Zaccaria Pasquale of Vicenza, confessed to having obtained a licence from the *Cattaveri* on false pretences by telling them that her age was forty when in fact it was only twenty-three or twenty-four. She had gone to work for the Jewish merchant Abram Papo, and professed to have actually succumbed to Judaism. Since it was she who had approached the Inquisition, she escaped with the obligation to abjure her offence; she asked pardon, and promised never to serve Jews again or to deny the Christian faith.[78] Casual outdoor contacts between Christian and Jew were acceptable, but anything savouring of domestic service or regular employment was subject to very strict surveillance, and should in theory be performed only by the middle-aged and not by the young and impressionable.

[75] S.U., b. 79, proc. 'Laghitelli todesca', ca. 20 Aug. 1620.
[76] E.B., b. 58, Not. 6, fol. 118, 13 May 1651.
[77] S.U., b. 107, proc. Careton, 15 Oct. 1658 to 26 Aug. 1660.
[78] Ibid., proc. Prudenza Pasquale, 19–20 May 1660.

At certain festival seasons, in the Christian and in the Jewish year, there was an especially strong need to demand the separation of the two peoples, as though to prevent the superseded religion from challenging the dominant one. This seemed essential both where analogous festivals coincided, as with Passover and Easter, and where they contrasted. On the fourteenth and fifteenth days of the Jewish month of Adar, Purim, commemorating the events of the Book of Esther, created an oasis of rejoicing in the desert of the Lenten city. Often called the Jewish carnival, although it lasted only two days, it meant drink, masquerades and rombustuous behaviour in the synagogues, and made Jewish customs alarmingly attractive to Christian libertines.[79] Christian Lent, too, was a season for Jewish weddings and dances.

One traditional and well-known method of enforcing separation at such times was the requirement in the *condotte* that Jews must stay in their houses in the Ghetto from sunrise on Holy Thursday to the hour of nones on Holy Saturday.[80] It was a means of demanding respect for a Christian festival, for the very appearance of the Jews, as the traditional villains of Passiontide, could be construed as an act of provocation. Festivals, exhilarating fellow believers and drawing them into unwonted unity in the face of outsiders, could well abolish the usual inhibitions which guarded against insult or even violence. To shut away the Jews at Easter was to protect them from harm and the city from scandal. And, in its milder way, the Passover bred rituals which led, not to serious violence, but to a momentary suspension of the usual deference of Jews towards Christians.

In the spring of 1571, the Holy Office was told of a strange ritual involving Jews and Christians immediately after Easter. Bettino, a Bergamasque porter from a neighbouring parish, described carrying baskets loaded with bread into the Jewish quarter, accompanied by two baker's journeymen. They passed through the Ghetto Nuovo to the Ghetto Vecchio, and were greeted with joyful cries of 'Bread, bread!' (*Pan, pan!*). But at the same time both he and the bread were pelted or beaten with mud and stones, and especially with *scovoli* – brushes impregnated with dust or filth. From other accounts it seemed that the crowd in the Ghetto Nuovo were mostly children (*forse mille putti*), and that this year they had a whole basketful of the brushes at the ready, specially bought for the purpose fifteen days before. One journeyman testified that this was an annual custom, enacted when the Jews returned from unleavened bread to ordinary bread at the end of the Passover. Apparently it was usual actually to carry bread into the Ghetto only at Easter time – a fact which

[79] On Purim see, for example, E. O. James, *Seasonal feasts and festivals* (London, 1961), pp. 121–3; Shulvass, *The Jews ...*, p. 176.

[80] As can be seen from Clause 29 of the *condotta* of 1624, published in Ravid, *Economics and toleration ...*, p. 119.

may suggest that the Christians involved were content to play their part in the game. Not, it seems, a questioning man, the journeyman Leonardo Ceteli said that he did not know whether this was a rite carried out in disrespect of Christians.[81] For some time the government had been inclined to frown on the traditional elements of violence and disorder in popular festivals, such as the celebration of Carnival Thursday (*Giovedi* or *Giobba Grasso*).[82] But the Inquisition showed few signs of taking the report seriously. Its records do, none the less, preserve for us a very rare instance of Jews acting together as a crowd. Stories of Jews as victims of carnival derision in Rome are very familiar, and references to carnival licences to wear the black hat suggest that in that season they might be considered fair game for Venetians also.[83] For once, however, Jews – though chiefly Jewish children – appeared as mockers and not as butts, thus briefly reversing the normal roles of Christian and Jew.

More reprehensible than impudent Jewish children were Christian adults who displayed over-familiarity, not only with the Ghetto itself, but with the rites, celebrations and religious food of the Jews. This problem was certainly in no way peculiar to Venice, and at various times in the late sixteenth and early seventeenth centuries it attracted the attention both of civil authorities and of inquisitors in the Duchies of Milan and Ferrara, and also in Rome.[84] In 1584 the Patriarch's Vicar-General examined in Venice a number of witnesses on behalf of the Inquisition in Capodistria, where several local Christian musicians had attended a wedding in the house of Cervo the Jewish Banker in the middle of Lent. Two of them, Cristoforo and Piero Piranese, had eaten meats, fats and eggs – foods which could then be permitted only to Christians equipped with a special licence on medical grounds. Such grave lapses appeared to degrade Christians in the sight of Jews: according to witnesses, 'as I understand, the Jews grumbled in their own language at the said Cristoforo and Piero, saying they were not good Christians,' or 'the Jews who waited at table laughed to see Christians eating meat during Lent.'[85]

Venice's most serious, or unfortunate, offender was one Giorgio Moretto. Born in the parish of the Madonna dell' Orto, he knew the Ghetto well from his childhood, though it was only about the year 1588

---

[81] S.U., b. 29, proc. 'Ebrei', 19–21 April 1571.

[82] Cf. E. Muir, *Civic ritual in Renaissance Venice* (Princeton, 1981), pp. 160–4, 174–8.

[83] On Jews and Roman carnival, see, recently, M. Boiteux, 'Carnaval annexé: essai de lecture d'une fête romaine', *Annales: Économies, Sociétés, Civilisations*, 32 (1977), pp. 360–1, 364, 372; cf. also above, p. 155.

[84] Stern, *Urkundliche Beiträge* ..., doc. 161, p. 175 (ca. 1600); Baron, *A social and religious history* ..., XIV, pp. 121–2; A. Balletti, *Gli ebrei e gli Estensi* (Reggio-Emilia, 1930), pp. 138, 141.

[85] S.U., b. 53, proc. marked 'Comedentes carnem', 6 April to 8 May 1584; for the quotations, test. Ottaviano de' Signorini and Antonio de' Languidis, 6, 8 April 1584.

that he became deeply involved with it. He was a sailor, who had spent six or seven months in Alexandria, but also a small trader or pedlar, and he spent much time 'broking' or acting as an unofficial go-between for miscellaneous purposes in the Ghetto itself. Five or six related charges were laid against him. He had attended at least two Jewish weddings during the Christian Lent, those of Solomon Maestro and Moses Moresco, and had behaved as the Jews themselves did, inviting guests in and receiving them. He had joined in the celebration of circumcisions and danced at these festivals, taking a full part in revels and masked balls. He had eaten flesh during Lent, once in a private house at a wedding, once at a furnace or oven where he took a capon off a spit and ate it, and once outside a Jewish butcher's shop. There were reports of his eating unleavened bread, and even of his being attacked and wounded by certain Christians for refusing to give them some matzos he had collected from Jewish houses: they evidently shared his curiosity about Jewish food, if not his thoroughgoing enthusiasm for the life of the Ghetto. He had compounded his crimes by being in the Ghetto at all hours of the night and disturbing its Christian porters or 'guardians', demanding with blasphemous imprecations that they let him out.

Equally offensive was his courtship of Rachel, the daughter of Isaac the Deaf. Giorgio resorted to one of the few defences available to him – that he intended to persuade her to convert, and then to marry her. But 'because her family noticed, they barred the doors and balconies and engaged in a thousand intrigues and were determined to injure me.' However, his conduct created a reasonable suspicion that, far from recruiting for Christianity, he was finding life among the Jews delightful, and might even be thinking of turning Jew to win Rachel. To the question, 'Does it seem good to you, as a Christian, to court Jewish girls and seek to lead them astray?' he replied: 'Yes, my lord, it does seem right, for I know my own conscience, and other girls have done it and been taken away and baptized, and so I hope to do with her and have her baptized, for these things are all present in my mind and heart.'

The Inquisition decided to meet the case by imposing a kind of suspended sentence: by solemnly forbidding Giorgio Moretto to enter the Ghettoes or loiter at their gates on pain of being sent for three years to the galleys. When, a couple of months later, he was found to have entered the Ghetto in defiance of orders, and to have worn the yellow hat of a Jew for a joke, the sentence was in fact imposed and he was sent to serve his term.[86] In all probability he was no serious judaizer, but rather a person so familiar with the Ghetto and so alive to its possibilities for entertainment that he could not bring himself to respect the social distances

[86] S.U., b. 64, proc. Giorgio Moretto, 8 April to 10 June 1589.

created by the state and the Church alike for the protection of the
Catholic faith and the proper observance of its dietary laws. His fun went
sour; was he an isolated figure, or did he represent a more widespread
fascination with the Ghetto? Parallels are not quite lacking. In 1626
Aron di Grasin of Udine, aged about sixty, denounced his landlord
Lieberman, a water-carrier in the Ghetto who also let rooms. It seemed
that he had held a soirée during Lent, at which he entertained a number
of Christian guests, persuaded them to dance to a fiddle, and gave them
forbidden foods with both meat and butter – including salami, poultry,
cakes and pastries. It was a very mixed company. There were Madonna
Sofia and her husband, a baker's journeyman; a 'good-time girl' (*donna di
tempo*) named Anna, who spoke Italian and German; a violinist; and two
poor Germanic Jews, one a water-carrier and the other a servant-girl.
Three German-speaking foreign gentlemen came to join the company and
danced a little, after which Lieberman offered them roast meats and a
cake made with butter and eggs, falsely assuring them that it contained
no fats. The inquiry was never followed up – perhaps because Lieberman
left for Amsterdam, although he subsequently returned.[87]

In Venice both the Church and the state were bent on a highly systematic
ordering of society, both on economic and on moralistic grounds. The
Senate was determined to control the economic activities of aliens in such
a way as to insert them into cracks and vacancies within a planned and
regulated system – one in which, as Sir Dudley Carleton once put it, 'The
lest thing hath his superintendent.'[88] Church and state alike were eager
to isolate all corrupting influences and sources either of unbelief or moral
pollution – assigning the Jews to their ghettos, attempting to cut at the
roots of prostitution, clearing the streets and churches of blasphemous and
insolent beggars enmeshed in the sin of idleness. At the same time these
corrupting influences were recognized at least tacitly as inescapable evils,
sometimes even as socially vital; those who practised them could always
be redeemed, the Jew through the house of converts, the prostitute
through the nunnery of the Convertite, the beggar through the discipline
imposed by the hospital of the Mendicanti.[89] Segregation was therefore a
vital condition of toleration, and it required a physical expression –
although, since one of the economic purposes of retaining the Jews was to
generate employment for Christians, the separation could never be perfectly neat and clean.

Where there seemed to be a real threat of heresy, apostasy or disregard

[87] S.U., b. 82, proc. Lieberman, 25, 30 June 1626.
[88] From his 'Particular notes of the government and state of Venice', probably of spring
1612, Public Record Office, London, State Papers 9918, fol. 340.
[89] Cf. Pullan, *Rich and poor* ..., pp. 362–70, 375–94.

of Christian dietary laws, the Inquisition became involved in the enforcement of segregation. Especially shocking and deserving of penalties were
forms of ambiguous behaviour, involving the juxtaposition of things
which ought to be kept strictly apart.[90] Francisco Olivier was sentenced
to the galleys in 1549 because, though a circumcised Jew, he had had
intercourse with a Christian woman, had confessed to a Christian priest
after being wounded in an affray, and had then had himself taken to an
inn in the Ghetto, where he had remained even after his cure.[91] When
the Levantine Jew Mair Lambros rented a house on Murano from a
Venetian patrician it seemed doubly shocking that it happened to be near
the monastery of San Pietro Martire.[92] And Giorgio Moretto's delator
seemed especially scandalized that he had consorted with Jews so soon
after performing pious Christian devotions. For he had scourged himself
on Good Friday, and the following day was at least near to the house of
the Jewish girl. Venetian society disliked and feared what it could not
classify, and resented any confusion of categories by marginal men who
would not label themselves – whether they were ambitious Jews, or incur-
ably frivolous Christians out for a good time even in Lent.

[90] On the fear of ambiguity and anomaly, see M. Douglas, *Purity and danger: an analysis of the concepts of pollution and taboo* (London, 1978), especially pp. 37–9.

[91] I.Z., p. 90, proc. Olivier, 8 Aug. 1549.

[92] S.U., b. 50, proc. marked 'Contra hebreos a Muriano eiectos', 7 July 1583.

10

The Senate and the Sephardim

Through the Levantine Jewish nation, which in theory consisted of transient Sephardic traders and of subjects of the Sultan, the Venetian Republic came into contact with the Marranos and former Marranos of Spain and Portugal – with Sephardic Jews who had once conformed to Christianity. For some of them the Venetian Ghetto was a haven in which they declared themselves to be Jews. For some the city was a point of departure from Europe to the Levant, or one of return from the Ottoman Empire to a vital trading-post on the edge of the western commercial world. For others (and these were most likely to fall foul of the Inquisition) the city was a place where they paused and dissembled, living still as Christians, but slowly winding up their affairs in Europe and building up new and profitable connexions within Jewry. The choice between Christianity and Judaism was not always easy to make. It was not only a choice between faiths, between the ancestral and the imposed religion. It was also a choice between a dominant Christian culture and the repressed sub-world created for Jews beneath it. And it could be a choice between Christian and Islamic civilizations.

In most years before 1589, there was only one safe way for Marranos to obliterate their past and win effective guarantees against prosecution for apostasy. This was to join the ranks of the Spanish-speaking Levantines, for the Venetians were disinclined to pursue those who plainly declared themselves to be Jews, and who, by accepting the constrictions imposed upon Jews, also accepted the Venetian concept of order.[1]

By the close of the fifteenth century it had become very difficult to

---

[1] Much of this chapter is a rewritten version of my article 'Religious toleration and economic decline: Venice and the Marranos', forthcoming in *Journal of Italian History*.

enforce the traditional ban – designed to reserve the trade to Venetian nobles and citizens – on Jews and Turkish subjects moving merchandise between Venice, the Venetian Adriatic and the Levant.[2] There were many eastern Jews trading on the routes between Venice and the Turkish provinces of the Balkans. In 1524, a decree long cited as a precedent recognized the principle that Turkish subjects would be entitled to transport goods between Venice and the Balkans; Jews would inevitably be among the principle beneficiaries of this concession.[3] Positive encouragement was offered by the Collegio and the Senate in 1541, when customs duties were reduced on certain goods originating in the Balkans, such as wool, hides and wax, and when the Jewish quarter was expanded by the enclosure of part of the Ghetto Vecchio, so as to provide a small and rather squalid fondouk for men of business in transit. Jews came to handle an impressive miscellany of goods which originated from the Balkan provinces or passed through them from much more distant places, including leather, hides, eiderdowns or bedcovers, 'Belgrade silk', and camlets and mohairs. In a somewhat hostile spirit, Jews were said in 1557 to be dominating the grain trade with the Levant.[4] And in the late 1560s, since the Republic had scant respect for the alum monopoly claimed by the Papacy, Joseph, son of Aaron Segura, of Constantinople, was able to make large purchases from the Sultan and import the alum, on an excessively ambitious scale, to Venice.[5]

Although supposed to be transients, the Levantine Jews developed by the second half of the sixteenth century into a body of permanent residents. They were useful enough to the economy for the Senate to forego altogether, or to enforce both leniently and erratically, its own laws forbidding them to reside continuously in the city;[6] the only serious disruption of good relations with the state was caused by the internment of Levantine Jews as Turkish subjects on the outbreak of war in 1570, and by the sequestration of their merchandise with heavy financial loss to some.[7] Mair Lambros told the Inquisition in 1580 that he had lived in Venice for twelve years at a stretch; Moses, son of Joseph Abenini, that he had done so for more than twenty years, broken only by the three-year

[2] See E. Ashtor, 'The Jews in the Mediterranean trade in the fifteenth century', in *Wirtschaftskrafte und Wirtschaftswege, I: Mittelmeer und Kontinent (Festschrift für Hermann Kellenbenz)*, ed. J. Schneider (Nuremberg, 1978), pp. 449–50.

[3] Ravid, 'Legal status ...', pp. 35–6, 230–1.

[4] Ravid, 'The establishment ...'; Pullan, *Rich and poor* ..., pp. 512–13; C.S.M., b. 62, fasc. 165, 20 June 1551, 17 Sept. 1557.

[5] N.V., VIII, pp. 258, 260–1, 267, 290, 298, 310 (9 Aug. to 29 Nov. 1567); cf. also N.V., XI, p. 561, 23 June 1576.

[6] Ravid, 'Legal status ...', pp. 69, 74, 121–2; for an attempt to enforce the law, C.S.M., b. 62, fasc. 165, 31 March 1565.

[7] N.V., IX, p. 226, 5 March 1570; Albèri, III/ii, pp. 83–4 (Jacopo Ragazzoni, 1571).

hiatus of the Turkish war; Moses Cardiel that he had spent thirty-five
years in the Venetian Ghetto, interrupted by a four- or five-year spell of
absence when he was virtually bankrupted during the war, but subsequently able to return and compound with his creditors.[8] Enjoying
Turkish protection, Levantine Jews could easily be presumed all to be
Jews by birth, and they were at this time little troubled by the Inquisition
– although five or six of them were fined in 1568 by the *Esecutori contro la
Bestemmia* for publishing and possessing unlicensed Hebrew books.[9]

In reality many Levantines were probably former Marranos. Most of
the Marranos who left traces on Venetian records in the sixteenth century
were Portuguese rather than Spanish, and were descendants of Jews who
had left Spain rather than conform in response to the expulsion decree of
1492.[10] They were heirs to the mass conversions imposed on Jews in 1497
by King Manoel. They were refugees or descendants of refugees from the
Inquisition introduced into Portugal in 1536, or from arbitrary acts of the
Portuguese monarchy against Christians of Jewish descent.

'Marrano' was an ambiguous word of uncertain origins. It had passed
into the Italian vocabulary of religious abuse and had even entered
Venetian official documents before the close of the fifteenth century. For
Marranos, said to be implicated in malpractices in the grain trade with
Sicily, were officially expelled from Venice for the first time in 1497.[11]
Most generally, perhaps, the term meant a dissembler – one who, even in
Italy, lived outwardly as a Christian but inwardly as a Jew; or one who,
by reason of his origins, was strongly suspected of this heresy. But the
epithet could also refer to persons now living openly as Jews who had in
other countries lived as Christians, or who might when visiting conformist
countries abroad revert to a Christian guise. A Spanish polemicist, Diego
de Simancas, wrote that the Jews of Rome employed the term disparag-
ingly to describe converts who returned to Judaism.[12] In practice it was
an insult reserved to Spanish or Portuguese Jews, and not applied to
Italian neophytes.

Frequently, too, Marranos were thought to be guilty of unbelief rather
than of practising secret Judaism – they were dangerous because they had
no firm faith by which to live or swear, and were godless, not as the result
of any intellectual process or theological argument, but simply out of a

---

[8] S.U., b. 45, proc. Gaspar Ribeiro, respectively 29 Nov., 29 Dec., 25 Aug., 23 Nov. 1580.

[9] E.B., b. 56, Not. 2, fol. 43r.–v., 22 Sept. 1568; Grendler, 'Destruction . . .', p. 115.

[10] Cf. the remarks on judaizers sentenced in Mexico, who were mostly Portuguese, in J. I.
Israel, *Race, class and politics in colonial Mexico (1610–1670)* (Oxford, 1975), pp. 125–6.

[11] See A. Farinelli, *Marrano (storia di un vituperio)* (Geneva, 1925), pp. 44–5; D.M.S., I,
col. 535, 733, 819, 3 March, 24 Aug., 13 Nov. 1497.

[12] Cited in J. Caro Baroja, *Los Judíos en la España moderna y contemporánea* (second edition, 3
vols., Madrid, 1978), I, p. 405.

desire to preserve their goods. 'Marrano' could be loosely employed as a pejorative version of the more neutral terms 'New Christian', *converso* or *confesso*, even where there was no specific evidence of judaizing tendencies. Indeed, it was once claimed in the course of a trial before the Venetian Inquisition that in common speech the word had no sinister implications, because it was merely a national nickname – whether ill-natured, satirical or just unthinking; Italian humour had it that the 'Spanish peccadillo' lay in not believing in the Trinity.[13] 'It is the custom in this city as in all Italy,' said Moses Cardiel in 1580, 'that when one is a Spaniard he is called a Marrano.' 'I have heard all Portuguese called Marranos,' said Don Simeone Castellaro, a Milanese merchant trading in Venice.[14]

A succinct statement on the subject was made by the Venetian patrician Antonio Tiepolo, on his return from an embassy to Spain in 1572:

> All those who descend from Jewish fathers are called New Christians. In the time of the King Don Emanuel they were forced to become Christians. From them, for the most part, come the people that in Italy we call Marranos; the towns in Italy are full of them, and that rascal João Miquez comes of this accursed and fickle people.[15]

His last remark contained one precise reason for Venetian fear and distrust of Marranos, in their supposed connections with those in positions of great favour and power with the Ottoman Sultan, and in the opportunities to commit treason against Christendom that they therefore seemed to enjoy.

It seems likely that many Marranos passed through Venice in the sixteenth century as transients bound for Salonica, Constantinople, Safed or Cairo, and subsequently returned as Levantine Jews. They thrust the Sultan's protection like a shield between themselves and the Inquisition, as if to obscure their Christian past in Spain or Portugal by a few years' residence in the Middle East. During his trial in Brussels in 1532, on charges of maintaining relations with Marranos in Turkey and aiding the escape of New Christians to Salonica, the financier Diogo Mendes admitted to sending the goods of New Christians, if not their persons, both to Ancona and to Venice – although he insisted in his defence that this was just an ordinary commercial transaction, and pointed out that the Adriatic ports were not the same thing as Salonica.[16] In 1555, a Jesuit

[13] Ibid., I, p. 315; B. Croce, *La Spagna nella vita italiana durante la Rinascenza* (second edition, Bari, 1922), pp. 214–17.

[14] S.U., b. 45, proc. Gaspar Ribeiro, 23–24 Nov. 1580, 28 Feb. 1581.

[15] Albèri, I/v, p. 211.

[16] See J. A. Goris, *Étude sur les colonies marchandes méridionales (portugais, espagnols, italiens) à Anvers de 1488 à 1567* (Louvain, 1925), pp. 562–7.

and a Spanish consul told the Inquisition of one Cardoso, a Portuguese who had once borne a sword and worn the dress of a Christian, and had now, after a spell in Cairo, appeared in Venice as a turbaned Levantine Jew.[17] So long as the Venetians harboured Levantines, they would never avoid sheltering heretics or apostates. A papal nuncio spoke in 1574 of 'many baptized Marranos who have returned to Judaism and call themselves Levantines, although for the most part they are really Westerners'.[18] A few years later a witness told the Inquisition that a standard procedure for Portuguese refugees was to go to Ferrara, have themselves circumcised there, depart through Venice for the Levant, stay there for three or four years, and finally return to Venice wearing a turban. One alternative tactic was to postpone circumcision until arrival at Skopje in Macedonia.[19] It was said of David Pas, who lived in the Ghetto Vecchio and kept a salon not disdained by Venetian patricians and Christians 'of most ancient lineage', that although he wore the turban of a Levantine Jew he was really the son of a Spaniard and had been baptized in Lisbon.[20]

But some New Christians, spurred by the uncertainties of life in Portugal and the Low Countries, having large fortunes and much to lose, came southwards with no clear or immediate intention of announcing themselves to be Jews. Even if they were destined for the Ottoman Empire, they would do well to negotiate the terms of entry. In the mid-1540s, the Venetian government was prepared to make special arrangements with prominent New Christians, as though suppressing its own doubts about their judaizing tendencies and calming the visitors' fears that these might become pretexts for arrest and confiscation of goods. In 1544, a safe-conduct was negotiated with the Council of Ten for the sisters Beatrix and Brianda de Luna, heiresses to the vast fortune of the Mendes; it had no time limit, and it embraced an entourage of twenty-five to thirty servants, familiars and agents.[21] Later events would show that a safe-conduct could be cancelled if its holder gave rise to suspicion or caused scandal, but that nevertheless he need fear nothing worse than deportation.[22] Enthusiasm for New Christians waned later in the decade, when the Republic was faced by a rising ride of immigration, caused by

[17] I.Z., pp. 227–8, 249, 251.

[18] N.V., XI, pp. 136–7, 23 Jan. 1574.

[19] S.U., b. 46, test. Giovanni Giacomo, neophyte, 23 April 1580; cf. also Stella–Bolognetti, pp. 289–90.

[20] S.U., b. 44, proc. 'Negromanti', test. Ruy Lopez, 23 July 1579; test. Francisco Oglies, 2 Sept. 1579; test. Antonio Saldanha, 12 Sept. 1579; also E.B., b. 56, Not. 2, fol. 179v., 3 Aug. 1581.

[21] I.Z., pp. 341–2. On their family and its connexions, see especially P. Grunebaum-Ballin, *Joseph Naci, Duc de Naxos* (Paris–The Hague, 1968).

[22] I.Z., pp. 263, 348–9, decision concerning Licentiato Costa, Aug.–Sept. 1555.

the increasing insecurity of New Christians in the Low Countries, and by Charles V's decision in 1549 to expel those arrived there within the past five or six years.[23]

As a good Catholic state, looking for inspiration and example from abroad, the Republic could choose between the repressive policies of the Emperor and the more liberal ones of the popes towards New Christians. In the late 1540s and the early 1550s, increasingly generous concessions were made by Paul III and Julius III in the hope of inducing New Christian merchants and other persons to settle as Jews in Ancona and do business from that city. These privileges began with a promise that in crimes of heresy, apostasy or blasphemy they would be subjected only to the Pope himself and not to any lesser authority, and they were then extended to include a guarantee that they would be subjected to no inquiries about religious actions committed before their arrival in the city – even if they had at some time lived as Christians. Such concessions promised to wipe Marrano slates clean; provided they showed consistency, and did not vacillate between Christianity and Judaism after their arrival, they could hope to shed their compromising past histories.[24]

Apart from the popes' pragmatic desire to promote the commerce of Ancona, there were two rather more high-minded justifications for their tolerant attitudes. Since the 1530s they and certain cardinals had proved quite responsive to the arguments of New Christian pressure groups, and had criticized the proposed arrangements for introducing the Inquisition into Portugal. They had held, as did Clement VII in 1533, that 'Those should not be considered as members of the Church who were forcibly baptized,' and had also pronounced that leniency ought to be shown to persons who, though not themselves forcibly baptized, had none the less lived at close quarters with forced converts.[25] A terse and hostile account of the Portuguese Marranos, written in 1564 and surviving among the Vatican manuscripts, alleged that the later and more generous papal privilege had been obtained from Julius III by means of the false statement that 'they had been made Christians by force, but were always Jews in their souls.' Many years later, Cardinal Albizzi, the seventeenth-century apologist, was also to allude to the argument of forced conversion. It was his contention that in the mid-sixteenth century it could indeed justify the Pope's decision to protect the Marranos from the Inquisition, but that it could not logically be invoked at a later date for the benefit of

[23] Goris, *Étude* ..., pp. 576–7; I. S. Révah, 'Les marranes', *Revue des études juives*, 117 (1959), p. 63; I. S. Révah, 'Pour l'histoire des marranes à Anvers', *Revue des études juives*, 122 (1963), p. 124.

[24] For the privileges of Paul III of 21 Feb. 1547 and Julius III of 6 Dec. 1552, see Albizzi, *Risposta* ..., p. 200 ff.; for a copy of Julius III's privilege, there dated 5 Dec. 1553, see Stern, *Urkundliche Beiträge* ..., I, doc. 106, pp. 108–12.

[25] Herculano, *Inquisition in Portugal*, p. 301 ff.; see pp. 329–30 for the Bull of 7 April 1533.

subsequent generations farther removed from the mass conversion of the late fifteenth century.[26] More explicitly, however, the Pope invoked the conversionist argument which could always be employed to justify the toleration of the Jews in a Christian society, speaking of his desire to 'attract Jews of this kind to the Catholic Church, outside which no one is saved, by all means possible, and to make suitable provisions against their departure to those nations which do not know our saviour Christ'.[27] Departure for the Islamic countries could be prevented, and the loss of souls forestalled, by grants of privileges rather than by penalties and confiscations. The Jew who remained in Europe was always a potential convert to the Catholic Church by legitimate means.

The Duke of Florence and the Duke of Ferrara followed the popes' example,[28] but for the time being the Venetians ostensibly inclined towards the imperial policy. There seemed to be no question of their offering general guarantees to New Christians, and in July 1550 they renewed the earlier decree of 1497 for the expulsion of the Marranos – now described as 'a people of infidels, without religion, and enemies of the Lord God'.[29] They were not, however, precisely defined, and it was not clear whether the expulsion decree was intended to apply to former Christians living in Venice as Jews, or only to Jewish immigrants posing as Christians. Explanations for the expulsion decree can be found in political and economic circumstances. Among them, no doubt, was the fear of Habsburg power; the recent decision to put teeth into the revived Roman Inquisition had been in part a response to warnings from the Imperial ambassador of the danger of flirting with heretics.[30] More positively, the Senate and the Council of Ten were probably confident enough in the expanding Venetian economy, and felt no need to compete with Ancona for the capital and skills of settlers. For Venice, sustained by a large body of native or long-settled entrepreneurs, was poles apart from Ancona – a port which depended chiefly on the willingness of those exporting goods from far-off countries to use it, and on the readiness of princes to issue privileges to foreign merchants.[31] In so far as the immig-

---

[26] Stern, *Urkundliche Beitrage* ..., I, doc. 133, p. 142; Albizzi, *Risposta* ..., pp. 214–15.

[27] Stern, *Urkundliche Beiträge* ..., I, doc. 106, pp. 110–11.

[28] See U. Cassuto, *Gli ebrei a Firenze nell' età del Rinascimento* (Florence, 1918), pp. 89–90; Balletti, *Gli ebrei* ..., pp. 77–8.

[29] For the documents, see D. Kaufmann, 'Die Vertreibung ...', pp. 525–30.

[30] See above, pp. 5, 17.

[31] On the Venetian economy in the mid-sixteenth century, see the evidence summarized in B. Pullan, ed., *Crisis and change in the Venetian economy in the sixteenth and seventeenth centuries* (London, 1968), and Pullan, *Rich and poor* ..., p. 287 ff. On Ancona, P. Earle, 'The commercial development of Ancona, 1479–1551', *Economic History Review*, second series, vol. 22 (1969–70), pp. 28–44; J. Delumeau, 'Un ponte fra oriente e occidente: Ancona nel Cinquecento', *Quaderni Storici*, anno 5 (1970), pp. 26–47.

rants to Venice were rich, they threatened to swamp the economy in such a way that Venetian patricians and citizens might lose control over it, and in so far as they were poor they presented a threat to public health and the food supplies. The image of the Mendes sisters threatened, at least in retrospect, to brush off on to all New Christian refugees from the Low Countries: Righetto told his judges in the early 1570s that at the time of Charles V's decree there were 400–500 Marrano families in Flanders, and that about 300 came to Venice, including some of the richest of all. Their wealth, he said, could have been valued at over 4 millions in gold, and the fortune of a single house might surpass 1 million.[32] But there had also been poor and humble New Christians in the Low Countries. A number of poor artisans and other insignificant people, some with their scanty savings sewn into their clothing, had been arrested in Zealand in 1540 by a public official, and many immigrants to Venice may well have conformed to this type.[33] Certainly, a diplomatic agent serving in Venice in 1550 saw many of the Marranos not merely as usurers but also as slum-dwellers plunged into a squalor which could threaten the physical as well as the spiritual well-being of the city. For they were grossly overcrowded, and living three or four families to a house.[34] Poor settlers could only be unwelcome at times of population pressure, when recurrent famines (there were dearths in 1549, 1550 and 1551) were causing heavy if temporary peasant migration into the city.[35] An estimate by the papal nuncio, that there were 10,000 Marranos living in Venice in 1550, may seem wildly exaggerated.[36] But it perhaps reflected the scale of the immigration anticipated by the Venetians, the height of the incoming wave their law was designed to break.

The Senate's decree was not a consequence of action by the Inquisition against Marranos on a large scale,[37] nor did it have the effect of unleashing a wholesale inquisitorial campaign against them. Indeed the law was probably designed – and in this it resembled an expulsion order issued in Naples in the early years of the century[38] – as an alternative to inquisitorial action, and not as a prelude to it. It might well have the incidental effect of guaranteeing the state a role in dealing with the

---

[32] S.U., b. 36, proc. Righetto, submission of 11 Sept. 1572.

[33] Goris, Étude..., pp. 571–4, 652–3.

[34] D. Kaufmann, 'A contribution to the history of the Venetian Jews', *Jewish Quarterly Review*, original series, vol. 2 (1890, reprint 1966), pp. 303–5.

[35] Pullan, *Rich and poor*..., pp. 288, 296 ff.

[36] N.V., V, pp. 87–8, 12 July 1550.

[37] The only two known cases of Marranism before the issue of the decree are those of Francisco Olivier (I.Z., pp. 79–91) and the denunciation by Juan Aloncigaria of Castile (ibid., pp. 93–4).

[38] Amabile, *Il Santo Officio ... in Napoli*, I, pp. 114–19.

Marranos, who could be claimed for its jurisdiction on the grounds that they were Jews simulating Christianity rather than renegade Christians.

At first the state entrusted the enforcement of the law to the lay magistrates called the *Censori*.[39] But the Senate caused alarm among the Rialto merchants both by its failure to define the term 'Marranos' and by its vague and sweeping veto on having dealings with them. Only at this second stage, in response to requests for definition and clarification, was an attempt made to involve the Inquisition. Its expertise was now invoked for the purpose of identifying secret judaizers, and at the same time the merchants were reassured that there was no intention to ban dealings with New Christian merchants abroad who might or might not be Jews at heart. The *Censori* were instructed to cause the inquisitors to inquire, in their presence and with their assistance, into 'those named as Marranos'. However, collaboration between the two bodies would not be easy to arrange. For the role of laymen in Inquisition proceedings was at this time the subject of fierce controversy,[40] and the nuncio and his colleagues, having already accepted three lay *Assistenti*, were probably reluctant to include any other magistrates. Some degree of collaboration must have been established between the Inquisition and the state, however, since the interrogations of Tristão da Costa, a member of Brianda de Luna's entourage, are recorded in the papers both of the Inquisition and of the Council of Ten[41] – the Ten, having issued the safe-conduct to the sisters, was in a strong position to claim jurisdiction over Brianda's servants and agents. Duarte Gomes and Agostinho Enriques sought to exculpate themselves before the Inquisition in 1555, but were later involved in other charges laid against them before the secular criminal court of the Quarantia, which acquitted them in 1557.[42] Though officially hostile to the Marranos, the state was anxious to preserve its own discretion in dealing with them.

As for the interpretation of the law, Righetto in his testimony to the Inquisition in 1571 implied that it was understood to mean that those New Christians who 'wished to live as Jews' must go to the Ghetto or else leave the city. His own uncle, the rich Enriques Nuñes, chose to depart for Ferrara, and he was certainly not alone in so doing.[43] In fact, the only known Inquisition cases are concerned with people who were maintaining a double identity in Italy as Christian and as Jew, and not with persons who had decided to be Jews and assume their uniform. A clear example

[39] For the appointment of the *Censori*, whose original purpose was to control electoral corruption, see D.M.S., XXIV, col. 659–64, 13 Sept. 1517.

[40] See above, p. 6.

[41] I.Z., pp. 252, n. 2, 263, 341–51.

[42] Ibid., pp. 225–47; I.Z. II, pp. 71–96; Kaufmann, 'Die Vertreibung...', pp. 531–2.

[43] S.U., b. 36, proc. Righetto, 4 Aug. 1571.

was Brianda's agent, who used on contracts his non-committal title of licentiate in law of the University of Salamanca, who answered sometimes to the Christian name of Tristão da Costa and sometimes to the Jewish one of Abraham Habibi, and who lived privately as a Jew not in the Ghetto but in the Gritti palace at San Marcuola, wearing the dress of a Christian in public.[44] Trials resulted, not from the kind of hostility on the part of the Venetian people that could have generated numerous denunciations, but rather from factional rivalries within New Christian circles. The special safe-conduct to the Mendes–de Luna sisters had survived the general expulsion decree, and Brianda's followers invoked it in their defence, although she was at last compelled to depart in 1555–56.[45] In these years it was still possible to disentangle oneself from Inquisition proceedings; Duarte Gomes, sometime physician to Beatrix de Luna and still handling some of her business after her departure for Constantinople, managed to clear himself by producing witnesses to his Christian acts in the face of some ominous signs to the contrary. A number of merchants, one Bolognese, three Florentines and a Genoese, closed ranks around him, together with a secretary to the Imperial ambassador and a secretary to the Duke of Florence.[46]

In a sense, Venetian policy towards Marranos was a compromise between the Imperial and the papal approaches. On the surface it resembled Imperial policy, but in practice it was directed only against dissemblers, and the presence of a body of officially tolerated practising Jews in Venice – unthinkable in Spain or the Low Countries – inevitably meant that discreet reversions to Judaism would be allowed. Here the Venetians were in reality not far from the papal position, although they shrank from offering any explicit privileges to Iberian Jews, and took no positive steps to encourage their settlement. A likely effect of their actions was that New Christians would tend to settle in Ferrara, but visit Venice in pursuit of their affairs. And with this populous New Christian community nearby, serving as refuge in case of trouble, it would in practice be difficult to eliminate Marranism – in the sense of dissimulation – from Venice.

Between 1550 and 1573, there was little reason for the Venetian government to revise its policy. Information laid before the authorities, clerical and lay, contributed to a stereotyped vision of the Marrano as a rapacious usurer lurking beneath a Christian skin, as a personification of the corrupting power of money, and as an entrepreneur whose wealth is merely extracted from the community around him, benefits it in no way and is indeed designed for export to enemy countries.

[44] I.Z., pp. 251–63.
[45] Ibid., and I.Z., pp. 342–51; Grunebaum-Ballin, *Joseph Naci* ..., pp. 54–65.
[46] I.Z., pp. 225–47.

. . . with their fine Spanish manners, their cunning and their abun-
dance of money [wrote the delator of Agostinho Enriques and
Duarte Gomes], they can do in the city all that they please, and
behind this cloak they hold states in their hands, for they have
correspondents and friends in Flanders, France, Constantinople and
all the provinces of the world, not only among merchants but also
among princes and great personages, and they are partners of those
Mendes women who fled to Ferrara. On Rialto they do business as
Christians, they send merchandise aboard galleys and ships, and
because they cannot do so on their own account they use the name
of a Venetian noble whom they support and who goes everywhere
with them, and they give money to the father – a great man – to
obtain the favours they desire, and they lend upon usury at a higher
rate than the professing Jews, thronging the house in such a way
that all the Ghetto has repaired to the Bridge of the Angel (at Santa
Maria Formosa) where they dwell.[47]

The most sinister implication of these charges was the suggestion that
with the aid of complaisant patricians – possibly the Procurator Marco da
Molin and his son Nicoló[48] – they were frustrating the intentions of the
stringent citizenship laws of the Venetians. These were designed to deny
participation in the Levant trade to all Westerners save those who had
resided in the city, paid its taxes for a period of twenty-five years and had
their claims to citizenship *de intus et extra* formally approved by the
government.

Whatever the truth behind this rhetoric, it was clear that at least one
prominent Venetian, the Procurator Antonio Priuli, had suffered through
his Portuguese connexions and through his bank's dependence on fickle
foreign depositors. He was a rare example of a Venetian entrepreneur
who held substantial assets in Portugal; for him the oceanic trade with
India and the Indies was not merely a rival to the Mediterranean–
oriental trade in which the Venetians were traditionally involved, but
rather an activity from which a Venetian could draw a profit. At his
bankruptcy in 1551–52, his own story was that his Portuguese clients
received news from their correspondents abroad of heavy losses on his
part, and although these were still unknown to any Venetian they withdrew their confidence and started a run on the Priuli bank which brought

---

[47] I.Z. II, pp. 71–2.
[48] The names of the Molin are high on the list of persons willing to vouch for him
presented by Gomes to the Holy Office in Ferrara on 31 Aug. 1555 (ibid., p. 90); they are
named by Licentiato Costa as his enemies on 15 July 1555, with a strong hint that they were
acting as frontmen for Beatrix de Luna and as allies of her agents Gomes and Enriques
(I.Z., pp. 256–7).

it down.[49] If they trusted in foreign capital, supplied by persons not deeply involved in the city but treating it as a square on a chessboard and all too ready to transfer their money out of it, the Venetians might see the stability of their own economy undermined. Portuguese connexions seemed to bring ill luck.

Furthermore, the unedifying affairs of the Mendes–de Luna family and their henchmen exposed the danger of Venice being used as a bridgehead for the export of wealth to the Ottoman Empire. Beccadelli, the papal nuncio, was appalled at 'the damage to Christianity, if such a fortune, made among us, were borne off into the hand of infidels'. Little but trouble resulted from the decision to shelter the Mendes, and it was not an encouraging precedent. For the Republic was too amenable to Turkish diplomacy, or perhaps too sensitive to Turkish threats, to prevent the elder sister, Beatrix, from departing eastwards in a galley bound for Ragusa. Machinations of supreme deviousness, intended to force her younger sister, Brianda, to join her in Constantinople, included the exploit of a cousin, João Miquez. This consisted of kidnapping Brianda's daughter, who was heiress to a part of the Mendes fortune, valued at 100,000 ducats.[50] It was the same João Miquez who was to rise to power and fortune at the right hand of the Sultan, to become Don Joseph Nasi, Duke of Naxos and the Archipelago. Although the sentence of banishment imposed for his crimes by the Republic in 1553 was withdrawn at his request in 1567,[51] he was widely believed to harbour a personal grudge against the Venetian state. Justifiably or not, Venetian historians thought him responsible for the Turkish attacks on Cyprus, and he was certainly interested in depriving Venice of the island, whether through war or through diplomacy.[52] Marranos were feared for their possible connexions with the Duke of Naxos, and for their hypothetical roles in his network of spies. Among Venetians the notion that the war of Cyprus was a Jewish war was current in 1570, when the Doge said it had been 'launched against them by the Turk on account of espionage and the evil machinations of Jews'. And the decree issued in 1571 for the termination of the Senate's contracts with the nation of Germanic Jews was stiff with

[49] S.T., filza 14, 26 Sept. 1551; reg. 1551–52, fol. 102v., petition of 29 May 1552.

[50] N.V., V, pp. 313–14, 316–17, 325, 14, 21 Nov., 5 Dec. 1551; VI, pp. 49–50, 196, 199, 213, 218, 13 Feb. 1552, 21 Jan., 4 Feb., 18 March, 15 April 1553; I.Z., pp. 342–4; Grunebaum-Ballin, *Joseph Naci* ..., pp. 45–65.

[51] N.V., VIII, p. 203, 12 April 1567; cf. Albèri, III/ii, pp. 66–7 (Alvise Bonrizzo, 1565); Grunebaum-Ballin, *Joseph Naci* ..., p. 83.

[52] C. Roth, *The House of Nasi: the Duke of Naxos* (Philadelphia, 1948), pp. 140–8; Grunebaum-Ballin, *Joseph Naci* ..., pp. 135–7, 142–7. See also Albèri, II/ii, pp. 90–2 (Jacopo Ragazzoni, 1571), where João Miquez is said to have upset the promising reciprocal arrangements between Venice and the Ottoman Empire for the release of interned merchants and their goods.

vituperation against the treachery of all Jews.[53] The prosecution of Righetto by the Venetian Inquisition in 1570–73 originated in the fear that, as a relative of João Miquez bound for the Levant, he would be likely to slip him information damaging to Christendom.[54]

In 1555–56, the papal tradition of qualified toleration of Jews and former Marranos was suddenly overturned by Paul IV. His notorious revocation of the safe-conduct granted to Portuguese Jews was soon followed by the failure of the retaliatory boycott of Ancona by Jewish traders and by the collapse of attempts to divert trade to the inadequate harbour at Pesaro.[55] It seemed as though anti-Jewish policies could be pursued with impunity, even in ports engaged in Levantine trade. Complementary to the attack upon the Sephardic community at Ancona was the potentially lethal decree of the Cardinal Inquisitors-General of 30 April 1556. Declaring oneself a Jew in Italy would confer no immunity: indeed, if any Portuguese had lived in Portugal and subsequently appeared in Italy either as a professing Jew or as a secret practitioner of Judaism, it must be presumed that he had apostatized from the Catholic Church – even if he denied under torture that he had been baptized, or that he had ever performed the acts of a Christian.[56] If strictly applied – and it was designed to be enforced by all branches of the Roman Inquisition – the decree would put an end to the studied myopia of an institution concerned only with a man's actions after he entered Italy. And there would be no need to undertake laborious inquiries for the purpose of proving baptism or establishing some other sacramental link with the Church.

Immediately after the war of Cyprus, however, Venice showed signs of positively advocating toleration for former New Christians who declared themselves to be Jews and held firmly to that position. To the embarrassment of a succession of papal nuncios, the Venetian government also began to justify this policy by alluding to the liberalism of Paul III and Julius III, and in effect pleading their concessions against the harsher attitudes towards Jews introduced by Paul IV. Changes had occurred in the Venetian economy, which could well instil into the Senate a more positive desire to attract foreign settlers, and at the same time reduce its

[53] N.V., IX, pp. 292, 295, 368, 17, 24 June, 14 Oct. 1570; Pullan, *Rich and poor* ..., p. 537; B. Ravid, 'The socioeconomic background of the expulsion and readmission of the Venetian Jews, 1571–1573', in *Essays in modern Jewish history: a tribute to Ben Halpern*, ed. F. Malino and P. C. Albert (Rutherford–Madison–Teaneck, 1982), p. 42 ff.

[54] Pullan, ' "A ship ..." ', p. 45.

[55] C. Roth, *The House of Nasi: Doña Gracia* (Philadelphia, 1947), pp. 134–75; A. Toaff, 'Nuova luce sui marrani di Ancona (1556)', in *Studi sull' ebraismo in memoria di Cecil Roth*, ed. E. Toaff (Rome, 1974), pp. 261–80; Delumeau, 'Un ponte ...', pp. 42–6.

[56] For the text, Albizzi, *Risposta* ..., p. 217; Stern, *Urkundliche Beiträge* ..., I, doc. 111, pp. 116–17; Pastor, 'Allgemeine Dekrete ...', p. 496.

anxiety to protect the jealously guarded spheres of interest of Venetian patricians and citizens. Between 1567–68 and 1576 the Republic lost most of the fleet of great armed merchant vessels which were legally entitled to navigate outside and beyond the Adriatic. By 1576 seven of the twenty-four surviving roundships (there had been forty-seven before the war) were on their last voyage and condemned to be dismantled.[57] The loss of Cyprus meant a reduction in the supplies of salt which, by providing ballast and a return cargo to the great ships exporting goods from Europe, had proved vital to the mechanics of overseas trade. Already in the mid-sixteenth century the merchant fleet had been revealing a tendency to shorten its range and concentrate on destinies in the central Mediterranean, retreating from the Atlantic, the Black Sea and Egypt.[58] In the last thirty years of the sixteenth century there was a still narrower focus on the Adriatic itself and on the Balkans. It was accompanied by devices for shortening sea routes, exploiting land routes into the Balkans from the Dalmatian harbours and protecting shipping within the Adriatic from the ravages of piracy. Since some Marranos were settling in the small Dalmatian ports, their services could be of use in the process. In 1577 the Heads of the Ten intervened vigorously on behalf of certain Marranos who had been sentenced by the Venetian governor at Split (Spalato), and ordered them a new trial.[59] Venice was not yet declining into a mere regional port, but the role of its own grand fleet in the trade conducted through Venice was dwindling, and it was being compelled to concede to foreigners a more prominent role in Levantine trade.

The ostentatious disapproval of Marranos, sweepingly expressed in 1550, had perhaps been the product of a self-confidence which was now beginning to evaporate. If rival ports were attracting Sephardic Jews and perhaps even giving them express guarantees against prosecution for heresy, Venice could hardly afford to discourage them. The closer the concentration on the Adriatic, the narrower the contraction of opportunities beyond it, the more intense became the fear of rivalry from the southern trading axis which passed from France and Italy through Ancona and Ragusa into the Ottoman provinces. During the war Ragusa had been a neutral port under international protection and as such exempted from the papal ban on trading with the infidel. Hence it had enjoyed special, though ephemeral, advantages over Venice, and Jewish textile importers trading with the West had channelled their merchandise

---

[57] See J. C. Hocquet, *Le sel et la fortune de Venise, II: Voiliers et commerce en Méditerranée 1200–1650* (Lille, 1979), pp. 580–90.

[58] Ibid., pp. 283–6, 316–30.

[59] D.N., filza 18, fol. 228r.–229r., 26 Oct. 1577; filza 19, fol. 39, 90r.–v., 10 and 3 May 1578 respectively. Cf. also F. W. Carter, *Dubrovnik (Ragusa): a classic city-state* (London, 1972), pp. 373, 377.

through it.[60] So long as hostilities lasted, the Venetians had been uneasily aware that there might be a Jewish commercial revival in Ancona. It was true that Paul IV had banned Marranos, but there were still Levantine Jews in the port, and through them the Papacy might in practice be enjoying the advantages of a Marrano presence. Policing the Adriatic, the Venetians had been determined to insist on parity of disadvantage, by ensuring that the Jews of Ancona should suffer prohibitions on trading with the enemy just as stringent as those inflicted on the Levantine Jews of Venice.[61] One possible solution was an agreement between Venice and the Papacy for the simultaneous expulsion of the Jews from Venice and from Ancona, and from 1570 onwards there was indeed a loose understanding of this nature. But mutual trust was never strong enough to make any such combined operation practicable.[62]

During the war another disquieting possibility had arisen. Emanuel Filibert, Duke of Savoy, proposed to develop Nice (Villafranca) as a port trading with the Levant, and also, it was rumoured, as a centre for manufacturing woollens, silks and soap which might become a rival to Venice. Proposals had been made to the Duke by Vital Sacerdote and his son Simon, Jews then resident in the state of Milan and said to be in close correspondence with New Christian families in Spain and Portugal. Christians turning to Judaism would have figured prominently, in company with Turks, Moors, Armenians and Persians, in the plans for the expansion of Nice. In September 1572 the Duke promised the Sephardim protection from 'inquisition, visitation, denunciation, accusation or other action' against them by inquisitors or other ecclesiastics, on the score of 'apostasy, hypocrisy or any other crime in matters of faith, even if they have at other times lived as Christians'. Such proposals were promptly recognized as highly offensive by the Spanish authorities in Milan, because baptized *conversos* could only be seen as heretics if they returned to Judaism, and if they were heretics they would also be rebels against God and the King of Spain; the dominions of the Duke, wrote the King himself, were in the midst of Christendom, and if they were peopled with heretics it could scarcely be a matter of indifference. In November 1573, bowing at last to the disapproval of Spain and the papal nuncio, the Duke announced rather disingenuously that he had been informed that the Jews permitted to settle in his states included 'some Marrano apostates, that is, persons who have been baptized but have subsequently abandoned our faith and taken up Judaism'. This being contrary to his

---

[60] Ibid., pp. 332–3, 358–9, 373.

[61] N.V., IX, pp. 292, 295, 368–9, 17, 24 June, 14 Oct. 1570; X, pp. 279–80, 334–5, 341, 13 Sept., 29 Nov., 6 Dec. 1572.

[62] N.V., IX, p. 295, 24 June 1570; X, pp. 167, 168–9, 22, 29 Dec. 1571.

intentions, he proceeded to give such 'Marrano apostates' six months' notice to quit.[63]

Within a month of the Duke's proclamation, the Venetian government made a positive but none too public attempt at offering concessions, as if it hoped to attract the apostates of Savoy. The Council of Ten and Zonta authorized the issue in the name of Doge Alvise Mocenigo of a safe-conduct to all Spanish and Portuguese Jews and other persons of Jewish descent then living in the West or in the territories of any Christian prince who might choose to settle in Venice within the next two years. In terms very similar to those used in Savoy it promised them protection against inquisition for past errors 'in the matter of faith', including apostasy and hypocrisy' (i.e. falsely passing as Christians). But at this point resemblance between the privileges ceased. For the Venetians expressly declared that their privilege would extend only to those declaring themselves to be Jews, donning the yellow hat, living as Jews in the Ghetto, and causing no 'scandal in matters of faith' after their arrival in Venice.[64] The Duke's concessions had seemed obnoxious to the Spaniards, not only on account of the security they offered to apostates, but also because there were no attempts to impose distinctive badges upon Jews, because guarantees were offered against the conversion to Christianity of any Jew under fifteen years of age, because the Jews would have been entitled to compensation for any slaves of theirs who were baptized, and because other infidels would have been entitled to live and trade freely in the Duke's lands.[65] Unlike the Duke the Venetians were not striving to develop a new port, but rather to compensate for some of the deficiencies of a fully developed economy, and to insert Jewish settlers into a carefully circumscribed social and economic sphere. There was no suggestion in Venice, as there was in Savoy, that immigrants would be allowed to live where they chose, to engage in any craft as well as in any form of trade, to own land and houses or to employ living-in Christian servants.[66] Even so the proposals were alarming to the nuncio Castagna, who foresaw that they would also result in immunities being granted to New Christians

---

[63] For the text of the privileges, found in the archives of the Jewish community of Padua, see M. Lattes, 'Documents et notices sur l'histoire politique et littéraire des juifs en Italie', *Revue des études juives*, 5 (1882), pp. 231–7; also S. Foa, *La politica economica della casa Savoia verso gli Ebrei dal sec. XVI fino alla rivoluzione francese: il portofranco di Villafranca (Nizza)* (Rome, 1962), pp. 14–20. For reports and correspondence by the Spanish authorities, and for the Duke's proclamation to the Marranos in November 1573, see the documents printed as Appendix to C. Beinart's Hebrew article, 'La venuta degli ebrei nel Ducato di Savoia e il privilegio del 1572', in *Scritti in memoria di Leone Carpi: saggi sull' ebraismo italiano*, ed. D. Carpi, A. Milano and A. Rofé (Jerusalem, 1967), pp. 86–119.

[64] C.D., Parti Secrete, reg. 10, fol. 159r.–v., 23 Dec. 1573.

[65] See clauses 7 and 25 of the ducal privilege; Beinart, 'La venuta ...', pp. 96, 101.

[66] See clauses 2, 14 and 29 of the ducal privilege.

living outside the Ghetto, and that they too would enjoy the luxury of a fresh start. When launching his protest early in 1574, the nuncio found himself embarking on the first of several fruitless debates (others would follow in 1602 and 1608) in which nuncios were hampered by having the concessions which the Papacy itself had made to Jews quoted to them in the Collegio, but not knowing precisely what these were or on what grounds they had been granted. He was realistic enough to understand that the Venetians would treat the affair 'as a matter of state, and as one of the privileges of their liberty, rather than as one for the Holy Office of the Inquisition'. His protests, he reflected, might make the government more discreet, but would make little substantive difference to the policy it actually pursued.[67]

Very likely the Venetians, since the peace terms of 1573 obliged them to admit Turkish subjects (including Levantine Jews) as traders to the city, could see no further arguments for excluding professing Jews of any culture or persuasion from the port. Instead, they concentrated on stabilizing and regularizing their economic position, whether as traders or as money-lenders, in such a way as to extract the maximum advantage from it for society and the state.[68] Over the next thirty or forty years the maxim that Levantine Jews were all Turkish spies was monotonously repeated, but this in itself could provide an argument for detaching them from allegiance to the Turk and freeing them of the need to acquire his protection.[69]

It seems very likely that over the next few years the Venetian government acted in the spirit of the document formulated in December 1573, even if the nuncio's intervention prevented it from advertising it widely. Fresh waves of immigration were now breaking on Venice and Ferrara, and newcomers were arriving from provinces in the Low Countries which had experienced, not just Calvinistic iconoclasm, but the breakdown of all religious discipline and certainty.[70] There was said to have been in Antwerp a Portuguese community of about 150 persons, or – by another estimate – of 94 'houses and chambers' before the great catastrophe of 1576.[71] Several of those who came to the attention of the Inquisition in

---

[67] N.V., XI, pp. 136–7, 141, 23 Jan., 6 Feb. 1574; Ravid, 'Legal status ...', p. 116.

[68] Cf. Pullan, *Rich and poor* ..., p. 539 ff.

[69] E.g., N.V., X, pp. 279, 303, 334, 341, 13 Sept., 18 Oct., 29 Nov., 6 Dec. 1572; N.V., XI, p. 283, 27 Nov. 1574; Albèri, III/iii, p. 316 (Gianfrancesco Morosini, 1585); D.N., filza 26, fol. 128, 20 Feb. 1588; filza 32, fol. 256v., 13 April 1596; Barozzi–Berchet, V/i, pp. 223, 242–3 (Simone Contarini, 1612).

[70] Cf. G. Parker, *The Dutch revolt* (London, 1977), pp. 154–5, 172 ff.; H. van der Wee, *The growth of the Antwerp market and the European economy (fourteenth–sixteenth centuries)* (3 vols., Louvain, 1963), II, p. 254 ff.

[71] For the first estimate, see the denunciation of Filipa Jorge, 1575, in S.U., b. 39; for the second, Goris, *Étude* ..., Annexe 5, pp. 614–16.

the 1570s and 1580s had in their recent past a spell in Antwerp or elsewhere in the southern Netherlands. By 1575 there was in Venice a tense circle of about a dozen Portuguese whose lives intertwined closely, who were regularly called upon to testify in cases of suspected Marranism, and who themselves suffered denunciation and even trial on account of their way of life. But it was only those living outside the Ghetto, and suspected of trying for materialistic reasons to get the best of both worlds, who were really in danger – at least until 1588.

It was put by the tribunal to Gaspar Ribeiro that he had posed as a Christian 'in order to live comfortably and securely here in Venice and attend to the business of a merchant, which he could not have done had he declared himself openly to be a Jew and one returning to the faith of the Jews'.[72] Those who reverted to Judaism as soon as they entered Venice might, like Consalvo Baes, an ex-broker of Antwerp, be abused at Rialto by Spanish merchants who recognized them.[73] But, perhaps baulked by the reluctance of the lay *Assistenti* to issue warrants, the Inquisition did not arrest them. Estevão Nogueira, officious, insinuating, claiming to be the son of an inquisitor of Coimbra, reported that threadbare arguments drawn from the forced conversions of the 1490s were rife in Venice and were being used to justify numerous transmutations:

> The said Jorge Lopez and Miguel Vaz told me that all who come from Portugal turn Jews when they are here, and that it is lawful for them to do so in Venice, for they say they were made Christians by force. This is utterly false, for their fathers were Christians and have always lived as such. . . .[74]

It was as if the status of forced convert had become hereditary, transmitted with the blood from one generation to another of the New Christian race; and as if the papal concession were forever valid, even when the popes themselves had sought to wipe it out. A Portuguese preacher from Lisbon heard alarming reports of more than one hundred Portuguese, formerly Christians, now living as Jews in the Ghetto. Seeing Senators at one of his Lenten sermons in San Geremia, hard by the Ghetto, he

> exhorted their lordships publicly from the pulpit to open their eyes, to remedy so grave an abuse, and to rid themselves of the Jews, for to keep them here was to entertain spies and usurers.[75]

[72] S.U., b. 45, proc. Ribeiro, 23 June 1580.
[73] S.U., b. 43, proc. Baes, test. Ruy Lopes, 22 March 1578.
[74] S.U., b. 44, proc. 'Negromanti', 20 Jan. 1579.
[75] S.U., b. 45, proc. Gaspar Ribeiro, test. 'Domenico de Pace', 28 Jan., 23 April 1580; cf. test. Gaspar Ribeiro, 10 March 1580.

Despite these edifying sentiments, and despite some argument on other grounds, the Jewish *condotta* was renewed within a few months, in August 1580.[76]

During the 1580s, however, the expanding authority of the Inquisition[77] created an obvious need to reassure the Jewish mercantile community by means of explicit and long-lasting guarantees. This was especially true after the arrest of the Jew Nemias by the Inquisition in 1588. It seemed to mark an ominous departure from previous policy. Serious charges had been brought against Marranos in the 1580s, against Gaspar Ribeiro and against the Filippi, but it could at least be said that they were persons who presented themselves as Christians and that they had committed 'scandalous' actions in Venice itself. But Nemias appeared to be a professing Jew in the correct uniform who lived in Ferrara and was only in transit through Venice. Furthermore, his offence was not that he had caused trouble in Venice but that he had posed as a Christian in Flanders. During the debate in the Collegio, the senior patricians present expanded with significant variations on the theme once tersely stated in the privilege of Julius III: that one must allure the Jews with privileges. They made no reference, as he had done, to the possibility of converting the Jews, but argued that it was vital to hold the Marranos in Europe, in order to stem a haemorrhage of wealth that would weaken Christendom. Matteucci was told that

> such people [Marranos] resolve to go to Constantinople and live under Turkish rule with their enormous wealth, even as Alvaro Mendes recently transferred himself thither with great riches. He gave 30,000 crowns just for the favour of being allowed to kiss the Sultan's hand, which is seldom permitted to Jews, and every day others follow his example and leave, to the terrible detriment of Christendom. Apart from the great profit they bring to our trade if they remain in these parts with their wealth, we can on occasion make use of them against the enemies of our faith. If it happens otherwise, the Turks feel the benefit of their riches, and make use of them to harm Christianity.[78]

By representing toleration as an action serviceable to the whole of Christendom, the Venetians sought to resolve the tension between material self-interest and religious duty. Well-chosen was the example of

---

[76] Pullan, *Rich and poor . . .* , p. 540.

[77] See above, pp. 73–8.

[78] C.E.R., reg. 4, fol. 4v.–6v., 20r.–21r., 23v., 140v.–141r., 26 March, 28 June, 15 July 1588, 28 Dec. 1590; D.N., filza 26, fol. 268r.–269r., 2 July 1588; also B.A.V., MS Barberino Latino 5195, fol. 77.

Alvaro Mendes, formerly financier and confidential adviser to Catherine de' Medici and brother-in-law to Queen Elizabeth's ill-fated physician.[79] The papal nuncio had been anxious to identify and perhaps arrest this opulent emigré when he passed through Venice in 1585, protected, it was said, by the clam-like discretion of the Portuguese residents.[80]

Instructed to put the Venetian case at Rome, the ambassador Giovanni Gritti held an inconclusive and guarded discussion with the Cardinal Santa Severina, head of the Roman Inquisition. From this it emerged that the Holy Office in Rome had been compiling a list or *catalogo* of all who had departed from Spain, with a view to tracing their movements across Europe. Some Marrano fortunes had been confiscated by the Inquisition in Florence and Genoa, others placed at risk in Ragusa. At the same time, the ambassador suspected that the Pope would show some sense of expediency, and 'would not willingly see such people absolutely barred from bringing their wealth into the states of the Church'. Though admitting to the existence of previous papal privileges, the Cardinal cut off discussion by pointing out that Paul IV had annulled them and by remarking that 'these are different times, and circumstances have changed, and if the Pope did such things today we would consider proceedings against him.'[81]

The Venetian government would scarcely be reassured either by the suggestion that the Roman congregation was compiling dossiers on Marranos or by the hints that some might be admitted to the Papal States or protected by the Duke of Ferrara. Measures more forceful than the bailing of Nemias were needed to restore the confidence of Jewish merchants of Spanish or Portuguese extraction. Attempts to reassure the Iberian Jews in Venice began to be combined with more positive steps to employ them to develop a new commercial link between Venice and Split. In the summer of 1589, the Senate issued a charter to prospective Sephardic settlers, which now had the effect of creating a third 'nation' of Jews which would take its place besides the two existing nations, that of the Germanic Jews and that of the Levantine Jews who were Turkish subjects. It would consist of Sephardim who owed no allegiance to the Turk, whether as 'Ponentines' they had come directly from the western world or whether as 'Levantines' they had returned to Venice from the East. They would now be officially entitled to bring their families and to acquire a settlement in the city. As did its predecessor of 1573, the new

[79] On Alvaro Mendes, cf. L. Wolf, 'Jews in Elizabethan England', *Transactions of the Jewish Historical Society of England*, 11 (1924–27), pp. 26, 29; J. Gwyer, 'The case of Dr Lopez', ibid., 16 (1952), pp. 165–6; Baron, *A social and religious history ...*, XIV, p. 101.

[80] D.N., filza 25, fol. 287v., 25 Jan. 1585.

[81] S.D.R.O., reg. 7, fol. 85v.–86r., 25 June 1588; S.S.D.R., 22, fol. 165v.–168v., 9 July 1588.

safe-conduct offered the newcomers safeguards against prosecution for religious offences. But, perhaps deliberately, it did so in a far more cryptic fashion. For its beneficiaries could merely be sure of 'not being molested on account of religion by any magistracy', and this was less than the petitioning merchants had sought.[82] The Holy Office would not normally be called a magistracy, though the term could have been applied to its lay *Assistenti*, with whom the responsibility for authorizing arrests would lie. This ambiguous phrasing may well have been designed to avoid diplomatic difficulties and provocative disrespect towards the Inquisition. On the surface it offered better guarantees against the *Esecutori contro la Bestemmia* than against prosecution for heresy. Most likely, the Venetians intended to claim, should the occasion arise, that Jews appearing in the guise of Jews – and only they would benefit from the privilege – could only be the concern of lay magistrates; and this was indeed to be argued in the case of the Jews of Verona a year or two later.[83] Hence, there would be no need to furnish express guarantees against the Inquisition. There would be safeguards against the immigration of undesirables, but the Jewish settlers were to be the judges in the first instance of the suitability of the newcomers, and there was no suggestion that they would be expected to invoke religious criteria. To ensure the recruitment only of 'law-abiding and reputable men' (*huomini civili e reputati*), they were formed into a corporation entitled to vet its own membership, subject to supervision from the Board of Trade, the *Cinque Savii alla Mercanzia*. Unlike its predecessor, the charter was to run for a maximum of ten years in the first instance, though the Sephardic Jew Daniel Rodriga would have liked more,[84] and it was to be the first of a long series of contracts and general safe-conducts for Sephardic settlers.

Surprisingly, the charter was not (it seems) challenged by the nuncio as the earlier patents had been; a Vatican document compiled in 1625 was later to suggest that it was issued in secret and not officially shown to him.[85] Protests from the Pope himself, in tones of indignation and regret, were to be made during the next decade and to be blandly answered by Venetian diplomats. They were the less disposed to take them seriously for their own suspicion that the Pope himself intended to do precisely the same thing, and that yet another attempt would be made to revive the

---

[82] For the charter and the petitions and recommendations that preceded it, see B. Ravid, 'The first charter of the Jewish merchants of Venice, 1589', *Association for Jewish Studies Review*, I (1976), pp. 187–222. The petition presented by Daniel Rodriga asked that merchants of Jewish race 'may live securely in their religion, without suffering inquisition from any office or magistracy, either ecclesiastical or secular' (see doc. C, p. 215).

[83] See above, pp. 86–8.

[84] See Rodriga's letter of 28 Aug. 1589, in Q.C., filza 105, proc. 84.

[85] B.A.V., MS Barberino Latino 5195, fol. 77r.–v.

flagging commerce of Ancona with the aid and advice of merchants described as 'Levantine Jews'. Clement VIII's attitude towards Jews who could bring capital into the Papal States was believed to be quite different from his feelings towards the 'lowly creatures of no account' whom he maltreated in Rome. Although the Congregation of the Inquisition in Rome was involved in the formulation of Jewish privileges in Ancona, it seemed that the Pope would be none too careful as to whom he attracted to his port. In 1594, the ambassador Paolo Paruta was astounded at the Bull which granted a free and perpetual safe-conduct to all Levantine Jews in Ancona, whereas previously it had been necessary to obtain from the Cardinal Chamberlain special licences made out to particular people for specified purposes,

> even though it is but a few days since the Pope . . . complained that Levantine Jews were received in Venice. Hence, to justify the Republic, I had to explain the reasons for it and to describe some of the measures applied in Venice, in order to obtain such profit as might be made whilst still avoiding scandal and disorder. So the same things are differently regarded, not in accordance with their true nature, but in the light of the gains one hopes to make therefrom.[86]

Renewed rivalry from Ancona underlined the need to maintain and encourage a Sephardic Jewish presence in Venice, and the attitudes of the Popes themselves continued to provide Venetian patricians with a strong justification for refuting criticisms from Rome, for any assemblage of Levantine Jews, not strictly vetted, would surely include some Marranos.

The motives behind the Venetian charter may not have been altogether worldly, since it could have been incidentally designed to reduce crypto-Judaism of the kind frequently reported to the Holy Office after the migrations from Flanders in the 1570s. Almost twenty years later, Doge Leonardo Donà would say, as though expounding a principle long implicit in Venetian policy,

> it is better they dwell as Jews in the Ghetto and wear the yellow hat, than that they dwell among Christians in a black one, frequenting the churches and sacraments in a spirit of falsehood, bringing dishonour to God and scandal to the city.[87]

---

[86] See G. De Leva, ed., *La legazione di Roma di Paolo Paruta (1592–1595)* (3 vols., Venice, 1887), I, pp. 156–7, 164, 179–80, 205–6, 246; II, pp. 329–30, 348–9, 362 (despatches between 3 April 1593 and 9 July 1594); also S.S.D.R., 27, fol. 250v.–251v., 5 June 1591; C.E.R., reg. 8, fol. 26v., 27, 13 June 1598.

[87] C.E.R., reg. 16, fol. 46v., 27 June 1608.

Better separation than syncretism; better a clean act of apostasy than the pollution of Christianity by Judaism.

It could be said that the charter was merely legalizing what had long been the surreptitious practice of the Venetian Senate. Those who governed Venice had long seemed reasonably happy if the ambiguity latent within the Marrano were firmly resolved by his revealing himself as a Jew, and so opting for one of the two categories in which his behaviour had placed him. But the emphasis of policies had changed; it had passed from expressing public disapproval of Marranism to taking positive steps to attract former Marranos to Venice. And it was surely not merely a reaction against the Inquisition's increasingly aggressive conduct, but also a reflection of a deep-seated economic process, whereby Venetian merchants were drawing in their horns and ceasing to maintain their own agents and branches abroad, even in the East. The corollary of this process was that foreigners had to be encouraged to settle in Venice itself to keep up the level of activity and maintain the revenue from customs and excise. Whether by treaty and charter, or by tradition and tacit understanding, they needed to be guaranteed against prosecution for religious beliefs discreetly held, and against prosecution for conduct outside Venice. In this respect, Venice's policy towards Sephardic Jews was broadly similar to its treatment of Protestant Grisons.[88] By the early seventeenth century it was to become broadly true, as Sarpi told the Burgrave von Dohna, that 'The Inquisition can do nothing to those who are not Italians'; or, as the English chaplain Bedell chose to put it, that 'noe man borne out of Italy is soe much as called in question by them unless he give great scandall'.[89]

For some considerable time, the Venetians had been less well represented in the western marts of Lyons and Antwerp than were the merchants of Genoa, Florence, Milan or Lucca, and the long history of the Fondaco dei Tedeschi bore witness to their lack of interest in penetrating Germany themselves rather than enticing foreigners to Venice.[90] Retreat from Levantine commerce, the most jealously guarded sphere, was a more recent development. Ambassador-consuls in the Turkish empire had for years been reporting that the Jews of Constantinople and the Turkish empire had established a monopolistic hold on Ottoman trade: they were buying up wool, controlling the trade in camlets, dealing in cloth and alum. Venetian firms in Constantinople had become too supine, too readily contented to use the Jews as middlemen whose high service charges

[88] Cf. D.N., filza 32, fol. 575, 2 Oct. 1603.

[89] Sarpi, *Lettere ...*, I, p. 124; Bedell to Adam Newton, 1 Jan. 1608, in Shuckburgh, ed., *Two biographies of William Bedell ...*, pp. 227–8.

[90] Cf. R. Gascon, *Grand commerce et vie urbaine au XVIe siècle: Lyon et ses marchands* (2 vols., Paris, 1971), especially I, p. 220; Goris, *Étude ...*, Annexe 7, pp. 618–21.

sliced the profits in half. It was said that the Jews demanded large dis-
counts for paying cash and conducted barter trade on terms highly dis-
advantageous to their customers. In 1560 there appeared to be only ten
or a dozen Venetian houses trading in Constantinople;[91] half a century
later, the number had dropped to five.[92] There could well be a temptation
to leave commerce in the hands of the Jews, but to increase control over it
by drawing a larger proportion of them towards Venice and its possessions on the Dalmatian coast. To judge by the reports of Venetian
observers abroad, the old idyllic relationship between the Turks and their
Jewish settlers was coming to an end, for they were no longer secure
against the whims of sultans, or against the violence of Janissaries. Used
by the Turks as tools of injustice and oppression, the rich 'Marrano Jews
of Portugal, who are very numerous, are in worse case than anybody else.
For the Turks bite them to the bone, and the native Jews seek to do them
down, and the poor creatures realize their error too late . . .' The belief
that Jews could be enticed from the Ottoman Empire and induced to
settle in Venice passed into the store of acceptable maxims passed down
from one Ambassador-consul to another.[93]

From the energy and persistence of Daniel Rodriga sprang the specific
arrangements of 1589. He was, *par excellence*, the Portuguese Jew committed to Levantine trade and taking as his province the Adriatic and the
Balkans – Ancona, Venice, Ragusa, the other Adriatic ports, Bosnia.[94]
His proposals now entailed linking the Dalmatian port of Split – in 1576
an obscure town of some 4,000 inhabitants – to Venice through the
collaboration of Jewish trading communities in both cities. Split would be
designed as a magnet for commerce within the Balkans, including goods
travelling westwards from Constantinople and the farther reaches of the
Ottoman lands. Reciprocal relations between the linked ports would be
fostered by tax concessions for goods passing between them, and would
depend on transport by armed galleys, which sometimes increased their
effectiveness as freighters by towing other ships.[95] These security meas-

[91] Albèri, III/i, pp. 101–2 (Bernardo Navagero, 1553); p. 182 (Domenico Trevisan, 1554); pp. 274–5 (Marino Cavalli, 1560); III/ii, pp. 53–4 (Daniele Barbarigo, 1564).

[92] Barozzi–Berchet, V/i, p. 235 (Simone Contarini, 1612).

[93] Albèri, III/ii, pp. 298–9, 301–2 (Maffeo Venier, Archbishop of Corfu, 1586); pp. 370–1 (Lorenzo Bernardo, 1592); III/iii, p. 389 (Matteo Zane, 1594, from whom the quotation is taken); Barozzi–Berchet, V/i, p. 32 (Agostino Nani, 1603).

[94] See R. Paci, 'La scala di Spalato e la politica veneziana in Adriatico', *Quaderni Storici*, 5 (1970), pp. 52–4.

[95] Ibid., p. 60 ff.; R. Paci, *La 'scala' di Spalato e il commercio veneziano nei Balcani fra Cinque e Seicento* (Venice, 1971), pp. 45–70; also D. Sella, *Commerci e industrie a Venezia nel secolo XVII* (Venice–Rome, 1961), pp. 2, 16, 55, 56, 58; F. Braudel, *The Mediterranean and the Mediterranean world in the age of Philip II*, trans. S. Reynolds (2 vols., London, 1975), I, pp. 286–8, 307, 373; II, p. 846. See also D.N., filza 21, fol. 254, 25 June 1580; filza 31, fol. 23r.–v., 4 Feb. 1595; filza 33, 25 Aug. 1603.

ures, not invariably successful, were designed to reduce the danger from piracy, and especially from the notorious Uskoks. Shortening the sea routes in this way was advantageous to Jewish traders. For their persons and merchandise were sadly vulnerable to 'pious' piracy, which partook sanctimoniously of the character of holy guerrilla warfare, and was intended to appropriate the goods of infidels.[96]

How effective in practice were the guarantees offered by the 1589 charter? Since comparatively few trial records have survived for the period from 1594 to 1616, it is hard to be entirely confident that no Marranos were tried by the Venetian Inquisition after its issue. But papal nuncios and curialists became very much aware that the state was blocking the Inquisition's path. 'There have almost always been insuperable difficulties in proceeding against Jews and Marranos,' wrote the anonymous compiler of some notes on the Venetian state's relations with the Inquisition from the 1590s to the 1620s.[97] Where serious arguments are known to have arisen, they were concerned with people who had blatantly changed their religion in Venice itself by living within its boundaries first as Christians and then as Jews, rather than switching hats discreetly at some earlier point on their odyssey. To pose as a Christian in Habsburg lands was an act of self-preservation, a concession to expediency which implied no binding allegiance to the Christian Church. To do so in Venice, where there was no such obligation to conform, might imply at best a cynical disposition to change loyalties for personal advantage and at worst the mentality of an atheist or heretic. The question is known to have arisen at least three times in the first thirty years of the new system, and in two of these cases the state intervened in defence of the accused and in a manner highly disconcerting to the ecclesiastical authorities.

When the *condotta* was first put into effect in and after 1589, difficulties were raised from within the Jewish community itself by the Germanic and Italian Jews. They disliked the exemption which the newcomers at first enjoyed from any obligation to contribute to the support of the loan banks. Understandably, too, they objected to sharing cramped accommodation with people who would not share their fiscal burdens.[98] If there was any analogy between Ancona in the 1550s and Venice in the 1590s, their antagonism may have had still deeper roots, for many Jews in Ancona had regarded Marranos with scant affection, seeing them as troublemakers who courted martyrdom by foolishly trusting in the promises of Christian princes and might easily involve other Jews in their

[96] See Tenenti, *Piracy* ..., pp. 8, 38, 41, 43, 48, 49, 178–9; and the many examples reported in the correspondence of the papal nuncios with the Cardinal Secretaries of State (D.N.).
[97] B.A.V., MS Barberino Latino 5195, fol. 76.   [98] Q.C., filza 111, proc. 121.

own downfall.[99] Sharing these suspicions or not, the Germanic and Italian Jews were said by Rodriga to be systematically opposing applications to the *Cinque Savii alla Mercanzia* to be allowed to settle in Venice, and also to be using their control over rented accommodation to prevent the newcomers from finding houses. Abraham Cabiglio, equipped though he was with letters of commendation from the Bailo in Constantinople, was ineffectively blackmailed on the grounds that he had lived both as Christian and as Jew in Venice itself. It may have been no more than an isolated intrigue, springing from Fior Alteras, a Jewess who believed that by denouncing him she could have her own husband's sentence of banishment rescinded. But it threw light on the circumstances in which an immmigrant might find himself in grave danger. Cabiglio remarked pointedly that all his relatives were looking to his case, to determine the advisability of settling in Venice. But he had not, he said, been seriously perturbed, and there the matter was allowed to rest.

In 1608, Moses and Joseph Masaod, who had lived continuously in the Venetian Ghetto since 1588, were denounced to the Inquisition as the former Antonio Rodrigues and Manuel da Costa. Manuel had, soon after migrating from Portugal to join his father in Turin, lived in Venice for a time as a Christian in the houses of fellow Portuguese at San Zulian and Santa Marina, and had transacted business in that guise.[100] Proceedings against him were firmly blocked first by the *Assistenti* and then by the Collegio. The oratory of the nuncio, Monsignor Gessi, urging the Venetians to discard the practical considerations which normally ruled them and to further wholeheartedly the service of God, was robustly countered by those familiar arguments in which the patricians seemed all too well rehearsed. The debate was chiefly remarkable for the Doge's personal contributions, which seemed designed to demonstrate his experience of things Spanish, and for his declaration that all forced converts and their heirs were unshakably and indelibly Jewish. Marranos were not in any meaningful sense Christians and could not be subject to the jurisdiction of the Holy Office. Scepticism concerning the information laid before the Holy Office, allegations of malicious prosecution and allusions to papal privileges closed the discussion. The Collegio, not for the first time, was intruding into the judicial process itself. Pursuing the matter with one of the *Assistenti*, Agostino Nani, Gessi was told that it mattered very little that Paul IV had cancelled the Ancona privileges; the Papacy had once seen the concessions as good in principle, and the fact could not be forgotten.[101]

---

[99] Cf. Toaff, 'Nuova luce ...', pp. 269–78.   [100] C.S.I., b. 4, fol. 175r.–176r., 28 May 1608.
[101] D.N., filza 38A, fol. 185v. and following, entries from 24 May 1608 onwards; C.E.R., reg. 16, fol. 44r.–v., 46r.–47v., 50v.–51v., 55r.–56r., 20, 27 June, 4, 18 July 1608; S.D.R.O., reg. 17, fol. 22v.–23, 28 June 1608.

Finally, the Diaz case of 1621 showed how generous the state magistracies were prepared to be in granting immunity to persons liable to charges of apostasy. It also showed how the state would react if its pliability were discovered by the Church. Jorge and Fernão Diaz, two Portuguese brothers, lived as Christians in the parish of San Marcuola in Cannaregio from about 1602 to 1615. They were merchants, said a local priest vaguely, 'but I know not what goods they deal in.' Jorge's children were baptized; a visiting relative died and was buried in the graveyard of the parish church; pictures of the Three Magi and an image of the Virgin, together with some Old Testament scenes, were glimpsed in the house; and like other good Christians, they would light two torches at their door on the evening of Good Friday. The worst thing said of them was that Jorge had once walked through the Servites' church without taking off his hat, though they were also reputed to holiday on Saturday and the girls of the household to bleach their hair on Sunday. Then the family moved, went abroad for a spell, and certain of the Diaz returned to Venice under Jewish names. In 1618 a privilege was issued to them in the names of Raphael Abendana, his son-in-law David Senior, and their respective families, 'notwithstanding the fact that they have for some years lived in this city as professed Christians in name and dress.' They were recognized almost three years later by someone who denounced them to the Inquisition, but on arrest they produced the safe-conduct. There was an embarrassing conflict of principles, which the Senate resolved high-handedly – much to the nuncio's chagrin – by destroying the safe-conduct but freeing the Diaz from gaol and ordering them to leave Venice.[102] Though tacitly admitting to an impropriety, the state kept its word and saved the Diaz from prosecution for apostasy, not merely frustrating the Inquisition but actually releasing its prisoners.

There was no logical reason why the charter of 1589 should have protected persons practising Judaism outside the Ghetto. But no prosecutions of dissembling Marranos are known to have taken place after its issue. It is hard to believe that all New Christians of judaizing inclination repaired promptly to the Ghetto. The psychological difficulties of transferring to that narrow, uncomfortable world could be considerable, relatives in Spain and Portugal might have been subjected to reprisal, and there were always difficulties in trading under Jewish names in those countries. But the issue of the charter may well have created a very convenient presumption that, because the opportunities of returning to Judaism so clearly did exist, nobody would now be likely to commit the offence of dissembling.

How far did the new privileges succeed in attracting the Sephardim to

[102] S.U., b. 77, proc. Diaz; C.E.R., reg. 19, fol. 52r.–53r., 57v., 23 July, 3 Aug. 1621; D.N., filza 42H, fol. 43v.–44r., Aug. 1621.

Venice and in stemming the currents of migration to the Ottoman Empire? It seemed unlikely that the Venetian charter, insisting on Ghetto conditions, would prove a strong enough net to catch councillors and financiers who wished to return openly to Judaism. There were fears in 1591 that João Lopes, 'so dear to Pope Sixtus', who had gained so much wealth 'from the blood of Christ', had departed for Salonica; large sums had been remitted for his benefit to the Venetian branches of the Florentine banks of the Strozzi and Capponi.[103] But from the beginning there were lesser triumphs, and there were signs of immigration both from Constantinople (whence came Abraham Cabiglio and his companion Joseph della Comare) and from rival ports in the West. For it was claimed in 1592 that Samuel Corcas or Carcos, 'who is the richest Jew, with the biggest business, in Ancona', had recently arrived in Venice.[104] Estimates of the Jewish share in Venice's Levantine trade are too disput able, sometimes too much clouded by polemic, to be repeated with much confidence. Moderate assessments of Jewish participation in maritime commerce in 1592–1609 have been made by an ingenious analysis of what is known about shipwrecks.[105] But these give too slight an impression of the Jewish share in all foreign trade, since the Jews were known for their part in overland trade through the Balkans and for their use of Split, which had special arrangements for transporting goods by galley.[106] A hostile witness, Alvise Sanuto, who at the turn of the century was one of the *Cinque Savii all Mercanzia*, asserted that three-quarters of the trade with Constantinople was now in the hands of Jews and Turks.[107] About 1608–9, there were in Venice 58 Levantine and Ponentine merchants privileged by the *Cinque Savii* in accordance with the terms of the *condotta*; visiting merchants, together with those who had applied for but not yet been granted such privileges, were said to raise the numbers to over 200.[108] How many of these were 'Marrano apostates' is not of course known. But it is worth recalling that Hector Mendes Bravo, who claimed to have lived in the Venetian Ghetto from 1607 to 1612, gave the Inquisition in Lisbon twenty-six names, those of six single persons and ten married couples, calling them 'the Portuguese living there whom the witness knows to have been baptized Christians'.[109]

---

[103] C.E.R., reg. 4, fol. 197v., 20 Sept. 1591; D.N., filza 27, fol. 293, 21 Sept. 1591.

[104] Q.C., b. 111, proc. 121, 7–8 Oct., 12–13 Nov. 1592.

[105] By B. Blumenkranz, 'Les juifs dans le commerce maritime de Venise', *Revue des études juives*, 120 (1961), pp. 143–51. Cf. the criticisms in Ravid, 'Legal status ...', pp. 214–18.

[106] See, for example, Barozzi–Berchet, V/i, pp. 239–40 (Simone Contarini, 1612) and 400–1 (Alvise Contarini, 1641).

[107] See Ravid, *Economics and toleration* ..., pp. 43–6.

[108] Ravid, 'Legal status ...', pp. 195, 203–4.

[109] C. Roth, 'The strange case of Hector Mendes Bravo', *Hebrew Union College Annual*, 18 (1943–44), pp. 230–2.

One clear effect of the charter was to bring about a silent revolution within the settled, tax-paying Jewish community of Venice, which came to be dominated by the Sephardic traders and not by the Germanic Jews. By 1636, however large or small the share of the Sephardic Jews in the total volume of overseas trade handled by the port of Venice, the contribution made by the Ponentine nation to the finances of the loan banks had become far larger than that of any other corpus of Jews. It was then paying 53.11 per cent of the bank tax, as compared with the Germanic Jews' 21.18 per cent, with 16.35 per cent from the Jews of the *Terra Ferma*, and with a modest 9.36 per cent from the Levantine Jews residing in Venice.[110] Levantine Jews who were subjects of the Turk, and therefore still classified as transients, did not pay this tax. In a style which almost anticipated Simon Luzzatto's attempts to evaluate the Jewish presence, leading Jewish traders priced themselves and their services before a criminal court in 1638. Isaac Monis claimed to have had 'the best business on the market' and to have paid customs for many years at the rate of 3,000–4,000 ducats per annum; Joseph, son of Abram Sachi, had 'brought more than 50,000 ducats profit to the prince'. And an honourable Levantine merchant at this time, Joseph Senior of Alexandria, enjoying excellent credit on the piazza, was said to have owned shares in two or three ships, to have rented a fine house for more than 80 ducats per annum and to have received with his bride a dowry of 12,000 ducats. This rumour seemed credible enough, said witnesses, because her father had a fortune of 50,000–60,000, and she was the only daughter.[111] Such a fortune would plainly be dwarfed into total insignificance by the assets of the most prosperous patrician families of the mid-seventeenth century, when a payment of 100,000 ducats was required of parvenu families as a condition of entry to the nobility, when there were said to be more than thirty old-established families with an income of 10,000–15,000 ducats, and perhaps ten families were believed to enjoy annual revenues of 20,000–80,000 ducats.[112] But 50,000–60,000 ducats was a considerable sum for a man who had, by the standards of the Christian world, no social position to keep up, and it admitted him comfortably to the ranks of those who, in terms of money but not of prestige, could be called solidly middle class.

Outside the Ghetto, one Spanish family, the Fonseca, had prospered well enough to aspire to noble rank during the war of Crete. They had

[110] Calculated from Ravid, *Economics and toleration* ..., pp. 80–1.

[111] I.R.E.C., Carte Diverse, 'Pie Case de Cattecumeni contro Università de gli Hebrei', fol. 35v., 43v., 86r.–v., 93v., 94v.–95r., 21, 25, 30 Jan., 24 Feb. 1637 Venetian style.

[112] These estimates of noble incomes – the basis for them is not known – are contained in an anonymous description of Venice written between 1659 and 1665 and printed at pp. 359–439 of P. G. Molmenti, *Curiosità di storia veneziana* (Bologna, 1919) – see pp. 416–18.

incurred the suspicion of being Jews, but in 1661 they obtained an elo-
quent testimonial to their devoutly Catholic habits from the parish priest
of San Geremia, where they lived suspiciously near to the Ghetto, and in
1664 they were aggregated to the patriciate, though in the face of substantial opposition.[113]

In the second third of the seventeenth century, there was little doubt
that the permanent Jewish community was expanding and renewing itself
chiefly through immigration from the eastern Mediterranean and from
those Italian ports which were most likely to shelter Sephardic Jews with
a Christian past. Between 1633 and 1666, the *Esecutori contro la Bestemmia*
are known to have made 45 grants of denization to immigrant Jews,
whether to individuals or to families. Almost all of these had resided in
Venice for ten years or more, and would now be released from the obligation to take out sojourn permits. Twenty-one of the grants were made
to recipients coming from Italian towns outside the Venetian dominions,
twelve to persons from the eastern Adriatic and eastern Mediterranean,
five to immigrants from Germany and Flanders and four to Jews from
within the Venetian *Terra Ferma*. There was no suggestion in the records
that anyone had come directly from Spain or Portugal, but Livorno, with
ten grants, Pisa, with three, and Ancona, Ferrara and Pesaro with two
each accounted for most of the newcomers from Italian sources. Prominent among migrating families were the Camis of Pisa and the Jesurum of
Livorno.[114] Very likely this was not a sign of Venice's superior attractions, but rather of the desire of Jewish merchants to build up links
between these ports. Simon Luzzatto wrote that the principal advantage
conferred by the Jews on Venice was that, in view of their relations with
correspondents in the western ports and emporia, a substantial proportion
of the trade now handled by foreigners could still find its way to it,
despite the massive geographical disadvantages which now afflicted the
city, and despite the natural primacy of Genoa and Livorno.[115]

At the roots of Venetian policy lay a conviction of the economic utility
of Jews, and it was to this that Luzzatto appealed when he undertook the
defence of the Jewish community. Sir Dudley Carleton once remarked
that 'Whereas other Governments are ruled by lawes the Venetian hath
little other than reason of state to which they doe resort in all occasions as
that which gives law to all other lawes.'[116] And yet the Collegio and the
Senate, in formulating their policies towards the Sephardim and making
them into a protected people, had never been content just to allude curtly

[113] See S.U., b. 106, test. Father Giovanni Cina, 10 May 1661; Cowan, 'The urban
patriciate...', pp. 125–6, 311.
[114] See below, Appendix II, p. 319.
[115] Luzzatto, *Discorso* ..., fol. 16v.–17.
[116] Public Record Office, London, State Papers 99/8, fol. 343v.

to interests of state or demands of commerce. Needing some higher justifications for their acts, some means of bridging the chasm between piety and expediency, they found them in the example of the popes, the elastic theory of the forced convert, the need to stem the flux of Marrano wealth from the Christian world, and the hope of saving the Christian faith from corruption by encouraging Marranos to separate themselves from it. Venice pleaded the old Papacy against the new, and sought to become for the Sephardim, whatever their past history, a terminus and not a place of transit. Years later, Cardinal Albizzi rebuked the Venetians, saying:

> To grant a free port to Turks, infidels, heretics born and bred in heresy, and Jews born into the Judaic faith is a dreadful thing, which is, however, tolerated for the sake of trade. But it is not in the power of any temporal prince to make such a concession to judaizing Christians, or to apostates, or to heretics, in such a way as to allow them to go unpunished. The Pope himself could not permit such a thing without giving scandal to the Church.[117]

But he spoke in vain, and the time-honoured practice of the Venetians gave his words the lie.

[117] Albizzi, *Risposta* ..., pp. 195–6, 217–19.

PART III

The Marranos of Iberia and The Converts of Italy

II

The Problem of Marranism

In its dealings with New Christians and Sephardic Jews, the Venetian Inquisition was hedged about by many constraints. Apostates whom it failed to prosecute far outnumbered those whom it actually tried. However, its records are extensive enough to contribute to the history of Marranism a number of strange individual stories of ambiguity and indecision. For its attention was devoted to those on the margin between two faiths, to those who temporized and hesitated, repented and relapsed; to those who embarked on voyages of exploration which took in religions as well as countries new to them. Venice was one of the cities in which the choice was most dramatically presented. For the exile from Spain or Portugal could now see the ancestral religion of Judaism openly practised, though under the degrading conditions of the Ghetto and the badge; and communities of Jews who had never touched Christianity could come face to face with those whose families had compromised or lived as 'idolaters'. And Venice was a place to take ship for the Levant, and thus, it might seem, to commit an irreversible betrayal of Christendom.

The nature of Marranism is a subject of controversy among writers who seek to generalize about the reactions of Jews to the experience of forced conversion and to that of living in strongly conformist countries where open adherence to Judaism was forbidden. Few would dispute that, where conversion was imposed en masse as in Portugal in 1497, and where communities of professing Jews were allowed to live alongside recent converts, as in fifteenth-century Spain, there could be a powerful sense of Jewishness, and much Judaism could be practised under the merest veneer of conformity. One thinks of Solomon-ibn-Verga's remonstrance with a king of Spain:

> It is of no use to Your Majesty to pour holy water on Jews and to
> call them Peter or Paul, while they adhere to their religion like
> 'Aqiba or Tarfon . . . Know, Sire, that Judaism is no doubt one of
> the incurable diseases.[1]

There come to mind, too, graphic accounts of the mass conversion in
Portugal such as that of Isaac-ibn-Faradj, an eyewitness writing some
years after the machinations of King Manoel in 1496–97:

> When the time had passed, and the Jews did not want to change
> their faith of their own free will, they were taken by force in all the
> King's provinces, and were beaten with sticks and straps and car-
> ried to the churches. There they sprinkled water on them and gave
> them Christian names, men and women alike . . .[2]

Sheer ignorance, as distinct from determined resistance, could prevent
first-generation converts from becoming good Christians. Having arrested
about a hundred Portuguese New Christians en route for Antwerp in
1540, the Receiver of Zealand found that, although only two proved to be
obdurate heretics, many understood not a word of the Paternoster and
Ave Maria they had been taught to recite in Latin; and when questioned
about the life of Christ, some knew that he was born in Bethlehem, but
did not know whether that town was in heaven or on earth.[3]

More questionable is the argument that Marranism entailed something
far more lasting than the practice of Judaism by a first generation of
defiant or bewildered converts. Influential Jewish historians have long
believed that it meant the secret transmission, from one generation to the
next, of a simplified version of the Jewish faith – one heavily dependent
upon the Old Testament rather than on the suppressed Talmud or on
rabbinical literature. Members of the families which had maintained the
faith in this way are said to have left Spain and Portugal when the
opportunity arose, and to have returned openly to Judaism, out of religious ardour, in the more liberal states of Italy or in the capital or provinces of the Ottoman Empire. Their journeys, to Constantinople, or
Salonica, or the holy city of Safed in Galilee, were the final manifestation
of a continuous and tenacious loyalty to Judaism.[4]

[1] Quoted in Baron, *A social and religious history* . . . , XIII, pp. 21–2.

[2] See A. Marx, 'The expulsion of the Jews from Spain: two new accounts', in his *Studies in
Jewish history and booklore* (New York, 1944), p. 104.

[3] Goris, *Étude* . . . , pp. 572–4.

[4] See especially C. Roth, 'The religion of the Marranos', *Jewish Quarterly Review*, 22
(1931–32), pp. 1–33; C. Roth, *A History of the Marranos* (Philadelphia, 1932). Cf. Révah, 'La
religion d'Uriel da Costa . . .', pp. 60–75, on the 'impoverished Judaism' of the Marranos in
the early seventeenth century.

But radical historians have offered very different interpretations of Marranism, founded partly upon distrust of the evidence communicated by the Inquisitions of Spain and Portugal, and partly upon the judgments of rabbis. It has been argued that Marranism of the kind just described did not exist in any objective sense. A cult such as Judaism which had once been practised openly and publicly could only wither away if forced underground; and it would surely be impossible to practise as an act of mere hypocrisy a Catholic religion one was compelled for several generations to follow in public. In most West European countries religious belief was determined by the authorities, and not by the 'spontaneous adhesion of souls'.[5] Hence, Marranism existed largely in the heads of the authorities and of those who became their accomplices and collaborators. It was the creation of all-powerful inquisitions and their dangerously elastic procedures; the Inquisitions of Spain and Portugal were tools of an ethnic majority, instruments of a traditional society, devices for the extension of royal power. They were given free rein, it is argued, because of the inability or reluctance of Spanish and Portuguese Old Christians to absorb competition from *conversos* or New Christians. The suggestion that New Christians were secret judaizers was a convenient pretext for attacking them.[6] In support of this thesis, it is certainly possible to find at least one example of the fabrication of evidence by a corrupt inquisitor. For in 1508 Diego Rodriguez Lucero, Inquisitor of Cordova, was found to have faked evidence of a vast conspiracy extending throughout Spain, and intended to undermine Christianity and replace it with the Jewish faith. The Cordovan authorities said he had had some of his prisoners instructed in Jewish prayers and rites, that they might seem to bear accurate witness even against Old Christians falsely accused.[7]

It seems, too, that eminent Jews, including the chief rabbis of Algiers in the fifteenth century, came to believe (however reluctantly) that many of the conversions which took place in Spain were not really forced, and in fact marked a lack of inner strength and self-confidence on the part of Spanish Jewry. Even where conversion was forced, it seemed to lead almost inevitably to assimilation.[8] If anything, the Inquisition became an instrument of God's providence, in as much as it offered the *conversos* a brutal proof that the gentile nations would never accept them, and rather than do so would falsely accuse them of judaizing. 'For although they assimilated among those nations entirely, they will find no peace among

---

[5] A. J. Saraiva, *Inquisição e cristãos-novos* (second edition, Oporto, 1969), p. 45.

[6] See, for example, Rivkin, 'The utilization ...'; Saraiva, *Inquisição ...*, *passim*; B. Netanyahu, *The Marranos of Spain from the late XIVth to the early XVIth century, according to contemporary Hebrew sources* (second edition, New York, 1973).

[7] Lea, *Inquisition of Spain*, I, pp. 190–211.

[8] Netanyahu, *Marranos ...*, pp. 22–54.

them,' wrote Isaac Arama shortly after the establishment of the Inquisition in Spain and its dominions, 'for they, the nations, will always revile and beshame them, plot against them, and accuse them falsely in matters of faith.'[9] Don Isaac Abravanel, who died in exile in Venice in 1508, wrote: 'It is the Sinners of Israel, whose forebears departed from our religion many years ago, against whom the nations level the most vicious libels, and whom they mercilessly burn alive by the hundreds and thousands.'[10] And when Marranos departed from Spain or Portugal, did they do so out of religious zeal and at the first opportunity, or did they really leave because security had been utterly destroyed and because excellent opportunities were opening up for them in the Ottoman Empire?[11] Did they travel with speed and determination to places where they could openly judaize? Or did they go first to Christian countries such as Flanders where they could not do so? If they did, was this an elaborate feint in the wrong direction, designed to disarm suspicion; or was it really an attempt to come to terms once more with a Christian society, and to temporize as long as possible before taking any irrevocable step? When such families declared themselves Jews in Ferrara, Salonica or Constantinople, were they announcing what they had always been at heart, or were they returning at an opportune moment to a faith which had been abandoned?

Seeking middle ground, it can well be argued that crypto-Judaism did exist, but did not survive just as a consequence of the unfailing loyalty of Jews to Judaism. The Inquisition had a part in the survival of secret Judaism, but it was not merely a crude and cynical forger of evidence. By the very questions it asked, by its Edicts of Faith, and by making the public aware of the possibility of secret Judaism, it helped to keep its memory alive.[12] It could also arouse curiosity about Judaism in persons who would not otherwise have thought seriously about it. Estevão de Arês da Fonseca was born in Coimbra in 1598 and confessed to judaizing in Lisbon in 1621, although he was later to admit to the Spanish Inquisition that he had then known nothing about the Jewish faith and had confessed only to save his own life. But the experience inspired him to undertake a tour of the Jewish communities of Europe. He was circumcised in Amsterdam, and his travels took him to' Venice, Livorno and Trapani, and then to the Ottoman Empire. Tiring of the experiment, he eventually chose to return to the Catholic faith in Rouen in 1633.[13]

[9] Ibid., pp. 154–5.

[10] Netanyahu, Don Isaac Abravanel ..., pp. 202–3.

[11] Cf. E. Rivkin, The shaping of Jewish history: a radical new interpretation (New York, 1971), pp. 140–58; cf. Netanyahu, Marranos ..., pp. 216–20.

[12] Révah, 'Les marranes', p. 54; Révah, 'La religion d'Uriel da Costa ...', p. 61.

[13] I. S. Révah, 'Autobiographie d'un marrane. Édition partielle d'un manuscrit de João (Moseh) Pinto Delgado', Revue des études juives, 119 (1961), pp. 81–3.

It may also be that a sense of Jewishness, if not a knowledge of Judaism, was kept alive not only by the Inquisition but also by other social devices, and particularly by the statutes disqualifying persons tainted with Jewish blood from municipal office, from certain guilds and brotherhoods, and from certain religious orders. Such measures drove the *conversos* to become, in a fairly high degree, an endogamous group holding itself apart from the Old Christians, and forming its own associations and clubs.[14] Yet there is equally powerful evidence that Spaniards of Jewish descent harboured a deep-seated loyalty to Spain, or a nostalgia for it, which survived expulsion or emigration. This found expression in the tombstones of Iberian Jews in Venice and Livorno, embellished with the arms of *hidalgos* and bearing inscriptions in Spanish, or in the synagogues of Salonica, called by the names of Castile, Aragon, Portugal, Catalonia, Evora or Lisbon.[15]

Marranos have been seen in at least three ways. They have been portrayed as a people who, though cut off from Judaism, are none the less deeply vowed to it: hence Carl Gebhardt's description of the Marrano as 'a Catholic without faith and a Jew without knowledge, though a Jew by desire'.[16] The late Israel Révah spoke of 'a secret, collective rejection of the Catholic outlook', embodying 'a stubborn desire to return to the Jewish tradition'.[17] But some scholars have portrayed Marranos as persons who would have been entirely happy to accept Catholicism, had they only been allowed to do so. And there is a third possibility, which finds plenty of backing in the polemics of contemporaries: that Marranos were devoted to neither faith; that they would profess either Christianity or Judaism as seemed convenient; that their experience had destroyed belief and made them men without a law by which to live. This mental condition could have been either a cause or a consequence of the rejection they sometimes suffered at the hands, not only of Christians, but also of professing Jews. Towards 1500, Isaac Caro, a rabbi in Portugal, spoke of a suspicion among the Gentiles that 'These people did not convert because they believed in our religion, but because they were afraid that we might kill them. Actually, they observe neither our religion nor theirs.'[18] And

[14] Cf. Baron, *A social and religious history* ..., XIII, pp. 84–91; H. Beinart, 'The *converso* community in fifteenth century Spain', in *The Sephardi heritage: essays on the history and cultural contribution of the Jews of Spain and Portugal*, ed. R. D. Barnett, I (London, 1971), pp. 428–37; H. Beinart, 'The *converso* community in sixteenth and seventeenth century Spain', ibid., pp. 457–8; Caro Baroja, *Los judíos* ..., I, p. 416 ff.

[15] See M. J. Benardete, *Hispanic culture and character of the Sephardic Jews* (New York, 1953), pp. 44, 56. Cf. Braudel, *The Mediterranean* ..., II, p. 809.

[16] C. Gebhardt, *Die Schriften des Uriel da Costa* (Amsterdam, 1922), p. xix.

[17] I. S. Révah, 'L'hérésie marrane dans l'Europe catholique du 15e au 18e siècle', in *Hérésies et sociétés dans l'Europe pré-industrielle: 11e–18e siècles*, ed. J. Le Goff (Paris–The Hague, 1968), p. 328.

[18] Netanyahu, *Marranos* ..., p. 167.

Isaac Abravanel addressed the Marranos, saying: 'you are considered as heretics and Epicureans and disbelievers in both religions – i.e. in the teachings of God and of the gentiles as well.'[19] Some definitions of the word 'Marrano' suggested only insincerity, and did not imply that Marranos held any beliefs at all. In his English dictionary of Italian words, compiled about 1600, John Florio called 'Marrano' 'a nick-name for Spaniards, that is, one descended of Jewes or Infidels and whose Parents were never christened, but for to save their goods will say they are Christians.'[20]

The most helpful approaches to the problem of Marranism are surely those which seek, not to generalize about collective behaviour, not to abandon altogether the attempt to trace some pattern in the history of the Marranos, but rather to identify and describe a range or spectrum of individual experiences. In his vast survey of the Jews of Spain, Julio Caro Baroja attempted to characterize eight types of *converso*. Among *conversos* who became genuine Catholics, he identified one group composed of apologists of the Christian faith who attacked the religion of the Jews; another consisting of persons who denounced crypto-Jews, whether from piety or from economic motives; and a third group containing those who satirized their former co-religionists. In the opposite camp appeared first a group of apologists for the religion of the Jews, second a select body of martyrs who suffered for the Jewish faith, and third a collection of satirists who took as their victims those New Christians who were genuinely loyal to Christianity. Beyond them, however, were two other kinds of person, the most unsettled and perhaps the most intelligent of all – those who became heretics within Christianity, and those who, being aware of conflict between the old law and the new, found a solution in denying both, and in the creation of new philosophies or personal systems of their own.[21]

Venetian evidence makes it possible to build up another, and a rather different, typology, consisting for the most part of studies in ambiguity and vacillation. This will not of course serve as an accurate reflection of the whole range of Marranism, because the evidence is itself naturally limited by the constraints on the institution producing it – for the Inquisition could only come to grips with the ambivalent, and not with those who were sure of themselves. But it should help to characterize the types of person who succeeded in uniting churchmen and Venetian patricians in common disapproval of their thoughts and deeds.

It is important, before looking at the biographies of individuals, to bear

[19] Ibid., pp. 193–4.
[20] In *Queen Anne's New World of Words* (London, 1611; facsimile edition, Menston, 1968), p. 300; quoted in Farinelli, *Marrano* ..., p. 63.
[21] Caro Baroja, *Los judíos* ..., I, pp. 293–5.

in mind that in the remarks of Venetian Christians and of Jews resident in
Venice, it is possible to find support for several of the opinions about
Marranism described above: certainly for the belief that crypto-Judaism
objectively existed, but also for the theory that it was perpetuated by
Spanish attitudes and policies rather than by its own tenacity, and again
for the suspicion that Marranos were not true Jews but rather dwellers in
a no man's land between two faiths.

Certain patricians who had actually been in Spain or Portugal felt little
doubt of the reality of crypto-Judaism. In this their opinions were probably the result of Spanish propaganda rather than of personal observa-
tion, but they could be critical of Spanish policies, both on the grounds
that they were un-Christian and on the grounds that they were inexpedi-
ent. They were certainly capable of implying that the problem of persistent secret Judaism was one of Spain's own making. Matteo Priuli served
with the papal nuncio in Portugal after 1542. Nearly thirty years later,
now enthroned as Bishop of Vicenza, he said of two prominent New
Christian merchants who had come to Venice in the late 1540s that

> they were living in this city, and pretending to live as Christians,
> although you might be certain that within themselves they were
> reverting to the Jewish faith. And many other such New Christians
> were doing the same thing in Venice . . .[22]

Leonardo Donà held similar opinions, but in the report he submitted on
returning from his embassy to Spain in 1573 he blamed the Spaniards for
their refusal to accept baptized Jews as anything other than Jews – a
policy which, though he did not say so outright, contrasted strongly with
the eagerness of Italian evangelists to absorb limited numbers of Jews into
Christianity. Describing the exclusive attitudes of the Hieronymite and
Dominican orders and their insistence on 'purity of blood', he remarked:

> It may well seem that Christian charity ought not to observe this
> distinction of persons, which has no meaning in the sight of God, for
> St Paul in his Epistle to the Romans gives equal status and honour
> to the Jew, the Gentile and the Greek who receive the law and turn
> Christian. But the generals of the orders say that their rules must be
> upheld for the sake of peace and quiet in the monasteries.

Indeed, the 'purity of blood' regulations served to keep alive 'old
memories of Judaism (*vecchie giudaizzanti memorie*) even in those who would
otherwise readily abandon them'. Furthermore, they threatened to create

---

[22] S.U., b. 36, proc. Righetto, deposition of 26 April 1571.

potential rebels, among people not deeply involved in society and the state, who saw themselves as outcasts.[23] Thirty-five years later, as Doge of Venice, Donà had occasion to lecture the papal nuncio on the true nature of Marranism; he seemed then to be stretching the term to comprise all forms of religious dissimulation in Spain, including that of the Moriscos. It was now important to emphasize, in order to justify Venetian policies towards former Marranos, that they were not and never had been anything other than Jews.

> At home and within themselves [he said] they live as Jews. All have a name, the men and the women too, either Turkish or Jewish, by which they are called at home; but outside their houses they have a Christian name. And if you ask one of the children, 'What is your name?' he will answer, 'At home they call me Abraham, but in the street Francesco.'[24]

Crypto-Judaism was sometimes thought real and potent enough to have penetrated the whole of Spanish society and to have created a kind of hollowness within its religious culture, infusing it with a spirit of hypocrisy. This thesis appears in the report of Paolo Tiepolo in 1563 and was several times repeated – that the Spaniards were a devout and even extravagantly pious people, but they seemed to treat religion as a drama which could at any moment deteriorate into comedy and farce, for even their festivals were like carnivals. Since many Spaniards were descended from Moors and Jews, it was probable that their hearts and souls were never in harmony with outward appearances.[25] It was a Venetian elaboration on the Italian theme of the judaizing inclinations of all Spaniards, and was expounded more strikingly in 1654 by a cheerfully malicious Spanish Jew who harangued a scandalized friar in the Venetian Ghetto. He told him with gusto that as the sacraments were in the hands of Jewish priests in Spain, the Church there was deeply penetrated by secret Judaism and many baptisms were invalid. Such were the 'ills and disorders' which came of 'the desire to make Christians by force and deprive us of our freedom of conscience'.[26]

[23] Albèri, I/vi, pp. 403–5; cf. Baron, *A social and religious history* ..., XIII, pp. 87–8.
[24] C.E.R., reg. 16, fol. 50v., 4 July 1608.
[25] Albèri, I/v, pp. 18–19; cf. also pp. 82–3 (Giovanni Soranzo, 1565) and I/vi, p. 410 (Leonardo Donà, 1573); likewise Barozzi–Berchet, I/i, pp. 76, 161 (Francesco Soranzo, 1602).
[26] S.U., b. 107, test. Fra Giovanni Battista Palliani, 20 April 1654, among the papers marked 'Valenza, Da Costa'. For the notion in the late fifteenth century of a corrupted body of *converso* priests, committing irregularities in the consecration of the Host and lending themselves to doctrinal error, see A. A. Sicroff, 'Clandestine Judaism in the Hieronymite monastery of Nuestra Señora de Guadalupe', in *Studies in honor of M. J. Benardete (Essays in Hispanic and Sephardic culture)*, ed. I. A. Langnas and B. Sholod (New York, 1965), p. 101 ff.

The Jews of Venice themselves seemed uncertain whether or not to accept Marranos or former Marranos as Jews. There is a little evidence which suggests that they applauded the expulsion order of 1550, for as the Estense agent remarked: 'The Jews of this city have done very well out of saying that these Marranos are malevolent and ill-favoured men.' At some point in the episode the Venetians were reminded that 'the Marranos are worse than Jews because they are neither Christians nor Jews.'[27] As we have seen, there was marked hostility on the part of the Germanic Jews towards the beneficiaries of the 1589 charter, and it was perhaps based on resentments and fears which predated the Sephardic Jews' exemption from contributing to the loan banks.[28] In a sense, these situations reversed that in Spain in the late fifteenth century, when (according to one pungent theory) the *conversos* in the city patriciates of Castile had borne a heavy responsibility for the expulsion of the professing Jews.[29] Towards 1580, delators and witnesses before the Inquisition stressed the Marranos' ignorance of the sacred language and their inability to use it either in public services or in domestic rituals – though Miguel Vaz, one suspected Marrano living outside the Ghetto, was said to be an exception to the rule.[30] 'Portuguese of this type,' said the neophyte Giovanni Giacomo, 'are neither Christians nor Jews nor Turks nor Moors . . . and when they go to synagogue they carry a book of offices in the Christian style in the Portuguese tongue. They are hated by the other Jews because they have nothing in common with Jews apart from the turban.'[31] Similar testimony was to recur at intervals over the next fifty years.[32] Chaim Saruc, consul of the Levantine nation, summoned as a witness in the case of Gaspar Ribeiro, did not doubt the ambivalent nature of Marranism: 'I took Gaspar for a Marrano by public reputation, and I have heard tell that he is a Marrano, and a Marrano, as I said, is one who steers by two rudders: that is, he is neither Christian nor Jew.'[33]

Gaspar Ribeiro had temporized and prevaricated; not all New Christians did so, and the attitude of Old Jews to those who returned

[27] Kaufmann, 'Contribution . . .', pp. 303–4.

[28] See above, pp. 192–3.

[29] See S. H. Haliczer, 'The Castilian urban patriciate and the Jewish expulsions of 1480–92', *American Historical Review*, 78 (1973), pp. 35–58; cf. Netanyahu, *Don Isaac Abravanel* . . ., p. 41 ff., for the attitudes of Spanish burghers to professing Jews, and Netanyahu, *Marranos* . . ., pp. 29–30, for the appearance of a group of converts who were actively turning against the professing Jews.

[30] S.U., b. 44, proc. 'Negromanti', den. Antonio Saldanha and Estevão Nogueira, 11, 20 Jan. 1579.

[31] S.U., b. 46, 23 April 1580.

[32] As in Roth, 'The strange case . . .', pp. 230–1, and S.U., b. 92, proc. Feliciana Diaz, test. Feliciana Diaz, 12 April 1635.

[33] S.U., b. 45, proc. Gaspar Ribeiro, 3 Sept. 1580.

openly to the Ghetto was not always as contemptuous as that described by Giovanni Giacomo. Moses Cardiel, Levantine Jew, testified that 'those who have been Christians and then become Jews are held by us to be Jews.'[34] Just as some Italian states inclined to more open acceptance of former Marranos at the turn of the sixteenth century, with the issue of the Venetian charter and the *Livornina*, even so the established Jewish communities seem to have made a more vigorous effort to re-educate Marranos in Jewish law and practice, and to have shown a much more accommodating attitude towards their ignorance of Hebrew.[35] Samuel Aboab, who moved from Verona to become Rabbi of the Ponentine community in Venice in 1650, was especially eager for the absorption of Marranos into the Jewish community. He declared that 'there should be in each and every city of Israel a special brotherhood for this purpose.'[36] Never, of course, had the rejection of Marranos by many professing Jews necessarily meant that the Marranos themselves rejected the Jewish faith. It can only be suggested that the suspicion they encountered both on the Christian and on the Jewish side manoeuvred some of them into a condition of religious neutrality, from which conviction, passion and a sense of belonging had entirely vanished.

[34] Ibid., 25 Aug. 1580.
[35] See Y. H. Yerushalmi, *The re-education of the Marranos in the seventeenth century* (Cincinnati, Ohio, 1980), pp. 8–12.
[36] Yerushalmi, *From Spanish court . . .*, p. 198.

12

The Marrano as Catholic
and as Jew

This chapter will discuss ten cases of Marranism taken from the files of
the Venetian Inquisition. Five concern people who were arrested and
imprisoned either by the Inquisition or by lay authorities on charges of
apostasy or dissimulation. Four are the outcome of 'spontaneous' confessions on the part of young people aged between eighteen and twenty-four,
who presented themselves to the Holy Office and sought reconciliation
with the Church. One was described by a young woman who, from the
guesthouse of the conservatory for imperilled virgins on the Giudecca,
denounced her father and stepmother for judaizing. For most of them,
Venice was only one stage on their travels, the place where they chose or
were forced to tell of their hesitations and deceits. The next chapter will
be devoted to a drama played out in Venice itself between 1570 and 1580
– to the troubled history of the Ribeiros of Santa Maria Formosa.

Apart from the story of the Ribeiros, accounts of Marranism depend
very heavily on autobiographical statements rather than on witness testimony; several of these, however, were volunteered, and they vary sufficiently to have a ring of truth. They suggest that New Christians of
Portuguese extraction – the kind who passed through Venice and got into
Inquisition records – should, if they are to be classified at all and not
merely treated as a series of individual cases, be placed in at least four
categories. And they suggest that Marranism was commonly associated
with two events or processes which are recurrent motifs in many personal
histories. One was a long, restless journey: it was not always a determined
pilgrimage to the Ottoman lands, but could well be a voyage in search of
oneself, of one's true religious identity, and of some way of achieving
security for persons and goods within a Christian or an Islamic society.
The other was a discovery made in adolescence – it might be that the

blood and religious allegiance of one's family were Jewish and not Christian; or it might be that one's parents, now Jews in Ferrara or Salonica, had once lived in a very different style in Portugal or Spain. Sometimes the news of a person's Jewishness was accepted in a way which marked the beginning of a long, sober career of dissimulation, which could only be resolved by emigration to some country where he could openly judaize. But the adolescent crisis could also provoke a rebellion which took the form of truancy, of suddenly breaking with one's family and embarking on a personal adventure, as though to try the experiment of retracing one's parents' steps and reversing their decision. Young men might do this by returning to Spain and Portugal to live for a time as Christians and to do things which Jews could not do, by fighting in wars or adorning court society. Or they might go on furtive pilgrimages to discover Judaism and to live for a time in the Jewish communities of northern Europe. For obvious reasons, this kind of roving rebellion was restricted to boys and youths. Young women, especially those who had been separated from their parents in childhood and brought up on strictly Catholic lines, sometimes reacted with sheer horror to the news of their parents' secret Judaism, or rebelled against the marriage plans hatched by Jewish kin. Lacking the opportunities open to males, they could escape only by surrendering to the Church.

These ten people range from those who professed to be convinced Jews to those who claimed to be firm Catholics, with at least two kinds of inconstant people in between. Tristão da Costa and Filipe de Nis were heads of households, mature men verging upon old age; never doubting that they were Jews, they were reluctant to court martyrdom, and seemed always inclined to balance the claims of their property and fortune against those of their faith. Righetto, 'Giovanni Pizara', João Batista of Lisbon and Fernão de Martin de Almeida Pereira all were, or once had been, adolescent rebels experimenting with the religion, the country and the style of life their parents had abandoned. In Francisco Olivier and 'Franciscus Hispanus' we can perhaps see a rather different character. Less wilful or headstrong, they may if anything incline to be Christians; but they belong to families part Christian and part Jewish and living in two or more Italian cities, and in times of misfortune they fall back on the Jewish relatives who happen to be closest to hand. Eminently suggestible, they fall in with their plans so long as they remain in immediate contact with them, but may reverse their decisions when they are not. Maria Lopes and Feliciana Diaz found themselves in the power of relatives who were secret or professing Jews, and who supposedly manoeuvred them into false positions in which they too had to dissemble, despite repugnance for Judaism and a desire for asylum with the Church.

The classic Marrano journey was from Lisbon to Flanders, with a spell in Antwerp or Cologne or both, followed by an overland trip southwards to the Adriatic cities of Venice and Ferrara, and then by a crossing to the Ottoman Empire, either into the Balkans or directly to Constantinople. The journey might well end in Salonica, or – for the pious – in the holy city of Safed. Stages in the journey sometimes marked steps in the spiritual progress of the traveller, or increasingly open and irreversible avowals of Judaism. Jewish names might be taken in Ferrara or Venice, though Christian names were still used for the purpose of trading with the Habsburg lands; the agonizing ritual of circumcision would entitle a man to put on the prayer shawl and the phylacteries.[1] Often the journey was a hesitant one, and there were long intervals between its stages, as though the travellers still hoped to settle in the Christian world and come to terms with it. And the physical journey could be reversed by the children of New Christian emigrants leaving Italy or Turkey and returning to Portugal or Spain. So could the spiritual. 'Franciscus Hispanus' converted in Italy back from Judaism to Christianity, and Filipe de Nis, to demonstrate his repentance, recalled his wife and maid from the Levant to reconcile them with the Church.

Tristão da Costa, otherwise Abraham Habibi, and Filipe de Nis, otherwise Solomon Marcos, most closely resembled John Florio's portrait of the Marrano. Both were men of some property, heads of households responsible for moving their families, compromising a shade prosaically between the claims of the faith and those of their goods. But they represented different generations. Tristão da Costa, born about 1497, presented himself as one who had as a child been caught up immediately in the brutalities of enforced mass baptism. He was a Jew, though not an especially devout one; perhaps it had never occurred to him to be anything else. Filipe de Nis, born about 1530, eventually told the Inquisition that he had not always known about his Judaism but had discovered it by degrees from his elders.

Tristão's story, told in Venice in 1555, was simply that he had always lived privately as a Jew, and had conformed to Christianity only out of expediency or fear. His father and brothers told him that he was snatched from the breast and then baptized. He grew up dissembling, during the long grace period granted by the King of Portugal, in which there would be no inquiry into the private religious practices of New Christians. After several years of arts and law at the University of Salamanca, he returned to his native town of Viana do Castelo in northern Portugal and married Francisca Pereira, who was likewise of Jewish race. His father had owned substantial assets in the form of land and houses, there was an inheritance

[1] Cf. Yerushalmi, *The re-education* ..., pp. 3–5; Pullan, ' "A ship ..." ', p. 47, n. 87.

to claim, and these considerations hindered departure even at such times as it was legally allowed. He was asked pointedly in Venice: 'What do you value more highly, the faith or your goods?' and prosaically answered: 'The faith, of course; but after the faith I want my goods, in order to have the means to live.' His method of keeping faith in both Portugal and Spain was to avoid as far as possible all contacts with the Christian sacraments, although he married according to the Christian rite, and had his children baptized in fear. Their birth roughly coincided with the introduction of a new and terrible rigour under John III of Portugal – 'Had I not had him [the eldest son] baptized, they would have had me burned.'

About 1543–44, the family left for the Low Countries, and soon afterwards headed south for Ferrara. Even in that city, fear of the introduction of the Inquisition was powerful enough to make Tristão da Costa, still living under a black hat, draw back from the irrevocable step of having his three sons circumcised. He then crossed the path of Brianda de Luna, who was embarking on interminable litigation with her sister Beatrix over the Mendes fortune, and he journeyed to Venice to become her agent. The safe-conduct granted by the Council of Ten seemed reassuring, and he went to Venice believing it 'a free city, with no inquisition' – none, at least, for him. Meanwhile, the family split up and the mother took the children to Salonica: it was there that she had their three sons, Manoel, Duarte and Francisco, renamed Isaac, Jacob and Benjamin, and she too was responsible for the decision to have them circumcised. But they then returned to the Adriatic, and two of the children were with Tristão in Brianda's household at the time of his arrest in 1555. The quarrel between the sisters had brought him to Venice, and it also proved to be his undoing, through the interfactional denunciations which it spawned. He admitted living in Venice for at least eight years as a Jew, disguising himself as a Christian for the purpose of conducting business. But, by his own account, living as a Jew did not involve the performance of Jewish ceremonies or the recitation of Jewish prayers; it really meant eating different foods from the rest of Brianda's supposedly Christian household, though Tristão often did so at the same table. If his statement is true, he was living in Venice in a condition which in fact came close to religious neutrality, seeking the society of New Christians, observing dietary laws but carrying out no formal acts of worship. Though it saved him from punishment, the safe-conduct allowed his deportation.[2] He was a Jew, but one who had clung to Europe, balancing loyalty to his faith against the need to make a living, and keeping up, even in Italy, his dual identity on the margins of the Christian and the Jewish worlds.

---

[2] I.Z., pp. 251–63.

Much the same odyssey, from Portugal to Flanders to Venice, was travelled by the family called Denis or de Nis, some of whom in their Venetian sojourn used the name of Filippi. About 1580, Maria, daughter of Diogo Lopes of Antwerp, went to Cologne on her father's instructions to join one Dr de Nis and his family for the journey to Venice. He was probably Tomé de Nis, who had migrated from Tangier to Antwerp, and had once been physician to Don Antonio of Portugal. To the girl's horror they lived as Jews on the journey, for they mocked at Christ, kept the sabbath, and avoided eating the innkeeper's food. Stopping at inns, they would go out on the balcony to pray in the Jewish manner; they would eat only kosher-killed poultry, and when eating meat would avoid the sciatic nerve; and they would change their clothing on Saturdays.[3] Arrived in Venice, however, Dr de Nis seems to have continued to live outwardly as a Christian, and to have died there some time between 1582 and 1585.[4] He had two brothers, known in Judaism as Isaac and as Solomon Marcos. Isaac passed rapidly through Venice en route for the Levant, but his son Jacob stayed behind and joined the household of his uncle, the third brother,[5] who kept up the tradition of living outside the Ghetto. Under the guidance of Solomon Marcos, the household behaved with extraordinary indiscretion, leasing a large house near but outside the Ghetto from the nobleman Francesco di Leonardo Contarini for the substantial rent of 130 ducats per annum.[6] Ill-concealed Jewish practices got most of the family arrested by the Inquisition at crack of dawn on 12 October 1585. The household then consisted of Solomon Marcos himself, of his wife Abigail and their two children Abigail and Anna, of Solomon's nephew Jacob, son of Isaac, of Francisco Dies, a young Spanish servant, and of the two maids Luna Maura and Speranza.

Realizing their error, members of the family none the less rallied and tried to fend off the Inquisition by denying their own baptism. Their case was that they were and had always been Jews. Solomon Marcos at first admitted only the civil offence of posing as a Christian for economic reasons, optimistically proposing that it was punishable only by a fine:

We called ourselves the Filippi because we wore the black hat and wanted to assemble our fortune, so that in Portugal and other places where I have assets they would not realize that I was a Jew.[7]

[3] S.U., b. 49, proc. Diogo Lopes and Catterina Mendes, 27 March 1582; b. 54, proc. Filippi, test. Filipe de Nis, 14 June 1586.

[4] S.U., b. 54, proc. Filippi, test. Gioseffo the tailor, 28 Sept. 1585.

[5] Ibid., test. Jacob, son of Isaac, and Filipe de Nis, 17 Oct. 1585.

[6] Ibid., tenancy agreement dated 22 Nov. 1584. For a description of the kind of middle-class housing for which one paid rents of 60–76 ducats per annum, in 1581, see P. Pavanini, 'Abitazioni popolari e borghesi nella Venezia Cinquecentesca', forthcoming in *Studi Veneziani*.

[7] S.U., b. 54, proc. Filippi, 12 Oct. 1585.

But when he and his household had failed with these tactics to convince their judges, Solomon Marcos finally determined to make a formal confession and offer an alternative autobiography. His story was now that he was born Filipe de Nis in Oporto about 1530, the son of a royal physician, baptized there as a child, lived in Lisbon from about 1537 to 1550, and thereafter spent most of his time as a trader on the island of São Tomé in the Gulf of Guinea, until, nearing the age of forty, he returned to Europe. He married Filipa Furtado in Lisbon about 1568–70, and then travelled to the north, where he moved between a base at Antwerp (ca. 1570–78) and another at Cologne for the next five years. From 1583 he was in Venice.[8]

His story suggested three phases in his conversion. When he was twelve or thirteen one of his brothers – probably the future Isaac – had approached him with a companion in Salamanca and told him

> that one must worship only one God in heaven; and they taught me, to put it plainly, to keep the sabbath and to fast all that day until the night came.[9]

He may not have followed these beliefs and practices continuously, but the secret interview in Salamanca probably gave him a lasting impression of his own Jewishness. He was cajoled into a double devotional life in Antwerp by Gaspar and Diogo Fernandes:

> They made me equivocate [*me prevaricavano el sentimento*] for all that I continued to go to Mass, and so did my wife.

In Antwerp and Cologne they both went to Mass and also to confession and Communion three or four times a year; unlike Tristão da Costa they did not evade the sacraments. Total abandonment of Christianity came only in Venice itself, at the instance of the physician Tomé de Nis, who inspired Filipe 'to leave the Christian faith with all my heart, causing me to eat meat from the Ghetto and sending me Jews to kill my chickens'. It was in Venice, too, that – falling sick and perhaps wishing to die as a Jew – he had himself circumcised. And it now appeared that the servant girl Luna was not, as he had said at first, a Jewess by birth. He now admitted to having bought her as a slave on São Tomé, 'where they live by the Christian faith', and to having had her baptized on that island.[10]

The game between the Filippi and the authorities had now been played to a finish. Filipe's confession was corroborated by no one outside his own

[8] Ibid., 14 June 1586.
[9] Ibid., 29 July 1586.
[10] Ibid., 14 June 1586.

family, and it may conceivably be no more deserving of trust than the original tale which he discarded. On deciding that surrender was the best course, he could have provided an over-elaborate account of his past, telling the tribunal at least as much as it wanted to hear, so that no one could charge him with incomplete confession. But there is no room for doubt that the family actually dissimulated to the extent of practising Judaism outside the Ghetto; their offence was well attested by Venetian witnesses, not Portuguese informers, and the Filippi never tried to deny it. There was the embarrassing testimony of a circumcision acquired in adult life. And there were subtleties, such as the three-stage process of conversion, which suggest that Filipe de Nis was something more than a liar drawing on a repertoire of standard fictions.

Unlike certain Marrano families, the de Nis seemed reasonably united, though they were never in total harmony. Travelling south from Flanders, Dr de Nis and his wife Isabella quarrelled over her desire to return to Portugal and live as a Christian with her brothers, though at other times, her mood changing, she seemed content to accompany the expedition.[11] Jacob had hesitated once at the moment of decision in Venice; his father Isaac had gone on to Turkey alone, only to die of grief on hearing that his brother Filipe was living outside the Ghetto.[12] It is possible that some of the de Nis intended to live as dissemblers in Venice, rather than to migrate and live openly as Jews in the Levant: though clearly the resolute Isaac did not intend to temporize in this way.

Enriques Nuñes, otherwise 'Abraham called Righetto' or 'Righetto Marrano', came of a very similar background and insisted just as forcibly on his identity as a Jew, likewise claiming that it ought to put him beyond the Inquisition's grasp.[13] But his talents lay in squandering a fortune, not in preserving and transferring it, and his tastes attracted him powerfully back to the Christian and courtly society from which his father and uncle had removed themselves – so often that one asks how sure he was of his own Jewishness, at least at such times as he had the means to live as someone socially exalted. He seems to introduce another new element into the pattern of Marranism – that of adolescent rebellion, of the sudden break away from parental authority, expressed in the dangerous adventure. Most likely his real place of birth was Lisbon, at some time between 1530 and 1537. His family, like that of Tristão da Costa, had begun its journey between 1543 and 1545, and had likewise travelled by way of

[11] S.U., b. 49, proc. Diogo Lopes and Catterina Mendes, test. Maria Lopes, 27 March 1582.

[12] S.U., b. 54, test. Jacob, son of Isaac, 17 Oct. 1585.

[13] What follows is a rewritten version of the account of Righetto's life in Pullan, ' "A ship ..." ', p. 40 ff.

Flanders. His father and uncle, New Christian merchants of substantial fortune, were driven out not only by the introduction of the Inquisition but also by the arbitrary actions of the monarchy. Righetto's father, Nuñes Enriques, was disastrously entangled in the affairs of Don Miguel da Silva, Bishop of Viseu and sometime secretary to King John III of Portugal. The King sought to ostracize the bishop and to extend his disgrace to anyone who had corresponded with him after his flight from Portugal to Italy, where he had accepted a cardinal's hat in defiance of the King's wishes. Nuñes was clapped in gaol and heavily fined, and on his release he determined to leave the country. From Flanders the family turned southwards towards Venice and Ferrara, and some of its members eventually crossed the water to Salonica. They probably had no clear and irrevocable plan for abandoning Europe, but hoped, in each of the places they settled, to come to terms with the Christian environment and achieve security unattainable in Portugal. Neither in Flanders nor in Venice, however, did they realize that hope, for Righetto's uncle was fined and imprisoned as a judaizer in Flanders, and the decree expelling Marranos from Venice in 1550 was not reassuring.

Migration beyond Ferrara, however, was slow, hesitant, and a matter for individual rather than collective family action. The family's style was aristocratic, given to conspicuous, indeed futile, consumption. Righetto and his elder brother Hieronimo preferred to waste money in the West rather than make elaborate arrangements to collect and export their cash and credits to Constantinople. It was only in the 1560s that the children of Nuñes Enriques began to arrive in Salonica, and his widow Violante, known as 'La Marchesa' while she lived in Ferrara, made the move only in 1568, when she was almost eighty. The decision to migrate may have been a consequence of poverty, which reduced the temptation to remain in the West in the hope of reinstatement. And the family did not obviously return to the Jewish faith at the earliest possible moment. When Righetto's elder brother made his will in Ferrara in 1552, he was still using his Christian name of Hieronimo rather than his Jewish name of Senior, and he made bequests to his sisters in Christian names also. As though with calculated ambiguity, his will expressed the desire that his body be buried in the place chosen by his mother, and that she set above the grave a silver lamp to the value of 250 gold ducats. Inheritances could not pass from Christian to Jew, and Righetto must have presented himself as a Christian in order to benefit by the will.

Righetto's rebellion against paternal authority occurred when he was perhaps nineteen or twenty, and was closely connected with his passion for courts and good company. His story was that from Ferrara he went to Mantua to see the festivals, and was reproved and beaten by his father; taking umbrage, he filched 2,000 crowns from the family coffers and began to pursue something still more splendid. He went to follow the court of Prince Philip from Italy to Augsburg and thence to Flanders and Spain, where he left the prince's suite at Valladolid in 1551 and went on to Lisbon by himself. It was the first of three expeditions back to Iberia. Apart from frivolity and a taste for a noble ambience, two other motives for his travels were mentioned by witnesses: to exact debts, and to encourage New Christians to leave for the lands of liberty. Most in evidence, however, was his growing addiction to gambling. On returning from his first adventure, about 1552, Righetto became administrator of the family patrimony, but he was no wise steward, and acquired a new notoriety in an Italian court which offered intimacy with the Spanish aristocracy. Here he won fame as the gambler who had lost 70,000 ducats at a single session in the salons of Cosimo de' Medici, Duke of Florence. His accumulated forfeits in 'this accursed gaming' were estimated at 170,000 ducats. Don Diego Ortiz de Vera, formerly a servant of the Duchess Eleonora, said of Righetto that

> He went to church with Don Luis de Toledo, my lady's brother, and with other Spanish Christians, and he went to Mass and knelt at the Mass with the rest of them. And all the servants of this Enriques were Christians, and he lived in the manner of a Christian, eating pork and other foods forbidden to Jews. And all his discourse was with Christians, and he spurned the society of Jews. And since he did not keep his own house he lodged in the households of Spanish Christian merchants and gentry, for it was his habit to come and go, and he would not stay. His bearing, style and habits were in all outward things those of a Christian, and he and his serving-men bore arms . . . and he slept and had to do with Christian women, who would never have taken him had they thought him a Jew.

Financial embarrassment after these costly adventures proved to be no obstacle to other visits to Spain and Portugal, though at least one was clouded by dejection – 'I went to Spain to die and not to live, for I had not the means to live, and I wanted to go to the Indies.'

Perhaps the tug-of-war in Righetto between his sense of Jewishness and his Hispanicity, between the merchant's heir and the wastrel gentleman, became so strenuous that he began to regard the Catholic and Jewish faiths as mere protective skins, to be donned and discarded at convenience. Literally he wore two hats; a gentleman's servant told at Lisbon of Righetto walking in the streets of Venice – 'when he saw Senators and persons of weight and dignity he put a yellow hat upon his head, and when he had passed them he took it off and put it under his arm, and placed on his head another hat or cap which was black. . . .' Throughout his trial, however, he insisted that he was a Jew. It is tempting to regard this as just a tactic, but only fair to point out that Jews in Venice and Ferrara did not reject him, and that he was kept alive in prison partly by their charity. His defence arguments were more consistent than those of the Filippi, and his encounter with the Inquisition ended in escape in August 1573.

Some similar ingredients can be discerned in the story of 'Giovanni Pizara', who came from his lodging in the house of converts to describe his career to the Inquisition in 1580. Much less is known about his antecedents. But he too was reversing his parents' decision to be Jews; he too was taking up pursuits – with him it was soldiering – which no professing Jew could have contemplated. Unlike Righetto, he allowed himself to be won over, at least for a time, to the Catholic faith. He was born in Salonica as Isaac, son of Moses Vasilai, and his wife Mazalta. Travelling to Portugal by way of Venice and Genoa, he had naturally to put on Christian dress, and he confessed to the friars and went to Mass, but never took Communion. Indiscretion in a barber's shop got him into trouble with the Inquisition in Portugal. An Indian came in, the barber asked if he had confessed and taken Communion, they discussed the Eucharist, and the barber said piously that the true God was in the sacrament. Rashly the traveller said he understood that God was in no place but in heaven. Soon afterwards he was arrested in Tomar, to the northeast of Lisbon, but managed somehow to talk his way out of trouble by saying that he had been baptized before emigrating from Portugal, and had now returned in the hope of being instructed in the Christian faith. It could fairly have been said that he had discovered this aim only after being detected, but he was sent for instruction to a monastery, and then went to fight against the Moors with Don Antonio or King Sebastian. For several months, until ransomed, he was a prisoner of war. To serve as a soldier was one way of being conspicuously un-Jewish, since arms were denied to Jews, and the soldier's profession was a dramatically new experience. To fight in a holy war was a means of authenticating conversion and claiming high standing among Christians. Portuguese Jews who had fallen under suspicion sometimes tried to disarm it by insisting on their roles in the royal service, military or civilian.[14]

Eventually, 'Giovanni Pizara' returned to Italy, and his doubts and hesitations began again, since he contemplated taking ship – presumably for the Levant. He spent more than a year in Soncino in the state of Milan. The matter of his baptism had still to be cleared up – he was a

[14] See above, p. 99, and below, p. 231.

crusading veteran, but had never been correctly admitted to the Church
– and he eventually made for Venice and sought an audience with the
Patriarch, who sent him to the house of converts. At this point his story
peters out; he was certainly questioned on his life history by the Holy
Office, but the record does not appear to survive.[15]

The autobiography of João Batista of Lisbon was more or less volunteered
to the Inquisition in 1582–83; he had probably been under considerable
pressure during his time in the house of converts. He depicted himself as
very much the adolescent rebel struggling in the face of his relatives to
return to Christianity but constantly frustrated by their power over him.
Remarkably, he seems to have made the classic journey twice, and to
have been at least briefly a convert to Islam. He was born about 1504 to
Francisco Rodrigues and Filipa Carlos, both 'Christians of the race of
Jews'. As a child his parents left Portugal and took him to Flanders,
thence to Ferrara (where he was circumcised) and finally to Salonica. His
name was changed to Abraham, son of David. He was only thirteen when
he made his first break, though his bald statement to the Holy Office
gives no clue to his motives:

Being inspired by the Holy Spirit, I departed and went to Rome,
where through the actions of certain Capuchin friars I was taken to
the Catecumeni, where I stayed for forty days. Having instructed
me in the faith, they baptized me and made me renounce the
Devil. . . .

After baptism the Bishop of the Algarve took him into service and with
questionable wisdom returned him to Portugal. One likely plan was to
discover whether he had been baptized before his parents' departure and
to perform a special ceremony if he had. But his Christian mentors exposed him to the influences which had acted upon his parents, and a
relative set in motion the process of migration all over again, sending him
by the same route and exposing him to withering reproach by other
kinsmen. At last he was sent out of Venice to Tripolis in Syria on board
the *Rosa Antica*, and thence to Safed to join another relative, Joseph
Cohen.
   João Batista was in Safed for about four years, and his stay was interrupted briefly and dramatically by a visit to Constantinople, in the course
of which he was seized by the Turkish police and forced, till ransomed by
his father, to wear the turban. By one reckoning, this was the fourth
change of religion, or at least of religious uniform, in a young life. He

[15] S.U., b. 46, proc. 'Giovanni Pizara', 6 April 1580.

broke away again from his family by saying that he wanted to visit his rich aunt in Venice. Arrived there, he went to the house of converts, and after a stormy spell in it was eventually reconciled to the Church on 8 February 1583.[16] Like most spontaneous confessions, his story was not corroborated, for Venice was simply the place where he chose to confess, and provided no evidence of its own. But his story, because it contained so much superfluous detail and was unnecessarily self-incriminating, deserves to be taken seriously; it exposed him to an unusually severe penance. He may have been engaged in a genuine struggle – more effective with increasing maturity – to assert against his relatives the right to choose his own life. In the free board and lodging offered by the houses of converts in Rome and Venice, he found an alternative to the charity of the Jews.

It was quite possible, in much the same spirit, for young men born Christians to experiment with Judaism, departing with equal abruptness from a Christian city. Fernão de Martin de Almeida Pereira was fifteen when he began his curious pilgrimage in 1619. He claimed to have been born in Lisbon of one of the noblest families in Portugal, and he never actually admitted Jewish descent, although it is difficult to explain his conduct and the Jews' reaction to him in other terms. In Spain he had been a devout Catholic and had taught Christian doctrine as a work of charity. There he was led astray by two fellow students of Jewish race. They told him they wanted to see Rome and look for relics, and he decided, impulsively, to go too without a word to his parents. His companions left him in Genoa, choosing, they said, to travel to Turkey. He took another ship to Flanders, and from Flanders made his way to the free city of Hamburg.

> And I asked if there were Spaniards and Portuguese there and was told where they lived, and I went, and found them to be Portuguese and German Jews. I stayed with them, saying I had thoughts of returning to Spain. But they persuaded me not to go, and preached at me that I must become a Jew, and so I did indeed become one, and stayed with them for two and a half years.

The rabbis of the synagogue in Hamburg had, at least to outward appearances, converted him; he was washed in running water and then circumcised, told that he must deny the faith of Christians and in future hold that of the Jews. Employing the kind of defence commonly used by people who had been captured by Muslims and forced or tempted into apostasy, he asserted that he had never denied the Catholic faith in his heart. He had yielded outwardly to Judaism only because

---

[16] S.U., b. 32, proc. 'Giovanni Battista' of Lisbon, 18 Dec. 1582 to 8 Feb. 1583.

there are no Catholics in the city of Hamburg, and because I did not have the means to return to a Catholic country, and because I had to live.

Eventually he decided to come south and see Venice, and there, still comporting himself as a Jew, he stayed in the hostelry of the 'German brotherhood' in the Ghetto. At last he resolved to reconcile himself with the Church, and the Holy Office received him charitably. He was allowed to abjure, and they imposed upon him annual Communion and confession for three years to come, together with the obligation to recite the Rosary once a week on bended knees.[17] Unfortunately for the historian they did not cross-examine him about his motives and seemed content to record his bald, factual account of his journey. Perhaps, like some obscure Uriel da Costa, he went to a northern city to seek out Judaism and at last found himself dissatisfied with it or merely nostalgic for Catholicism. It seems most unlikely that he became a Jew just to claim Jewish charity, or that the Jews of Hamburg converted a visitor they had no reason to claim as kin.

Marrano types are not always sharply distinguishable, and they often shade into each other, forming a spectrum or continuum rather than a series of categories. Francisco Olivier and 'Franciscus Hispanus' seem to have been isolated members of families which consisted predominantly or partially of professing Jews. If anything they inclined towards Christianity, but the chief characteristic exposed by their misfortunes was not an independent spirit but a kind of pliability. In times of trouble – of isolation, poverty or illness – they fell back on assistance offered them by Jewish relatives, though this did not necessarily imply a firm return to Judaism, and there could be further vacillations which got them into serious trouble. Francisco Olivier was the first Marrano known to have been sentenced by the Venetian Inquisition. His tactics were opposed to those of Tristão da Costa, Righetto or Filipe de Nis, in that he insisted on his allegiance to Christianity, though he failed to convince his judges. Jews had called him 'a gentleman and one who has commanded in the field'.[18] But a series of witnesses pronounced themselves quite uncertain of his religious identity. 'I know not, I know him only as one of those Marranos from Portugal,' said Vittorio da Pesaro,[19] and others echoed the non-committal statement with slight variations. It was certain, how-

[17] S.U., b. 78, proc. Fernão de Martin de Almeida Pereira, 28 July 1623.
[18] I.Z., p. 87, test. Antonio di Benedetto di Giovanni, a merchant from Aviano di Friuli, 27 July 1549.
[19] Ibid., p. 81, 23 July 1549.

ever, that he had professing Jewish relatives. They included a brother David, who was a merchant moving between Venice, Ferrara and Ancona; some others in Ferrara; and some others who had departed for the Levant. Jews had befriended him after a wounding in Venice: 'I had no money or means to live, and was taken in at the Ghetto, where I have many Jewish relatives, and till now I have lived there in the inn of the Jews and my relatives have paid for me.'[20] There was some evidence that he had not left promptly after his cure, which doubtless helped to convince the Inquisition that he was a Jew. The Jews may have wanted to help rather than to proselytize, but such subtleties did not save the accused from a galley sentence.

In January 1581 'Franciscus Hispanus', a prisoner in the galleys, was interrogated by the Inquisition about his relatives the Ribeiros and about Marranos in Ferrara and Venice. Although a Christian he was still relying on his Jewish relatives to intercede for him, and ingenuously confessed to the court that he had asked a friend named Joseph Sasson, living in the Ghetto, to write to his father. He stands for the Marrano who returns to Christianity in Italy, and goes on vacillating helplessly between the two faiths, highly susceptible to pressures from those around him, especially in times of penury and isolation. He was, he said, born Isaac, the son of Abraham de Almeda, a Portuguese emigré already secretly circumcised in Lisbon, who had come to live in Ferrara. There the witness was born about 1552, and there at the age of twenty-four or twenty-five he became a Christian. A year or two later he found himself in Venice, impoverished and suffering from a scabious itch. He then appealed to his father, who sent 4 crowns from Ferrara by one Joseph, a Levantine Jew, and encouraged the young man to leave and join his father's sisters in Constantinople, there to live as a Jew. On the eastward voyage, 'Franciscus'/Isaac was treated with the rest of the passengers on the ship *Barbara* to a miracle, and they resolved, as though in unison, to go on pilgrimage to the Madonna of Zante, Venice's currant-growing colony in the Ionian sea. Here the refugee repented and confessed to a Franciscan that, although a baptized Christian, he had been heading for Constantinople to return to the Jews. He allowed his confessor permission to reveal the sin to the bishop with a view to getting him absolution. But the bishop thought otherwise and had him arrested, and on the arrival of the Provveditor Salamon, the Venetian Governor, 'Franciscus Hispanus' paid the penalty for a pathetic if not tragic indecision and was awarded a galley sentence. Converts in Italy were ordered to shun the company of Jewish friends or relations, but this one showed no sign of having absorbed the lesson.[21]

[20] Ibid., pp. 84, 89–90, test. the prisoner, 23 July, 1 Aug. 1549.
[21] S.U., b. 45, proc. Gaspar Ribeiro, 26–28 Jan. 1581.

Only young men could venture upon the kind of adolescent rebellion which was expressed through the long experimental journey to a distant country. Young women were capable of showing great strength of character and of rejecting both the religion and the tutelage of relatives who practised Judaism. Women were probably more constant than men, binding themselves more firmly to the faith in which they had been raised, whether Jewish or Christian. Those living as Jewesses in private could scarcely avoid attendance at church services altogether. But they had less reason than men to engage in elaborate pretences for the sake of a business, a career or an inheritance. Tension between the differing demands of the household and the piazza, of the public and the private life, was less acute for them. Filipa Jorge, a mysterious Marrano woman of mature years who attracted inquiries in the 1570s, was among the few of her kind who seem to have moved about Europe on their own.[22] Matriarchs from Portugal sometimes seemed more determined than their husbands to cling to the dietary laws and other practices of Judaism. As we shall see, Isabella Medina, first wife of Gaspar Ribeiro, was perhaps a case in point;[23] and the mother of Feliciana Diaz may well have been another. Conversely, the daughters of well-to-do families who had been separated from parents and brought up in nunneries sometimes proved capable of rejecting Judaism. Their placement in convents may have been a prudent act of conformity on the part of persons not fully committed to Judaism; it may have been intended as camouflage; or it may simply have been the only suitable method of caring for girls whose families were in transit across Europe, with the adults going ahead as pioneers. Be this as it may, it was understandable that their upbringing should draw them closer to the Church than to their own parents or relatives. There are rough analogies between the case of Maria Lopes in the 1580s and that of Feliciana Diaz in the 1630s. Both were convent-educated, both claimed to have been forced into dissimulation by Jewish relatives, and both threw themselves on the mercy of the Church in their efforts to escape.

Eighteen years old in 1582, Maria Lopes deposed in a volunteered statement to the Holy Office that she was the daughter of Diogo Lopes of Antwerp by Anna of Malines, eight miles from the city. Her parents had been betrothed but had never married, because her mother discovered her father's Judaic leanings, and had subsequently married a 'Lutheran' and become a Protestant herself. At the age of twelve, about the year 1576, Maria was boarded out for an annual fee by her father to a convent of Augustinian nuns; she spent four years there, and the Catholic faith became a rock to cling to. A serving woman brought the seemingly slanderous news that her father and his stepmother were living as Jews. At

---

[22] S.U., b. 39, proc. Filipa Jorge, 1575.

[23] See below, pp. 233–4.

first she dismissed the idea, but came to realize in retrospect that they had been observing the sabbath and on Fridays putting the house in order for it. Her father left her in Flanders while he went to explore new ground in Florence, where he took a wife, Catterina Mendes, and lived for a time in the palace of Don Luigi, brother-in-law of the Grand Duke. If, as this suggests, he had some taste for an aristocratic style of life, he would be in no hurry to return openly to Judaism, whatever he might do in private. But great distance, and perhaps distrust of her stepmother, would surely increase Maria's sense of alienation from her father. Her southward journey to join him, in the company of Marranos – it was she who described the travels of Doctor de Nis – was a repugnant experience. After a discreet interval of saying nothing, which lasted for three months, her father and stepmother began to press her to live as they did, the father threatening to disinherit her if she refused to live in his household as a Jew.

> They used to say to me that I should believe in only one God, and not in the Mass or the sacraments of Holy Church, for these things had not been ordained by God, and that he who died was not the true Christ but a false prophet. . . .

To this she replied that

> I wanted to believe as I was taught in the nunnery, and I knew that my soul could not be saved if I believed what they said, and for this my father and stepmother could not stand the sight of me, and my stepmother was accustomed to curse the nuns who had instructed me in the Christian law.

Maria's chance to break away from the family came when they moved to Venice. She made her statement to the Inquisition from the guesthouse of the Casa delle Zitelle on the Giudecca, a pious institute founded on Jesuit inspiration for the shelter of children who might be sold into prostitution; she had taken refuge there at the urging of her confessor.[24] The teachings of the Church had made a far deeper impression upon her than had the exhortations of a father she had long scarcely known.

Feliciana Diaz, half a century later, belonged to a family of Iberian extraction which had been domiciled for some time in Italy. She and her immediate family lived in Tuscany, but her mother's close relatives, by blood or marriage, were Jews of Venice. Despite apparent religious differ-

---

[24] S.U., b. 49, 27 March to 18 April 1582. On the Pia Casa delle Zitelle, see Pullan, *Rich and poor . . .*, pp. 385–91.

ences, they kept in close touch and maintained business connections; when she sank into poverty, the power of her Jewish relatives over Feliciana began to increase. She said that she was born in Pisa about 1611. Her mother was a Jewess, her father a Christian and a Spaniard. 'Before the people, that is, outwardly', her mother lived 'as a Christian, on account of her husband, my father, who was a Christian'. At the age of seven, Feliciana was lodged with the Hospitaller Sisters of St John of Jerusalem, where, like her sisters, she remained for six years. At first her father was reasonably well off, and she and her sisters (there were four girls in all) could look forward to marriage portions of 10,000 ducats each. But much of the family fortune was entrusted to Jewish relatives who were either incompetent or unlucky men of business   including Joseph Senior, who was one of her mother's brothers or brothers-in-law. Feliciana told the Holy Office in Venice that Joseph had lost the family some 40,000 crowns, and that her father 'died in despair' in Pisa in 1629. After his death, she and her mother, perhaps as distressed gentlefolk or *povere vergognose*, were under the protection of the Archduchess in Florence. She confirmed the close tie with the Church by maintaining Feliciana in the nunnery of Sant' Elisabetta for three years, and then she gave her a small dowry of a few hundred ducats. With this Feliciana contrived to marry a Spanish Christian merchant doing business in the city, but he died within two years and left her a young son, Rinaldo Attilio, born on 1 April 1634.

It was then that her mother's relatives began to take an interest in her and to talk of arranging a second marriage. Her goods had dwindled, and were now valued at a paltry 200 ducats. Having deposited them with a Spanish correspondent of her uncle's in Florence, she set out for Venice at a leisurely pace in the company of two Jews. On the way they were detained by the Inquisition in Ferrara, and to escape trouble Feliciana committed her first serious deception, by claiming – as did her companion Jacob Lima – to be a Jew by birth.

Feliciana and her companions eventually reached Venice about March 1635. She thought that her uncle's conscience was pricking him, as well it might, into organizing a second marriage for her; his Portuguese brother-in-law, Abram Aboaf, made it abundantly clear that this could only take place within the Jewish faith, for 'he could not do any favours for one who lived in idolatry.' She came at last to a decision, saw her opportunity, and on 30 March 1635 spoke to a Christian glazier who had come to work at her uncle's house, lamenting that for the first time she was celebrating the Passover and not Easter, and begging him to have her removed from the 'hands of the Devil, and from these animals'. He went to the Inquisition, and once the glazier's apprentice had confirmed his story Feliciana was removed from the Ghetto with the aid of the secular arm. On 17 April 1635 she was ordered to abjure *de levi*, to confess and take Communion as soon as possible, and to perform certain spiritual penances.[25]

In this chapter the spectrum which began with the convinced Jew has ended, seemingly, with the convinced Christian. Parents' religious decisions were sometimes – who knows how often, or how rarely? – challenged by their children: sometimes in a spirit of experiment and curiosity, sometimes in a spirit of disgust. Sometimes we have seen individuals striving, with different degrees of determination, for a religious identity of their own in the face of heavy family pressure, from parents, uncles or other kinsmen. The next chapter will try to show the diversity of behaviour and of attitudes towards Christianity and Judaism that could arise within a single family of parents and grown-up children living in Venice under the same roof.

[25] S.U., b. 92, 5–19 April 1635.

13

The Marrano Family

Marrano families were not always cohesive units capable of imposing collective choices upon their members. The richer families — married brothers and their wives, children and servants – moved themselves and their assets cautiously over long distances, some forging ahead as scouts or pioneers to test the situation in a new centre of operations, others remaining behind to wind up affairs and exact debts in an old one. Discipline and co-operation could be maintained over great distances, but separation was also liable to encourage the habit of acting as an individual and making highly personal choices. Children of poorer families, which sometimes moved more quickly and directly from West to East, could be treated in a surprisingly cavalier fashion. They might be left behind, uneasily poised between the Ghetto and the house of converts, by parents who could not afford their passage. In Venice, about 1585, Manuel Dies from Peñafiel in Old Castile had not enough money to transport himself and four adolescent children to the Levant, and proceeded to raise it by pledging the eldest, Francisco, to a year's service with the Marrano family of the Filippi.[1] Manuel Ferrante and his wife Caterina travelled in the mid-1580s from Lisbon to Venice; his humble trade was cleaning cloths. Still dressed as Christians, they departed for Ancona, leaving their son Miguel, eleven years old, behind in Venice. He was still below the normal age of apprenticeship to a skilled trade, but was probably thought capable of fending for himself through odd jobs and domestic service.[2]

Outward religious differences within an extended family of brothers

[1] S.U., b. 54, proc. Filippi, test. Francisco Dies, 13 Nov. 1585.
[2] S.U., b. 61, proc. Miguel Ferrante, 15, 22 March 1588; cf. Beltrami, *Storia della popolazione* ..., p. 198.

and cousins, living under different roofs and sometimes in different cities, did not necessarily imply the severance of friendly relations. Such differences may even have been contrived, for division between Christianity and Judaism could enable brothers to maintain connexions both in the Christian and in the Jewish worlds. Was this the strategy of the Galindos? Fernão Galindo, formerly a goldsmith in Flanders, changed his name to Moses in Ferrara. Of his four sons the eldest lived as a Christian in Venice and 'traded with the fortune of his father, for he is a man who has some 20,000 ducats'; Samuel, Juda and Jacob were loyal to their father's profession and worked in Ferrara as goldsmiths or as jewellers.[3] Partnerships between Christian and Jew may have existed within the Ribeiro cousinhood, and they certainly did, though with unhappy results, between the Diaz of Florence and their relatives in Venice.

But it was equally true that, within a nuclear family of parents and children, religious differences were often concomitants of bitter domestic struggles. Antipathy towards fathers or stepmothers could be expressed by rejecting their religious beliefs and practices. Adolescent rebellion, eagerness to escape from domestic claustrophobia, sometimes accounted for experiments with an alien faith. Conversely, religious conflict could engender or stimulate these family tensions, exposing incompatibilities of temperament that might otherwise have lain concealed. Marked divisions arose within the immediate family circle of Gaspar Ribeiro of Santa Maria Formosa. A prominent feature of it was a breakdown of paternal authority through Gaspar's advancing age, confusion and possibly senile dementia, which allowed his strong-minded son and daughter to make their own decisions.[4]

Accounts of Gaspar's life before he came to Venice at the age of nearly seventy, somewhere about the year 1560, depend very heavily on his own statements. But a reasonably coherent account of his last ten years, from about 1570 to his arrest in 1580, can be pieced together from the remarks of a large number of Christian and Jewish witnesses, appearing both for the court and for the defence. By way of caution it has to be said that he was deeply unpopular with the Jewish community and, by implication, with the Portuguese as well, because his long memory might equip him to inform the authorities who had been a Christian in Portugal and a Jew in Venice.[5] He quarrelled bitterly both with Righetto and with the Levantine consul Chaim Saruc, though there is no evidence that his statements to the Inquisition, some of them very generalized, did serious

---

[3] S.U., b. 45, proc. Gaspar Ribeiro, test. 'Franciscus Hispanus', 26 Jan. 1581; cf. the list of Marranos in Ferrara and Venice offered by Antonio Machado, ibid., 31 May 1579.

[4] For much of what follows, see Pullan, 'The Inquisition ...', p. 221 ff. I have provided references here only to establish points not made in that article.

[5] S.U., b. 45, proc. Ribeiro, test. Nicolò da Ponte of Savona, 19 Jan. 1581.

harm to any individual.[6] Like anyone of unlovely habits – his ruling vice was an almost pathological meanness – he was a magnet for malicious testimony. But there is enough variety and consistency in the evidence, taken as a whole, to provide a convincing family history.

It seemed that Gaspar was born in or near Lisbon in 1493 or 1494; his father was Arês Ribeiro of Palmela, five leagues from the city. Hoping, perhaps, to authenticate his Christian status, Gaspar liked to insist on his past service to the royal family. The earliest event of which he spoke was a journey to Fez between 1527 and 1532, afterwards called 'the time when I was the King's ambassador to the land of the Moors for the recovery of Christian slaves'.[7] Articles drawn up by his advocate in 1580 declared that he had transacted business with the French King on behalf of King John of Portugal (presumably John III), and that in Italy he had carried out the instructions of the late Cardinal of Portugal and of the Prince of Parma.[8] About 1560, he and his wife, Donna Isabella, had arrived in Venice from Ratisbon with the permission of the child King's great uncle, Cardinal Henry. The Ribeiros were merchants, and Gaspar claimed to have traded with many parts of the world, including both India and the Far East, and also Portugal, Paris, Lyons and Venice. In extreme old age he liked to discuss 'the affairs of Spain and Portugal, and the places where pepper and cane-sugar grew'; and, chatting by the fireside in his last days, he liked to think 'that he had ships abroad which sailed on his account'.[9]

At first, Gaspar lived with his wife and his daughter Violante in the parish of Santa Marina.[10] About 1563, after a move to Santa Maria Zobenigo, his son João arrived in Venice, where father and son traded under their joint names. Their interests were varied, and not always legitimate. They undoubtedly dealt in pearls and rubies, and might take other exotic items, such as consignments of nutmeg, as security for loans and themselves sell them. About 1570, they managed between them the city's meat supply, advancing the government a lump sum for the con-

[6] S.U., b. 36, proc. Righetto, test. Ribeiro, 6, 9 Aug. 1571; b. 39, proc. Filipa Jorge, test. Ribeiro, 19 July 1575; b. 45, proc. Ribeiro, test Chaim Saruc, 26 Jan. 1579.

[7] S.U., b. 36, proc. Righetto, test. Ribeiro, 6 Aug. 1571; b. 45, proc. Ribeiro, test. Ribeiro, 15 March 1580.

[8] Ibid., Aug. 1580. Note his son João's pointed allusions at moments of difficulty to his role in the royal service – A.S.V., Giudici del Piovego, b. 1 (Capitolare 1254–1568), second foliation, fol. 73, probably of Jan. 1568. On 23 July 1579 he rebuts the accusations of Saldanha, calling himself 'a man of reputation, a merchant of Rialto, as may be seen from letters of my lady of Parma and of the Infante of Portugal' – S.U., b. 44, proc. 'Negromanti'.

[9] S.U., b. 45, proc. Ribeiro, test. Marsilio de' Marsili, a priest of San Barnabà, 27 May 1581.

[10] Ibid., test. Giovanni Cornuca, 21 Nov. 1580.

tract and hoping to clear a profit on the excise. Gaspar once quarrelled with a customer on Piazza San Marco over meat he was reserving for himself, and exclaimed in his persistent Portuguese, as rendered by a Venetian witness: 'Estas becharia me costas vinticinques milles schudi, e voi voles questas carnes' ('This butchery costs me 25,000 crowns, and you want that piece')![11] João, too, probably invested some of his capital in speculations on the yield of the excise on wine.[12] And the Ribeiros' example could reasonably have been cited by those who argued that Marranos were usurers. Their only identifiable victim, however, was Abraham Abencini, a Levantine Jew who was forced as the condition of a loan to purchase a grossly over-valued box of pearls, the difference between their real and their fictitious value representing a concealed payment of interest.[13] This was not their sole business connexion with Levantine Jews, who might become associates as readily as they became clients, for about 1569–70 João formed on his own a partnership with Moses Cardiel, and it lasted some eighteen months.

Prophetically, a report on their usurious activities proclaimed:

> We see by experience that many foreigners flock to this city, and among them are some who have no respect for the laws of God or man, and to the deadly peril of their own salvation seek to lend upon usury and drink the blood of those who fall into their hands; and having amassed great wealth they depart from this city. . . .

In later years witnesses would speak of the Ribeiros' intention to use time in Venice, as did the Filippi, to tidy up their business before emigration to the Levant. One of them said of Gaspar that 'he had scattered his goods throughout the world and that he wished to assemble them and come to Saphet in Constantinople [sic!] to live in the manner of the Jews.' If the Ribeiros seriously entertained the plan, they went about it in at least as leisurely a fashion as the de Luna–Mendes or the Nuñes Enriques, and it seems quite credible, as was suggested by an informer, that they were aiming at Venetian citizenship. Citizenship de intus et de extra, normally obtainable on petition to the government only after twenty-five years' residence, was necessary to all – other than Levantine Jews – who wished to transport goods between Venice and the East without employing intermediaries. For the time being the Ribeiros relied on collaboration with such as Moses Cardiel, and probably shipped their goods with the aid of

[11] Ibid., test. David David, 20 Dec. 1580; test. Hieronimo di Francesco Leffo, 9 Feb. 1581; test. Lauro de' Cremonesi, 18 Feb. 1581.
[12] Ibid., test. Pietro di Santino, 25 Feb. 1581.
[13] A.S.V., Giudici del Piovego, b. l. second foliation, fol. 61v.–74v.

Giulio di Priamo Balanzan, a Venetian citizen and merchant of San Barnabà.[14]

Religious division within the family broke the surface in 1569, the year the Ribeiros were first denounced to the Inquisition. It received reports of an ugly scene in which Gaspar's daughter Violante burst forth from the family house and made for the canal to escape a beating inflicted by her brother, screaming to the neighbourhood: 'Signori, help me, these dogs would give me by force to a Jew and for this they are thrashing me!' Plans were afoot to marry her into a distinguished Jewish family, the Abravanel, and these contrasted starkly with an earlier proposal involving Filippo da Rhò, a Milanese gentleman known to Gaspar in Lyons. The Portuguese priest who knew the family best attributed the impious plan to the son, João, and believed it inspired by certain Jews of Ferrara.[15] João treated Violante 'always in the manner of a Jewish dog, and it was he who perverted his father, for the father, it seems to me, is neither Christian nor Jew nor Turk, and could not himself tell you what law he follows, save that of making money.' According to one later story, the Abravanel negotiations had already broken down because Gaspar's fist was too tight to release a sufficient dowry. He responded meekly enough to the priest's rebuke, agreed to a Christian marriage for Violante, and the Inquisition took no further action. Within three years, Jessica to her father's Shylock, she married Vincenzo Scrova, a nobleman of the subject city of Vicenza. Arrogant, violent and impulsive, he made her neither an equable husband nor a pious one, for he was often banned from the communion table. But Violante's marriage gave her family a toehold among nominal Christians of moderate prestige. Vincenzo Scrova disliked the society of Jews and despised his cantankerous father-in-law, but he loved the prospect of his wife's inheritance. Violante's role as the most devoutly Catholic member of the family, shocked into protest at the sight of its judaizing intentions, bears some relation to that of Maria Lopes.

Isabella de Medina, Gaspar's wife, also emerges as firmer in her religious allegiance than the men of her family, although she inclined towards the faith of the Jews. To the book-keeper Francisco Gomes she had said: 'Poor little chap, what will you do? Can you not see that the Christian faith is not sound?' Exhorted on her deathbed to think of God and the Madonna, she replied, 'Of the God who made the world, yes; but of others, no.'[16] And a relative repeated family tradition in 1581, saying

---

[14] S.U., b. 45, proc. Ribeiro, test. Balanzan, 1 Dec. 1580.

[15] S.U., b. 24, proc. Ribeiro, test. Enrique de Mello, 19 Oct. 1569; cf. b. 45, proc. Ribeiro, test. Moses Cardiel, 23 Nov. 1580.

[16] S.U., b. 24, proc. Ribeiro, test. Enrique de Mello, 18–19 Oct. 1569; some of this was repeated in the delation he made in Rome on 31 Oct. 1575 (b. 45).

she would observe the Jewish faith and eat meat brought her from the Ghetto, or so my stepmother told me, saying that this Isabella de Medina had always been a Jewess at heart and strove always to perform the rites of Jews whenever she could. . . .

Accounts by Christians of her husband's and son's conduct were often equivocal. Accounts of hers were not.

By 1569 Gaspar's first wife had died, and he seemed readier to conform to Catholic practice, if not to accept Catholic belief. Perhaps a year after the first encounter with the Inquisition, the family moved to a new parish, Santa Maria Formosa, and Gaspar became a pillar of parochial affairs through his election as *Gastaldo* or chief officer of the fraternity of the Blessed Sacrament. Such parish brotherhoods had been encouraged by the Franciscan Observants and later by the Jesuits and by the more zealous bishops of the Counter-Reformation. In the last quarter of the sixteenth century they existed in about one-third of Venetian parishes. Their main purpose was to ensure that the consecrated Hosts in the churches were kept not merely decently and reverently but in splendour, and that on their journeys through the streets to visit the sick they had an impressive following. No social distinction was required of office-holders (indeed the brotherhoods had once been dismissed by the haughty as only fit for smiths and cobblers),[17] and Gaspar went swiftly to the top, where he succeeded a dyer. In his time the fraternity commissioned a fine tabernacle for the Host, he caused 150 to 350 ducats to be spent on the operation and on the decoration of the chapel, and – he told the tribunal – he earned a commemorative inscription, 'Gaspare Ribiera ha fatto fare', in the church. 'Were I a bad Christian, I would never have had that done,' he reminded his judges.

Gaspar lent hangings to the church, usually seeking a receipt, for he was very careful of his property; he would take a torch or candle and follow the sacrament on Good Friday; and he gave alms to the Hieronymite monastery of Santa Maria delle Grazie when the friars came to knock upon his door.[18] There was some evidence that he had taken Communion, if not very often, and this would imply that his link with the Church was a sacramental one, and not forged only through charity, church attendance and ceremony. It would be ungracious to suspect him of doing these things just as a form of camouflage, but his activities savoured a little of the over-conformity to which suspected judaizers, as in Majorca, would sometimes resort.[19] In subsequent years the evidence

[17] Cf. B. Pullan, 'Natura e carattere delle Scuole', in *Le scuole di Venezia*, ed. T. Pignatti (Milan, 1981), pp. 12–13.

[18] S.U., b. 45, proc. Ribeiro, test. Nicolò da Ponte of Savona, 19 Jan. 1581.

[19] Cf. Moore, *Those of the street . . .*, pp. 22, 42–3, 152.

cited in his defence bore a close resemblance to that urged on behalf of Vincenzo Valgrisi, a bookseller of the nearby parish of San Zulian, churchwarden and *Gastaldo* of the fraternity of the Sacrament, in 1570.[20] The last thing expected of a judaizer or a heretic would be deliberate association with the body of Christ.

Gaspar went so far as to take a Venetian Christian wife. In 1574 he married Elena, daughter of the late Giorgio Teodori, jeweller at San Zulian, who had been introduced to him by a local advocate's wife. True, it could be seen as a calculating act, a marriage of convenience between two elderly people designed to improve Gaspar's chances of obtaining citizenship. But if he intended to practise Judaism he was taking an extraordinary risk; though loyal to him the old woman seemed conventionally devout, and she could hardly be totally unaware of his habits. Though at least one of the living-in book-keepers employed by the firm was Portuguese and conceivably a New Christian, the domestic servants employed at Santa Maria Formosa were Italians. The evidence given at the trial both by the wife and by the maidservant Mattea was inconclusive. The servant thought her master's sole irregularity in diet was to eat eggs and fats during Lent, although – like Brianda de Luna before him – he claimed to have an ecclesiastical licence to do so.[21] Family tradition had it that whenever Gaspar proposed to eat chicken he would personally cut the fowl's throat with a knife kept for the purpose. 'But I do not know,' added the witness judiciously, 'whether he did this to make it tastier [*per farlo più pollo*] or to perform the rites of the Jews'.[22] Other testimony established that Gaspar had become so eccentric as to assume the management of the household and cook for himself, going personally to market in fine weather. It suggested a determination to control the household's diet and conceal his own menu from the servants, but there was (as usual) another explanation. Asked why someone so rich should do these things for himself, a former employee said: 'He is so miserly that he trusts no one and fears that everybody would destroy him.'[23]

Mattea could testify that Gaspar kept in his room a gilded image of the Madonna, rather larger than the one in the room where she was being interrogated. Asked whether Gaspar actually knelt before it to pray, she replied:

The truth is that of an evening he would stand upright in the

---

[20] See Sforza, 'Riflessi ...', II, p. 186.

[21] S.U., b. 45, proc. Ribeiro, test. Mattea da Rippa Sicca, 7 April 1580; cf. I.Z., p. 261, proc. Licentiato Costa, test. Paolo Mogliani, 15 July 1555.

[22] S.U., b. 45, proc. Ribeiro, test. 'Franciscus Hispanus', 28 Jan. 1581.

[23] Ibid., test. Catterina, wife of the boatman Francesco, 7 April 1580; Nicolò da Ponte of Savona, 20 Oct. 1580; Bartolomeo da Bassano, 5 Nov. 1580; Moses Cardiel, 23 Nov. 1580.

middle of the room while I warmed the bed, and I think he was saying the prayer because he moved his lips and kept his hands joined, but he stayed on his feet and not on his knees. And he faced the image of the Madonna, but from afar off, and I never saw him kneel, not even at Mass, where he went, not often, but every fifteen or twenty days, saying that he could not go [more frequently].

Madonna Elena claimed to have heard the prayer, which ran: 'To God I give myself, to the Holy Spirit I commend me, my sin is great, but great is your mercy.' It is tempting to believe that he was creating a private synthesis of his own between Judaism and Christianity, although there is nothing to suggest that it was a sophisticated one, and it could well have been born of confusion rather than of intellectual effort. When tested by the Inquisition, his knowledge of Christian worship seemed imperfect. As the record reported, he

said the Ave Maria in the Portuguese or Spanish vernacular, but with some Latin words; and he said the Pater Noster in Latin, but he left some words out and omitted 'Forgive us our debts.' But the Creed he could not say, crying 'Pardon me, gentlemen, for I am not in my right mind.'

At the same time Gaspar appeared to be keeping in touch with Jewish relatives and contributing to Jewish charities, though much of the evidence on this point came from Jews engaged in litigation with Gaspar and responsible for the inquiry into his conduct. Piety towards Jewish kin would not of course be incompatible with an essential commitment to Christianity, though it would excite suspicion. Embarrassing and even potentially damning to Gaspar was his rejection of a nephew who had turned to Christianity and come to Venice to ask him for money. But he had his reasons, and prophesied grimly:

That young man who has returned to the faith will never stand firm in Christianity, and with time you will see that I say true. And for that reason I do not want him in my house.[24]

But if Gaspar was moving tentatively towards Christian conformity and merging with his hosts the Venetians, he had no real ability to carry his son with him. Relations between the two were tense, and their clerk preferred to eat in the counting-house because it was their habit to quarrel at mealtimes.[25] During the 1570s effective control of the business

[24] Ibid., test. Gaspar Ribeiro, 21, 23 June 1580.
[25] Ibid., test. Nicolò da Ponte of Savona, 14 June 1580.

passed to João, whilst Gaspar retreated into household management, though both would sign the firm's letters. It was once suggested that João would forge his father's signature in order to enhance his own credit at Antwerp or at Besançon.[26] Gaspar's interventions were confined to peevish outbursts whenever he disliked the contracts concluded and he was capable of visiting the bank at Rialto with instructions that João should no longer be entitled to sign on the firm's behalf. Too weak to sustain these protests, he would soon countermand his orders. Many bore witness to decay in Gaspar's mental powers, speaking of pointless rudeness and petulant rage, of unreliability, childishness, inconsequential and rambling speech. Unable now to read, he could be deceived about business or any other matter. His consul called him 'a man of little wit, for he was always complaining and beating the servant girls and making a lot of noise.'[27] Hence his son's freedom to act on his own.

Unlike his father, João Ribeiro seems to have been cheerful, generous with tips, sociable, and a sexual libertine. 'My son did not hate Jews,' said Gaspar, 'and he got on well with everyone, both with Christians and with Jews.'[28] He was also capable of cunning and ruthless action against those who threatened him, as witness his moves to discredit the informer Saldanha.[29] There was evidence of punctiliousness in devotion, including the taking of Communion and visits to a confessor. Other testimony, however, pointed in a different direction – that he was, as had been said of his father, a man without law and a Marrano, not in the sense of being a secret judaizer, but rather in that of an unbeliever and a traitor who had no faith to pledge.

Even so, João committed one action which appeared to draw him firmly into the camp of the Jews. About August 1575, he secretly married a young Jewess according to the Jewish rite in the house of Giorgio Cornaro, a Venetian nobleman, on the island of Murano.[30] He did not bring her to Santa Maria Formosa, but would leave home to stay with her in the Ghetto for several days at a stretch.[31] Very likely the match was a renewal of the earlier project to marry among the Abravanels, a counterweight to Violante's marriage with a Scrova, and also a measure to ingratiate the Ribeiros with the Marrano élite in the Ottoman Empire. For the time being, life in Venice was comfortable enough, but the decree for the expulsion of the Marranos had never been rescinded; no doubt it was desirable to take out insurance, and provide against enforced emi-

---

[26] Ibid., test. Moses Cardiel, 25 Aug. 1580.

[27] Ibid., testimony of eleven witnesses, 21 Nov. 1580 to 2 March 1581.

[28] Ibid., 15 March 1580.

[29] See above, pp. 103–6.

[30] S.U., b. 45, proc. Ribeiro, test. Lissebona Berrão, 24 March 1580.

[31] Ibid., test. Chaim Saruc, 26 Jan. 1580; test. Mattea da Rippa Sicca, 7 April 1580.

gration to the East. João's bride, Alumbra, had much to commend her. Her mother claimed to be second cousin to the Duke of Naxos and said that she had a sister named Rena, who at the time of the match had been on the point of departing for Constantinople to join the Duke. Although the extent of the Duke's influence on the Sultan Murad III was some-times questioned, he was still a desirable protector, he still controlled the wine excise, and kinship with him could still confer prestige. Later Alumbra called herself niece to the Duchess of Naxos, and she may indeed have been related both to the Duke and to his wife.[32]

For these connexions the Ribeiros were prepared to pay, but in a grudging fashion. A family of rich non-noble merchants could expect to attract a dowry of 10,000 ducats, approximately half that paid at the time by patricians of procuratorial rank.[33] In her genteel poverty Alumbra could only offer 1,400. Since the match would be advantageous to the Ribeiros, they offered to supplement the dowry themselves to the tune of a further 3,000 ducats.[34] Should Alumbra outlive her husband, at least part of this sum would be repaid from his estate and used for the support of herself and of any children of the marriage. Alumbra, her mother and friends later told the Inquisition that João, less miserly than his father, had offered to raise the sum promised her to 13,000 ducats. But Moses Cardiel confessed that he and Alumbra's aunt had tampered clumsily with a letter from João to the Duke, announcing his intentions, and had amended the 3,000 ducats he mentioned to a more seemly 13,000.[35]

Whatever the sums involved, João's calculations seemed clear enough, at least to one of his relatives. He

took this wife to ennoble himself, and for her beauty, and that he

---

[32] Ibid., test. Lissebona Berrão, 24 March 1580; test. Mattea da Rippa Sicca, 7 April 1580. On 8 March 1580 Gaspar Ribeiro describes Alumbra as the daughter of Francisco Valdaran and as a Jewess of Lisbon. On 12 April the Jew Joseph Sarafarin testifies that she was born in Ferrara. From S.U., b. 44, proc. 'Negromanti', 15 May 1579, it appears that Isabetta, a Spanish or Portuguese neophyte, told the Inquisitor of Ferrara that João Ribeiro was married to a Jewess, the niece of Arès de Luna; in the Ribeiro trial, on 6 Sept. 1580, Saldanha refers to Alumbra and her family as the 'Lunas'. On the position of the Duke of Naxos, see Albèri, III/ii, p. 166 (Marcantonio Tiepolo, 1576); but cf. Grunebaum-Ballin, *Joseph Naci* ..., p. 161.

[33] Gaspar grumbled that João could have had a Venetian gentlewoman to wife with a dowry of 10,000 ducats, and implied that arrangements fell through because João was known to have a Jewish mistress (S.U., b. 45, 15 March 1580). On dowries at this time, see B. Pullan, 'The occupations and investments of the Venetian nobility in the middle and late sixteenth century', in *Renaissance Venice*, ed. J. R. Hale (London, 1973), pp. 389–90. On the function of dowries, see Cowan, 'The urban patriciate ...', p. 187 ff.

[34] S.U., b. 45, proc. Ribeiro, test. Chaim Saruc, 26 Jan. 1580; test. Lissebona Berrão, 24 March 1580.

[35] Ibid., test. Moses Cardiel, 23 Nov. 1580; test. Gabriele Cavazza, 16 Feb. 1581.

might say he was a relative of the Great Duke, and because she was of good blood, and he had promised he would assemble all his wealth and property and they would go to Constantinople and live there as Jews.

Husband and wife had at least one quarrel which implied that he wanted to borrow money from the Duke, perhaps to pay the dowry he was supposed to have promised.[36] Neither this nor his pledge to migrate was ever honoured, and he died in Venice four years after the marriage. The circumstances of his deathbed were characteristically ambivalent. He was attended by 'a Levantine Jewish doctor who wore the yellow turban and was a Portuguese', and said that he consulted him because he was Portuguese and not because he was Jewish. João confessed two or three times, but did not take Communion because his tongue was swollen and he was choked with vomit – though it was hinted that the vomiting was self-induced.[37]

The Ribeiros' downfall came through litigation over the dubious dowry. Understandably if unwisely, Gaspar refused to pay the sums demanded by Alumbra, and, trusting in her own immunity, she applied to the *Avogadori di Commun*, who had jurisdiction over marriage contracts. Founded on tangible documentary evidence, the case was transferred to the Inquisition. The fact of the marriage was not disputed, but there was room for argument about the extent of Gaspar's complicity. His defence – apart from senility – was that the contract of betrothal bearing his signature was a forgery and the product of a malevolent conspiracy among the Jews. He had of course been aware of João's association with Alumbra, but had taken her simply for the latest of a series of concubines;[38] his elderly wife said he had spoken of plans to make Alumbra a Christian.[39] Whether or not he had personally concluded the contract of betrothal and celebrated it with eggs and fish, there was ample evidence – and not only from Jewish sources – that he had acknowledged the woman as his daughter-in-law and that they had exchanged gifts. She had sent him 'things made of sugar and honey', and he, calling her 'Madam daughter' (*signora fia*), had sent her 'pepper, cane-sugar, spices, powdered sugar, flour, wine, firewood and salted fish', always personally preparing the pepper and spices. She had stitched handkerchiefs and shirts for Gaspar out of materials he had sent her. It was suggested, too, that he had invited her to live in the house at Santa Maria Formosa to care for his son during

[36] Ibid., test. Alumbra, 2 July 1580.
[37] Ibid., test. Fabrizio Locatelli, parish priest, 26 Nov. 1579; test. Flaminio Riccheri (a Jesuit), 26 Jan. 1580.
[38] Ibid., test. Gaspar Ribeiro, 8 March 1580.
[39] Ibid., test. Elena, 12 April 1580.

his last illness.[40] Gaspar's bitterness against Alumbra at the trial seemed boundless; he called her 'that bitch' (*questa cadena*), and vowed he would rather have presented her with a rope than a dress.[41]

Understandably, the tribunal remained unconvinced by Gaspar's energetic defence. Witnesses spoke of him, in his last days, unctuously professing repentance. Alert to inconsistency, the Inquisitor asked one of them sharply 'if he believed that a man held to be out of his mind would ask on several occasions to be allowed to confess and take Communion and ask pardon for his son and other persons involved in these troubles?'[42] Certainly the Inquisition saw with its own eyes nothing but a denial of responsibility which persisted to the end. On 12 May 1581 Gaspar died in a house at San Barnabà where he was still in custody after fourteen months. His corpse was placed in a wooden coffin and lodged in a storeroom on the ground floor by night and without the presence of clergy or any ceremony of the Church. Inquiries into the deathbed were launched. Released from the sense of urgency instilled by Gaspar's living presence, the tribunal came slowly to its conclusions. Over three years later his memory was finally condemned as that of an apostate and a judaizer, and his body was marked for shameful burial, without light and in unconsecrated ground. For another year or more, the corpse was still kept in a storeroom, now in a house at Santo Stefano, where Gaspar's son-in-law was living. On 12 February 1586 officials of the Holy Office opened the coffin, found that the body had not been totally consumed, and briefly locked the room again. On 13 February, at dead of night, the chief constable of the Inquisition buried the corpse of Gaspar 'in the place where the bodies of dead Jews are buried'.

Each member of the Ribeiro family could well be cited in support of a favourite theory about the nature of Marranism. Donna Isabella seems to confirm the suggestion that secret Judaism tended to be transmitted by wives and mothers rather than by husbands and fathers, her daughter Violante to support the argument that *conversos* could well be ready and willing to turn to the Catholic faith. João Ribeiro seems to illustrate, above all, the calculating, strategic element in Marranism. He seems to have been a successful merchant laying plans to migrate if he needed to do so, but he was in no hurry, and was content to take out insurance. Both he and his father were seen by some acquaintances, not as secret Jews, but as men without law, who believed in nothing. Gaspar may, in his unintellectual way, have groped towards a personal synthesis of

[40] Ibid., test. Canaan of Città di Castello, 22 March 1580; test. Lissabona Berrão, 24 March 1580; test. Mattea da Rippa Sicca, 7, 8 April 1580; test. João de Medina, 26 April 1580; test. Alumbra, 2 July 1580.
[41] Ibid., 10 May 1580.
[42] Ibid., test. Matteo di Giovanni Maria of Belluno, 27 May 1581.

Christianity and Judaism, although he possessed a full understanding of neither. His epitaph could well be the words of Moses Cardiel: 'Of Gaspar I know nothing, save that I found him a good Christian. God alone can know the secrets of the heart.' Much of the evidence was highly ambivalent, as though it related to persons well accustomed either to prevaricating or to disarming suspicion; only the marriage contract provided firm evidence of the acts of a secret Jew.

Trial transcripts are always incomplete sources for the history of crime. They portray the indiscreet, irresolute and incompetent who get caught, and the penitents and exhibitionists who confess; above all they depict the type of crime which gets reported and punished, which bears an uncertain relationship to the whole range of offences actually committed. Inquisition records dealing with Marranism, whose prosecution was so deeply influenced by political and economic considerations, are no exception to this rule. Inevitably, the papers used in these chapters have over-stressed the elements of indecision, confusion, materialism and hypocrisy which formed a part, but only a part, of its make-up. Their territory is the twilit zone of those who tried to be men of two worlds. Venice had its own version of dissembling Marranism, and it also – as a place where wanderers paused to tell their life stories – heard much about the kinds of secret Judaism held to be practised elsewhere. Its own Marranism was not of the kind which depends on the transmission of a simplified clandestine religion. It coexisted with professing Judaism, and its alleged practitioners often had business connexions with Jews, or lived close to the Ghetto, or both. However, they were probably alienated from Old Jews (even from Levantines) by differences of experience, accusations of trimming and ignorance of Hebrew. Their decision to live as Christians was perhaps rooted in at least four considerations. Economic calculation suggested that they set their affairs in order, exact payment from their debtors, continue trading as far as possible with Spain, Portugal and their rulers' dominions, safeguard foreign assets against confiscation and protect relatives in those lands from reprisals. For all these things the name of a Christian was required. The richer the family, the more complex the preliminaries to any transfer to the East. Conservatism made them cling to Europe, and sometimes their departure turned from a short-term goal to a beguiling promise they never fulfilled. Repugnance at the constraints and humiliations imposed on Jews might well keep them out of the Ghetto. And, simultaneously, a form of prudence (which, paradoxically, entailed considerable risks) prompted some of them to build up connexions in the Ottoman Empire, and to insure against possible expulsion.

The tales of adventure abroad can carry a picaresque air and a smell of romantic fiction. Plainly, Marranos did use cover stories which had the obvious purpose of suggesting that their subject was outside the jurisdiction of the Holy Office. But there are also stories containing much elaborate detail whose function – if it was false – is less easily discerned, unless it was designed to protect the teller against any suggestion of incomplete confession, or intended to give good value to the house of converts in return for its charity. Their chief claim to authenticity lies in their variety; they portray no single stereotype, and they bring us, in several guises, the young man who wanders to find and prove himself and to retrace the steps of his parents, reworking their decisions.

Clearly not all Marranos were systematic practitioners of secret Judaism or in their own minds Jews by desire. Some may well have regarded Christianity and Judaism, not as mutually exclusive faiths making total claims, but rather as equally valid systems of devotional practice, depending more upon ritual and upon dietary laws than upon inner conviction: as habits which one followed for the sake of profit, self-preservation or even pleasure. Marranism is surely best seen as a series of individual choices, often subject to revision, sometimes complicated by youthful uncertainty, and best not portrayed in terms of any collective resolve.

14

Neophytes of Italy:
the Conquest of Souls

It fell to the Inquisition to deal, not only with Marranos, but also with the casualties of Italian campaigns to transform Jews into good Christians. Italian converts were described as 'neophytes' or 'Jews turned Christians' (*ebrei fatti cristiani*). Even in their more ambivalent moments they were not called Marranos. In the process of conversion, the Inquisitor and his colleagues were both auxiliaries and disciplinary officers. Occasionally they would be called upon to investigate the motives of converts or to authenticate conversions. They might warn or punish those who tried to divert prospective converts or reclaim those who had already made their decision. During the 1580s they would sometimes avenge insults to neophytes, and they would support the Pia Casa dei Catecumeni, the house for recruits to the faith, by enforcing its discipline or upholding its right to claim Jewish children for instruction. They would punish neophytes who showed signs of returning to Judaism and hence of overturning the religious hierarchy, the order whereby the superseded faith of the Jews was inferior to that of the Christians, and movement should therefore be made only in one direction: through promotion from Judaism to Christianity. But the harshest penalties were reserved for those who deliberately exploited the credulity of the faithful and stole their alms by repeatedly converting to Christianity. They were guilty, not only of fraud, but also of grossly abusing the sacrament of baptism, in such a way as to deny its decisive and indelible character and exploit it for the sake of material gain.

Large-scale forced conversion was not a grave problem in Italy, and Italian campaigns – increasingly persistent and highly organized from the time of Paul IV – produced a type of unsatisfactory convert who seems, at first sight, quite different from the ideal or model Marrano. In the minds of sixteenth-century writers, and in subsequent tradition, the Marrano is commonly seen as one who has suffered forced conversion, either in his own person or through his forebears. Illogically enough, however, he is regarded by hostile observers not as the victim of forced conversion but rather as its material beneficiary, now enabled to acquire great wealth and a degree of social acceptance by virtue of his Christian façade. Hence, like Enriques and Gomes,[1] as depicted in the vehement delation of 1555, he is linked with the complementary notions of religious deceit and of the corrupting power of money. Real Marranism was of course more complicated than this caricature suggests, and many Marranos were poor; but there were occasions when the image bore some relation to reality, the actual to the ideal.

Jews who had converted in Italy – the kind who figured in the records as prisoners, delators or prosecution witnesses – appeared to cluster round two contrasting ideal types. The first of these was neither a forced convert nor, even potentially, a rich man. In turning Christian, he was generally yielding to persuasion rather than force, and his qualities were either weakness or low cunning. Inquisitors, churchmen and certain Jews were troubled by awareness of the shabby creature who would embrace Christianity in response to the pressures of poverty; not strong enough to endure humiliation and privation in the hope of the Messiah, he would surrender to the blandishments of the missionary who promised him a better life. But having crossed the frontier between faiths, he might also lack the perseverance to become a good Christian. 'Madam, if one has not been a good Jew he cannot become a good Christian,' said Solomon, harpsichordist, music teacher and German Jew, to a Venetian noblewoman in 1555.[2] 'I have little faith in such people, and have been deceived by them several times,' wrote Archbishop Carlo Borromeo, returning a prospective convert to Brescia, '. . . for I have found that on the pretext of coming to our faith many of them sought and had other purposes, and were with fraud and trickery pursuing worldly gains.'[3] Ingeniously, if at times obscurely, Browning evoked the down-at-heel neophyte and the atmosphere of the Roman conversion sermon, ca. 1600, in two verses of the mordant *Holy Cross Day*:

---

[1] See above, pp. 177–8.

[2] I.Z., pp. 155, 158, proc. Elena de' Freschi Olivi, test. Paola Marcello, test. Solomon, 26, 28 March 1555.

[3] Carlo Borromeo to Giovanni Dolfin, 5 March 1584, in R. Segre, 'Il mondo ebraico nel carteggio di Carlo Borromeo', *Michael: on the history of the Jews of the Diaspora*, I, ed. S. Simonsohn (Tel-Aviv, 1972), pp. 254–5.

See to our converts – you doomed black dozen –
No stealing away – nor cog nor cozen!
You five that were thieves, deserve it fairly;
You seven that were beggars, will live less sparely;
You took your turn and dipped in the hat,
Got fortune – and fortune gets you; mind that!

Give your first groan – compunction's at work;
And soft! from a Jew you mount to a Turk.
Lo, Micah, – the selfsame beard on chin
He was four times already converted in!
Here's a knife, clip quick – it's a sign of grace –
Or he ruins us all with his hanging-face.

Venetian records suggest that his vision was not entirely satirical fantasy
or historical fiction.

A second species of convert, by nature prosecutor and not prisoner, is
the zealot who allies aggressively with his adoptive church. Unlike the
model Marrano, he is no traitor to the Christian world, but rather an
enemy of Judaism. Not content to abandon the ancestral faith himself and
to perfect his own Christianity, he tries to win acceptance and disarm
suspicion of himself and his motives, making himself one of the Church's
experts on Jewish affairs, rounding on the culture of the Jews, or becoming an ardent conversionist. Venetian examples, approximating to the
type, were Dr Giovanni Battista de' Freschi Olivi, physician, theologian
and foe of the Talmud; Don Eusebio Renati, a governor of the
Catecumeni in the 1580s and 1590s, several times a willing witness in
Inquisition cases; and Don Giulio Morosini, formerly Samuel Ben-
Nachmias, who converted in 1649 and many years later published a
voluminous treatise for the assistance of conversionist preachers and dis-
putants.[4]

As with the Marranos, these images, models or ideal types have their
uses and are not divorced from reality. As with the Marranos, the reality
is far more complex: Inquisition and other records do reveal the existence
of converts who were certainly not poor in the sense of being without
property at the time of conversion, and they undoubtedly hint at a great
many others who were neither delinquents, nor backsliders, nor fanatics.

For all these apparent contrasts, the neophyte of Italy and the Marrano
of Spain and Portugal were not wholly dissimilar. Some who converted in
Italy claimed to have previously experienced forced conversion to Islam

---

[4] G. Morosini, *Via della fede mostrata a' gli ebrei* (Rome, 1683); for his appearance as a
witness before the Holy Office on 26 April 1661, see Ioly Zorattini, 'Note e documenti ...',
pp. 337–9. On Freschi Olivi, see above, p. 115, and below, pp. 282–8; on Eusebio Renati,
above, p. 127, and below, pp. 265, 281, 289–90.

in the lands of the Turk. This may well have induced in them a cynicism, or a sense of detachment from any official religion, which came close to that of certain Marranos. As the stories of 'Franciscus Hispanus' and João Batista of Lisbon have shown, it was quite possible for descendants of Marrano families to convert to Christianity in Italy. Although his family arrived in Venice from Salonica, the famous Nachmias-Morosini was of Marrano stock. Distinctions between conversion by persuasion and conversion by duress could not easily be drawn, and the children and dependants of adult converts could hardly be said to have chosen freely for themselves. And there were echoes of fifteenth-century Spain in the conversionary tactics employed by the Counter-Reformation Papacy, which were analogous to the methods of Pedro de Luna, the Spanish Avignonese Pope in the later days of the Great Schism.[5] Crucial to both was the practice of enforcing the legal restrictions which emphasized the servile status of those who followed the superseded faith of the Jews. Paul IV's Roman ghetto was the most tangible expression of this approach, since it imposed a squalor and humiliation which could be escaped only through acceptance of the Christian Messiah. Conversion must come, not through violence, but through the eloquence of the preacher and strict attention to the canon laws governing the relationship between Christians and Jews.

In early modern Europe the conversion of the Jews was envisaged on two quite different levels. It might be imagined as a miraculous and splendid event, in which, as prelude or sequel to the Second Coming, the whole Jewish nation or a mere remnant of it would at last be turned to faith in Christ, in fulfilment of the prophecies contained in the eleventh chapter of St Paul's Epistle to the Romans. Or, more prosaically, it could be seen as a series of individual conversions, each one a triumph laboriously gained by rational argument, biblical scholarship and Christian charity over the general obstinacy and blindness of the Jews, most of whom would persist in error throughout foreseeable future time. The dichotomy was well expressed by the English divine, Joseph Mede, when he wrote in 1629:

> They will never believe that Christ reigns at the right hand of God, until they see him. It must be an invincible evidence which must convert them after so many hundred years settled obstinacy. But this I speak of the body of the Nation; there may be some *Praeludia* of some particulars converted upon other motives, as a forerunner of the great and main Conversion.[6]

[5] See K. R. Stow, *Catholic thought and papal Jewry policy, 1555–1593* (New York, 1977), p. 278 ff.; cf. Y. Baer, *A history of the Jews in Christian Spain* (2 vols., Philadelphia, 1966), II, p. 166 ff.

[6] Quoted in D. S. Katz, *Philosemitism and the readmission of the Jews to England, 1603–1655* (Oxford, 1982), p. 93.

Some heroic attempts have been made to distinguish sharply between Catholic and Protestant attitudes to the conversion of the Jews, and to suggest that only Protestants – and particularly English Baptists and Independents in the wake of the Civil War – were buoyed up with millenarian hopes of the conversion of the entire nation.[7] These arguments are not wholly convincing. Italian Catholics may have had more opportunity to become disillusioned with missionary work, since they regularly practised it in large cities which continued to shelter Jews. But Catholicism had its own deep-rooted millenarian tradition, and Pope Paul IV himself saw portents of the Second Coming in the conversion of Gentile nations beyond the seas, which would itself become the prelude to the conversion of the Jews, as though in fulfilment of the prophecy: 'Blindness in part has fallen upon Israel, until the fulness of the Gentiles have come in, and then the whole of Israel shall be saved' (Romans 11: 25–6). And the argument was vigorously pursued by Marquardus de Susannis, a jurisconsult of Udine, in the polemical sermon he included in his influential *De Iudaeis et aliis infidelibus*, published in Venice in 1558: with the Second Coming at hand, even the perfidy of the Jews would be turned to Christ.[8] In the middle and late sixteenth century, anti-Jewish measures may well have gained a new fervour because they were not merely repressive but rather evangelical in intent, spurred on by the prospect of success. Talmuds were burned, not merely to ensure respect for the Christian religion, but also to drive Jews back to the fundamentals from which they had been distracted, and to return them to the intensive study of the Old Testament, which held the key to the new faith.[9]

There was no clear indication at first that the repressive measures of the Venetians in the sixteenth century were designed to convert the Jews. When the Senate imposed the Ghetto on the Jewish population of the city some forty years before Paul IV, its main motive appeared to be to protect Christians from contamination rather than to win Jewish recruits. If there was any deeper religious motive behind it, the segregation of the Jews may well have been designed to propitiate God at a crucial moment in the Italian wars, when the fate of the Duchy of Milan hung in the balance.[10] It is true, however, that the establishment of the Ghetto was urged by Lenten preachers who had shown some interest in winning Jews over to Christianity, and had sometimes crowned their polemics against Judaism with the baptism of converts in popular churches or such great

[7] E.g. by R. M. Healey, 'The Jew in seventeenth-century Protestant thought', *Church History*, 46 (1977), p. 77; M. Scult, *Millennial expectations and Jewish liberties: a study of the efforts to convert the Jews in Britain, up to the mid-nineteenth century* (Leiden, 1978), pp. 2–3.

[8] Stow, *Catholic thought* ..., pp. 63 ff., 131 ff., 242 ff.

[9] Stow, 'The burning of the Talmud ...'.

[10] See R. Finlay, 'The foundation of the Ghetto: Venice, the Jews, and the War of the League of Cambrai', *Proceedings of the American Philosophical Society*, 126 (1982), pp. 140–54.

public squares as Campo San Polo.[11] A house for catechumens and converts was founded in Venice in 1557, as though in imitation of the institution established in Rome in 1543 by Ignatius Loyola.[12] And it is true, again, that in 1571 the decision to terminate the Jews' *condotta* was accompanied in the Senate's file by a small but revealing piece of legislation which gave a new degree of official recognition to this house of converts. For it then became one of the institutions which Venetian notaries were obliged to mention to testators when drawing up their wills, and it was also added to the list of charities to which the Collegio would regularly contribute alms.[13] Admittedly the Catecumeni may have owed its new status to the number of Turkish prisoners-of-war then in Venice, but the precise timing of the decree suggests that the proposed removal of the Jews from Venice was incidentally expected – as was the expulsion of the Jews from Spain eighty years earlier[14] – to bring in substantial numbers of converts.

As is well known, the conversion campaigns were developed under Pope Gregory XIII: in 1577 he founded the Collegio dei Neofiti to train converts for missionary work, and seven years later issued a Bull urging Christian authorities who sheltered Jews to provide conversion sermons for their benefit.[15] To guard converts from insult and discouragement was one of the aims of the Bull of 1581 which extended the jurisdiction of the Holy Office over professing Jews; though causing concern to the Venetian Collegio, it seems to have been sporadically enforced during the 1580s.[16] Venice's response to other papal proposals is less evident. It seems certain that before this pontificate sermons to small numbers of Jews had been delivered in the great Mendicant churches of the city. On Palm Sunday, 1519, Fra Giovanni d'Agnolina had addressed fifteen Jews in the Frari.[17] About 1569, Isaac Pugliese of Vigevano was induced by his noble patron, Antonio Boldù, to attend a sermon in Santi Giovanni e Paolo, uttered by a 'preacher most learned in the Hebrew tongue'. In the audience was another patrician, Pietro Loredan, who was evidently a connoisseur of such sermons and urged him at suitable moments: ' "Mark this pass-

---

[11] For examples of Lenten baptisms, and of the activities of Fra Rufino, see D.M.S., VIII, col. 70–71, 79, 88, 6, 10, 15 April 1509; XII, col. 98–9, 121, 2, 18 April 1511; XVIII, col. 51, 123, 19 March, 9 April 1514; XXII, col. 65, 72–3, 23, 26 March 1516.

[12] See *Capitoli ed ordini per il buon governo delle pie case de' Catecumeni di Venezia* (Venice, 1737), pp. 4–5; I.R.E.C., fragment of an eighteenth-century Catastico, fol. 424r.

[13] S.T., filza 58, 18 Dec. 1571.

[14] Cf. Baer, *Jews in Christian Spain*, II, pp. 435–6.

[15] See B.R., VIII, pp. 188–91, 487–9; cf. Peña, pp. 74–5, and Stow, *Catholic thought ...*, pp. 208–9, 214–15, 281.

[16] See above, pp. 73–4, 76–7.

[17] D.M.S., XXVII, col. 182, 17 April 1519.

age!" '[18] But the Venetian government was unlikely to agree to anything so bold as compulsory sermons for all adult Jews. Archbishop Matteucci, nuncio in 1588, was eager to see them introduced; the Patriarch Priuli was still awaiting them in 1596–97.[19] But the state could hardly have countenanced such a measure at a time when it was especially eager to attract Sephardim to the city and guarantee them liberty to practise their religion.

Being chiefly concerned with weakness, irresolution and failure, Inquisition records can suggest all too strongly that the artificially imposed poverty of the Ghetto, and the proposals to relieve it by means of Christian charity, were the principal weapons in the conversionist's armoury. Some Jews, however, claimed with conviction that their conversion had been a disinterested intellectual process, the outcome of study and disputation rather than of merely listening to sermons. In 1528, Camillo, a learned Jew, was said to have been converted by reading the Epistles of St Paul, and he acknowledged his debt by taking the name of Paolo at the font.[20] The arguments of pious Christians, springing from common ground in the Old Testament, were designed to prove to the Jews that the Scriptures were fulfilled in Jesus of Nazareth, who must be acknowledged as the Messiah; the most popular of the standard texts and prophecies on which they focused was without doubt Genesis 49: 10. About 1555, Matthias Gutich, a physician from Pomerania, saw one dressed as a Jew attending a Capuchin's sermon in the fashionable church of the hospital of the Incurabili. Knowing some Hebrew himself, he

> seized the chance to reason with him. To overturn his law, I quoted him the dictum of the prophet Ezekiel, where he says in the person of God, 'I have given them a law which is not good, and statutes which are not good, whereby they shall not live.' Then, said I, it was necessary that one should come to fulfil it; and that this is true and that he is now come appears from the blessing of Judah, where it is said: 'The sceptre shall not depart from Judah until Messiah comes.' Now you have neither king, nor kingdom, nor lordship, nor any of these things; therefore, the Messiah has come.[21]

The powerlessness of the Jews, evinced in the society of the Ghetto, was itself an instrument of persuasion and the demonstration of a prophecy. Isaac Pugliese, afterwards Marcantonio degli Eletti, gave pride of place to

[18] I.Z. II, pp. 104–5, proc. Marcantonio degli Eletti, test. the prisoner, 15 Nov. 1569.
[19] D.N., filza 26, fol. 198, 30 April 1588; S.T., filza 141, 31 Jan. 1596 Venetian style.
[20] D.M.S., XLVI, col. 501–2, 19 Jan. 1528.
[21] I.Z., p. 295, proc. Gian Giacomo de' Fedeli, 15 Sept. 1558. The first quotation is from Ezekiel 20: 25.

the same text during his trial for repeating baptism, in a written submission intended to demonstrate how well he had absorbed the lessons of Christianity:

> They have no house or tribe of Judah, no field or vineyard, and there are no lords or captains among them; how then can they think the Messiah is still to come? If they have nothing in their hands, how then can they lose it?[22]

By way of a textbook, his patrons had urged upon him the *De arcanis catholicae veritatis* of the Franciscan Pietro Colonna or Petrus Galatinus, first published in 1518. It was a much read memorial to the belief that the best way to convert the Jews was to confound them out of their own writings, and not only by invoking the Mosaic law but also by resort to the cabbalah, the oral tradition which uncovered the secrets of the law. The convert's submission was embellished with quotations in the original Hebrew, and there were suggestions that he had indeed been influenced by the most characteristic arguments of the Christian cabbalists, – by the mysteries contained in Hebrew letters, in the tetragrammaton and in the names of God. He spoke with enthusiasm of the prophecies of Rabbi Elias or of the 'house of Eli', that the world would last for 6,000 years, divided into three great epochs; 2,000 years of nature, before the giving of the law; 2,000 years of Scripture; 2,000 years of the days of the Messiah. When 1,569 years of the third epoch had already passed, how could the Jews refuse to acknowledge Jesus?[23]

In 1579 Estevão Nogueira gave the Inquisition an account of secret disputations between Jews, secret Jews and Christians which may well have been wholly spurious, but still has some value as further confirmation of the list of texts round which such a debate could have been expected to develop. Should such passages as 'Behold, a virgin shall conceive' and 'Unto us a son is given' be understood to refer to the Virgin Mary and to Jesus of Nazareth, and what should be made of the text in Daniel 9: 24–7, concerning the seventy weeks?[24] Over the next seventy years, the conventions governing such discussions changed little, to judge by the account of his own conversion furnished by Morosini, late Nachmias. He explained that he turned out of admiration for the good customs of Christians, because he had heard their goodness praised even by Leon Modena, the most fashionable Jewish preacher of his day, and because he had come to believe that the Scriptures were fulfilled in Jesus

---

[22] I.Z. II, pp. 105–7, 110–14, 15 Nov., Dec. 1569.

[23] Cf. Secret, *Les kabbalistes* . . . , pp. 8–11, 84–5, 102–4.

[24] S.U., b. 44, proc. 'Negromanti', den. Antonio Saldanha and Estevão Nogueira, 11, 20 Jan. 1579; references are to Isaiah 7: 14, and Isaiah 9: 6.

of Nazareth. Crucial to his decision was, he said, a disputation over the seventy weeks in the Book of Daniel, in which even Rabbi Simon Luzzatto, the famous apologist, had come close to conceding victory to the Christians. As though anticipating all the standard charges against converts, Morosini emphasized that at the moment of conversion he was a mature and highly educated man of thirty-seven, and that he came of a distinguished and well-to-do Sephardic family.[25] Hence he could hardly be accused of espousing Christianity out of ignorance, juvenile impulsiveness or greed for Christian charity.

But for poor Jews and indifferent scholars there undoubtedly were material incentives to conversion, which might outweigh all other considerations. The Church had not only to impose upon professing Jews constraints and humiliations which proved that Judaism did not pay, but also to hold out inducements which suggested that Christianity did. For the *vera fides* of Christians was a spiritual state superior to the *perfidia* of Jews, and there ought therefore to be a superior social condition, the wider world of Christianity spreading beyond the confining walls of the Ghetto, which corresponded with it. Christian charity would be the visible demonstration of the providence of God. Since the thirteenth century, Popes had issued legislation which commended poor converts from Judaism to Christianity and urged Christians to make them better off by virtue of their transformation.[26] In the seventeenth century the *Nuper ad Fidem Conversus* was still deserving enough to be listed by the Neapolitan jurist Giovanni Maria Novario among his many categories of privileged poor.[27] As well as their general recommendations, the popes from time to time issued briefs in favour of rich Jews and their families converting to Christianity, such as that granted by Clement VII to Jacob, son of the banker Asher Meshullam, in 1530, which entitled him to keep his property provided he restored, by one means or another, all usurious gains.[28]

A new charter for converts, influential but not wholly original, was devised in 1542 by Pope Paul III in the Bull *Cupientes iudaeos*; many printed copies of the document survive among the records of the Casa dei Catecumeni in Venice, and it was sometimes cited in Inquisition proceedings.[29] Dealing both with the propertied and with the poor, the Bull

[25] Morosini, 'A' i dispersi figliuoli d'Israele della presente Cattività', preliminary address to his *Via della fede* ....

[26] Stow, *Catholic thought* ..., p. 51; Nicholas III, *Vineam sorec*, 4 Aug. 1278, and John XXII, *Cum sit absurdum*, 19 June 1320, B.R., IV, pp. 45–6, 294.

[27] See A. Musi, 'Pauperismo e pensiero giuridico a Napoli nella prima metà del secolo XVII', forthcoming in *Timore e carità: i poveri nell' Italia moderna* (Cremona).

[28] D.M.S., LVIII, col. 567–9, entry for 15 July 1533.

[29] See Peña, *Literae apostolicae* ..., pp. 86–7; B.R., VI, pp. 336–7. There are references to the Bull in the cases of Gian Giacomo Fedele (I.Z., p. 273, a delation of 1558) and of Mendlin of Sacile (S.U., b. 52, test. Giovanni Daniele Bastiati, 25 Feb. 1585).

provided *inter alia* that even those who had converted against their parents' wishes should be entitled to their share of the patrimony. Clergy and laity were exhorted 'by the bowels of God's mercy' to give aid to poor converts. Bishops must defend them against insult and injury; they must exhort Christians to help them; and they must themselves grant them assistance from ecclesiastical revenues, including those set aside for the poor. Jews should become 'citizens' – whatever that might imply – of the places in which they were baptized. Having become 'citizens of the holy places and servants of God', how much more should they enjoy their rights in the city on earth. They would not be encouraged to marry with other converts, but rather with persons born Christians who would strengthen them in their resolution. If scrupulously followed, such policies would prevent the perpetuation of the ghetto outside the ghetto's walls, through the persistence of endogamous groups of newcomers to Christianity deprived of normal opportunities for social advancement.

At the start of the sixteenth century, conversion was already well endowed with public rituals, and there were well-tried methods of giving the convert a good start in the Christian world. He would at least be provided with a suit of clothes, which was not only a charitable gift but also the symbol of a new and dramatically altered life. 'Clothing' a Jew, in Sanuto's vocabulary, was equivalent to baptizing him.[30] A collection would be taken for the new Christian, sometimes in more than one place; Giovanni Battista from Portogruaro received 25 ducats at the Madonna dell' Orto and another 'goodly sum in alms' on Campo San Polo.[31] In 1521, David, aged fifteen, grandson of Cervo of Verona, was baptized Constantino Marco in the Doge's box or 'pulpit' in St Mark's. His godfathers, the Doge's nephew and twenty other noblemen, gave him 1 ducat each, and a collection round the Church brought the complete takings to 51 ducats. Lest the young man's motives be misunderstood, the diarist hastened to add that 'he was a rich Jew, and was moved by the Holy Spirit to be baptized.'[32] Rich and poor alike received their alms and promises of support. When Vivian, aged seventeen, son of Jacob and grandson of Anselmo del Banco, was baptized in the Frari in 1528, boxes were placed at the doors as if it were a Jubilee, though not more than 20 ducats were found in them. Although his father had assured him that he would not go in want, his Christian benefactors still drew up a subscription list to buy him an annuity:[33] it was as though giving fulfilled a need

---

[30] D.M.S., VIII, col. 79, 10 April 1509 – Fra Rufino 'vestirà, zoè baptiserà, uno ebreo zovene'.

[31] Ibid., VIII, col. 88, 15 April 1509.

[32] Ibid., XXXI, col. 291, 24 Aug. 1521.

[33] Ibid., XLVI, col. 501–2, 19 Jan. 1528.

in them, even where there was no conspicuous material need in the convert.

A poor convert would more likely be furnished, especially by a bishop or abbot, with a patent confirming his status as a former Jew now turned Christian and commending him as an especially deserving object of charity. Thus, the document issued in 1548 to Aaron of Sarzana, baptized Francesco at the Camaldolese abbey of Vangadizza in the Polesine, exhorted all Christians that

> when the aforesaid Francesco approaches you, you should treat him
> charitably and kindly, assisting him who has been deprived of all
> worldly goods and become naked even as he came forth from the
> womb, that he may truly know how generous is the providence of
> God, and see that God never abandons one who trusts in him, but
> rather endows him with every kind of good; and that when he
> understands this he may continually go forward to better things;
> and that others, moved by his example, may have recourse to the
> mercy of God and come to the Holy Catholic Faith in the know-
> ledge that just as there is one true God even so there is one true way
> to his Kingdom, and that is the Gospel of Christ.[34]

The patent was a florid, literary version of the licence to beg. This was one of the less fraud-proof devices used by city authorities for identifying the deserving poor;[35] unlike the licence, however, the patent was an aid to begging rather than an indispensable qualification for the activity – to judge, at least, by Giovanni Battista Cividin, who managed to raise 46 lire from various Friulian townships and villages at Christmas 1577 without the benefit of a patent from the bishop.[36] Some seventeenth-century converts had such documents and exploited them. A woman said of Stefano Valetta in 1644 that 'Now he's a second-hand dealer, but before that he used to go seeking alms, and publicly displaying his converted Jew's patent.'[37] And Salvatore da Caglione, baptized in Vicenza in 1642, came to Venice two years later with a woman and a small girl, put up at the Sturgeon on the Riva del Carbone in the parish of San Silvestro, whose host was himself a former Jew, and spent four or five weeks working the city and its religious houses.[38] His was a form of licensed begging

[34] I.Z., p. 69, proc. Aaron Francoso, document dated 27 March 1548.

[35] On this see Pullan, *Rich and poor* ..., pp. 221–2, 238.

[36] See the text of his trial in P. C. Ioly Zorattini, 'Un giudaizzante cividalese del Cinque-cento: Gioanbattista Cividin', in *Studi storici e geografici*, I (Pisa, 1977), pp. 203, 205.

[37] S.U., b. 101, proc. Stefano Valetta, test. Francesca della Fonte of San Giovanni in Bragora, 17 March 1644.

[38] Ibid., proc. Salvatore da Caglione, note from the Inquisition of Vicenza, 30 Dec. 1644, and test. Battista Molin, 21 Feb. 1645.

which outlasted the most vigorous attempts to enclose the poor in the all-embracing hospital of the Mendicanti.

Converts and conversions provided entertainment and spectacle which ranged from great theatrical occasions to lively sideshows. Every place in the Frari was taken at Vivian's baptism in 1528, and Sanuto guessed the crowd at 10,000.[39] Towards 1580 three young Paduan converts, Zanetto, Antonio and their cousin Menego, joined the mountebanks in Venice and made money without selling anything, but just by talking in Hebrew for the delight of the bystanders.[40] Small wonder, then, that conversion should become a trade for the *furfante*, the rogue and vagabond who lived by exploiting the credulity of the pious and needed a good story to tell. From the end of the fifteenth century, if from no earlier time, sensational treatises on the underworld had identified the Iucchi or rebaptized Jews at a kind of sub-guild within the huge, sprawling confraternity of professional beggars which they loved to depict. As Teseo Pini described the Iucchi in his *Speculum Cerretanorum*,

> They are called 'rebaptized' because they repeat baptism: they pretend they were once Jews grown fat upon usurious lending, but they say that they have seen awe-inspiring visions and scarcely credible miracles. Inspired by these they have, in the manner of the apostle, abandoned everything to follow the poor Christ in poverty and perfection.[41]

There is little evidence that fraudulent begging was really an organized business, but the conversion game undoubtedly was, in life as well as in art, a standard ruse for those living by their wits. Some of its practitioners had never in fact been Jews and had not actually taken baptism. Santo of Venice, who travelled with a donkey and carried a halberd on his journey through the Veneto, had a mate, Leonora, a squat and unlovely woman who called herself a Mantuan, but was very likely a Piedmontese and in flight from her husband in Vercelli. When the pair came to Verona in

[39] D.M.S., XLVI, col. 501–2, 19 Jan. 1528. For the baptism of Lazarus near the Vendramin bank at Rialto, ibid., LII, col. 318, 2 Dec. 1529.

[40] S.U., b. 59, proc. Marco di Francesco of Padua, 22–23 Oct. 1587.

[41] See P. Camporesi, ed., *Il libro dei vagabondi* (Turin, 1973), pp. XCII–XCIII, CLVI, 44–5, 140–1, 358, 367. Pini's treatise was written about 1485 and remained in manuscript for over a century, though it was probably rediscovered about 1585 when the Papacy grew increasingly concerned with the problem of mendicity in Rome. It was eventually published by the Dominican Giacinto Nobili, who used the pseudonym Rafaele Frianoro, and did something to adapt it and bring it up to date. The first known edition is that of Viterbo in 1621. Ibid., pp. XX–XXII, CLVII–CLVIII, CLXVIII–CLXIX, 167–78; cf. B. Pullan, 'Poveri, mendicanti e vagabondi (secoli XIV–XVII)', in *Storia d'Italia: Annali I. Dal feudalesimo al capitalismo*, ed. C. Vivanti and R. Romano (Turin, 1978), pp. 1011–14.

August 1587, Santo sent her to seek alms, and she did so as a Jew turned Christian. Arrested at the suit of the Vicar-General of the diocese, she was found to be a false beggar, kept in prison for two or three days, and then released after seeing her bogus certificate destroyed.[42] In Venice in 1611, one Lorenzo of Verona was said to be visiting monasteries and other churches and begging in the guise of a Jew turned Christian, compounding his offence by lamenting that the Casa dei Catecumeni had taken all the moneys collected at his baptism and sent him away with nothing.[43] To lay hands on patents was not difficult. Antonio Giustinian, a convert who offered to eliminate frauds and improve the finances of the Catecumeni, explained that bishops would all too readily give them and that they were often lent, sold or otherwise passed from hand to hand.[44] Travelling in the Veneto as authorized collector to the Catecumeni, he observed that 'in all the Bresciano there are only five who are really Jews turned Christian, but there are a thousand seekers of alms who say they are converts to Christianity.'[45] Those detected were, like Leonora, liable to be punished, but none too harshly, by the secular authorities.[46] Persons who had actually been Jews but had repeated baptism for mercenary ends would come within the purview of the Inquisition, and were liable to much harsher penalties, for they had passed beyond fraud and into the abuse of sacred things.

The Pia Casa dei Catecumeni stood for a less haphazard approach to the problem of conversion; it was designed to scrutinize the intentions of prospective converts, to see them properly instructed, to eliminate fraud, and to provide the emotional and other support necessary to preventing lapses. Intended as a haven not only for Jewish converts but also for Turks and Moors, it embodied many of the ideals of the more advanced Catholic philanthropy of the mid-sixteenth century.[47] Its charity was to

---

[42] S.U., b. 59, proc. Marco di Francesco of Padua, testimony of the prisoner, 22–23 Oct. 1587.

[43] I.R.E.C., Not. F, fol. 18, 2 May 1611.

[44] Ibid., fol. 147, 6 June 1619. Cf. a report from the Inquisitor in Capodistria, 28 Aug. to 23 Sept. 1636, which describes how Giuseppe Bon, alias Francesco Maria Leoncini, had passed patents to another Francesco Maria, who accepted them in payment of a debt and in exchange for a promise of help (S.U., b. 94, proc. Giuseppe or Iseppo Bon). For other references to fraudulent begging, I.R.E.C., Not. D, fol. 29v., 10 Feb. 1593 Venetian style; Not. F, fol. 93v., 1 Oct. 1615.

[45] I.R.E.C., Carte Diverse, 'Arricordi de Antonio Giustinian', fol. 44, 14 Nov. 1619.

[46] Ibid., fol. 42, 43v., 29 Oct., 14 Nov. 1619.

[47] For the original Roman house of the Catecumeni, see B.R., VI, pp. 353–8; A. Milano, *Il ghetto di Roma: illustrazioni storiche* (Rome, 1964), p. 283; Stow, *Catholic thought* ..., p. 52. On the Catholic philanthropy of the period, see Pullan, *Rich and poor* ..., p. 372 ff.; B. Pullan, 'Catholics and the poor in early modern Europe', *Transactions of the Royal Historical Society*, 5th series, 26 (1976), pp. 28–30; B. Pullan, 'The old Catholicism, the new Catholicism and the poor', forthcoming in *Timore e carità*....

be directed towards the sublime purpose of conquering souls from ignorance, infidelity and sin, and to be enlisted in a domestic struggle which corresponded modestly to the sweeping campaigns being fought in overseas continents. Venice's Jews and infidels could hardly be recruited on so vast a scale as the Indians, but each soul won for Christ at home and without holy violence would mark a triumph of the highest quality. Pius V's nuncio, Facchinetti, as though a trifle weary of the Jesuits' heroics, reminded them of successes which could comfortably be scored on the 'great crowd of Turks' in Venice.[48] And in their petition of 1571 the governors of the Casa declared that

> we seek to recover lost souls. If other good works deserve assistance and support, this one is especially meritorious. In others they deal only with the maintenance of the body; but in this we are concerned with the maintenance of the body, the conquest of souls, and the acquisition of faith. Your Serenity makes every effort to uphold the faith, and at present is seeking to extend and extol it.[49]

The Catecumeni was first established in rented accommodation at San Marcuola in 1557. It then moved twice; each move took it further from the Ghetto, and towards the peripheral zones of the Zattere and the Giudecca where the new religious orders and the new charities of the Counter Reformation – the Jesuits, the hospital of the Incurabili, the houses of the Zitelle and Convertite – were finding vacant land and cheap sites, at the cost of some remoteness from the hub of city life. After a spell at the Santi Apostoli, the institution came to rest at San Gregorio in 1571 and began with time to purchase premises of its own.[50] In early days it was chiefly concerned with Jewish converts; in 1563, there were some fifteen male inmates, eight of whom were catechumens under instruction, whilst seven were baptized Christians, and only one, described as Abraham the Moor, appeared not to be Jewish.[51] Traditions of the house, repeated in the eighteenth-century statutes, suggest that the proportions changed during the war of Cyprus and Lepanto, when large numbers of slaves were brought to the city and the Turkish intakes began to increase.[52]

---

[48] N.V., IX, pp. 142–3.

[49] S.T., filza 58, 18 Dec. 1571.

[50] *Capitoli ed ordini ...*, pp. 4–6; G. Tassini, *Curiosità veneziane, ovvero Origini delle denominazioni stradali* (new edition, ed. L. Moretti, Venice, 1964), p. 154; I.R.E.C., Catastico 71 (1504–1698), fol. 29–30, 42.

[51] As appears from the investigation of Aaron and Asher, I.Z. II, pp. 31–48, 8 May to 4 June 1563.

[52] *Capitoli ed ordini*, p. 5.

Unlike most Venetian fraternities, hospitals and charities, whose administration was strictly under lay control, with the clergy confined to the roles of chaplains or spiritual advisers, the Catecumeni was tied to the Patriarch and managed by a congregation of governors which included substantial numbers of clerics. The foundation meeting was held in the palace of the Patriarch Diedo, and he gave official approval to the institution.[53] Connexions with Jesuit neighbours were strong in the later sixteenth century, and their advice was sought, together with the Patriarch's, on many delicate cases.[54] Their expulsion during the verdict of 1606–7 breached the institution's ranks, and the Patriarch Vendramin had subsequently to be invited to appoint other religious to examine Jewish children before baptism.[55] Occasionally the Patriarch would himself baptize converts,[56] and he would sometimes preside over arguments between the governors of the Catecumeni and the Jewish relatives of young persons who had declared their intention to convert.[57] On the board of governors were represented the three higher estates of Venetian society – the clergy, the nobility and the citizens or merchants – and at any one time there would be three executive officers or *Presidenti*, chosen in rotation from the congregation, one drawn from each estate. On 21 May 1592 the three *Presidenti* were the parish priest of Sant' Angelo, the noble Benedetto Zorzi and a citizen or merchant named Alvise Stella. On that day thirteen other brothers attended the congregation, including the parish priests of San Vio, San Lio and San Maurizio and two other clerics. Of the eight laymen, two were described as *Clarissimi* and were presumably noblemen.[58] Surviving minutes-books record very systematic procedures, the congregation deliberating among much else on the admission of candidates and the timing of their baptisms, and deputing named persons to carry out clearly defined tasks. Supervision of the 'children of the house', as all inmates and ex-pupils were called, was – during their time within the walls of the house – the business of a Prior and a Prioress. As a minute impeccably stated, the Prior ought to be 'a reverend priest of good life and character, with some degree of learning, for the benefit and salvation of souls'.[59]

So far as is known, the Catecumeni was financed entirely by voluntary contributions, by bequests, gifts or alms handed to collectors, and did not

[53] Ibid., pp. 4–5, 15.

[54] I.R.E.C., Not. D, fol. 8r., 8v., 21, 46, 50, 85, 92, 94v. (between 24 Sept. 1592 and 11 June 1599).

[55] Ibid., Not. F, fol. 85v., 4 Sept. 1614.

[56] Ibid., Not. D, fol. 41v., 24 Nov. 1594.

[57] Ibid., Not. F, fol. 25v., 21 July 1611.

[58] Ibid., Not. D, fol. 1r.–v.

[59] Ibid., fol. 15, 11 March 1593.

benefit by any dues or taxes similar to those levied on the Jewish communities of the Papal States.[60] Dutiful notaries, obeying the decree of 1571, would very likely draw from testators a number of small bequests in the form of lump sums in cash.[61] A few benefactors founded trusts, providing much larger sums which were to be invested to obtain an income, either for the house itself or for its pupils or former inmates. A pioneer among them was Vincenzo Garzoni (ca. 1547–94). By his will of 1588 he declared that 'having always thought it good to invite infidels to the waters of holy baptism and to give them assistance', he wished a total of 500 ducats to be dispensed annually in perpetuity 'to the honour and glory of the Five Wounds of Our Lord', and to be shared among twenty Jews, Turks or Moors, male or female, so long as they were over twelve years of age on coming to the font. This proviso was plainly intended to eliminate children baptized at their parents' request, and to confine the benefits to those who had chosen Christianity of their own free will. The bequest would be advertised by the Guardian of the Franciscans of San Nicolò, who was expected to print particulars and circulate them to all places, within and outside the Venetian dominions, which contained Jews or infidels. By a codicil the income was doubled, the benefits increased to 50 ducats per head per annum, and the trust – administered by the Patriarch, the Guardian of San Nicolò and the two oldest members of the noble and citizen estates among the governors of the Catecumeni – came into operation in 1594.[62]

Other testators adopted similar tactics. In the mid-seventeenth century Giacomo Galli left the Catecumeni 20,000 ducats to be 'cautiously' invested, the income to be used to make once-and-for-all gifts of 50 ducats apiece to Turks, Moors, Jews and other infidels who came to baptism, 'that they may have reason to persevere in good works and pray to God for my soul'.[63] Using a different formula, benefactors interested in the progress of particular children of the house could make bequests to them personally; two former Jewesses, Cattarina and Betta, inherited modest sums from Venetian noblewomen, and, about 1600, had them invested on their behalf by the governors of the Catecumeni.[64] And the institution itself did, as might be expected, receive outright gifts or assignments of income to be used at its discretion to improve the lot of its pupils.[65]

In 1618, some sixty years after its foundation, the 'ordinary' income of

---

[60] Cfr. Stern, *Urkundliche Beiträge* . . . , I, docs. 134–5, pp. 143–5.

[61] Cfr. Pullan, *Rich and poor* . . . , pp. 415–16.

[62] I.R.E.C., Catastico 71, fol. 61–2, 65r., 107r.–v., 109r.–v., will of 11 Aug. 1588, codicil of 5 Aug. 1591; Not. D., fol. 39, 42, 15 Sept., 5 Dec. 1594.

[63] I.R.E.C., Catastico 71, fol. 141, 10 Feb. 1648 Venetian style.

[64] Ibid., fol. 70v.–71r., 73v.–74r.

[65] E.g. those of Cattarina Mocenigo, 1608–9, ibid., fol. 76v., 88r.–v., 96r.–97v.

the house was estimated at 360 ducats per annum, 'ordinary' expenditure at 370 ducats.[66] Plainly, however, this represented only a small proportion of the expenditure on converts in Venice, since it did not include the moneys supposed to be dispensed each year from the coffers of the Garzoni trust: these 1,000 ducats were left to the converts themselves and not to the house, which merely participated in the administration of the bequest. Even if converts enjoyed income of only 1,400 ducats a year, it was – on the restricted scale on which all charity must be measured – an ample sum to be shared among a small corpus of privileged poor. In the better years of the early seventeenth century, the richest of the charitable fraternities, the Scuola Grande di San Rocco, dispensed about 5,000 ducats a year, principally in alms and dowry payments, but its clientele was much larger and more vaguely defined.[67] Furthermore, the term 'ordinary' revenue may well include only revenue from investments, and not the average sums gained annually from gifts, small bequests and collections. We know, also, that some of Venice's large new foundations, such as the Incurabili and the Mendicanti, relied very little on investment income,[68] and the Catecumeni, though much smaller and more specialized than these big hospitals, may have conformed to the same pattern. Regular and predictable income could be supplemented by windfalls such as the 100-ducat fine imposed by the *Ufficiali al Cattaver* on Solomon Portogallo, probably for approaching a child in the house and trying to lure him away.[69] Converts in general relied for support or extra benefits upon collecting alms, in churches or public places or from door to door, either for themselves personally or for the institution.

Ambitious attempts to organize the process, not only in Venice itself but across the whole mainland state, were made in and after 1619 by the convert Antonio Giustinian. His scheme was an attempt to replace altogether the old laissez-faire arrangements whereby each convert collected for himself, and whereby the citizens and villagers of the mainland were chronically vulnerable to the importunities of the *furfante*. In response to his proposal the governors of the Catecumeni called in all patents they had themselves issued, and bishops were requested – they could scarcely be instructed – to desist from handing out these dangerous documents. Giustinian would now become chief agent and co-ordinator of a central scheme whereby the Catecumeni would have the monopoly of all begging and collecting on behalf of converts, and all newcomers to the Church would be instructed to apply to it for aid. Giustinian had something in him of the showman, the mountebank, perhaps even of the *furfante*, for he

---

[66] I.R.E.C., Not. F, fol. 122v., 27 June 1618.

[67] See Pullan, *Rich and poor* ..., pp. 165–6.

[68] Ibid., pp. 412–13.

[69] I.R.E.C., Not. F, fol. 20r., 20v., 27, for 26 May and 4 Aug. 1611.

had a splendid story to tell of his own conversion by a vision of the Virgin Mary; no doubt, too, he could personify vividly the inmates of the house he represented, thus saving the procedures from becoming drab and colourless. But he was also something of a bureaucrat or commissar, keeping in touch with the governors by correspondence (though not so regularly as to allay their suspicions), and enlisting coadjutors and sub-delegates with the aid of local authorities, both of the Church and of the state. He and his helpers were remunerated as commission agents; 5 per cent of the proceeds would be his, and 10 per cent would go to them, under the original arrangements of 1619.[70] In all probability, Giustinian told those who already held patents to seek the benefits of the Garzoni trust. This can be inferred from an aggrieved letter, written from Padua to the governors by one Paolo d'Anatolia:

> He says we shall get 50 ducats each, but we have not received them, and hence there is mutiny in the city, and there are Christians here who used to be Jews and have gone to complain to the Most Illustrious Bishop. He has sent them away, saying that they should have patience until Easter.[71]

Their discontent reflected the tensions and contrasts between two approaches to conversion – between the traditional haphazard arrangements, dependent on freelance begging, and a newer system dependent on a specialized institution which would exercise close supervision over its 'children'. Neither was able to triumph over the other, and products of both processes were, from time to time, to attract the attention of the Holy Office.

The highly formalized process of conversion instituted by the Catecumeni fits almost too snugly into Van Gennep's famous analysis of the rites which marked the passage of an individual from 'one defined position to another which is equally well defined'.[72] It was marked by a decisive, preliminary separation of the potential convert from the world of the Jews, involving his physical removal to the other side of the city and his enclosure in the Catecumeni, there to pass through a transitional period of instruction in the elements of Christian faith and worship. From this liminal state, poised between Judaism and Christianity, the convert could be expected to proceed to baptism, which was at once a further rite of separation from evil and a ritual of incorporation with Christ and the Church. Such solemnities would surely declare the need to forsake the

---

[70] Ibid., fol. 146v.–152v., 6 June to 8 July 1619; Carte Diverse, 'Arricordi di Antonio Giustinian'.

[71] Ibid., 'Arricordi', fol. 58v.–59r., 9 March 1620. Cfr. also fol. 42r.–v.

[72] See A. Van Gennep, *The rites of passage*, transl. M. B. Vizedom and G. L. Caffee (Chicago–London, 1960), especially pp. 3, 10–11, 17–21, 63, 93–4.

Jewish world, emphasizing it as the older and more casual procedures had not, and would likewise stress the unique and decisive character of baptism, making more heinous the offences of those who debased it in any way.

At its most formal, conversion might well begin with a solemn declaration of intent on the part of the prospective Christian. When Simon Luzzatto resolved to change his religion in 1592, he signed a paper which was probably addressed to Father Rocca, preacher at San Geremia:

> Reverend father, I am most ready to come to the faith of Jesus Christ and to believe with all my heart and to observe, with all its consequences, everything that may be taught me. May it therefore please your reverence to declare from the pulpit to what place I must go in order to be instructed in the faith; and I beg that my good intention may be fulfilled as soon as possible, that the Devil, who is the enemy of all good deeds, may not impede this most worthy operation. . . .

Shortly afterwards he added a personal declaration to the effect that he had come to Christianity because he knew it to be the true faith. He applied – probably through the Holy Office, in whose files the records of this transaction survive – for an order giving custody of two small children, a son of seven or eight years and a daughter aged two or three, who would be delivered to him with a view to their being baptized with him. That the preacher would order him to the Catecumeni was a foregone conclusion. An inventory of his property was taken, and a government tipstaff solemnly proclaimed for his benefit that no Jew might dare to approach the Casa or send to it any emissary of any faith or condition, or loiter or transact business in the streets nearby. In due course Simon Luzzatto was transmuted into the Christian Hieronimo, doubtless taking his name from the church where his pious purpose had been announced.[73]

In his compilation of laws concerning Jews, Marquardus de Susannis recalled that a Jew ought to wait forty days to receive baptism after first expressing the desire. Once the probationary period had been a mere eleven days, but at that time many Jews had returned to Judaism soon after baptism. It was true that as students of the old law Jews would require less instruction than other infidels; but their conversion should still be delayed out of respect for the faith.[74] Hence, conversionists might well think themselves generous in the time they allowed to Jews to reflect

[73] S.U., b. 69.
[74] Stow, *Catholic thought* . . . , p. 171; Marquardus de Susannis, *De Iudaeis et aliis infidelibus* (Venice, 1558), fol. 131.

on their decision: they could surely not be charged with rushing them into an irrevocable step. However, it was not necessary to spend all the days elapsing between declaration and baptism actually within the walls of the Pia Casa. In the late sixteenth century spells of residence in the institution varied considerably in length. The secretary who served the congregation of governors in 1595 fortunately had clear and consistent habits in recording dates of acceptance by the governors and dates of eventual baptism. These show that the briefest intervals between the two were then of about three weeks, whilst the longest far exceeded the prescribed forty days.[75] Preliminaries could clearly be protracted in difficult circumstances, should there be serious doubt concerning the aspirant's intentions or his account of his origins and life. Paolo Loredan, formerly a Cretan Jew, told the Inquisition that he had been three months in the Catecumeni, from December 1586 to March 1587, before being baptized.[76] In the early seventeenth century forty days became the accepted minimum period between acceptance and baptism. Samuel, a Jew from Poland who had reached Venice via Bosnia and been lodged in the house of a noble patron, Giovanni Barbaro, was received by the governors on 14 April 1611; on 19 May it was decreed that he be baptized ten days later on the day of the Most Holy Trinity.[77] Israel, aged fourteen, son of Isaac of Lonigo, was accepted by all sixteen votes of the congregation assembled on 14 July of the same year. Two or three weeks later, arrangements were made to parade him before the Patriarch for examination, and on 25 August the governors resolved that he be baptized on 4 September.[78] 'Sara, a foreign Jewess, come from the Ghetto of this city' was accepted on 2 May 1614; but, since inquiries had to be made to satisfy the governors that she had not previously been baptized, she did not come to the font until 8 September of that year.[79] Later in the century, very brief spells in the Catecumeni could again be considered sufficient, for Nathan Cohen, son of Chaim, of Corfu, was baptized only eleven days after admission, in February 1658.[80] If the allegations soon made against him were justified, his sponsors might well have devoted more time to scrutinizing his motives. It is tempting to say that short probationary periods implied haste and long ones thoroughness and deliberation. In fact there were pitfalls in both, for the prospect of several months' free board and lodging could enhance the Casa's attractions for the opportunist and the ne'er-do-well.

[75] I.R.E.C., Not. D, fol. 45v.–60r.

[76] S.U., b. 60, proc. Paolo Loredan and Chiara Pisani, test. 15 Oct. 1587.

[77] I.R.E.C., Not. F, fol. 16v., 19v.

[78] Ibid., fol. 25, 26v., 27, 29v.

[79] Ibid., fol. 82v., 85v.

[80] S.U., b. 114, proc. Nicolò Dolfin, test. Michael Cosunovich of Split, Prior of the Catecumeni, 17 June 1660. See also below, pp. 309–10.

Information about the instruction offered in the Catecumeni, before and after baptism, is not abundant; the minutes, bald if businesslike, are silent on the point. Judicial and inquisitorial records can create flashes of insight, by revealing not only deviant behaviour but the pious background against which it was committed. In the early days, the techniques of the house for teaching children, and its notion of basic Christianity, seem to have resembled those of the Schools of Christian Doctrine, another important concern of the new religious orders in the middle and later sixteenth century.[81] In 1563 the child Gabriel of Ancona explained that the Prior would allow the boys and men one hour's recreation a day, and that the boys would spend the precious time enacting a religious procession through the house and singing the litanies of the Madonna. He himself carried an image of her and a banner embellished with portraits of St Roch and St Sebastian, twin protectors against the plague. The young Jew Asher, arraigned before the Advocate Fiscal of the Curia Patriarcale, said that in processions 'they say the Ave Maria, the paternoster, and another prayer which he does not know.' He was charged with heretical blasphemy, for among other things he had thrown a penny ball which hit the Madonna and had snatched the banner and waved it about like any common flag.[82] Piety was no less piety, images demanded no less reverence, for forming part of a game. Forty years later, in reluctant tribute to the efficiency of Catholic methods, the English chaplain Bedell dryly commented upon a similar scene:

noe sooner do their Children almost creep out of their Cradles, but they are taught to be Idolators. They have certain childish processions, wherein are carryed about certain puppets, made for their Lady, and some boy that is better Clerke than his fellows goes before them with the words of the Popish Litany; where the rest of the fry following make up the quire. A great tyrant is custome, and a great advantage hath that discipline which is suck'd in with the mothers milke. But to convey superstition into the minds of that tender age under the form of sport, and play, which it esteemeth more than meat and drinke, is a deeper point of policy, and such, as wise men would profitably suck somewhat out of it for imitation to a right end.[83]

Something about the practices of conversionists can also be deduced from an account of instruction given in the Augustinian monastery of Santa

[81] Cfr. Pullan, *Rich and poor* ..., pp. 401–4.

[82] I.Z. II, pp. 34–5, 45–7, 8, 25 May 1563.

[83] William Bedell to Adam Newton, 1 Jan. 1608, in Shuckburgh, ed., *Two biographies of William Bedell* ..., p. 229.

Maria degli Angeli in Sacile to Mendlin or Mandolino, the local Jewish banker, who had declared his wish to become a Christian. The friars' pupil knew the Our Father, Hail Mary and Creed; they were teaching him the Salve Regina; he heard Mass in the morning from the organ loft; he had adored the sacrament and 'revered the image' of Christ or the Madonna, and he was said to believe in the twelve articles of faith which had been declared to him.[84] And when Mariana the Pole objected to entering the Catecumeni of Venice in 1624 because she already knew very well 'how to live as a Christian, the duties of a Christian, and a number of prayers',[85] she was probably furnishing an accurate summary of the curriculum of the Catecumeni for adults and children alike.

When the catechumen came to baptism it was still a time for rejoicing, but it seems likely that in the later sixteenth century the baptisms of Jews, occurring more often and being more systematically organized, ceased to be such special occasions. Despite the prospect of winning Mendlin of Sacile, there were fewer prosperous Jewish bankers to bring to Christ amid promises of restoring usurious gains, and seldom could conversions be said – as were those of the Meshullam family in the 1520s and 1530s – to entail substantial reductions in the wealth of the Jewish community. In the dominant city, loan-banking had been reduced to the rank of broking in pawn. In accordance with Tridentine prescriptions, opposed to the formation of large squads of co-godfathers,[86] the number of godparents had diminished. For all this tendency to create routine rather than spectacle, some magnificent ceremonies were still performed in great churches as though to remind the faithful of the good work in progress. On 14 May 1598 it was resolved that a Jewish boy be baptized next Sunday in the church of Santi Giovanni e Paolo, 'with two trumpets and the pipes', as in the olden days.[87] Baptisms could be celebrated, 'either privately or with solemnity, as is the custom of this house'.[88] Collections were still taken at baptisms, but in the early seventeenth century converts were strictly forbidden to remove the proceeds and devote them to their own immediate uses.[89] Whether they applied them to the needs of a particular convert, or to those of the house in general, the governors were determined to control the moneys themselves; and this represented yet another

[84] S.U., b. 52, proc. Mandolino da Sacile, test. Fra Giovanni and Sartorio Galeota, 23 Feb. 1585.

[85] S.U., b. 79, proc. Mariana of Poland, test. Don Peracci, a *Presidente* of the Catecumeni, 13 June 1624.

[86] Cfr. J. Bossy, 'Blood and baptism: kinship, community and Christianity in Western Europe from the fourteenth to the seventeenth centuries', in *Sanctity and secularity: the Church and the world*, ed. D. Baker, Studies in Church History, 9 (Oxford, 1973), pp. 132–5.

[87] I.R.E.C., Not. D, fol. 85v.

[88] Ibid., Not. F, fol. 18, 2 May 1611.

[89] Note the case of Ephraim Pichio, baptized Francesco on the island of Murano, who made off with his collection – ibid., fol. 141, 147, 151, 21 March, 6 June, 4 July 1619.

move to subject the process of conversion to the discipline of an institution.

Given the modest premises of the Catecumeni and the need to examine the motives of each candidate, the operation could never be carried out on a vast scale. The Catecumeni could only knock chips off the rock of Judaism; conversion could never compensate for the increases in the number of professing Jews through immigration in the late sixteenth and early seventeenth centuries.[90] It seems that in the calendar year 1595, nine adult Jews presented themselves at the house; the governors had dealings with two persons in custody who could not come to the place but were none the less adopted as its 'children'; and the records mention the baptism of one Jewish child. We can think in terms of at least eight actual baptisms in that year.[91] Records for 1611 convey a similar impression: twelve Jews were formally accepted by the house; two young children and a boy were certainly baptized; five adults did at least come to the point of baptism.[92]

Once achieved, baptism meant the assumption of a new identity and the beginning of a new life. Christian names taken by converts sometimes commemorated the churches which were the scene of their baptism or the religious orders which took care of them. A Jew received by the congregation on St Bartholomew's day, 24 August 1595, became Bartolomeo.[93] Allegorical names were sometimes used to symbolize the change wrought and the hope revealed by baptism. Hence, at a uniquely magnificent ceremony in 1533, Jacob Meshullam was girded, spurred and decked out as the Cavalier Marco Paradiso.[94] 'Renato' was used as Christian name, surname or suffix, announcing its owner's rebirth, and retained its popularity in Venice and elsewhere from the sixteenth to the middle of the seventeenth centuries. Eusebio Renati, formerly Bonaventura, born a Jew in Ferrara, was an assiduous worker for the Catecumeni, of which he became a governor, and he also performed many services for the Holy Office. He supplied information, he encouraged others to do so, and he was also called in to inspect circumcisions, to exhort prisoners to repent, to censor Jewish books, and to make inquiries about candidates for baptism – a range of activities which served to justify his name.[95] When four

[90] See above, pp. 156–7.
[91] I.R.E.C., Not. D, fol. 45v.–59v.
[92] Ibid., Not. F, fol. 16v.–32v.
[93] I.R.E.C., Not. D, fol. 54v., 55.
[94] D.M.S., LVIII, col. 564, 15 July 1533.
[95] S.U., b. 51, which contains several of his reports, of 1583, 1589 and 1592; b. 52, proc. Mandolino da Sacile, 22, 26 Feb. 1585; proc. Solomon della Regina, 3 Aug. 1585; b. 54, proc. 'Jewish exorcists', 11 Sept. 1584; proc. Filippi, 21 Oct. 1585, 9 June 1586; Ioly Zorattini, '"Mif'aloth Elohim"', pp. 67–8; I.R.E.C., Not. D, fol. 2, 22, 23, 51, 59v., 29 May 1592, 5 Aug. 1593, 29 June, 8 Feb. 1595 Venetian style. For other persons called Renato, I.Z., p. 301, proc. Gian Giacomo de Fedeli, 2 June 1559; for Paolo Renati of Mantua, S.U., b. 88, 92, proc. Carlo Antonio Barberini, 6 July 1632, 11 Sept. 1636.

Jews were baptized in San Marcuola about 1660, one of them took the name of his godfather, the French ambassador, and became Renato Argenson. In the moment of transition, given names were almost always changed, though 'Jacob' could be transformed into 'Giacomo'.[96] Jewish surnames, such as de' Salvi and Colombo, occasionally survived baptism.[97]

In Venice, the Papal States and Florence it was fashionable for converts to take the names of their eminent patrons and godfathers, as though becoming second selves and acquiring some of their virtue and piety, if not their social standing. Some neophytes aspired even to that. Invited to intercede with Gian Giacomo, who had taken the proud patrician name of Pisani, a Rialto broker answered 'that I did not wish to tangle with the gentry, for Gian Giacomo was making himself a gentleman'.[98] Sponsoring converts was a good work just as popular with the provincial gentry as with those of Venice itself, although the practice of transferring the names of great godfathers to humble converts proved, in subject cities from Verona to Cividale, to be less than automatic.[99] Godfatherhood could imply charity, patronage, protection, something more than short-lived benevolence at the moment of transition. Aspirants to the Catecumeni were sometimes described as emerging from the house of such and such a nobleman, where they had been sheltered. Samuel or Simon of Mantua, once baptized Marcantonio in Verona about 1583–84, was said to be bemoaning his fate as he starved in Salonica, a Jew once more, and nostalgically recalling the good days spent in the house of Signora Lugrezia Fregosa.[100] The dubious Isaac Spagnoletto allegedly lived during the 1620s both in the town house of Signora Elisabetta Cornaro in Venice and in her country villa.[101] When a Venetian convert tangled with the law in 1617 and 1624, his Roman patron, Cardinal Scipione

[96] Ioly Zorattini, 'Note e documenti ...', p. 338. On that occasion Jacob Boncompagno took the name of Giacomo.

[97] Q.C., filza 109, proc. 113, test. Giovanni de' Salvi, 13 Nov. 1590. For the transformation of Mazo Colombo into Andrea Colombo, see I.R.E.C., Not. D, fol. 47, 61v., 13 April 1595, 4 April 1596.

[98] S.U., b. 46, proc. Gian Giacomo Pisani, test. Hieronimo Coruzzo of Dulcigno, 27 Aug. 1580.

[99] See the case of Giovanni Battista Cividin, whose godfathers (1573) were 'meser Nicola Galli' and 'meser Brandis, a nobleman of Cividale' – Ioly Zorattini, 'Un giudaizzante ...', p. 205; that of Giovanni de' Salvi, n. 94 above, whose godfathers in 1550 were the Cavalier Boldieri and Count Amerigo Bevilaqua; and that of Grassino, son of Liberale Vito, whose godfather in 1589 was Count Marcantonio dalla Torre, but who took the name of Agostino, probably in honour of the religious order which was educating him at the time of his disappearance (Q.C., filza 109, proc. 113, test. Rabbi Matthias Bassano and Angelo/Arcangelo Padavino, 8, 27 Nov. 1590).

[100] Ibid., test. Abraham, son of Matthias Bassano, 13 Nov. 1590.

[101] S.U., b. 77, proc. Isaac Spagnoletto, letter of the Inquisitor of Ferrara, 3 Aug. 1622.

Borghese, interceded effectively on his behalf through the papal nuncio.[102] Where no splendid godfathers were forthcoming, governors of the Catecumeni in the early seventeenth century were obliged to perform the duty themselves,[103] so that the personal and emotional tie between godfather and godchild blended into the instutionalized after-care extended by the Pia Casa to its pupils. Antonio Giustinian, chief collector for the Catecumeni on the mainland, probably owed his sonorous name to a nobleman chosen a governor in February 1619.[104]

The Casa's conception of aid to converts went far beyond the simple notion of giving alms. Patents issued to converts might depict them romantically as pilgrims leaving everything for the sake of Christ. But the Catecumeni tried to ensure that those who had property would in fact lose nothing other than usurious gains and the respect of Jews. Following principles enshrined in Paul III's *Cupientes iudaeos*, they would conduct litigation with the relatives of converts, in order to recover inheritances, dowries or other payments, which were not to be cancelled out by the change of identity from Jew to Christian. Thus modest sums were spent in the 1590s to help Paolo Gradenigo assert his rights to the goods of a deceased brother, that 'the favour of inheritance may come to those Jews who have come to the faith of Our Lord.'[105] Two governors were deputed in 1611 to obtain justice for a 'German girl' who had been a servant in the Ghetto and was owed 20 ducats' back pay.[106] Indeed, a well-to-do Jewess, who had no wish to enter the Casa to be catechized or enjoy its charity, still wanted to use it as a kind of benevolent solicitor, and sought to inscribe herself and her child on its rolls that it might look after their affairs.[107]

Contests, potentially bitter, were softened by the appearance of professional mediators between the Catecumeni, the converts and the Jews, among them Marcus Moses Jonah Levi, one of the few Jews permitted on the premises of the Pia Casa. It was he who persuaded Jacob da Caprilis, banker in the great fortress of Palma in Friuli in 1635, to pay 500 ducats towards endowing his daughter Ghella or Galla, who became a Christian and went to the Catecumeni under the name of Marietta; and he who conjured 350 ducats out of Missier Ventura Grassini in 1637 for the benefit of another renegade or refugee from the Jewish faith.[108] Some-

[102] C.E.R., reg. 18, fol. 146; reg. 21, fol. 52v.–53r.
[103] I.R.E.C., Not F, fol. 121, 31 May 1618.
[104] Ibid., fol. 138, 19 Feb. 1618 Venetian style.
[105] Ibid., Not. D, fol. 17v., 81v., 29 April 1593, 2 Jan. 1597 Venetian style.
[106] Ibid., Not. F, fol. 31, 15 Sept. 1611.
[107] Ibid., Not. F, fol. 121v., 15 June 1618.
[108] I.R.E.C., Carte Diverse, 'Pie Case de Cattecumeni contro Università degli Ebrei', fol. 61v., 62, 66r.–v., 69r.–v., 72v.–73r., 75r.–v.; Atti Giudiziari, 'Salumieri e casaroli', fol. 47 ff.

times the more prosperous potential converts were found making discreet inquiries as to how much of their wealth they would be permitted to retain.[109] Coryat, the English traveller, was certain that the obligation to restore the profits of usurious lending must act as a serious deterrent to conversions; but he did not know that a large proportion of the Jews' modest riches came from other sources.[110]

More positively, the Catecumeni would seek to obtain employment for its boys and men and to negotiate contracts for the marriage of its girls or for their placement in nunneries. It was not designed as a terminus, a refuge of final resort, but rather as a bridgehead between infidelity and Christianity. Its slender revenues could not support the dead weight of many persons who did not work, and it was from expediency as well as principle that it adopted the newer concept of philanthropy which urged benefactors to provide opportunities to labour, rather than permission to seek alms. Asher of Chelm, who tried to leave the Catecumeni in 1563, was depressed by a gloomy prophecy of the Jew Solomon, whom he met on Piazza San Marco on an illicit excursion – 'the most you'll get if you're baptized is that they'll teach you a trade and then let you go.' For he feared it would only mean going in rags.[111] Vincenzo Garzoni, the most important benefactor of the house, was scarcely politer to converts than was Cardinal Borromeo, but he saw some hope of redeeming them by discipline.

> I would have them come to the faith,' said he, 'not for the sake of the legacy, but to save their souls and to acquire paradise. I beg the trustees to reprove and even deprive those who are vicious, idle and impious [*vitiosi, vagabondi et non devoti*] as most of such people have proved to be in the past, and to put in their place others who may seem to be better Catholics and worthy of a better life.

He bequeathed pensions to neophytes, but they were not intended to eliminate the need to work. Rather, their purpose was to increase independence, 'that they may be able to support themselves by some employment until they die.'[112] For a time at least, the governors took seriously their task of enforcing discipline. Two of the first beneficiaries suffered a magisterial admonition from the Archbishop of Split, who threatened deprivation if they misbehaved. Soon the same Giovanni and Andrea were disciplined again for disobedience and for dealings with women of dubious reputation, and it was stipulated that they might leave the house

---

[109] I.R.E.C., Not. F, fol. 128v., 26 Sept. 1618.
[110] Coryat, *Coryat's Crudities*, I, pp. 373–4.
[111] I.Z. II, proc. Aaron e Asser, p. 43, 25 May 1563.
[112] I.R.E.C., Catastico 71, fol. 61, 107r.–v.

only to go to Mass in the Prior's company, until such time as they were found suitable lodgings outside its semimonastic walls. Giovanni should be found a place as a butcher, and some other job should be sought for Andrea.[113]

Younger boys could look forward to apprenticeships, or at least be given a chance with local craftsmen. Jocanam, son of Solomon Portogallo, was baptized Bernardino in 1611. Ten months after admission the governors sent him for eight days' trial with 'the tailor at San Maurizio who makes women's clothes'. Should he prove his aptitude, arrangements would be made to apprentice him to the craft.[114] More ambitiously, Alessandro (probably 'Alessandro Pozzo renato', son of the Levantine Samuel Pichi) was sent to Rome to spend six years with the painter Marcello Cecchoni; the Casa was ready to pay for clothing and equipping him, for the expense of the journey and for Alessandro's maintenance during his apprenticeship.[115] Girls might expect a substantial contribution to a modest marriage portion, or (in accordance with practices common to several of the newer institutions of the sixteenth century) they might be placed in nunneries.[116] Aware of the vulnerability and isolation of the convert, cut off from his relatives and deprived of the protection afforded him by Jewish charity, the paternalistic house sought to provide its sons and daughters with guarantees of stability: a job, a marriage partner, the insulation and discipline of a convent.

It was true that poverty might tempt a person to apply for the superior status of a Christian, and hence it was a somewhat two-edged weapon in the conversionist's hands. Should grinding poverty persist after conversion, the recruit might be drawn back to the Jews once more. Francesco Colonna confessed to the Holy Office in 1553 that when he found himself in Venice with no occupation and so poor that he had to sell his sword-belt, proud symbol of his new standing as a bearer of arms, he yielded to the persuasions of certain Levantine Jews from the Ghetto Vecchio who persuaded him to take ship for the East.[117] Venice's Catecumeni had little need of the memorandum read in 1598 by Pope Clement VIII to the Venetian ambassadors, reminding them

[113] Ibid., Not. D, fol. 48v., 52v., 18 May, 24 July 1595.
[114] Ibid., Not. F, fol. 20, 46, 26 May 1611, 23 March 1612.
[115] Ibid., Not. F, fol. 54v., 55, 30 Aug., 6 Sept. 1612.
[116] E.g. ibid., Not. D, fol. 6v., 13 Aug. 1592, where the governors resolve to borrow 400 ducats at interest 'to marry daughters of the house, in order to relieve it of the heavy expenditure it incurs on their account'. See also fol. 8v., 8 Oct. 1592, where all available governors are to see the Patriarch about 'the girls to be made nuns'; fol. 18v., 13 May 1593, a reference to arranging a marriage between 'Missier Gieronimo and Isabetta', not more than 90 ducats to be given them on behalf of the Catecumeni.
[117] I.Z., p. 96, 28 Nov. 1553.

that on many occasions infidels came to holy baptism, and since they frequently had nothing to support them and lacked the means to live, they were compelled to leave and return to Judaism or else go to Turkey.

Many people of this kind dwelt or tarried in the States of the Church, and His Holiness did not fail to provide them with the means to live, by making them grooms, or putting them in the light cavalry, or setting them on work at digging the earth or at carrying stones as the opportunity may arise. Being unable to meet all needs, however, he recommended that they be assisted by the *Serenissima Signoria*, for this is a good work most acceptable to the Lord God, and worthy of the piety and charity of the Republic.[118]

A few children of the house were destined by the governors, with varying degrees of success, for careers in the Church. Angeletto, about 1580, lasted a year as a Dominican and then became a tentative Capuchin; but he afterwards decided 'that the state of a religious will not do for him', and was sent to Milan to resume his studies and shelter from his parents, Venetian Jews who were allegedly trying to suborn him.[119] For seven years, from 1592 to 1599, the governing body was regularly occupied with the minutiae of maintaining one Zanetto throughout his course at the Patriarchal Seminary and afterwards with placing him with one of the newer and more evangelical religious orders, such as the Theatines or the Somaschians.[120] More taxing, more prolonged, and eventually soured by petty disputes, were the arrangements for accommodating the family of Strassoldo in various ecclesiastical niches. Lazarin, son of Jacob Belgrado, a physician of San Daniele di Friuli, brought with him to Christianity in 1608 three daughters and a son, and took the name of Giovanni Giuseppe Strassoldo. The Catecumeni assisted him in exacting various sums from relatives, and particularly in obtaining from his uncle, Caliman Belgrado, the sum of 2,600 ducats made over to him by deed of gift in rather different circumstances, as long ago as 1583. Moneys due to the father were handed over in trust to the Catecumeni, which served as tutor to the children, raised additional sums to place one of the daughters in the nunnery of San Marco and Sant' Andrea di Murano with a suitable dowry of 800 ducats, and saw to the education of the son, Paolo, so long as he remained in Venice. A priestly tutor and a seminary were duly tried for the boy. By 1615 the father, after a spell in Rome, was

[118] C.E.R., reg. 8, fol. 26r.–v., 13 June 1598.
[119] The governors of the Catecumeni to Carlo Borromeo, 11 Aug. 1582, in Segre, 'Il mondo ebraico ...', p. 236; cf. also pp. 233, 235–6.
[120] I.R.E.C., Not. D, many entries.

clearly hatching plans to become a priest, and a small annuity was arranged for him 'in accordance with the constitutions of the Council of Trent, lest he be forced to beg for a living and thereby bring the priesthood into disrepute'. The former Jewish physician became a chaplain or Mass-priest in the cathedral at Treviso, and in 1647 the son and one daughter were still living, he being a 'reverend father' and a beneficiary of the Garzoni trust, and she remaining among the nuns on Murano. The Strassoldi provide a striking example of systematic aid being extended to persons by no means penniless, and being used to cement a whole family of converts into the safest places for them to be in; an instance, too, of charity being insistently exploited, for the governors became deeply irritated by Giovanni Giuseppe's obvious reluctance to make proper contributions to the support of his daughter.[121]

The more advanced charity of the sixteenth century was directed towards outcasts no less than towards respectable persons, and the governors of the Catecumeni were prepared to approach prisoners and grant them baptism. They did not do so on a vast scale, and in 1595 only two out of the eight clearly recorded baptisms of Jews were performed on such people. Baptism did not bring immediate release – authority was not so naive – but a prisoner's conversion was a point that could be argued in his favour, and any such argument, any move to secure influential Christian protectors, was valuable at a time when convicts were often kept in the galleys by debts and friendlessness for years after the official expiry of their sentences. Mazo Colombo presented himself at the Catecumeni in April 1595, announcing that he wished to become a Christian and to take the name of Andrea. Arrangements were then made to visit his brother, 'Colombo the Jew', who was on one of the penal galleys, and ask if it was also his wish to become a Christian. The convict was eventually baptized about the beginning of July, and in April 1596, a year from his own conversion, Andrea Colombo was given a certificate of good character for the purpose of obtaining a 'grace' for his brother.[122]

Designed to control the process of conversion, the Catecumeni inevitably had its failures. The pressures it imposed could make it hard for a prospective convert to withdraw during the interval between expression of intent and baptism, and could create a new form of conversion under duress. Surviving records, however, suggest that the Inquisition was used to enforce the discipline of the Catecumeni rather than to accuse its former inmates of lapsing into Judaism; and that, where charges of heresy

[121] Ibid., Not. F, many entries, and Atti Giudiziari, 'Pro Catecumeni contro Ebrei Ponentini', fol. 2 onwards; on Caliman and Jacob Belgrado, see also F. Luzzatto, *Cronache storiche della università degli ebrei di San Daniele di Friuli: cenni sulla storia degli ebrei del Friuli* (Rome, 1964), pp. 39–43.
[122] I.R.E.C., Not. D, fol. 47r.–61v., several entries from 13 April 1595 to 4 April 1596.

or suspicion of heresy did arise, they were usually directed either against beneficiaries of the older and more casual types of arrangement for converts, or against people who had converted, whether through a Casa dei Catecumeni or not, in other towns or cities. Pupils of the Venetian house were soundly instructed in the rules, and if they wanted to lapse or to earn a dishonest penny by repeating baptism would be well advised to leave town – for the likelihood of detection, if they sinned in Venice, would be too strong. There were exceptions, but not many are recorded. Moses, a prospective Christian, was enticed away by the Jew Merlin in 1574, and the Prior and one of the governors reported the matter to the Holy Office.[123] Anna, an inmate or protégée of the Casa, fled to the Ghetto after baptism in 1615.[124] Logic demanded that such treachery be treated as apostasy, but the charge was reluctantly brought against persons who had converted in Italy. Proof of irredeemable desertion of the faith came only from departure for the Levant, and this effectively removed the apostate from the Inquisition's grasp. Buonaiuto, son of Leon Viterbo, a tailor in the Ghetto, became a Christian about December 1633, baptized by the Prior of the Catecumeni, who would later become his accuser. After conversion he drifted from one job to another, earned his living selling malmsey for about a fortnight, then worked as a tailor and at other trades and finally returned to the Ghetto. Denounced by the Prior, he was apparently not brought to trial, and it was believed that his father had funded an escape to Constantinople.[125]

The link between the Catecumeni and the Inquisition became especially strong during the 1580s, and the interventions of the Holy Office promoted it from an ordinary charity to an institution which could invoke penal sanctions. Hence, in 1582, when João Batista of Lisbon proved unduly inquisitive or argumentative about the Scriptures, he was reported to the Holy Office for insolence by the Prior and governors and sent to cool his heels for three or four weeks in prison.[126] Michele, formerly a Jew, removed his son Angelo from the care of the Catecumeni, contrary to its wishes; suspected of lapsing, he too was gaoled for a time and then released on surety.[127] If the Catecumeni used the Inquisition, it was equally true that the Inquisition used the Catecumeni: it was a suitable place of confinement for children who attracted the attention of the Holy Office – among them a Jewish boy, born in Seville and presumed to have been a Christian, who was forcibly separated from his father in the Ghetto in 1586.[128] Neophytes and the governors and staff of the

---

[123] S.U., b. 37, proc. Moisè, den. 5 Oct. 1574.
[124] I.R.E.C., Not. F, fol. 93v., 24 Sept. 1615.
[125] S.U., b. 90, proc. Buonaiuto, den. 27 June 1634.
[126] S.U., b. 32, proc. 'Giovanni Battista' of Lisbon, 11 Jan. to 8 Feb. 1583.
[127] S.U., b. 53, proc. Michele, 3 March to 21 Aug. 1584.
[128] S.U., b. 57, proc. 'Giorgio' of Seville, 9–13 Aug. 1586.

Catecumeni picked up gossip about the peccadillos of Jews turned Christians and could be expected to retail it to the Holy Office. A recruit to Christianity could prove his sincerity by making such reports, although there is no sign that the Inquisition treated them as privileged information, more likely to result in action than any other. In the seventeenth century, when seeking assistance over such matters as the detention of the wives and children of converts, the Catecumeni would more likely resort to secular magistrates, such as the *Avogadori di Commun* or the Quarantia Criminale.

Even in Venice itself, the Catecumeni had no monopoly of the processes of catechizing and baptizing converts. The governors wished to be informed of the baptisms of Jews and infidels,[129] but they did not claim that all neophytes must become children of the house. Abram, already catechized by a priest, could be baptized 'according to the style of the congregation' if he wanted to be entered on the books as a 'son of the house'. Otherwise 'he can have himself baptized as he chooses, but without enjoying any benefit of any kind from this house.'[130] And, of course, Venice saw many former Jews who had been converted in other places. Some had been through Case dei Catecumeni, although these were established in few Italian cities, and indeed the printed statutes for the Venetian house listed only three others which had survived into the eighteenth century – Loyola's house in Rome, founded in 1543, that of Ferrara (1584) and that of Reggio Emilia (1630). For a time at least there had been another in Bologna, erected in 1568.[131] In one or two other cities converts might be found among several categories of deserving poor admitted to institutions of wider scope: in Mantua, from 1574, they became eligible for the orphanage of Sant' Antonio, and in Genoa for the huge Albergo dei Poveri established in the mid-seventeenth century.[132] Elsewhere, converts were prepared, not necessarily inadequately, by nonspecialists, secular priests, laymen or religious houses. Methods and results varied. The dubious Giovanni Battista Cividin was instructed for forty days in the house of a priest in charge of a local church.[133] Mendlin of Sacile was first instructed in the faith for two months by the bailiff of a Venetian nobleman who held land in the region, and he then moved into

---

[129] I.R.E.C., Not. D, fol. 5, 23 July 1592.   [130] Ibid., fol. 89, 7 Oct. 1598.

[131] *Capitoli ed ordini* ..., p. 6. Balletti, *Gli ebrei* ..., pp. 208–9, 216, mentions a foundation in Modena (1629) and another in Reggio Emilia (1632). For the foundation in Bologna, see P. Tacchi Venturi, *Storia della Compagnia di Gesù in Italia* (2 vols. in 4, Rome, 1950–51), I/i, p. 405.

[132] See U. Cappellazzi and D. Ferrari, 'Repertorio di fonti archivistiche per lo studio del pauperismo in Mantova (sec. XIII–XIX)', forthcoming article in *Timore e carità* ..., and Scheda 50 circulated at the Cremona conference on which the volume is based; E. Grendi, 'Pauperismo e Albergo dei Poveri nella Genova del Seicento', *Rivista Storica Italiana*, 87 (1975), p. 659.

[133] Ioly Zorattini, 'Un giudaizzante ...', pp. 197, n. 13, 205.

the local Augustinian monastery both for better insulation from his Jewish relatives and for more intensive instruction (the two friars in charge of him slept in his cell at night).[134] Should there be no house of instruction conveniently to hand, a convert could be sent to Venice – a wise move for the banker's daughter from Palma, since the manner of her leaving the Jewish faith, with jewels and other wealth taken from her father as a device to guarantee payment of her dowry, was calculated to evoke ill-will.[135]

It seems clear that in the sixteenth and seventeenth centuries the conversion business functioned on two levels. In a few large Italian cities endowed with populous Jewish communities it became a highly professional process, governed by strict rules and almost bureaucratic routines. Assistance, going beyond mere almsgiving, was used to reassure the well-to-do Jews and to open to the poor the prospect of a better life. Elsewhere, in towns such as Vicenza which had no resident Jews, or those such as Sacile which contained only a Jewish banker and his family, conversion could be marked at one end of the spectrum by carelessness born of credulity and inexperience, and at the other by intense enthusiasm on the part of a whole neighbourhood which had enjoyed no chance to get bored with the process. The bishops' persistence in using the old method of doling out patents undoubtedly opened the way to fraud. But the pitfalls were not entirely on the side of tradition. Even benefactors such as Garzoni realized the dangers inherent in making spiritual and material advantage closely coincide. The policies of the Catecumeni, by reducing the element of sacrifice in the process of conversion, risked laying it open to persons of less moral strength and conviction. Like most zealots, like most persons who dole out conditional charity, like many officials accustomed to routines, the governors were prone to resent changes of heart and to attribute them simply to bad faith. They could supervise neophytes in their own cities, but could not prevent them from departing elsewhere and returning to their old ways. Certain casualties both of the older and of the newer processes of conversion will appear in the pages which follow.

---

[134] S.U., b. 52, proc. 'Mandolino da Sacile', test. Daniele della Rovere and Fra Giovanni, 22–23 Feb. 1585.
[135] I.R.E.C., Atti Giudiziari, 'Salumieri e casaroli', fol. 47–58.

15

Neophytes of Italy: Conversion
and Reclamation

Adult Jews in Italy were normally exposed to conversion by persuasion, rather than to conversion by duress. Heavier pressure was exerted upon two kinds of people, who were sometimes reduced to a state of bewildered uncertainty and sometimes driven into subterfuge. It was applied to those who had expressed an intention to convert, but had then begun to waver; and it was felt, too, by the dependents of adult male converts. Wives, children and sometimes elderly parents might have changes of faith thrust at them by the decisions of household heads and breadwinners, who were used by the Church as instruments for the conversion of their own immediate families, and were required to perform this pious action as proof of their own good faith. Wives were often steadfast in resisting the proposed change. Children short of puberty, who had not officially arrived at the age of reason, had no lawful right to do so. For them Jews were most likely to claim the status of forced convert; with them they were most likely to continue affectionate relations. It was they who, like certain Marranos, were most liable to be caught in a field of tension between the Jewish and the Christian worlds. Where the adult convert faced only the indifference and contempt of his former co-religionists, the child was more likely to become the subject of a contest for souls between Christian and Jew, certainly before and possibly after his enforced recruitment to a new creed.

The Catecumeni exhaled, not only a smell of the monastery, but also a whiff of the prison-house, and it was at its most zealous where the souls of adolescents or children were at stake. It was certainly possible in principle for adults who had changed their minds to withdraw from the Catecumeni. Vincenzo, who had 'decided to be a Jew and not a

275

Christian', was to be given his clothes and allowed to go wherever he pleased.[1] Raphael of Mantua, who had once left the house of his own accord, was evidently forgiven, for he was received back and allowed a fresh start.[2] But children were jealously guarded, and one prior was sacked for letting two of them escape.[3] When Aaron and Asher, two young Jews from central Europe, chafed against the discipline and wanted to leave, this mild rebellion, together with reports of blasphemous utterances and disrespect for religious images, got them removed to the district lock-up at San Giovanni in Bragora and earned a grilling from the Advocate-Fiscal of the Curia Patriarcale, who accused them of being 'false Catecumeni'.[4]

In confused and uncertain circumstances, the Inquisition applied heavy pressure to the Jew Alessandro Ferro in 1586. It resisted his attempts to retract a proposal to convert with an exceptional sternness, probably explained by its fear of losing the opportunity to claim his young children. Cecilia, wife of the schoolmaster Andrea Diedo of Santa Fosca, who taught Jewish children in the Ghetto, told the Inquisition that Alessandro had joyfully announced to her husband the 'good news' that he intended to become a Christian, and to bring his children with him to the faith. The schoolmaster and his wife duly agreed to become godparents, and Alessandro promised to convert as soon as he had paid off a debt. He asked the Diedi to find the money for him, and he eventually obtained it from Cecilia. Her story was that the Jew then removed one child, aged two, from her mother's care on the pretext of buying her a pair of shoes, handed the little girl over to Cecilia, and approved a proposal to take her to the Catecumeni. Alessandro's version of these events was entirely different. He had made no promise to become a Christian, and had merely borrowed an urgently needed 40 lire. To leave human pledges for debts was seemingly quite common at this time, and he had, as it were, merely left the child in pawn, returning within four hours to repay the loan. A harrowing scene then followed, in which (according to the Diedi) the Jew's wife came and begged for her child, only to be met with the sententious answer that 'one must not pluck the rose that has been offered to the Lord.' The Catecumeni would not surrender the child and invited the Jewess in, but she would not cross the threshold. Arraigned before the Inquisition, Alessandro was told that a promise to convert was binding upon him,

> that he is denying the truth, that the contrary has been established, and that in this he is a criminal, since having promised Christ to

[1] I.R.E.C., Not. D, fol. 73, 26 Nov. 1596.
[2] Ibid., Not. F, fol. 64v., 24 Jan. 1612 Venetian style.
[3] Ibid., Not. D, fol. 46, 47, 29 March, 13 April 1595.
[4] See above, p. 263, and below, pp. 296–7.

become with his children a Christian he can no longer think better of it. And if in the secret recesses of the heart he had said it falsely for the purpose of obtaining money from the woman [Cecilia] he would not be excused, for the Holy Church does not judge the heart but rather the words expressly pronounced. . . .

He was then committed to prison and after five days yielded, saying that after all he wished to become a Christian. His children, Filomena, the two-year-old, and a small son of four months, would be baptized with him. Just over three weeks later, he was found to be missing from the Catecumeni.[5] But his children presumably remained behind.

The greatest bitterness was commonly aroused by the tactics used to claim for Christianity the wives and especially the children of men who had announced their intention to convert. It was a longstanding doctrine that the consent of one parent was sufficient authority for the baptism of children. In Venice this usually meant that they were gathered in by the authority of the father, often opposed by a more conservative (or more steadfast) wife determined to hold the Jewish faith. In one case, after the death of both parents, the consent of an uncle sufficed in the eyes of the Holy Office to justify taking a six-year-old child and lodging him with the Patriarch Priuli, in defiance of the wishes of his other relations and co-religionists.[6] Moreover Venice, like Rome, knew cases of Jewish children who had for some reason been baptized without the consent of either parent. In 1615 the nuncio brought to the Collegio the affair of Savia, daughter of Allegra, a Jewish prostitute who had admitted to having intercourse with Christians, and had boarded her child out with a Christian foster mother in a neighbouring parish. Seemingly in danger of death, the girl Savia was baptized by a parish priest without parental consent. Since a number of delicate legal issues arose, the state referred the matter to its most distinguished *consultor in jure*, Paolo Sarpi himself. He ruled against the arguments by which the nuncio had urged that the baptism was valid, but conceded that there might be others, of a vaguer and more sweeping character, which justified treating the child as a Christian. Sarpi asserted that it was only since the sixteenth century that such baptisms had been considered valid at all. Opinion had changed in order to legitimate large-scale conversion by zealous missionaries and colonists overseas, and particularly 'on account of many Indian children who were so baptized by the Portuguese'. As on many occasions, he

---

[5] S.U., b. 57, proc. Alessandro Ferro, 7 June to 5 July 1586. Cf. Stow, *Catholic thought* ..., pp. 173, 174, and above, p. 68.
[6] Stern, *Urkundliche Beiträge* ..., I, doc. 161, p. 173 (1593); cf. de Susannis, *De Iudaeis* ..., fol. 133v.

invoked the older traditions of the Church against more recent practices, and opined that there was no reason to remove the child to the Catecumeni,

> save that it is a more pious action, and one both favourable and respectful towards the holy faith and religion, not to leave the child, now that she has (however improperly) been baptized, in the hands of her mother, who will bring her up in the error of Judaism.[7]

However exasperating to the nuncio, Sarpi's opinion did not offer decisive protection to the child. The fate of Savia is not known.

More often recorded, however, is the drama in which the father offers himself and his children to Christ, but the mother or some friend or agent hastily gathers them up and takes flight to a strange country abroad in the hope of escaping the Church's attempts to claim them; the Ottoman Empire is the only certain refuge. And the Jews, it seems, close ranks around them; at the least they enter a conspiracy of silence, at the most they secrete them on ships to further their escape, or make passionate pleas to the Venetian authorities on behalf of the children.[8] No wife could be converted by her husband's authority, but she could be subjected to gruelling ordeals designed to persuade her. Protesting his sincerity as a Christian, Odoardo Dyes, who had converted about 1562, boasted that

> I kept my Jewish wife, Madonna Zogia, daughter of Gratian Levi, for forty days in the women's prison at San Marco so that she might turn Christian, and then, seeing that she did not wish to do so, I left her and became a Christian myself.[9]

Holding to the Jewish faith, a mother could expect divorce and separation from her children, though the choice in the matter would lie with her husband; unless formally repudiated by him she could not, as Leon Modena took pains to point out, marry again.[10]

---

[7] I.R.E.C., Not. F, fol. 90v., 91, 11, 14 May 1615; C.E.R., reg. 18, fol. 83v., 14 May 1615; Cecchetti, *Republica di Venezia* ..., II, doc. XIX, pp. 368–70. Cf. Milano, *Il Ghetto di Roma* ..., pp. 285–90; Balletti, *Gli Ebrei* ..., pp. 197–200; Stow, *Catholic thought* '.., p. 173; Stern, *Urkundliche Beiträge* ..., I, doc. 161, pp. 176, 180.

[8] For examples, see N.V., V, pp. 150, 157, 163, 174, 182, 204 (25 Oct. 1550 to 7 Feb. 1551) – the case of Deborah, wife of the physician Teodoro Sacerdote of Orvieto, converted as Lodovico Carretto; D.N., filza 34, fol. 141v.–142v., 10 July 1599; I.R.E.C., Carte Diverse, 'Pie Case de Cattecumeni contro Università de gli Hebrei', 1637–38.

[9] S.U., b. 43, proc. Odoardo Dyes, test. 11 Sept. 1578.

[10] Leon Modena, *Relatione*, IV. 6: 'Should a Jew become a Christian or a Turk, his wife cannot remarry, unless he frees her by repudiating her in the proper form, even though he has passed to another law.' Cf. the opinion of a Christian jurisconsult of the seventeenth

Where both parents left the faith, other Jews might take matters into their own hands. When a husband and wife turned Christian together in Ferrara in the early seventeenth century, another Jew spirited away the children, a boy and two girls, aged four, seven and nine; it was rumoured that he had brought them to the Venetian Ghetto or taken them to Padua. On that occasion, trying to spur the Collegio to action, the nuncio expounded for its benefit the law governing the conversion of Jewish children. 'Since they are small children who do not have the use of reason [*non habent usum rationis*], they must also become Christians in the faith of their parents [*in fide parentum*]. If they were twelve or thirteen and had the use of their reason, then they would have to be interrogated and examined, to be left subsequently, however, in whatever condition they might choose.'[11] His speech implied that there was no exact definition of the age from which a child's consent would be required. It seems, though, that in the late sixteenth century boys and girls were differently treated for this purpose, and girls were deemed to acquire the use of reason earlier in life. When a Cretan Jew converted in Rome and took the illustrious name of Guglielmo Sirletto, cardinal-protector of neophytes and Catecumeni, it was assumed that his eldest girl, aged twelve, would be entitled to refuse conversion, and in fact she proved unwilling to join her father.[12] Paolo Loredan, likewise a former Cretan Jew, was asked: 'Why have you not had your children baptized, especially the boy under fourteen and the girls under twelve, of whom you could freely dispose . . . ?'[13] The reasons for such discrimination were not stated; it may have revealed a greater anxiety to recruit male children to the Church, the authorities adjusting the age of reason in order to allow themselves more latitude, or it may have reflected a more disinterested belief that girls matured earlier.

Unquestionably, it was the duty of the neophyte to bring in his children; every convert might give the Church a purchase on a household. In the mid-sixteenth century, before the establishment of the Catecumeni in Venice and the consequent introduction of specialized machinery for the

---

century – 'It cannot be said that baptism invalidates marriage, because marriages between infidels are true marriages, even though they are not so firm and indissoluble as those between Christians ...' (*consulta* of Giovanni Maria Bertolli, in I.R.E.C., Catastico 71, fol. 149v.).

[11] C.E.R., reg. 18, fol. 39r.–v., 43, 48, 21 Feb. 1613 Venetian style, 14 March, 4 April 1614.

[12] S.U., b. 46, proc. Guglielmo Sirletto, 31 Oct. 1579. From the judgment of the Holy Office it appears that his wife and two girls, aged nine and five, came to Venice, but the wife was persuaded to flee by her brother Mendlin of Uderzo, who had her sent to Ferrara. She was then extradited, returned to Venice, and placed in the house of Missier Leone Bembo, where she eventually resisted conversion.

[13] S.U., b. 60, proc. Paolo Loredan and Chiara Pisani, 15 Oct. 1587.

conversion of the Jews, the husband could be allowed much latitude in approaching his family and in the tactics used to win them over. Giovanni Battista de' Freschi Olivi was granted permission to wear the yellow hat of a Jew even after his conversion, thus disguising himself 'in order to recover his children'; it was said that he wore it for as much as three years. Simile of Montagnana, who became the Christian Giovanni Giacomo de Fedeli in 1553, was likewise authorized to approach his wife and children in Conegliano under a false colour,[14] though progress was slow and his good faith became suspect: his official goal, the baptism of the children Mendlin and Bella, was attained only in 1558. The convert continued to visit his Jewish wife in Montagnana or Conegliano, saying that 'he had to do with her in order to make her pregnant, and having done so he intended to bring her here to a nunnery to see whether or not she could then be converted.'[15] The threat of separation from a child as yet unborn would surely prove a powerful one.

The ambivalent behaviour of Simile/Gian Giacomo might well cause conversionists to reassess their methods. It seems likely that after the institution of the Catecumeni such devious tactics were eschewed. There was a more open resort to force rather than cunning, more invocation of police powers, more direct collision between Christian authorities and Jews; and all of these things followed logically from a greater reluctance to entrust the task of recovering the children to the converts themselves and hence to allow them to mingle with their former associates. In this, as in other branches of its activity, the Catecumeni sought to transfer responsibility from private initiative to institutional action and itself assumed responsibility for bringing in the children, now treating the pioneer adult convert as a frail being who must be shielded from contact with Jews, lest he himself be decoyed from his pious resolve. In the early seventeenth century the governors would enlist the aid of secular magistrates rather than of the Inquisition. It was the *Avogador* Basadonna who took charge of the search for Jewish children removed from Ferrara in 1614.[16] In the following year, 'in the matter of Giovanni Battista's sister, now that her father has written to say he has become a Christian', certain governors were charged with going to the Heads of the Ten 'to have her taken from the Ghetto'.[17]

There was little doubt that Jews would exert themselves to save children from conversion by paternal fiat. Uneasily aware of ships departing for Turkey, whose holds might carry refugees or even the victims of

[14] I.Z., pp. 278–9, 281–2, proc. Gian Giacomo de Fedeli, test. Gian Giacomo de Fedeli and Andrea Pasqualigo, 11, 17 Aug. 1558, citing the case of Freschi Olivi as a precedent.

[15] Ibid., p. 308, test. Matthias Gutich, 7 Sept. 1560.

[16] C.E.R., reg. 18, fol. 43, 14 March 1614.

[17] I.R.E.C., Not. F, fol. 90v., 11 May 1615.

kidnapping, the nuncios and the henchmen of the Holy Office pressed the public authorities to track the children down. Giovanni Giacomo Pisani raised illicit fees by posing as an officer of the Inquisition empowerd to search the ships moored at Castello and Sant' Antonino for Marranos and for neophytes bent on departure for the Levant. He was severely reprimanded for bringing 'the Holy Office into disrepute by suggesting that it might have agents who sought to exact payments from departing merchants.'[18] But he had been able to play upon real fears that the Inquisition might act in this way. Indeed, Eusebio Renati, a governor of the Catecumeni, remembered an occasion on which the chief constable of the Holy Office had paid a fruitful and timely visit to a Turkish ship in the port of Venice.[19] Anyone who, however inadvertently, assisted plots for the removal of Jewish children before or after baptism would court severe disfavour. Another governor was threatened with dismissal in 1615 for leaking to a Jew in the Ghetto the information that the Catecumeni were pursuing two children of 'minor age', sought by their baptized father, with the result that the children were sent away. It was, said the Congregation, 'a diabolical, not to say scandalous, operation'.[20] And the rhetoric of the *Avogador* Morosini, prosecuting in 1637, pungently denounced the fact that

> in the midst of the city of Venice, in the very bosom of the Prince, the wife and children of the former Leon Luzzatto have been seized and stolen by those means already well known to the law, as if in this city, a haven of security, children had been kidnapped by the pirates of Tripoli, Algiers and other towns of Barbary. . . .[21]

He was, needless to say, alluding to the tactics ascribed to the Jews, and not to those employed by the Catecumeni and other ardent conversionists.

Decisions to convert could have implications, not only for the convert's children, but for all his economic and emotional dependants. They might well be manoeuvred into espousing the Christian faith, not, it is true, by compulsion, but still by considerations far removed from genuine conviction. Fear of loneliness was surely a powerful incentive to convert, for the gulf between neophytes and Jews was greater than the gulf between Christians and Jews in general. An elderly mother, pressed into comply-

[18] S.U., b. 46, proc. Giovanni Giacomo Pisani, 27 Aug. 1580 to 14 Jan. 1581.

[19] S.U., b. 51, report of Eusebio Renati on the removal of Christian children in Turkish vessels, 4 July 1592.

[20] I.R.E.C., Not. F, fol. 94v., 95, 15, 29 Oct. 1615. The resolution to dismiss him was cancelled after he had produced some arguments in his defence. He was allowed to resign and eventually reinstated on 14 March 1619 – fol. 140v.

[21] I.R.E.C., Carte Diverse, 'Pie Case . . .', fol. 39, 21 Jan. 1637 Venetian style.

ing with the wishes of her son, but still drawn by a natural conservatism to her customary devotional and domestic routines, was more liable to be forced into false positions than was a wife sustained by her blood-relations and enjoying some prospect of remarriage. A notable casualty of the process was Elena de' Freschi Olivi, some seventy years of age, who was denounced to the Inquisition for heretical blasphemies committed in her parish church of San Marcilian in March 1555.[22]

Some five years before, her son Lazarus the physician and his brother Isaac, a surgeon, had converted to the Christian faith and taken the names of Giovanni Battista and Giovanni Giacomo de' Freschi Olivi.[23] It seemed that the doctor was a convert of irreproachable motives. He could hardly be accused of converting out of economic necessity, for as a physician he already exercised a valued skill, although he could, by virtue of his new religion, hope to escape some constraints and humiliations. It could not be said of him, as it was of certain converts, that he had shifted his religion out of carnal love for a Christian or for the purpose of divorcing an unwanted partner. Efforts were duly made to convert his wife Valorosa or Bella Rosa to the Christian faith, but in vain, and after their divorce she married Lazzarino, a banker in Reggio Emilia.[24] For three years or more the doctor hatched no plans to marry a Christian wife, and it seems that he eventually did so only to secure a governess for his children, after falling out with Donna Margarita, the married woman he at first hired to do the job.[25] After conversion he extended his intellectual achievements by taking a doctor's degree in theology at the University of Padua,[26] and became a notorious enemy of the Talmud. With Christian clerics he was appointed to a small commission whose business it was to describe the Talmud, and to define those works dependent upon it which were condemned, by the papal and Venetian decrees of 1553, to be burned.[27] 'I have persecuted, and continue to persecute, those blas-

[22] For a sensitive and penetrating account of the case, based on the documents in S.U., b. 12, see N. E. Vanzan Marchini, 'Il dramma dei convertiti nella follia di una ex ebrea', *Rassegna mensile di Israel*, Jan.–Feb. 1980, pp. 3–30. The full text of the surviving materials, including those contained in b. 159, is now published in I.Z., pp. 151–224.

[23] Giovanni Battista is identified as the former Jew Lazarus in the testimony of Maddalena, widow of Giovanni Marco de' Brachi, 30 April 1555, I.Z., p. 197, and Giovanni Giacomo as the former Isaac in that of the maid Agnese, ibid., p. 198, 2 May 1555.

[24] I.Z., p. 323, den. Giacomo de' Freschi Olivi, 12 Aug. 1560, in the case of Giovanni Battista Moretto (see below, pp. 287–8).

[25] I.Z., pp. 165–6, proc. Elena de' Freschi Olivi, written submission of Giovanni Battista de' Freschi Olivi.

[26] I.Z., Introduzione, n. 134, pp. 51–2.

[27] Stern, *Urkundliche Beiträge* ..., I, doc. 105, pp. 106–8; Kaufmann, 'Die Vertreibung ...', pp. 533, 537; cf. I.Z., p. 203, test. Antonio de' Morandi, chaplain of Santa Maria della Misericordia, in the case of Elena de' Freschi Olivi, 4 May 1555, and above, p. 82.

phemies and insults that are contained in the books of the Jews, and will go on so doing as long as I live, and after death if that is possible, taking no account of danger, enmity, retaliation, or injuries to my body.'[28] Such heroics were, perhaps, a means of authenticating his own conversion and winning acceptance in the Christian world, of repelling all suspicion which might attach to him; a means, too, of justifying to himself an act of seeming treachery, by reviling the religion he had left.[29] He appeared to have brought six souls to Christ – his mother, his brother and his four daughters, one of whom took the veil.[30] But two were to cause his brother and himself an embarrassment which bordered on poetic justice.

From the beginning the conversion of the doctor's mother had presented problems. For she was at best eccentric and at worst insane; acquaintances who had observed her both in Jewish and in Christian days called her 'feeble-minded' (*'scema di cervello'*), 'off her head' (*'fora di cervello'*), 'possessed' (*'inspiritata'*), 'simple' (*'sempiu'*) or 'mad' (*'mata'*). Hence, there was reason to doubt the propriety of her baptism: was she fit to make so momentous, so irrevocable a decision? But if she did not turn to Christianity, what would become of her? She was not continuously deranged, and so conversion could be contemplated. A woman in her middle sixties, mentally unstable, could hardly view coolly the prospect of sudden separation from sons and grandchildren, especially as she had no independent income and looked solely to the doctor for support.[31] She was torn between the prospect of isolation and the need to foresake the faith and rituals of a lifetime. By her own account, her sons' decision came as a shock, and at first she resisted fiercely, but then allowed herself to be persuaded to convert.

> One morning there was a great noise in the Ghetto, and I asked what it was, and was told that my son and his brothers wanted to be baptized. I begged him not to do this evil thing and inflict such shame upon the Jews, but he told me 'Bear with me, for I wish to be baptized.' So as not to leave my sons, for I am a widow, I chose to go out with them, and there came both friars and women of the third order [*pizochere*] and they had so much to say to me that I came to the faith of Christ and was baptized and now I live as a Christian.[32]

[28] I.Z., p. 175, submission of 21 June 1555.
[29] Cf. Vanzan Marchini, 'Il dramma ...', pp. 6–7.
[30] I.Z., pp. 165, 178, 171.
[31] In a written submission of 21 June 1555, Freschi Olivi calls her 'essa povera vedova vecchia et inferma gia vinti anni, la quale vive sotto l'ombra delli mei sudori, senza cavedale ne intrata alcuna di fermo ...' (I.Z., p. 178).
[32] See her examination on 21 March 1555, ibid., p. 192.

None the less, according to Agnese, the maid who knew her best, she continued to waver until the last minute, and went with her sons and granddaughters to the church of San Basso saying that she would accompany them only to the point of baptism, and then she would go to Jerusalem. Intentionally or not, Agnese herself turned the emotional screws upon the old woman. Madonna Elena took up a position at or near the church where she could not actually see the ceremony; Agnese brought the newly baptized girls to her one by one, and reported on the proceedings. On hearing that Isaac, the younger son, was even now becoming the Christian Giacomo, his mother, as though her resistance were broken, finally agreed to take baptism herself. The maid did not know if the old lady had ever repented of her baptism – 'I have heard her say only that God found a way to have her baptized when she did not wish it.'[33] Asked the same question by the Inquisition, Elena had already answered, 'How should I know? I don't remember, I don't remember!' But then, as though recalling her situation, she had added:

> Why do you want me to repent, to go and turn Jew again? Do you want me back in the Ghetto, becoming a Jewess? I have not forsaken God, and when I say 'in the name of the Father and of the Son and of the Holy Spirit' I have found God. I am a good Christian, and became one of my own accord, and was persuaded by nobody.[34]

Whatever her real state of mind at the moment of conversion, Madonna Elena succeeded in learning quite competently a range of new devotional practices and good works, although her behaviour remained strangely contradictory. She seemed to have responded well to the two friars who had told her, 'Madam, you have to believe that Christ is God and was born of the Holy Ghost and of the Virgin Mary.'[35] She also seemed to have acquired the devotional habits expected of a pious widow, for she now knelt to say her prayers, she lit candles in church, she took confession and Communion, she gave alms to priests and poor, she would recite the office of the Madonna and read Vespers in her own house, and her instruction to her grandchildren seemed flawless. When the girls went to bed she told them to say the Our Father, and the barber-surgeon Michele marvelled at it, saying to himself, 'Hark to this woman who has been a Jewess, how well she brings up these children!'[36] On the other

---

[33] Ibid., pp. 198–200, 2 May 1555.
[34] Ibid., p. 194, 20 April 1555.
[35] Ibid., p. 192, 21 March 1555.
[36] Ibid., p. 206, 16 May 1555; the other points were established by many witnesses.

hand, there were signs that she found far more difficulty in changing her diet and culinary habits to meet the demands of a new religion. It was as though the body rebelled where the mind could be disciplined, at least to the extent of memorizing new dogmas and such florid sentiments as 'at the Mass I am so consumed with devotion that I seem to have entered into the Holy Spirit, and when I hear the organ it seems to me that God has come to listen to the Mass.'[37]

A sympathetic witness said that Elena insisted on fasting rigorously.[38] But Margarita the governess suggested that the old lady was practising deceit. She, Margarita, was not one of those who considered Elena mad; she professed to think her merely odd and given to talking to herself. There was a rationale behind the widow's conduct: she was an unrepentant Jewess. From the two elder girls the governess knew that their grandmother would commandeer any meat or broth left over in the house on Thursday evening and consume them on Friday and Saturday. When the doctor bought meat on Saturday for Sunday she would furtively make herself chops and eat them that same day. The girls were caught in the cross-fire of household antagonisms; they were beaten by their father, nervous and easily embarrassed, for telling the governess everything, and they were beaten by the governess for accepting the forbidden foods proffered by their grandmother.[39] Admittedly the governess was hostile and her testimony suspect. But a far more friendly witness, the maid Agnese, recalled that the old woman had rejected certain meats and delicacies bought by the doctor, flinging them in disgust down the latrine.[40] And there was no doubt that she clung to the old ritual in slaughtering chickens, cutting their throats and throwing their heads away – if only, as she told the inquisitors, because she was frightened of wringing their necks.[41]

Such indiscretions could have been contained within the household. Disgruntled servants might have betrayed them, but their stories could well have been dismissed as malicious gossip. However, the old lady's misconduct became embarrassingly public when she was believed to be uttering blasphemies against the Virgin Birth and the consecrated Host, not merely in the attics of the family house but also in the local churches. The scandal broke when she exclaimed 'You lie in your teeth, you're a bastard, son of a harlot!' or similar words in the church of San Marcilian at the moment in the celebration of Mass when the priest had reached the words 'et incarnatus est de spiritu sancto ex Maria virgine et homo factus

[37] Ibid., p. 194, 20 April 1555.
[38] Ibid., pp. 159–60, test. Donna Agnese, 1 April 1555.
[39] Ibid., p. 157, test. Donna Margarita, 27 March 1555.
[40] Ibid., p. 199, 2 May 1555.
[41] Ibid., pp. 195–6, 27 April 1555.

est'.[42] This vituperation, seemingly addressed either to the priest or to the Host itself, came very close to the usual style of blasphemy ascribed by Christians to Jews in the years following the destruction of the Talmud. One witness, Paola Marcello, a nobleman's widow living in the parish, soon recollected rumours of the old lady slipping into the Ghetto for purposes more sinister than pawning goods: 'she goes to the banks to weep, and she would like to emerge from this accursed faith and return to her own.'[43] Paradoxically, Dr Freschi Olivi, the censor of Jewish blasphemy, was constrained to argue that his mother's words could not be construed as a sign of judaizing 'because the Jews who at present live among Christians neither use such words themselves nor teach anyone else to use them, on account of their fear of Christians. Full of evil intentions they may be, but they do not reveal them.'[44]

More charitable explanations of Elena's behaviour could be tendered, and her son hastened to urge them upon the tribunal. Were his mother not a former Jewess no one would have seen in her anything worse than a common if distressing form of madness.[45] Witnesses spoke of her inconsequential speech, her soliloquies, her sense of persecution, her habit of wrestling with invisible opponents, meanwhile reliving old resentments and abusing the empty air with threats to have the law upon her enemies, her indifference to surroundings or onlookers, her expensive habit of ripping up good shirts and throwing the rags down the latrine. Here again her behaviour seemed to fall into contrasting and irreconcilable halves; she would retreat into a private world of invisible foes, but was never beyond recall from it. Some thought her mad only in these private soliloquies; answering questions she proved entirely lucid, and indeed her appearances before the Inquisition seemed to demonstrate the fact, for she was guilty then of nothing worse than excitability and occasional evasiveness. She had her own explanation of the affair: she had been praying to the Madonna to deliver her from the importunities of a servant who wanted to marry her, and he was the lying bastard to whom she had referred ('Sto bastardo mulazzo, el mente per la golla, perche non lo voglio per marito').[46] Eventually the Inquisition accepted the argument that her remarks were delirious ravings rather than deliberate acts of blasphemy, and since there was no madhouse in Venice and no place

[42] Ibid., test. Pietro Pianella, parish priest of San Marcilian, 18 March 1555, pp. 151–2; test. Donna Lucrezia, Donna Cattarina and Paola Marcello, 19, 25–26 March 1555, pp. 153–5.
[43] Ibid., p. 155.
[44] Ibid., p. 188.
[45] Ibid., p. 172, submission of 18 April 1555.
[46] Ibid., p. 193, 21 March, 20 April 1555.

could be found at the great hospital in Treviso, it was agreed that she be confined in perpetuity in a bedroom of her son's house.[47]

The old woman's madness, if such it was, was no direct consequence of the strains imposed by her conversion: indeed, it seems to have antedated her trial by thirty years or more, when her mind had been unhinged by the loss of a child.[48] But in one sense her madness may have served her well, for it removed the need to reconcile the contrasts between the old Judaism and the new Christianity, and it perhaps allowed her – until it caused too flagrant a scandal to the faithful – to enjoy the indulgence extended to the insane, and to express a lasting antipathy towards her son's new faith in terms forbidden to the normal. Dr Freschi Olivi wrote of the tolerance extended to a woman possessed by demons, an *inspiritata* who was regularly brought on Fridays to the church of San Rocco and was allowed – with the understanding and pity of most of the congregation to spit and make vulgar gestures at the sacrament.[49] The plea of insanity served him well too, for it enabled him to display his new-found Christian erudition and, by exonerating his mother from a part of the blame, to repair his own battered reputation.

The doctor's daughter Orsetta was likewise poised uneasily on the frontier between Christianity and Judaism, for it was possible that the girls' mother, alive, comfortably off and not very far away, might claim their loyalty. Orsetta and one sister were married to Christian artisans or tradesmen, the first a dyer at the Madonna dell' Orto and the second a 'distiller of waters' at San Canciano. In accordance with *Cupientes iudaeos*, these marriages were doubtless intended to procure steady husbands who would bind their wives firmly to Christianity. But the dyer, Giovanni Battista Moretto, proved to be a disappointment. He ran short of money, dressed up his wife as a man and smuggled her out of Venice on a trip to Reggio and Ferrara.[50] The worst construction put on his actions was that he and been suborned by the Jews into restoring her and possibly her sister to them for money. Casual boasting to a friend threatened to cost him dear. He had shown coins to a grocer's apprentice and had told him: 'If you let them circumcise you, as I shall let them circumcise me, you will get even more than that!'[51] Happily for him the Inquisition accepted his story that he and his wife had merely gone to borrow from her

[47] Ibid., pp. 189–91, 218–24, 12 Sept. to 16 Nov. 1555.

[48] Ibid., pp. 197–8, test. Maddalena, widow of Giovanni Maria de' Brachi, 30 April 1555; test. Marco Trevisan, boatman and ferryman, 30 July 1555, ibid., p. 216. Cf. ibid., p. 205, test. Menega, wife of Moretto, 14 May 1555; ibid., pp. 212, 214, test. Donna Lucia and her husband Paolo, the Ghetto watchman, 18, 30 July 1555.

[49] Ibid., p. 164, submission of 26 March 1555.

[50] Proc. Giovan Battista Moreto in I.Z., pp. 321–35.

[51] Ibid., pp. 326–7, test. Alfonso Borgognon, 13 Aug. 1560.

mother,[52] that the money he showed came not from the Jews but rather from signing on board a ship, and that if he had indeed left her behind in Ferrara – a city of many Jews – he had done so for no deeply improper purpose. He had merely left her in pledge for a debt of one and a half crowns, which he owed to the host of the 'Sun'. Feckless and unchivalrous he might be, perhaps even anxious to dump a wife whose dowry had been quickly spent. But there was no proof that he had conspired to make his wife an apostate, still less that he had ever acted as an agent of the Jews.[53] Orsetta's role had been a passive one, but she showed no sense of impropriety at the prospect of visiting her mother. Her father's conversion had divided her family into parties alienated in faith but conscious of some lingering obligations and some expectations of aid and charity created by ties of blood. Movement within the family, liable to excite suspicion, could no longer be a matter of indifference to the Church.

Orsetta's case raised the question whether the Jews would really take the risks involved in reclaiming persons already turned Christian, as distinct from children on the verge of conversion by their father's decree. Would they even wish to reclaim them? Churchmen, conceiving of a ceaseless battle between Jewish obduracy and Christian faith, proclaimed their belief that Jews would always strive, by force or cunning, to entice converts back to the religion of their ancestors. They would do so not simply out of evangelical fervour, or out of forgiveness for strayed sheep, but rather as an act of revenge upon Christians and a measure to keep the number of Jews constant. Jews might, it was said, conspire against converts, offering false evidence to the courts, out of sheer vindictiveness; or, more deviously, they might get them into trouble to break down their defences and increase the possibility of winning them back. Defending the cardinal-nephew's protégé, Scipione Borghese, who had suffered in the penal galleys, the nuncio declared that he had been persecuted by the Jews, 'who cannot abide that one should become a Christian'. Later he added that 'Could they contrive it that he returned afresh to Judaism, they would take him for a saint.'[54] To snatch back their children would be a sweet revenge on those neophytes who had collaborated with Christians in attacking the Jews or destroying their culture. Converts had undoubtedly been encouraged to believe in the possibility. Francesco Colonna described the attempts of Isaac Cohen and Rabbi Sabbatai to enveigle him back to the Ghetto and ship him off to the Levant. These were made, he said, on the very day the Talmud was burned at San

---

[52] Ibid., p. 329, test. Donna Franceschina, 17 Aug. 1560.

[53] Ibid., pp. 331–3, test. Giovan Battista Moretto, 5 Sept. 1560.

[54] C.E.R., reg. 18, fol. 130, 133, 27 Jan., 17 Feb. 1616 Venetian style; cf. also reg. 21, fol. 28v., 11 May 1624.

Marco and Rialto; his seducers were consumed with fury, and raged at the witness's father and at another baptized Jew, Fra Alessandro da Foligno, who were blamed for the persecution.[55] Giovanni Battista de' Freschi Olivi was known to certain Jews as 'the man who helped to get our books burned'.[56] His brother accused them of trying to reclaim the late doctor's daughter Orsetta, 'in contempt of this most holy faith, because the girl's father was utterly opposed to their crimes [*tristitie*]'.[57]

A few converts told stories of Jews who specialized in reconversion and in organizing escapes to the Levant. If the Inquisition could be persuaded to believe in such persons, strong in their nefarious designs, it would serve to excuse the weakness of the neophyte who had lapsed. Moses Israel/Iseppo Bon told of a certain Elias who had picked up four women in Livorno who were 'Jewesses become Christians', brought them to Venice and shipped them to the Levant to return to Judaism. One of his techniques, it seemed, was to threaten to sell them into slavery. A certain Lavinia, having been told that conversion to Judaism would save her from this fate, yielded and became a Jew in Skopje in Macedonia.[58] But the story went unconfirmed.

Converts and conversionists thus fostered, if they seldom proved, the notion of the embattled forces of Jewry, engaged in guerrilla warfare for the souls of converts and their children, the Ottoman Empire and its wastes of un-Christian territory serving as refuge or prison for those the Jews had reclaimed. And the Jews too were interested parties. They must have borne in mind not only their own fate, but also the future of their communities: this would surely be jeopardized by any suspicion that they were systematically recovering converts. They professed before the authorities an attitude of indifference or contempt towards deserters from their faith. Those who crowned their protean careers by attempting to return to the faith of the Jews would, they said, be the more deeply despised for it. Eusebio Renati, baptized Jew and governor of the Catecumeni, told the Inquisition that he had sent something to be pawned in the Ghetto, and that at the bank Solomon della Regina had said to the brokers acting for Eusebio, 'Do you take account of these *meshumadim*?' Reporting the insult, Eusebio explained, 'This word is used by Jews in abuse of baptized Jews, and it means those who are destroyed, made as nothing, and struck out of the book of God in this world and the

---

[55] I.Z., p. 97, proc. Francesco Colonna, test. 28 Nov. 1553; cf. Joseph Hacohen and the Anonymous Corrector, *The Vale of Tears (Emek Habacha)*, ed. and transl. H. S. May (The Hague, 1971), pp. 87–8.

[56] I.Z., pp. 157–8, proc. Elena de' Freschi Olivi, test. 28 March 1555.

[57] I.Z., pp. 323, 324, proc. Giovan Battista Moreto, den. Giacomo de' Freschi Olivi, 12 Aug. 1560.

[58] S.U., b. 92, proc. Iseppo Bon, test. 14 Feb. 1636.

next. . . .'[59] That Jews would never think such nonentities worth reclaiming was the theme of members of the community in Verona in 1590, accused of stealing away the neophyte Agostino. It was most learnedly and tortuously pursued by Grassino, son of Marco Bassano, who was just beginning to earn the title of rabbi. Glad to expound the law of the Jews, however unsympathetic his audience, he told his judges:

> In our house, Signor, we have this custom: that when a Jew becomes a Christian, we want to know no more of him. And since our sages say, taking the sentence from the Talmud, that a Christian who becomes a Jew is transformed from evil into good and begins to live according to the good law, all the more, then, must we do good works in our own law, and all the less do we take account of a Jew turned Christian, and we do not concern ourselves with him.[60]

Rabbi Marco, his father, adopted a less oracular style:

> when one of our Jews becomes a Christian, I love him no more, but I do not hate him: I look upon him with repulsion (*l'ho a schifo*), I have nothing to do with him, and I do not care to speak with the man. I have all the less trust in him when he returns to being a Jew. . . .[61]

Their story failed to convince the civil authorities, though it may have given the Inquisitor pause, and by the standards of proof which the Holy Office demanded there was no satisfactory evidence in this case of conspiracy to reclaim converts. On the whole it seems unlikely that Italian neophytes, unless converted as children, were exposed to the same dilemma as the offspring of the Marrano families, for these were often advised in adolescence or adulthood of their Judaism and urged by relatives or friends to return to it. If adult Italian neophytes returned to Judaism, they seem to have done so less because Jews were eager to have them back than on account of their own loneliness and their desire to use the narrow, intimate world of the Ghetto to find lodgings and employment in a strange city.

Such motives seem to underlie the pathetic story of Solomon, once a Jew from Cameo. The son of Angelino of Ferrara, he was baptized in Rome on 18 November 1630 by the Spanish cardinal Sandoval. From him he received a pension of 3 ducats a month and the name Pietro

---

[59] S.U., b. 52, proc. Solomon della Regina, 3 Aug. 1585.
[60] Q.C., filza 109, proc. 113, 28 Nov. 1590.
[61] Ibid., 29 Nov. 1590; see also above, pp. 86–7.

Vincenzo Maria. In mid-August 1632 he arrived in Venice from Ferrara and put up in the Ghetto in the hostel for the poor maintained by the Fraternity of the German Jews.[62] A young Jew from Rome then found him work with a tailor, Giovanni Pio of Pirano, whose shop was in Corte di Ca' Zappa in the parish of San Geremia, where the Ghetto stood.[63] Surprisingly, since this man was himself a convert, he at first saw nothing wrong with employing a journeyman who wore the red hat. By his account, his new assistant returned the next day, saying he had been expelled from the Fraternity's hostel because they had discovered him to be a Jew turned Christian. If this was true, the act of rejection may have marked a dislike of converts, a fear of spies or a reluctance to incur the Christian authorities' displeasure. Homeless, the pariah journeyman took lodgings for about nine days with a poor Christian woman, an artisan's wife in the next parish, and followed his employer's advice to change his hat for a black one. But Giovanni Pio was not satisfied that the proprieties had been resumed, and he went to San Domenico di Castello to report the whole affair to the Inquisitor, saying that old habits were refusing to die, for his assistant was absent on Saturday and had tried to work the following day.

Making no formal defence, the tailor was sentenced to imprisonment and, despite his poor health, sent to serve on the prison ships. He fell ill and died on the galley *Pasqualigo* about four months later. At this point, however, one piece of unambiguous evidence appears. If the Jews had rejected him in life, they did not do so in death. The prisoner – should he be called Solomon, or Pietro Vincenzo Maria? – made his confession in the galleots' hospital, and most of his fellow convicts thought him a genuine convert to Catholicism.[64] But, through an elderly soldier serving as a freeman on board the galley, he managed to send a message to a young Jew in the Ghetto Vecchio, and Jews visited him several times before he died.[65] The convict-warder said that he would not interfere, and allowed them to remove the corpse in a gondola for burial in the Jewish cemetery on the Lido. Appealed to as an expert, Giovanni Pio the tailor suggested that to satisfy themselves of his Jewishness the Jews would have searched the body for sacred things – a book of offices, phylacteries, a prayer shawl. It was clear that the prisoner had taken the initiative in approaching the Jews; it was not that the Jews had actively sought to reclaim him.

[62] S.U., b. 89, proc. Pietro Vincenzo Maria Sandoval, test. Giovanni Pio, Moses, son of Leon Luzzatto, and the prisoner, 31 Aug., 7 Sept. 1632.

[63] Ibid., and test. Emanuel Lattes, 7 Sept. 1632.

[64] Ibid., test. Daniel of Crete and Bartolomeo Bassarin of Tarvisio or Treviso, 15 Feb. 1633; test. Don Guerruccio Orlanducci da Campiglio, a Florentine priest, 21 Feb. 1633.

[65] Ibid., test. Tommaso di Giovanni Battista Stenti, 21 Feb. 1633.

If out of prudence or conviction Jews held back from adult converts, there are a few indications that they showed less detachment from those converted as children. The evidence of Francesco Colonna of Mantua lacks corroboration. But it is worth recalling his statement that Isaac Cohen, on discovering that Francesco had been baptized as a child of about ten, made much of two points: that his father had had him baptized 'by force' and that his mother, Sara Boccazza, living in Mantua, was still a Jewess. 'Poor you,' said Isaac Cohen, 'you have a Jewish mother, and you want to stay like this?'[66] Valorosa, formerly the wife in Judaism of Dr Freschi Olivi, was content to lend a little money to her christianized daughter and son-in-law.[67] Marco, son of Jacob Bassano, accused of snatching his nephew Agostino from his monastery in Verona, gave the impression that the boy was good for nothing. As an adolescent, fourteen or fifteen years of age,[68] he was officially presumed to have had the use of his reason at the time of his conversion. But not all his relatives were totally indifferent to him. Indeed, the novice-master described how a relative had come to speak to the boy shortly before his disappearance, and had said, 'Father, blood was never water, and for my blood that is in him I love him still' ('Padre, il sangue non fu mai aqua, et del mio sangue gli voglio bene').[69]

Andrea Nunciata, born Abram Teseo in 1609 and baptized at the age of ten, declared himself torn as a child by the pull of his benefactors towards Christianity and the pull of his father towards Judaism, although it was plain that when he was in his twenties and had an inheritance to claim his blood relations showed no enthusiasm for his return to their faith. By his own account, he was born in Florence to Guglielmo Teseo and his wife Allegra. His father was a businessman, and in Ferrara had dealings with two silk and textile merchants, Bernardino della Nunciata and his son Andrea. Taking a fatherly interest in the boy, they eventually procured his baptism in the cathedral on 17 July 1619. Either the act was performed without parental consent or else his father came to regret the permission given, for he tried to reclaim him and spirited him back to a subterranean hiding-place near their home in Florence, where he hatched plans to send him to the Ottoman Empire. After one false start, the boy was sent to Bosnia, where (or so he said) he managed to live as a Christian because neither Jews nor Christians were compelled to wear distinctive badges. His own tangled story was that he provoked the

[66] I.Z., p. 96, test. 28 Nov. 1553.
[67] I.Z., p. 332, test. Giovanni Battista Moretto, 5 Sept. 1560.
[68] Q.C., filza 109, proc. 113, test. 29 Nov. 1590; for the boy's age, test. Emmanuel, son of Jacob di Porto, 9 March 1592.
[69] Ibid., test. Arcangelo Patavino, 27 Nov. 1590.

enmity of his uncle Joseph Teseo when he returned to Italy in the early 1630s after his father's death in the great plague, adopted the guise of a Jew in order to claim his patrimony, removed his sister Stella from Modena to Venice, and introduced her to the household he had recently set up with a newly married Christian wife. Poised like a double agent between Christianity and Judaism, he was denounced by his uncle to the Holy Office, got into trouble with the criminal law in Venice and was eventually sentenced to one year's imprisonment as 'vehemently suspect of heresy'. Treated by his father as a forced convert worth reclaiming, noisily protesting his loyalty to Christianity, proving it by denouncing a former servant to the Inquisition, lamenting to his uncle that he was in dire straits for 'desiring to maintain the law of the Jews, which was my first law', he showed an ambivalence and perhaps a confusion greater than those of many Marranos.[70]

There were few mass conversions in Italy, but there were many small multiple conversions, spreading outwards from many scattered nuclei, from the head of a household to his family circle. It suited some churchmen to believe in a contest of good and evil, to hold that the Jews, as the relentless embodiment of the principle of evil, were proselytizing and joining the battle for souls with no less ardour than themselves. Their own efforts became the less trivial and prosaic, their vigilance over converts in the beleaguered fortress of the Catecumeni took on the colours of heroism. Indifference may have been the real reaction of the Jews to adult converts; if these returned to Judaism the act was more an expression of their own needs than the result of determined efforts to recover them. It was the child or adolescent convert, exonerated from the full moral responsibility for his choice, who found himself most confusingly placed between the two worlds of the Christian and the Jew, and closest to the dilemma of the Marrano. By the seventeenth century the Venetian authorities had officially resolved to regard the Marranos *en bloc* as forced converts. They continued, understandably, to treat the former Jews of Italy as persons recruited to Christianity by legitimate means, and the state was not known to intervene to rescue italianate converts from the Inquisition. A few personal histories, such as those of the Freschi Olivi family, suggest that many were converted, not by physical force, but rather by their own dependence (emotional, financial or legally sanctioned) upon a zealous household head, and these examples blur the simple distinction between coercion and free choice.

[70] S.U., b. 91, proc. Andrea Nunciata, 26 April 1633 to 24 Jan. 1636.

16

Neophytes of Italy:
Casualties of Conversion

This chapter will try to reconstruct the circumstances and the mentality of a few converts whose personal histories have been preserved by the Inquisition. Accounts can be given of nine relatively poor converts and of three comparatively rich ones. Only the poor were actually punished, incurring sentences which ranged from a public penance before St Mark's to a spell of twenty years' penal servitude in the galleys; the richer converts were merely investigated. Over all of them there hung the suspicion that they had become Christians for materialistic, carnal or worldly reasons, and that in so doing they had exposed the weakness of conversion strategy. The poorest persons had converted, not for spiritual gain, but for physical survival, seeking a respite from the struggle to exist; the richer had done so, not for survival, but for betterment, as part of a plan entailing marriage to a Christian wife, the acquisition of property, and some advancement in the world. For all of them, perhaps, conversion promised to be a liberating act which opened up prospects and offered to cast off old entanglements – debts, petty lawsuits, prison sentences, the tyranny of an oppressive father or the demands of an unloved wife.

Five of the poorer converts came before the courts between 1548 and 1587, the other four between 1629 and 1637. Westerners predominated in the first group; the others were all Sephardim from the Levant. Most of the nine were – or were accused of being – social undesirables in a fairly broad sense, and they were all persons living by their wits, or doing odd jobs and acting as go-betweens, or otherwise engaged in dubious and unproductive occupations. Their social utility was not conspicuous, they were far removed from Marrano merchants, and the secular power would have no economic incentive to offer them protection against the Inquisition. Indeed, they had something in common with the vagrant, the restless figure who haunted the consciousness of social legislators in the sixteenth and seventeenth centuries, inverting as he did the values of the settled, industrious society. In Catholic countries at least, vagrants tended to be treated not only as threats to public order and health, but also as a religious problem: they throve on the credulity of pious persons whose alms they stole, their pitches were often in churches, they disturbed order in church, they blasphemed, they were ignorant of the most elementary Christian doctrine, and they died on the streets without benefit of the sacraments of the Church. Out of ignorance or design, the delinquent convert sometimes became a trader in sacred things. This felonious tendency would make him a criminal far more reprehensible than most sturdy beggars. Conversion was sometimes one symptom of an outlook which dreamed of getting rich quickly through windfall profits, perhaps by supernatural and highly suspect means.

Like the Marranos, the delinquent converts defy simple classification. No two prisoners of the Inquisition showed identical characteristics, but these could overlap: hence the possibility of arranging them along a continuum. This can well begin with the person who proposes to convert to escape extreme poverty or trouble with the law, and who incurs suspicion because his enthusiasm begins to flag. Beyond him stands the man who becomes a professional convert, discovering the benefits which can be obtained regularly from presenting himself as a Jew turned Christian. This status may become his principal asset; however genuine, it can lead him into the company of professional beggars who engage in pious fraud. There are degrees of this, however, and the man who sells bogus ecclesiastical bric-à-brac and false indulgences is committing a less serious crime than the one who actively 'sells baptism' and so becomes the walking parody of the evangelical campaign for the conversion of the Jews. Repeating baptism may for a time be a principal means to live, or it may supplement earnings from a precarious occupation, such as peddling cheap goods and trinkets. Some delinquents deliberately chose repeated conversion. Others – especially the much travelled Levantines charged before the Inquisition about 1630 – had suffered the dislocating experience of conversion under force or fear from Judaism to Islam in childhood or youth. Though not in general closely resembling the professional converts, they shared something of their restlessness, lack of roots, and lack of steady application, and they showed ominous signs of treating religious divisions as frontiers that could be crossed at will. For most of them, travelling, shifting a religion and putting on a new identity were things inseparably linked.

Apart from a select band of well-to-do merchants, second-hand dealers and bankers, most Jews were poor. If they behaved suspiciously after conversion their detractors could easily suggest that their only motive in converting had been to escape poverty. Even the banker could change his hat out of worldly ambition. Before embarking on tales of suspect converts, it is only fair to point out that a few Jews turned to Christianity on their deathbeds, at a moment when they were surely beyond material concerns. Michael, a Jew of Padua, felt the plague upon him in the pesthouse during the terrible epidemic of 1575–77, called the two Franciscans who had the cure of souls in the Lazzaretto, and asked for baptism for himself and his children.[1] In 1584 Francesco Bono, sacristan of St Mark's, was asked by increasingly large and insistent deputations of noblemen to baptize the Jew Joseph, who was dying of typhus in the galleot's prison, and had said that for twenty years he had wanted to become a Christian. He had never made his confession, but he had come to believe in the Trinity. He recited the paternoster, Ave Maria and Creed with the priest, who testified:

> I began to read the service of baptism, and he rejoiced, saying, 'O Jesus Christ, you have given me this grace,' kissing my hands and constantly thanking God and the most holy Trinity.[2]

The psychology of such deathbed conversions is hard to fathom. They may have been the last acts of persons who had long entertained the idea of conversion out of genuine conviction, but had been deterred by the social complications inherent in the change, and by the difficulty of breaking with relatives. At the moment when society ceased to matter, they made their choice at last.

No such detachment could be ascribed to Aaron and Asher, two young Jews from central Europe. They were among the poorest of the poor who came to the Catecumeni in its early days, hoping to find in it a stepping-stone to a better life on earth.[3] They had travelled far greater distances than most of the 'subsistence migrants' known to have come to sixteenth-century Venice.[4] Asher, the stronger of the two characters, told the authorities that his home was in Chelm, to the east of Lublin in Poland, where his father was an eye-doctor and glazier. Asher made two visits to Venice, with an intervening spell in Lombardy, and on the first he carried water and firewood and minded a small child for a widow in the Venetian Ghetto. Aaron, called in the notary's record a 'German from Prague in Bohemia', said that he had no trade and lived by begging among the

---

[1] S.U., b. 59, proc. Marco di Francesco of Padua, test. Marco, 22–23 Oct. 1587.
[2] S.U., b. 53, proc. Joseph, 13 March 1584.
[3] Cf. Pullan, 'The old Catholicism ...'.
[4] Cf. Pullan, *Rich and poor* ..., p. 297.

Jews, though he also did odd jobs and lived by beating cloth and carrying water. It was hard to say where casual work ended and Jewish charity began. Eventually, desperate for something better than this precarious existence in a strange land where he could scarcely speak the language, Asher was tempted into the Catecumeni, and Aaron followed him. They liked neither the confinement nor the discipline and began, too late, to suspect that the path would be far from smooth. Asher slipped out and met Jews who tried to persuade them both to leave, or dropped ominous hints that after baptism the Casa's obligations to them would end; when he returned the prior deprived him of food by way of penalty for his illicit expedition. The closed institution probably seemed no less constricting than the Ghetto. The blasphemies ascribed to Asher were perhaps less acts of calculated disrespect for Christianity than expressions of childish frustration and boredom. Since he and his friend were surrounded by impressionable young people, they were hastily removed to a local prison and questioned with a suspicion that seemed to betray, not merely a lawyer's professional hostility, but also the misgivings of Christian authority concerning the hazards built into its own conversionary policy. Aaron was called a *ribaldo*, one moved to enter the Catecumeni not by the spirit of God but rather by the Devil, bent upon seeking the goods of this world, 'seeing that you lived wretchedly by serving the Jews and performing the lowliest tasks, as you have stated'. Asked what he expected to gain from turning Christian, Asher seems to have replied that 'he thought he would be well and prosperous, and have a good trade, and put all his relatives out of mind.' The interrogator duly admonished the boys:

> Have you not been instructed in the faith of Christ, that he takes care of everyone, even of the birds? Do you not know that you must forsake everything for his love and that he will abandon no one who puts his trust in him?[5]

Pious rhetoric idealized the convert as the pilgrim who set all worldly things at naught and trusted absolutely in the providence of God. Some, having neither wealth nor possessions to sacrifice, could see conversion only as a means to gain.

Conversion might also get a man out of trouble; governors of the Catecumeni shunned neither the gaols nor the galleys. Admittedly, Paolo Loredan, once described as 'that little Spaniard brought up among Greeks who is a Jew turned Christian',[6] would have rebutted any sugges-

---

[5] I.Z. II, pp. 31–48, 7 May to 4 June 1563.
[6] S.U., b. 60, proc. Paolo Loredan and Chiara Pisani, test. Chiara Pisani, 3 Oct. 1587.

tion that his motive was to escape either punishment or poverty. An immigrant from Crete, he claimed to own property on the island, and to be a scholar now convinced that 'Jesus Christ is truly the Messiah and came to save our souls.' He was at pains to show that he had been bent on conversion even before he left Crete, and reminded the former governor respectfully of the fact when once he saw him on a balcony at carnival time.[7] But his conduct was subject to less favourable interpretations. After coming to Venice he was imprisoned by the public prosecutors, the *Avogadori di Commun*, for illegally selling weapons, and was said to have become a Christian, together with Samuel, his eldest son, in order to gain his freedom.[8] His wife and five children remained in Crete, and he did nothing beyond expressing a vague desire to fetch them or a hope that the Senate would send for them and place them in the Catecumeni.[9] Staying on in the city, he showed no signs of getting a steady job, and probably lived on fees or tips for performing magical rituals with the aid of wax effigies and an obliging spirit.[10] After baptism he had gone to live in the house of Chiara Pisani, a gold-thread-spinner of San Pantalon, but their relations deteriorated to the point where each began to denounce the other. Preferring tangible evidence to wild allegation, the Holy Office seemed most interested in the books he had chosen to keep by him, which included Jewish books of offices, biblical commentaries and Hebrew grammars. He had a rosary, which he showed the tribunal, but 'no books of the Christian faith other than what the Catecumeni taught me'. It was put to him that 'His keeping the daily offices of the Jews and not possessing the Christian book of offices shows that he is a bad Christian who holds to the law of the Jews.'[11] Nothing was proved, however, and he was released with a warning not to depart from Venice without permission. There was a little evidence that he had tried to sell the books, and no corroboration of his supposed remark that 'he wanted to turn Jew again, and what he had done he had done out of poverty.'[12] None the less he leaves the impression of a man without integrity, turning his hand to many things to scrape a living. Conversion was not the least of these expedients.

Though many accusations were launched against Loredan, and against Aaron and Asher, it was never suggested that they intended to become professional converts. Marco of Padua was one of these, though in a

[7] Ibid., test. Paolo Loredan, 15 Oct. 1587.

[8] Ibid., and ibid., test. Joseph Mocato, 17 Nov. 1587.

[9] Ibid., test. Paolo Loredan, 12 Dec. 1587.

[10] Ibid., test. Chiara Pisani, 3 Oct. 1587.

[11] Ibid., 15 Oct. 1587.

[12] As suggested in a petition of Chiara Pisani to the Holy Office; cf. test. Joseph Mocato, 17 Nov. 1587.

modest way of business. He had been converted in an emergency by his father's decision, he had not been apprenticed to a craft or received any basic instruction in Christianity as the Catecumeni prescribed, and he had no backing other than a certain claim on Christian charity. This, however, led him into the world of the *furfante*, the charlatan who gulled the pious. Born Elias or Lissan after 1565, he was baptized at the age of about eleven when his father offered himself and his children to the Church in the pesthouse at Padua, and perhaps another ten years passed before he was educated in basic Christianity – by no house of converts, but at the general hospital in Milan. Of Marco's three brothers, two graduated to keeping a lodging-house in Treviso, but one remained a beggar 'for the love of God'. Marco himself, about 1584–85, joined a company of strolling players who kept him but paid him no wages, and stayed with them till they reached Turin, whence they left for France. Eventually the wanderer returned to Padua and, finding little to do but trade on his status as a converted Jew, himself went begging. With time he decided to improve his chances by obtaining a licence, and was passed down the line from the Dominican convent of Santa Corona at Vicenza to the local inquisitor, who in turn obtained from the bishop's vicar-general a patent entitling him to seek alms. His credentials were genuine, but he soon embarked on disreputable activities. He began to purchase from a shady Vicentine printer, from stalls in the market-place and from a fellow pedlar sheets of paper which offered false indulgences, and also to acquire rosaries embellished by beads falsely supposed to have been blessed. He could neither read nor write, but had learnt the indulgence sheets by heart. They bore the title 'The indulgences and graces of the Ave Marias blessed by Pope Adrian VI on 25 December 1523, and confirmed by His Holiness Pope Sixtus V in the first year of his pontificate . . .'. Their extravagant tone was set by the opening paragraph: 'Whosoever carries upon him one of these blessed Ave Marias and recites one time the paternoster and the Ave Maria will on that day liberate three souls from Purgatory.' Arrested at Belluno, he was found guilty of having 'sold in several places summaries which falsely included the name and authority of the Supreme Pontiffs, and also beads attached to the rosaries, which you sold on the pretence that they had been blessed', and sentenced to two years in the galleys or three in a closed prison.[13] Marco's crime was never represented as a lapse into Judaism or inflated into a serious attempt to undermine the Catholic faith, but it can well be seen as the product of a hasty conversion outside the strict regime of the more advanced institutions created by Catholic reform. Isolating him from fellow Jews but doing nothing to integrate him with settled and respect-

[13] S.U., b. 59, proc. Marco di Francesco of Padua, 22–31 Oct. 1587.

able Christians, it seems to have led him into a rootless, drifting existence marked by the ignorance which betrayed him.

Marco's offences did not include the most heinous crime in the professional convert's book – the repetition of baptism. It was this misdeed that translated into reality the literary image of the *Iucchi*; the exploitation of a sacrament was far worse than the touting of false rubbish. Offenders of this type were at large in the mid-sixteenth century and were still encountered in the 1630s. Aaron Francoso of Sarzana, then subject to Siena, was born after 1528 to Raphael Francoso and his wife Stella. At the age of nineteen, he said, he was persuaded to become a Christian by a priest in Padua, and was baptized Giacomo in the church of San Geremia in Venice. For a time he taught a little Hebrew to three scholars, but they left him within a month, and – having discovered the financial if not the spiritual benefits of conversion – he took to repeating the performance. In September 1547 he took the name of Paolo in Modena; in Ravenna, about four months later, he was newly baptized Battista; and on Palm Sunday 1548 he was baptized Francesco in the abbey of Vangadizza in the Polesine. The gains were tiny – 14 lire in Venice, 2 crowns at Ravenna, 6 ducats and some clothing at Vangadizza. On the last occasion, however, he did acquire a beggar's patent, which promised more cash. His penny profits were large enough to keep him from starvation, but the penalties for such abuse of baptism were heavy indeed. Reported to the papal nuncio and arrested by the Venetian Inquisition, the young man made a prompt confession. 'I had myself baptized because my clothes were in tatters, and I did it to get a bit of shelter.' Candour did not save him; the authorities, aware of the threat of Anabaptism, were perhaps especially anxious at that time to assert the unrepeatable character of the sacrament, and to inflict exemplary punishment on anyone who abused it. The prisoner was sentenced to twenty years at the galley's oar, to have his ear split as a mark of infamy, and to perpetual banishment from Venice and its dominions once the sentence was served.[14] At this time fraudulent begging in churches or elsewhere by bogus cripples or the falsely blind was earning much milder penalties, which did not in theory stretch to more than eighteen months in the prison ships.[15] They, like Aaron, had abused the credulity of the pious, but they had not misused a sacrament.

In the summer of 1636, a Franciscan described a conversation aboard the courier's boat from Ferrara to Venice, in which the Jews were called

[14] I.Z., pp. 67–78, proc. Giacomo Francoso, 3–10 April 1548.
[15] Pullan, *Rich and poor* ... , pp. 296–307.

'sellers of baptism'.[16] Anyone acquainted with the misdeeds of Moses Israel would have echoed the sentiment. This name will do as well as any; he had several others. In the Ottoman Empire he was a Jew, in Italy a Jew turned Christian. His trade was that of a mercer, a pedlar in haberdashery, though he also combed wool for a living and admitted reluctantly to selling gunpowder. Following these precarious occupations, he would travel great distances to scrape a living, and he described to his judges three adventures which started with sea trips from the Levant to Italy and sometimes involved long sojourns in Venice. The first voyage took place about 1618, when he travelled to Venice by way of Corfu and stayed there for about five months, buying 'materials, combs, needles, paternosters from Murano, and other such things'. Stocked up, he returned to the Levant in a Slav ship by way of Split. Three or four years passed, and he came again to buy similar merchandise, and returned to the Levant by way of Corfu. A third journey began in 1632 with three months in Venice, followed by five in Corfu, and then eight months in Venice again. He left for Livorno, and from Livorno made his way to Rome.[17]

These voyages tended to coincide with experiments in Christianity which gave access to Catholic charity and helped the traveller to renew his wardrobe: his natural mobility made repetition of baptism easier to contemplate. Whether or not, as his detractors suggested, he had first been baptized Francesco Maria in 1624 by Cardinal Ludovisi, Archbishop of Bologna,[18] there was no dispute that he was baptized in Rome about 1634 in the church of San Giovanni Laterano, after the statutory period of forty days in the Catecumeni. He was seen in the street by a Jewish tailor,

> dressed in black, but with white stockings, shoes and girdle, and I asked him what he had done with the rest of the white outfit. He answered that he had borrowed one from the Rector of the Catecumeni in order to get the money from the papal tailor who provides raiment for Jewish neophytes.[19]

After this, the convert lived for four months in a series of lodging-houses near San Francesco in Trastevere, trading as a mercer. He said that he was then enticed back to Judaism by Elias of Rome, a professional recon-

---

[16] S.U., b. 92, proc. Carlo Antonio Barberini, den. Fra Girolamo Bonezzi of Reggio, 27 Aug. 1636.

[17] S.U., b. 94, proc. Iseppo Bon, test. the prisoner, 3 April 1636.

[18] Ibid., correspondence with ecclesiastical authorities in Bologna, 18 Feb., 4 March 1636.

[19] Ibid., test. Elias of Rome, 22 Jan. 1636.

versionist, and induced to go East once more. Old habits, and a sound if hubristic knowledge of the techniques of survival in Italy, lured him back to the West a fourth time, in March 1635. He still had his patent from Rome, which offered him protection in the name of Francesco Maria Leoncini, neophyte, but he chose to seek baptism again, certainly for the second time and possibly for the third. Not content with the dribble of alms which could be attracted by showing the patent, he wanted the quick initial returns which could be expected from another conversion. He was now accompanied by a kinsman, Daniel Levi of Salonica, and having arrived in Venice by way of Zante they headed for Vicenza. Significantly, they chose a town that had no Jews: attempts to dissuade or even report them by co-religionists would be less likely, and the authorities, less used to dealing with converts, might prove to be less suspicious. The travellers proved plausible enough, and both the Venetian governors, Podestà and Capitano alike, stood godfather to them at their baptism in the cathedral of Vicenza by the archpriest. For two or three months they roamed the town and its territory, 'going begging as Jews converted to Christianity in order to live', in company with a third convert of advanced years. Already in trouble in Venice for breaking a ban imposed upon him when still a Jew, the former Moses Israel – now dignified by the Podestà's name of Giuseppe Bon – was seized in that city in December 1635,[20] and his difficulties were soon aggravated by the delation of Andrea Nunciata, who had once employed him as a servant in Salonica.[21] His pleas that the last baptism was the result of misunderstanding, and that he had believed it necessary to expunging the sin of reconversion to Judaism, convinced nobody. He was found 'violently' suspect of heresy and sentenced to seven years in the galleys or twelve in a close prison.[22]

Poverty and restlessness do not furnish complete explanations for the behaviour of all the converts who attracted the attention of the Inquisition – even for that of all the poorer ones. Most of the former Jews involved with the Holy Office in the late 1620s and the 1630s were persons who had moved between Italy and the Levant, and in their histories there was sometimes another ingredient – conversion from Judaism to Islam.

There was some disagreement among the learned as to whether the Inquisition could properly judge a Jew who converted to Islam. Castagna's *Repertorium* had cited an opinion to the contrary, on the

[20] Ibid., 14, 21 Feb., 8 April 1636. The statement concerning baptism is confirmed by two clergymen of Vicenza cathedral, 20 Sept. 1636.
[21] Ibid., Jan. 1636, 11 March 1636.
[22] Ibid., 22 Jan. 1637.

grounds that Judaism was worse than Islam, and therefore any change represented progress; Cesare Carena, a Cremonese appointed to the Roman Inquisition by Urban VIII, held that such a conversion would be an offence against the common beliefs of Jews and Christians, and would therefore expose the Jew to prosecution under Gregory XIII's Bull *Antiqua Iudaeorum improbitas*.[23] In Venice, no Jew was actually charged with such an offence – known conversions had all occurred in a foreign state – but reports of such moves probably aroused interest in that they provided evidence of an inconstant and frivolous mental condition. Furthermore, some Venetians believed that to become a Muslim every Jew must pass through an intermediary stage as a Christian. Hence every Jew turned Turk must also be a renegade from Christianity, and so liable in theory to Inquisition proceedings. The surviving summary of Agostino Nani's report on the Ottoman Empire, delivered in 1603, includes the statement that 'They do not allow Jews to become Muslims, unless they first become Christians.'[24] Almost sixty years later Loredan, in his defence of the Jews, repeated the commonplace that 'The Turk allows no Jew to become a Turk, unless he turns Christian first.'[25] Practice, however, did not seem to correspond with this theory, for in 1632 Giovanni Battista Bonaventura denied it to the Inquisition.[26] Behind it may have lain the belief that Islam was a synthesis between Judaism and Christianity, and hence the Jew must overcome his hostility to Christ before he could enter upon Islam. Years earlier, Gianfrancesco Morosini, ambassador-consul in Constantinople, had bluntly declared that Mohammed 'took it into his head to invent a kind of law which promised to licence loose behaviour in order to attract sensuous men, and which could give satisfaction both to Christians and to Jews'.[27]

In the 1620s and the 1630s there were several good reasons why the Inquisition and its host state should closely scrutinize travellers and settlers from the East. The establishment of the Fondaco dei Turchi in 1621 marked a desire to discipline the Turkish community in Venice,[28] an ambition which could well extend to all who had lived in Turkey or had once been Muslims. Given the decline of Turkish power, the Venetians could afford to be less tender in their treatment of the Sultan's subjects, especially of obscure ones. Since the early 1620s, the proposals of Antonio

---

[23] See *Repertorium Inquisitorum* ..., p. 493; C. Carena, *Tractatus de Officio Sanctae Inquisitionis et modo procedendi in causa fidei* (Bologna, 1668), pp. 208-9; cf. Stern, *Urkundliche Beiträge* ..., I, doc. 161, p. 181, and above, pp. 73-4.

[24] Barozzi–Berchet, V/i, p. 36.

[25] C.S.M., b. 62, fasc. 165.

[26] S.U., b. 89, proc. Giovanni Battista Bonaventura, 3 Aug. 1632.

[27] Albèri, III/iii, pp. 270-1 (1585).

[28] Cf. Preto, *Venezia e i Turchi*, p. 132 ff.

Giustinian had focused attention on fraudulent begging by persons claiming to be converted Jews.[29] Levantine Jews could be descended from Marranos, from a deeply suspect people; prosperous merchants adhering firmly to Judaism and paying their taxes were clearly exempt from prosecution for religious offences, but lesser and more inconstant men were not. And during the 1630s there were moments when the future of the whole Jewish community in Venice appeared to be threatened, not least by the arrest of all the heads of the Ghetto on charges of conniving at the removal of a convert's children to the Levant.[30]

On 8 July 1635, Moses Abdula was baptized Francesco by the Prior of the Catecumeni in the church of the Theatines, and then, it was thought, he went for a soldier on the *Terra Ferma*. Various indiscretions of his had stuck in the minds of other inmates of the house, and there were rumours that he was a professional convert who had blasphemed against the sacrament of baptism. In the Rialto fish market a Jew told the Prior: 'You made a nice mess of things, baptizing that Jew; he was done before, in Rome.' At first the Prior dismissed the tale, 'supposing that Jews are no lovers of those who get themselves baptized'; but he pricked up his ears on learning that Moses Abdula had 'become a Turk' five times in the Ottoman Empire, and began meditating on the familiar saying that 'the Turks will receive no persons into their sect unless they declare themselves Christians first.' There were stories, too, of Moses trampling on his baptismal certificate and calling the ceremony 'a pantomine where you put a pinch of salt in the mouth and a drop of oil and water on the head'. Reasonably enough, a former Turk suspected the man 'had become a Christian more for the sake of new clothes and a gain of 100 ducats than for any better reason'. Moses was recruiting for Christianity, but his recruits seemed no more constant than himself, and Abram, baptized Vincenzo, was on the verge of apostasy.[31]

Movements between the three religions of Christianity, Judaism and Islam were equally characteristic of two other Jews, converted in Italy and suspected of treating their experience lightly. Samuel Levi, son of Abram, was born in Salonica in 1598 or 1599. On arrest in Venice, he was described as 'a Spaniard, a tall man of some thirty-four or thirty-five years, thin, and with a ruddy complexion. I found him,' said the chief constable of the *Cattaveri*, 'with a black hat, a sword at his waist, and a dagger.'[32] In this he resembled, at least superficially, those Marranos who

[29] See above, pp. 255, 259–60.
[30] See Ravid, *Economics and toleration* ..., p. 10 ff.; I.R.E.C., Carte Diverse, 'Pie Case de Cattecumeni contro Università de gli Hebrei'.
[31] S.U., b. 92, proc. Moisè Abdula, 27 July to 30 Aug. 1635. Cf. also Preto, *Venezia e i Turchi*, p. 229.
[32] S.U., b. 87, proc. Felice Magalotti, test. Luca di Battista, 4 Sept. 1629.

were consumed with curiosity about their parents' ancestry and retraced their steps towards Spain, assuming the dress of the arms-bearing Christian gentleman. Be this as it may, Samuel's first move had not been towards the Christian world. He had turned Turk at the age of thirteen or fourteen, for fear of a brutal schoolmaster. He was received into the Muslim faith in a mosque and then led round the city, accompanied by a rejoicing crowd, with a stick or cane attached to one finger which he held on high. They gave him alms and told him he must believe no more in the law of Moses, although he insisted that despite conformity in externals he never inwardly forswore the Jewish faith. 'For all that I wore the white head-dress as the Turks do, I never believed in my heart in the law of Mohammed. Rather, I believed always in our own law, and for that reason I left Turkey and strove to come to Venice.'

Samuel's travels began about 1620, when Salonica was partially destroyed by fire and many of its Jews dispersed. He went to Monastir, now Bitolj in Yugoslavia, and there, according to her story, he met his future wife, Mazalto, called in Italian Bonaventura. It was probably she who inspired the plan to return to Judaism. They seem to have travelled independently to Venice, where he married her in July 1627.[33] The following year both were arrested in Ferrara with several other culprits (on what charge is not clear), and there they fell into the hands of the Inquisition, which exhorted them to become Christians. Samuel Levi was already familiar with the hypocrisies which authority could force on a man. He yielded, but his wife did not.[34] They divorced, it was said, not only because he had turned Christian, but because his real name turned out to be Joseph Sabai[35] and he had a wife and children living in Belgrade. However, he was sufficiently attached to his wife – or anxious enough to touch her for a loan – to pursue her into the Ghetto of Venice. Indiscreet visits led to his arrest and condemnation on suspicion of heresy. Sentencing him to eighteen months in the galleys in May 1630, the Inquisitor and his colleagues may well have reflected on the early experience of conversion in the Ottoman Empire, which – the accused implied – had taught him the art of dissembling, and of remaining loyal to Judaic law, despite all outward appearances.

There was no proof that Giovanni Battista Bonaventura, tried for heretical blasphemy in 1632, had converted to Christianity out of self-seeking,

[33] Ibid., test. the prisoner and his wife in Ferrara, 23 July 1627 or 1628, 2 June 1628.

[34] Ibid., letter of the Inquisitor of Ferrara to his colleague in Venice, 26 Aug. 1629; certified copy of an entry in the records of the cathedral in Ferrara, showing that Levi was baptized by the archpriest on 19 Nov. 1628. His godparents were Cardinal Lorenzo Magalotti, Bishop of Ferrara, and the Marchioness Felicia Sassatella Bevilacqua.

[35] He used the name occasionally in Venice – see a note from the records of the *Esecutori contro la Bestemmia*, ibid., 27 July 1629.

self-preservation or cynicism. But he too had experienced conversion to Islam, and he too was one who lived precariously, hoping for fortune without hard work. If conversion was indeed one of several devices on which he pinned his hopes of a new life, the reality was disillusioning, for it brought him marriage to a flighty wife who resented his savage jealousy and his attempts to hold her in oriental seclusion. His own story was that he was born in Damascus about 1598, or at least lived much of his early life there, the son of Raphael Anaf. At fourteen he went to Jerusalem to visit the holy places, was seized by the Turks, and converted to Islam to escape death by fire.[36] An aged broker of Venice retailed rumours, stemming from a Cairo Arab, that 'Giovanni Battista was first a Jew, then he became a Christian, then he turned Turk, then he returned to Judaism, and in the end he became a Christian yet again – for in those countries Jews do not become Turks without being Christians first.'[37] Most of these changes were denied; Giovanni Battista claimed to have given a frank account of his conversion to Islam to the parish priest of Santa Sofia. About 1626–28 the priest baptized him in his church, together with one small son; he left in the Ghetto a Jewish wife who refused to follow him. Before his conversion he had shared those preoccupations of the Venetian people with magic and superstition which the nuncio Bolognetti had described some fifty years before. For him as for them the purpose of magic was not to discomfit enemies but to make gains. Father Turrati, the priest, remembered that 'he wanted to find treasure on the Lido, and before his baptism we burnt a whole basketful of writings on magic and spells for him.'[38] No professional necromancer, he none the less had books of spells or formulae 'with which, or so he said, he would have made demons come to show him treasure, and now that he is making no money he would use those books if he had them.' Giovanni Battista claimed to be unlettered, at least in the Italian language, and indeed he was to sign his abjuration with a cross. But he admitted to once owning some 'little books' in Hebrew – one of astrology, another of dreams, another of medicines, another of 'certain houses of the planets'.[39] After baptism he earned his living precariously as a broker with the Turks, and was rumoured to engage in vicious occupations on the side. Most of the evidence smacked of malice too strongly to have much chance of sticking, and after months in gaol under investigation he escaped with spiritual penalties alone, for

[36] S.U., b. 89, proc. Giovanni Battista Bonaventura, test. the prisoner, 3 Aug. 1632.
[37] Ibid., test. 8 July 1632.
[38] Ibid., test. Giovanni Turrati, 8, 15 July 1632; confirmed by several witnesses. Cf. Stella–Bolognetti, p. 286.
[39] Ibid., test. Meneghina, the prisoner's wife, 3 Aug. 1632. His mother-in-law, Angela, said she had heard Giovanni Battista say that 'if he had them now he would have no need to work' – ibid., 15 July 1632.

he was eventually treated as nothing worse than a loose-tongued Christian. But he provides another variation on the theme of unsteadiness and restlessness, sometimes coupled with dreams of easy money, often linked with the convert of Italy.

Not all converts were poor. Relatively well-to-do Jews, including physicians, bankers and professional mediators such as the solicitor Marcus Moses Jonah Levi, often had more far-reaching contacts in the Christian world than had poor Jews sunk in the lower depths of the Ghetto. Clients, associates or patrons might wish to benefit a business acquaintance by introducing him to Christianity, the greatest favour they had to bestow; Isaac Pugliese was converted largely through the efforts of the nobleman who had got him a licence to work outside the Ghetto at night, making reflecting glass globes on Murano, and a governor of the Catecumeni said of Marcus Moses, 'In truth I think him a gentleman, who deserves to be a Christian, and I hope in God to see him become one.'[40] If the poor were enticed by windfalls, the rich could think in terms of advantageous marriages. Conversionists intended marriages between Christians and former Jews to act as a steadying influence on the converts, but conversions might be improperly inspired by carnal love, and the renunciation of usurious gains might be more than balanced by a good match and a solid dowry. Such suspicions arose in three Inquisition cases which all concerned Jews deeply involved in commerce, or money-lending, or both these things.

Born about 1528, Simile of Montagnana enjoyed substantial backing from a group of Christian creditors headed by the nobleman Andrea Pasqualigo. His function seems to have been to interpose himself between Christians who put up capital and others who wanted to borrow at interest, thus disguising Christian implication in usurious transactions. The Inquisition's files contain references to forty-three usurious contracts concluded at Montagnana, some of them in company with Pasqualigo.[41] Such arrangements were common enough in the mid-sixteenth century for the Senate to legislate against them – as witness a decree of 1553 which forbade Christians to buy up Jewish credits or exact debts payable to a Jewish banker.[42] At some time between 1551 and 1553, Simile's creditors persuaded him to become a Christian. The baptismal ceremony took place in secret, and Simile was afterwards allowed, like Dr Freschi Olivi, to continue wearing the yellow hat of the professing Jew in order to approach his wife, two young children and his sister Ricca, aged seventeen. It was before the days of the Catecumeni, and Simile – now offi-

---

[40] I.Z. II, proc. Marc' Antonio degli Eletti, pp. 101, 104–5, 12, 15 Nov. 1569; I.R.E.C., Carte Diverse, 'Pie Case ...', test. Carlo di Domenico Contarini, 3 Feb. 1637 Venetian style.

[41] I.Z., p. 275, proc. Gian Giacomo de Fedeli.

[42] S.T., reg. 1553–54, fol. 19v., 9 May 1553.

cially Gian Giacomo de' Fedeli – lived in Andrea Pasqualigo's house for five or six years. He was instructed in the faith by Matthias Gutich, a German doctor and a tutor in Greek, Latin and Hebrew who taught in the house.

Over the next few years there was much unkindly speculation about Simile's motives, and a statement by a friar suggested that the principal bait for him was Cecilia Gabriel, the chief creditor's stepdaughter, with whom he had slept before his baptism. Knowing that his patron's benevolence would not extend to having his house guest as son-in-law, he had put him off the scent by inviting Cecilia to become godparent to one of his Jewish daughters: spiritual kinship would act in law as a bar to marriage. Neither this, nor his failure to divorce his Jewish wife, prevented him in practice from going through a form of marriage with Cecilia.[43]

At the time of his all-too-discreet baptism, Simile had professed a desire to recover property or debts, 'that we, his creditors, might not forfeit what was ours when he changed his hat, and that he might have the means to live and to support his children . . .'[44] He made a show of honourable behaviour and used it to excuse his retention of the yellow hat. But it was urged against him that

> it would have been far more advantageous to collect his own as a Christian, rather than as a Jew. For under Pope Paul the Farnese it was granted that a Jew who has turned Christian may possess the property he enjoyed as a Jew.[45]

There was, none the less, an exception to that rule, which demanded the restoration of usurious gains. Simile/Gian Giacomo would have been unable, had he appeared openly as a Christian, to exact his credits as a money lender, nor could his Christian creditors (barred by the legislation of 1553) have lawfully done so either. It seemed, in fact, that he was using his marginal position between the two faiths in a highly disingenuous manner:

> if he had to obtain money or goods from Jews or other persons he collected them as a Jew, and when he claimed payment for himself he called himself a Jew. But when he himself had to pay he would use the excuse of being a Christian, and so he mocked at both faiths.[46]

---

[43] I.Z., proc. Gian Giacomo de' Fedeli, various testimonies, pp. 279–84, 286–7, 295–6, 300–1, 303–6, 17 Aug. 1558 to 5 Sept. 1560. However (see pp. 308–9), Gutich testified on 7 Sept. 1560 that Gian Giacomo was reluctant to take Cecilia, and did so only after much discussion with Andrea Pasqualigo.

[44] Ibid., pp. 281–2, test. Andrea Pasqualigo, 17 Aug. 1558.

[45] Ibid., p. 273.

[46] Ibid., p. 268, den. Carlo Querini, 5 Aug. 1558.

Unlike the poorer converts, Gian Giacomo seemed thoroughly worldly-wise, seeking with his creditors' initial collusion an ambiguous status, and exploiting it even to the point of maintaining two wives. He fell under enough suspicion to be gaoled for a month or two by the Heads of the Ten in 1558, but he could always disarm hostility by agreeing to the baptism of his children or reminding the authorities how he had furthered the conquest of souls by enticing to the font a brother aged twenty-five and a sister aged eighteen.[47] Even after his breach with Pasqualigo he seems to have remained a mediator between Judaism and Christianity sufficiently useful to escape dire penalties. In 1565 he was respectable enough to be asked to provide the Inquisition with certified translations of writings in Hebrew.[48]

Seemingly less dubious and more carefully scrutinized was the conversion in 1585 of the banker Mendlin of Sacile. The worthies of the small town and its surrounding district took an interest in the event, perhaps because it offered a rare chance to take part in a fashionable good work, perhaps because they liked Mendlin for himself. Locally there was no secret that Mendlin's spiritual aspirations could be related to his fondness for Angela, a young Christian woman of the neighbourhood. Suggestions that he might have been bewitched by incantations or love-philtres brought the Commissario of the Holy Office to the township, but townsmen, friars and Mendlin himself knew enough about the proprieties to testify that these were being strictly observed: his Jewish wife would have her dowry, usurious gains would be restored, a papal brief had been obtained through two Venetian patricians to entitle him to keep the rest. The love of Angela, it was pleaded, was incidental to the banker's love of the Christian 'law'. Having failed to discover locally any evidence of duress, unfair persuasion or corrupt motive, the Commissario departed, and the transformation of Mendlin into a Christian was no doubt permitted to proceed.[49]

A final instance of the richer convert who falls under suspicion is provided by Nathan Cohen, who moved between Venice and the colony of Corfu. Born in 1630, he was the son of Chaim Cohen of Corfu, who was evidently both a merchant and a money lender: so much appears from a judicial decision which spoke of Nathan's removing from the family '20,000 ducats or more in money, silk, oil, leather, grain, bread, credit notes, gold, silver, and pledges'.[50] Nathan went to Venice about 1656,

[47] Ibid., pp. 296–8, 12–22 Sept. 1558, pp. 312–13.
[48] I.Z. II, p. 51, proc. Samuel Ventura.
[49] S.U., b. 52, proc. Mandolino of Sacile, 22–25 Feb. 1585.
[50] S.U., b. 114, proc. Nicolò Dolfin of Corfu, 2 Feb. 1660.

perhaps on business, and was baptized there in February 1658, with Nicolò Dolfin of San Pantalon as his godfather. In accordance with custom he adopted this patrician name. Subsequently he divorced his Jewish wife and married a Christian, Cateruzza Muazzo. These are the only apparently indisputable facts in the case. Unfortunately, the record is especially lop-sided, since the Inquisition, though moved by the dossier sent to it from Corfu to issue a warrant for his arrest, did not apparently succeed in bringing him to trial. Suffice it to say that his new wife promptly declared the conversion a pretext to get his hands on her property – it was a substitute for litigation, since her family had owed money to Nathan's father.

> . . . he and his brother [she said], insinuated themselves into my house. And little by little he acquired dominion over my own person by outwardly becoming my husband, to which arrangement I agreed through fear of his rigorous threats and not of my own free will. And when I thought to detect in him some spark of Christian feeling, I discovered that it was a total pretence and that he was truly a Jew. For the first thing he did was to try to persuade me to make him a donation of my father's and mother's goods and wholly renounce all rights in them . . .

She showed a notarial document to this effect and described actions which seemed to indicate quite plainly his adherence to the faith of the Jews.[51] If there was a family conspiracy it did not go smoothly, because in February 1660 Nicolò Dolfin was in dispute with his Jewish relatives concerning the assets he had seized at his conversion. From judge-arbitrators he obtained a decision obliging his family to finance a company of soldiers with himself as captain, provided he left an inheritance – a fortune gained partly through usurious lending – in their hands. His conversion therefore opened to him a prestigious profession and a gentlemanly style of life, and the settlement would enable him 'to serve the Doge as he desires, and to maintain himself honourably for the rest of his life with the stipends and other payments customarily made to captains'.[52] When the scandal broke on the island, Nicolò Dolfin wisely departed, and was believed to have fled to Venice.[53]

These three cases modify the conventional picture of the shady Italian convert as a pauper warding off starvation or a petty criminal escaping

[51] Ibid., a petition addressed by Cateruzza Muazzo to the *reggimento* of Corfu before 2 Feb. 1660, with a notarial document dated 28 Dec. 1659.

[52] Ibid., judgment of the *Capitano in Golfo* and a galley commander as *Giudici Arbitri*, 2 Feb. 1660.

[53] Ibid., 30 April, 25 May, 22 June 1660.

trouble. They do not destroy it altogether, and they further stress, and perhaps over-emphasize, those materialistic motives which could so easily sully a change of faith, for the prosperous as for the poor.

In most of the twelve cases discussed above, the convert had in some way exposed the flaws in the conversion campaign and had threatened to deprive Christianity of its triumph over Judaism. Inherent in the mission to the Jews was a serious dilemma. Intellectual argument would not be enough to produce converts; material incentives, the prospect of social advancement, emergence from the Ghetto, must be offered too. But would it then prove possible to establish the sincerity of the candidate, to be sure of his readiness to put spiritual things first? Investigation, admonition and sometimes punishment at the hands of the Inquisition were necessary in order to make the intentions of the campaigners, their demands for sincerity, disinterestedness and firm adhesion to Christianity, clearly understood.

By themselves, the records of the Inquisition are unlikely to provide a balanced account of the psychology of the convert. They can, however, build up a strong impression of the type of person most likely to attract the attention of the Holy Office, and most likely to seem to its lay attachés, concerned for the interests of the Venetian state, a suitable candidate for prosecution and punishment. Among the poorer persons, the suspect was almost always far from his native place – Chelm, Prague, Sarzana, Crete, Salonica, Damascus. Marco of Padua, who was not, still had a history of wandering with only precarious means of support. Only Giovanni Battista Bonaventura had kept a house in Venice for any length of time. Both the old, haphazard method of issuing converts with patents and the newer, more ambitious system of instructing and training them within the Catecumeni produced their casualties. Moses Israel took advantage of both of them. In the Ghetto Jews had had little chance to acquire manual skills, and few adult converts were likely to be successfully trained as artisans capable of competing in the Christian world. They were still effectively confined to the rather disreputable spheres of the pedlar and the broker. The highest hopes had really been for the children, and perhaps contributed to the ardour with which they were pursued, for their prospects were brighter than those of the father who decreed their change of faith. Adults, such as Loredan or Bonaventura, dreamed of treasure; conversion did not bring it. In delinquent converts there was often a sense of drift coupled with a disintegration of strong and immediate family ties – one thinks, especially, of Asher's indifference to his relatives, whom he had left hundreds of miles behind him, of the death of Marco's father, of the divorce and possible bigamy of Samuel Levi, of Bonaventura's troubled household. Not violent criminals, delinquent converts tended to be adventurers, travellers and solitaries, and as such were at least vaguely undesirable socially. Whatever the expectations it created, conversion to the dominant faith seldom actually provided more than temporary relief and a short spell as an important and cherished person; frustrated hopes on the part of those without conviction could tempt them to return to the narrower but less bleak world of the Jews, or else to escape to the Ottoman lands.

Conclusion

Venice was bound to be a place of transition for those passing between western Christendom and Islamic Turkey – an escape route, a centre of espionage, a trading-post, a place to temporize and hesitate before taking irrevocable steps. At all times it was eager to maintain an unequivocal character as a Catholic state; on this it staked its survival and its title to obedience from its subjects. It might be a lay state, excluding clerics from public office and from formal influence on policy; but it was never a secular state, in the sense of one frankly devoted to worldly and material ends, or one which saw itself as a man-made growth, without divine consecration and protection. It needed formulae to reconcile religious duty with political independence and economic interest. Its open quarrels with the Papacy in the early seventeenth century gave it a lasting reputation among Protestants and anticlericals, but many of its religious and charitable institutions were of Roman origin and inspiration, and compromise – founded on common interest – was far more usual than were conflicts between Church and state.

At most times the Inquisition in Venice was an embodiment of compromise, devoted to regulating if not forestalling conflict; its constitution and the conventions governing appointments were directed towards that end, though there could be periods in which the tribunal was seriously constrained in its attempts to deal with certain types of case. Church and state entertained notions of good order which generally overlapped, but were capable of diverging, and the Inquisition's treatment of the Jews helps to illustrate both coincidence and divergence of view. From the time of Paul IV the Roman Church was interested in the heresy or apostasy of all persons who had deliberately withdrawn themselves from the faith of their birth and upbringing, and in the collection of evidence from any country which could throw light on their conduct; hence its pursuit of what the Duke of Savoy termed 'Marrano apostates'. However discreetly committed, apostasy remained apostasy. The state would condemn heresy in so far as it could see a connection between heresy, rebellion and treason. But its representatives could see some brands of heresy, such as Marranism, as the outcome of questionable policies on the part of state and society in Spain and Portugal, rather than as faults inherent in individuals. And in the early seventeenth century heresy was not merely an insidious force which threatened to destroy the state: the state's own champions, its theologians and consultants from the interdict years, were themselves in danger of heresy charges. Furthermore, the state's Catholicism was in a sense 'nationalist' rather than 'universalist'. It was concerned, less with the detection of those who had offended the Catholic faith in other countries or in the course of journeys, than with the discipline of those who had 'scandalized' the particular body of Christians under its care. The famous liberty of Venice meant, among much else, the chance to leave one's past outside the city, so long as one did not create new troubles within it.

Under the combined influence of churchmen and lay patricians, the Inquisition became chiefly concerned with offences involving a clear public interest, which removed them from the region of personal crises of conscience, domestic disputes and personal vendettas; in the punishment of people who were social undesirables in a fairly broad sense and sometimes had criminal records already; and in the punishment of specific actions which constituted flagrant breaches of the conventions governing acceptable behaviour. Often the Inquisition's activities seemed to be an extension of those of the lay magistracies concerned with the maintenance of public order and morality – its prisoners included the blasphemer whose words smelt of heresy, the companion of Jews who abused the sacrament of marriage, the professional beggar who exploited the sacrament of baptism for the sake of clothing, shelter or alms.

Because it had to serve two masters, because there were other magistracies dealing in a more summary fashion with religious offences, and because it could pursue only those whose prosecution would not harm the interests of the state, the Inquisition tried only a small number of cases involving Jews and judaizing. The reasons why it did not prosecute are as important as the reasons why it did. But the quality of the evidence it transmits is enhanced by the fact that it had to account to two different authorities in Rome and in Venice, by the need to compile full written records for the purpose, and by the fact that cases involving Jews did not decline to the level of routine trials based upon stereotypes. The Inquisition was a court directed by a highly trained and experienced professional judge, applying an unusually full and elaborate body of written rules. It is, to an unusual degree, possible to scrutinize the methods by which it achieved results and arrived at conclusions. The trials studied in this book are searchlights which play briefly on a few individuals singled out from a huge, dark, anonymous crowd of uncertain extent. They can never become a comprehensive guide to the mentality and circumstances of those converts who changed from Christianity to Judaism or from Judaism to Christianity. But they can build up an impression of the type of person who offended against the concepts of order entertained by the state as well as by the Church. It was the inconstant and indecisive who fell foul of the Inquisition, together with those who could not or would not accept the debased role of the Jews in the economic and social order sanctioned by the policies of the Senate — those not what they seemed to be, those who did not know their place, those who were aware of their Jewishness but could not accept the Ghetto, and those who had once aspired to a position in the larger and bleaker Christian world, but fell back on the Ghetto in a desperate search for support. Italian neophytes who returned to Judaism were inverting the hierarchical relationship between the dominant and the defeated faith, whereby all Christians ought to be demonstrably superior to all Jews; but Spanish or Portuguese *conversos* who went discreetly to the Ghetto could be defended on the grounds that they were only revealing themselves as the Jews they had always been, that they were dispelling dissimulation, saving Christianity from pollution, and accepting the Venetian sense of order.

Venetian policies towards Jews were seldom justified in crudely economic terms alone; the state's practice of circumscribing them economically was easy to reconcile with ecclesiastical policies which advocated the debasement and segregation of Jews in order to prove that the sceptre had departed from Judah and the Messiah had long ago come. And the presence of Jews in Venice was the occasion for conversion campaigns designed to avoid the excesses of Portugal and Spain. They were supposed to rest on incentives rather than to depend on fear, though those incentives were strengthened partly by imposing an artificial poverty upon Jews, and thus enhancing the contrasts between the Jewish and the Christian worlds. The Inquisition dealt with those whose conduct revealed too painfully the flaws inherent in this approach. There was little disagreement about the punishment of backsliders who had been converted in Italy, according to the proper rules: defences based on forced conversion and enforced conformity were not available to them. Paradoxically, for all its ardent Catholicism, the Venetian state allowed a large number of technical apostasies to outweigh a small number of conversions achieved according to the Italian rules, the Jewish population growing through the attraction of Sephardic immigrants, some of whom had a dubious Christian past. More than anyone else, the Jews had a sharply defined place within the Venetian order; they were set apart from Christians, and the bridges between the dominant religion and the superseded faith could be crossed only in specified ways. Born of the state's need for consecration and of the Church's need for sanctions, the Inquisition defended the concepts of right order on which both could agree.

APPENDIX I

Fiscal Obligations of the Jews in the mid-Seventeenth Century

In 1658 the *Università degli Ebrei* stated its annual obligations as follows (S.T., filza 660, 12 Feb. 1658 Venetian style):

Annual obligations of the whole corporation of Jews in this city

On maintaining the banks and their dependencies	duc. 8,367 (14.08%)[1]
'Voluntary offering'	9,000 (15.14%)
The taxes called *taglioni*: three were paid this year, each of 9,500 ducate	28,500 (47.96%)
'Gradual tax' [*tansa insensibile*[2]]	960 (1.62%)
Eight galleots this year, at 200 ducats each	1,600 (2.69%)
Extraordinary expenditure of the corporations on public lodgings and other occasions, and the expenses of the nations considered separately, in an average year	5,000 (8.41%)
To atone for the failure of bankrupts and others who could not pay the *taglioni* and offerings	6,000 (10.10%)
	59,427 (100.00%)

In addition to the obligation to deposit money in the Mint.

[1] Percentages added by the author.

[2] The *tansa insensibile* mentioned here was probably the tax imposed in 1639 to enable guilds and corporations to build up reserve funds, to help meet their obligations to finance galley crews (see F. Besta, *Bilanci Generali della Repubblica di Venezia*, Milan, 1912, doc. 232, p. 542).

The Loredan speech of about 1660 (C.S.M., b. 62, fasc. 165) states that by 1649, after five years of war, the state had received 256,060 ducats from the Jews, in *taglioni, quarti d'affitti* (taxes based on rents), voluntary offerings, consignments of grain from foreign countries and payments for the support of the banks.

To this, the writer says, should be added 30,000 ducats for 'silver placed in the Mint', and six assignments of 64,000 ducats each, which the Jews were compelled to deposit in the 7 per cent loan funds in the Mint.

These sums amounted to a total of 670,060 ducats paid to the state over five years only, which lends weight to the Jews' claim that between 1644 and 1659 they had contributed 1.3 million ducats to the fisc.

See Balletti (*Gli ebrei* . . . , p. 81) for evidence of Jews, frequently of Portuguese descent, migrating from Venice to Reggio Emilia about 1654 to escape the heavy taxes demanded in the Venetian state.

APPENDIX II

Jewish settlement in Venice in the Seventeenth Century

From 18 July 1612 all Jews newly arrived and lodging in Venice had by law to be registered with the *Esecutori contro la Bestemmia*; their hosts were to inform the Heads of the Ghetto, who would accompany them to the office of the *Esecutori*.[1] For several years afterwards the newcomers would be obliged to take out *bollettini* permitting them to remain in Venice. But in 1628 three Jews and their children obtained formal exemption from the obligation to seek such a certificate;[2] from 1633 it became clear that these exemptions would be granted when a Jew had kept house in the city for ten years or more. These grants of denization were made in 1633–66 to persons of the following provenance (grants made to households, or families, or on the same day to two or more persons bearing the same surname, have been counted as a single grant):

Provenance of Jewish settlers in Venice, 1633–66[3]

	Grants
Italy, outside Venetian dominions	21
Italy, within Venetian dominions	4
Eastern Mediterranean	12
Germany and Flanders	5
Unknown or uncertain	3
	45

[1] E.B., b. 54, Capitolare, fol. 68r.–v.; b. 57, Not. 4, fol. 266r.–257v., 12–13 Aug. 1612.
[2] Ibid., b. 58, Not. 5, fol. 150, 1 Sept. 1628.
[3] Taken from ibid., b. 58–9, Not. 4–7.

Manuscript Sources

This list includes only those manuscript sources not already mentioned in the list of abbreviations.

Public Record Office, London: State Papers 99/8, fol. 340–4: Sir Dudley Carleton, 'Particular notes of the goverment and state of Venice, *cum observationibus minimarum rerum*, as they come by discourse, withowt observacion of time or congruitie'

B.A.V., MS Barberino Latino 5195: 'Raccolta di alcuni negotii e cause spettanti alla Santa Inquisitione nella Città e Dominio Veneto. Dal principio di Clemente VIII sino al presente mese di luglio MDCXXV'

B.A.V., MS Vaticanus Latinus 10945: 'Anima del Sant' Offitio spirata dal sopremo tribunale della Sacra Congregatione, raccolta dal Padre Predicatore F. Giacomo Angarano da Vicenza l'anno del Signore MDCXLIV'

Bibliography

Albèri, E, ed. *Relazioni degli ambasciatori veneti al Senato* (15 vols., Florence, 1839–63)

Albizzi, F. *Risposta all' historia della sacra Inquisitione composta già dal R.P. Paolo Servita* (second edition, probably of Rome, ca. 1680)

Amabile, L. *Il Santo Officio della Inquisizione in Napoli* (2 vols., Città di Castello, 1892)

Amram, D. W. *The makers of Hebrew books in Italy, being chapters in the history of the Hebrew printing press* (Philadelphia, 1909)

Ancona, C. E. 'Attacchi contro il Talmud di Fra Sisto da Siena e la risposta, finora inedita, di Leon Modena, rabbino in Venezia', *Bollettino dell' Istituto di Storia della Società e dello Stato Veneziano*, 5–6 (1963–64), pp. 297–323

Aquinas, Thomas *Summa Theologica, with the Commentaries of Thomas de Vio Caietanus*, in *Opera omnia iussu impensaque Leonis XIII P.M. edita* (16 vols., Rome, 1882–1948), vols. IV–XII

Ashtor, E. 'Gli inizi della comunità ebraica a Venezia', *Rassegna mensile di Israel* (Nov.–Dec. 1978), pp. 683–703

Ashtor, E. 'The Jews in the Mediterranean trade in the fifteenth century', in *Wirtschaftskrafte und Wirtschaftswege, I: Mittelmeer und Kontinent (Festschrift für Hermann Kellenbenz)*, ed. J. Schneider (Nuremberg, 1978), pp. 441–54

Baer, Y. *A history of the Jews in Christian Spain*, transl. L. Schoffmann (2 vols., Philadelphia, 1966)

Balletti, A. *Gli ebrei e gli Estensi* (Reggio-Emilia, 1930)

Barbiero, G. *Le confraternite del Santissimo Sacramento prima del 1539* (Treviso, 1941)

Baron, S. W. *A social and religious history of the Jews* (second edition, 17 vols. to date, New York, 1962–onwards)

Barozzi, N., and Berchet, G., eds., *Relazioni degli stati europei lette al Senato dagli ambasciatori veneti nel secolo decimosettimo* (10 vols., Venice, 1856–78)

Barozzi, N., and Berchet, G. *Delle accoglienze ai Principi di Savoia fatte dai veneziani, 1367–1722* (Venice, 1868)

Battistella, A. *Il Santo Officio e la riforma religiosa in Friuli: appunti storici documentati* (Udine, 1895)

Battistella, A. *Il Santo Officio e la riforma religiosa in Bologna* (Bologna, 1905)

Beck, H. G., Manoussacas, M., and Pertusi, A., eds., *Venezia centro di mediazione tra oriente e occidente (secoli XV–XVI): aspetti e problemi* (2 vols., Florence, 1977)

Beinart, C. 'La venuta degli ebrei nel Ducato di Savoia e il privilegio del 1572', in *Scritti in memoria di Leone Carpi: saggi sull' ebraismo italiano*, ed. D. Carpi, A. Milano and A. Rofé (Jerusalem, 1967), pp. 72–119

Beinart, H. 'The *converso* community in fifteenth-century Spain', in *The Sephardi heritage: essays on the history and cultural contribution of the Jews of Spain and Portugal*, ed. R. D. Barnett, I (London, 1971), pp. 425–56

Beinart, H. 'The *converso* community in sixteenth- and seventeenth-century Spain', ibid., pp. 457–78.

Beltrami, D. *Storia della popolazione di Venezia dalla fine del secolo XVI alla caduta della Repubblica* (Padua, 1954)

Benardete, M. J. *Hispanic culture and character of the Sephardic Jews* (New York, 1953)

Benzoni, G. 'Una controversia tra Roma e Venezia all' inizio del '600: la conferma del Patriarca', *Bollettino dell' Istituto di Storia della Società e dello Stato Veneziano*, 3 (1961), pp. 121–38

Benzoni, G. 'I "teologi" minori dell' Interdetto', *Archivio Veneto*, serie V, vol. 91 (1970), pp. 31–108

Besta, F. *Bilanci generali della Repubblica di Venezia* (Milan, 1912)

Biasio, L. De 'Note storiche sul Santo Officio di Aquilea e Concordia', in Menis, ed., *Mille processi . . .*, pp. 83–100

Blumenkranz, B. 'Les juifs dans le commerce maritime de Venise', *Revue des études juives*, 120 (1961), pp. 143–51.

Boiteux, M. 'Carnaval annexé: essai de lecture d'une fête romaine', *Annales: Économies, Sociétés, Civilisations*, 32 (1977), pp. 356–80

Bossy, J. 'Blood and baptism: kinship, community and Christianity in western Europe from the fourteenth to the seventeenth centuries', in *Sanctity and secularity: the Church and the world*, ed. D. Baker, Studies in Church History, 9 (Oxford, 1973), pp. 129–43

Braudel, F. *The Mediterranean and the Mediterranean world in the age of Philip II*, transl. S. Reynolds (2 vols., London, 1975)

Braunstein, P. 'Remarques sur la population allemande de Venise à la fin du moyen âge', in Beck and others, eds., *Venezia centro . . .*, I, pp. 233–43

Brown, H. F., Brown, R., and Hinds, A. B., eds., *Calendar of state papers and manuscripts relating to English affairs, existing in the archives and collections of Venice, and in other libraries of Northern Italy* (London, 1864 onwards)

Brulez, W. *Marchands flamands à Venise, I: 1568–1605* (Brussels–Rome, 1965)

Bullarium diplomatum et privilegiorum sanctorum romanorum pontificum taurinensis editio locupletior facta (24 vols., Aosta, 1857–72)

Burke, P. *Venice and Amsterdam: a study of seventeenth-century élites* (London, 1974)

Burke, P. 'Witchcraft and magic in Renaissance Italy: Gianfrancesco Pico and his *Strix*', in *The damned art: essays in the literature of witchcraft*, ed. S. Anglo (London, 1977), pp. 32–52

Burke, P. *Popular culture in early modern Europe* (London, 1978)

Butler, K. T. 'Giacomo Castelvetro, 1546–1616', *Italian Studies*, 5 (1950), pp. 1–42

Caietanus (Thomas de Vio) *Commentaries*. See Aquinas, Thomas

Camporesi, P., ed., *Il libro dei vagabondi* (Turin, 1973)

Canale, Cristoforo. *Della milizia marittima libri quattro*, ed. M. Nani Mocenigo (Venice, 1930)

Capitoli ed ordini per il buon governo delle pie case de' Catecumeni di Venezia (Venice, 1737)

Cappellazzi, U., and Ferrari, D. 'Repertorio di fonti archivistiche per lo studio del pauperismo in Mantova (sec. XIII–XIX)', forthcoming in *Timore e carità* ...

Carena, Cesare *Tractatus de Officio Sanctae Inquisitionis et modo procedendi in causa fidei* (Bologna, 1668)

Caro Baroja, J. *Los Judíos en la España moderna y contemporánea* (second edition, 3 vols., Madrid, 1978)

Carpi, D., ed., *Minutes book of the Council of the Jewish community of Padua, 1577–1603* (Jerusalem, 1973)

Carter, F. W. *Dubrovnik (Ragusa): a classic city-state* (London, 1972)

Cassuto, U. *Gli ebrei a Firenze nell' età del Rinascimento* (Florence, 1918)

Cecchetti, B. *La Republica di Venezia e la Corte di Roma nei rapporti della religione* (2 vols., Venice, 1874)

Cohen, M. R. 'Leone da Modena's *Riti*: a seventeenth-century plea for social toleration of Jews', *Jewish Social Studies*, 34 (1972), pp. 287–319

Cohn, N. *Europe's inner demons: an enquiry inspired by the great witch-hunt* (London, 1975)

Coryat, Thomas *Coryat's Crudities* (2 vols., Glasgow, 1905)

Cowan, A. F. 'The urban patriciate. Lübeck and Venice, 1580–1700' (University of London Ph.D. thesis, London School of Economics and Political Science, 1981)

Cozzi, G. *Il Doge Nicolò Contarini: ricerche sul patriziato veneziano agli inizi del Seicento* (Venice–Rome, 1958)

Cozzi, G. 'Federico Contarini: un antiquario veneziano tra Rinascimento e Controriforma', *Bollettino dell' Istituto di Storia della Società e dello Stato Veneziano*, 3 (1961), pp. 190–220

Cozzi, G., ed., *Stato, società e giustizia nella Repubblica Veneta (sec. XV–XVIII)* (Rome, 1980)

Croce, B. *La Spagna nella vita italiana durante la Rinascenza* (second edition, Bari, 1922)

Croft, P. 'Englishmen and the Spanish Inquisition, 1558–1625', *English Historical Review*, 87 (1972), pp. 249–68

Cugnoni, G. 'Documenti chigiani concernenti Felice Peretti, Sisto V, come privato e come pontefice', *Archivio della Società Romana di Storia Patria*, 5 (1882), pp. 1–32, 210–304, 542–89

Davis, J. C. *The decline of the Venetian nobility as a ruling class* (Baltimore, 1962)

Delumeau, J. 'Un ponte fra oriente e occidente: Ancona nel Cinquecento', *Quaderni Storici*, anno 5 (1970), pp. 26–47

Derosas, R. 'Moralità e giustizia a Venezia nel '500–'600: gli Esecutori contro la Bestemmia', in Cozzi, ed., *Stato, società e giustizia* ..., pp. 431–528

Douglas, M. *Purity and danger: an analysis of the concepts of pollution and taboo* (London, 1978)

Earle, P. 'The commercial development of Ancona, 1479–1551', *Economic History Review*, second series, vol. 22 (1969–70), pp. 28–44

Eymeric, Nicolau *Directorium Inquisitorum, cum scholiis seu annotationibus eruditissimis D. Francisci Pegnae Hispani, S. Theologiae et Iuris Utriusque Doctoris* (Rome, 1578)

Eymeric, Nicolau *Le manuel des inquisiteurs*, ed. and transl. L. Sala-Molins (Paris–The Hague, 1973)

Farinelli, A. *Marrano (storia di un vituperio)* (Geneva, 1925)

Fedalto, G. *Ricerche storiche sulla posizione giuridica ed ecclesiastica dei greci a Venezia nei secoli XV e XVI* (Florence, 1967)

Finlay, R. 'The foundation of the Ghetto: Venice, the Jews, and the war of the League of Cambrai', *Proceedings of the American Philosophical Society*, 126 (1982), pp. 140–54

Firpo, L. *Il processo di Giordano Bruno (Quaderni della Rivista Storica Italiana*, I: Naples, 1949)

Florio, John *Queen Anne's New World of Words* (London, 1611; facsimile edition, Menston, 1968)

Foa, S. *La politica economica della casa Savoia verso gli ebrei dal sec. XVI fino alla rivoluzione francese: il portofranco di Villafranca (Nizza)* (Rome, 1962)

Frede, C. De 'L'estradizione degli eretici dal Dominio Veneziano nel Cinquecento', *Atti dell' Accademia Pontaniana*, nuova serie, vol. 20 (1970–71), pp. 255–86

Friedberg, E., ed., *Corpus Juris Canonici, Pars Secunda: Decretalium Collectiones* (Leipzig, 1922)

Fumi, L. 'L'Inquisizione romana e lo Stato di Milano: saggio di ricerche nell' Archivio di Stato', *Archivio Storico Lombardo*, serie iv, anno 37 (1910), vol. 13, pp. 5–124, 285–424; vol. 14, pp. 145–220

Gaeta, F., and others, eds., *Nunziature di Venezia* (Rome, 1958 onwards)

Gascon, R. *Grand commerce et vie urbaine au XVIe siècle: Lyon et ses marchands* (2 vols., Paris, 1971)

Gebhardt, C. *Die Schriften des Uriel da Costa* (Amsterdam, 1922)

Gennep, A. Van *The rites of passage*, transl. M. B. Vizedom and G. L. Caffee (Chicago–London, 1960)

Georgelin, J. *Venise au siècle des lumières* (Paris–The Hague, 1978)

Ginzburg, C. *I Benandanti: ricerche sulla stregoneria e sui culti agrari tra Cinquecento e Seicento* (Turin, 1966)

Ginzburg, C. *The cheese and the worms: the cosmos of a sixteenth-century miller*, transl. J. and A. Tedeschi (Baltimore–London, 1980)

Goris, J. A. *Étude sur les colonies marchandes méridionales (portugais, espagnols, italiens) à Anvers de 1488 à 1567* (Louvain, 1925)

Grendi, E. 'Pauperismo e Albergo dei Poveri nella Genova del Seicento', *Rivista Storica Italiana*, 87 (1975), pp. 621–65

Grendler, P. F. *The Roman Inquisition and the Venetian press, 1540–1605* (Princeton, 1977)

Grendler, P. F. 'The destruction of Hebrew books in Venice, 1568', *Proceedings of the American Academy for Jewish Research*, 45 (1978), pp. 103–30

Grendler, P. F. 'The *Tre Savii sopra Eresia*, 1547–1605: a prosopographical study', *Studi Veneziani*, nuova serie, 3 (1979), pp. 283–340

Grunebaum-Ballin, P. *Joseph Naci, Duc de Naxos* (Paris–The Hague, 1968)

Gwyer, J. 'The case of Dr Lopez', *Transactions of the Jewish Historical Society of England*, 16 (1952), pp. 163–84

Hacohen, Joseph, and the Anonymous Corrector *The Vale of Tears (Emek Habacha)*, ed. and transl. H. S. May (The Hague, 1971)

Haliczer, S. H. 'The Castilian urban patriciate and the Jewish expulsions of 1480–92', *American Historical Review*, 78 (1973), pp. 35–58

Healey, R. M. 'The Jew in seventeenth-century Protestant thought', *Church History*, 46 (1977), pp. 63–79

Herculano, A. *History of the origin and establishment of the Inquisition in Portugal*, transl. J. C. Branner in Stanford University Publications in History, Economics and Political Science, I (1926), pp. 189–636

Hocquet, J. C. *Le sel et la fortune de Venise, II: Voiliers et commerce en Méditerranée, 1200–1650* (Lille, 1979)

Ioly Zorattini, P. C. 'Note e documenti per la storia dei marrani e giudaizzanti nel Veneto del Seicento', in *Michael: on the history of the Jews of the Diaspora*, ed. S. Simonsohn, I (Tel-Aviv, 1972), pp. 326–41

Ioly Zorattini, P. C. 'Il "Mif'aloth Elohim" di Isaac Abravanel e il Sant' Offizio di Venezia', in *Italia: studi e ricerche sulla cultura e sulla letteratura degli ebrei d'Italia*, I (1976), pp. 54–69

Ioly Zorattini, P. C. 'Un giudaizzante cividalese del Cinquecento: Gioanbattista Cividin', *Studi storici e geografici*, I (Pisa, 1977), pp. 193–208

Ioly Zorattini, P. C. 'Processi contro ebrei e giudaizzanti nell' archivio del S. Uffizio di Aquileia e Concordia', *Memorie storiche forogiuliesi*, 58 (1978), pp. 133–45

Ioly Zorattini, P. C. 'Note sul S. Uffizio e gli ebrei a Venezia nel Cinquecento', *Rivista di Storia della Chiesa in Italia*, anno 33 (1979), pp. 500–8

Ioly Zorattini, P. C., ed., *Processi del S. Uffizio di Venezia contro ebrei e giudaizzanti (1548–1560)* (Florence, 1980)

Ioly Zorattini, P. C. 'The Inquisition and the Jews in sixteenth-century Venice', *Proceedings of the Seventh World Congress of Jewish Studies* (Jerusalem, 1981), pp. 83–92 (English version of 'Note sul S. Uffizio ...', above)

Ioly Zorattini, P. C., ed., *Processi del S. Uffizio di Venezia contro ebrei e giudaizzanti (1561–1570)* (Florence, 1982)

Israel, J. I. *Race, class and politics in colonial Mexico (1610–1670)* (Oxford, 1975)

Jacoby, D. 'Les juifs à Venise du XIVe au milieu du XVIe siècle', in Beck and others, eds., *Venezia centro ...*, I, pp. 163–216

James, E. O. *Seasonal feasts and festivals* (London, 1961)

Katz, D. S. *Philosemitism and the readmission of the Jews to England, 1603–1655* (Oxford, 1982)

Kaufmann, D. 'A contribution to the history of the Venetian Jews', *Jewish Quarterly Review*, original series, vol. 2 (1890), reprint 1966, pp. 297–310

Kaufmann, D. 'Die Vertreibung der Marranen aus Venedig im Jahre 1550', *Jewish Quarterly Review*, original series, vol. 13 (1901), reprint 1966, pp. 520–32

Kaufmann, D. 'Die Verbrennung der talmudischen Litteratur in der Republik Venedig', *Jewish Quarterly Review*, original series, vol. 13 (1901; reprint 1966), pp. 533–8

Kieckhefer, R. *European witch trials: their foundation in popular and learned culture, 1300–1500* (London, 1976)

Langbein, J. H. *Prosecuting crime in the Renaissance: England, Germany, France* (Cambridge, Mass., 1974)

Langbein, J. H. *Torture and the law of proof: Europe and England in the Ancien Regime* (Chicago–London, 1977)

Laras, G. 'Diego Lorenzo Picciotto: un delatore di Marrani nella Livorno del Seicento', in *Scritti in memoria di U. Nahon* (Jerusalem, 1978), pp. 65–104

Lattes, M. 'Documents et notices sur l'histoire politique et littéraire des juifs en Italie', *Revue des études juives*, 5 (1882), pp. 219–37

Lea, H. C. *A history of the Inquisition of Spain* (4 vols., New York, 1906)

Lea, H. C. *The Inquisition in the Spanish dependencies* (London, 1908)

Le Roy Ladurie, E. *Montaillou: Cathars and Catholics in a French village, 1294–1324*, transl. B. Bray (London, 1978)

Leva, G. De, ed., *La legazione di Roma di Paolo Paruta, 1592–1595* (3 vols., Venice, 1887)

Luzzatto, F. *Cronache storiche della università degli ebrei di San Daniele di Friuli: cenni sulla storia degli ebrei del Friuli* (Rome, 1964)

Luzzatto, Simon *Discorso circa il stato de gl'Hebrei, et in particolar dimoranti nell' inclita Città di Venetia* (Venice, 1638)

Mackenney, R. S. 'Trade guilds and devotional confraternities in the state and society of Venice to 1620' (University of Cambridge Ph.D. thesis, 1982)

Mansi, J. D., and others, eds., *Sacrorum Conciliorum nova et amplissima collectio* (55 vols., Florence and elsewhere, 1759–1962)

Maranini, G. *La costituzione di Venezia* (2 vols., Venice, 1927–31; reprint, Florence, 1974)

Martin, R. 'Witchcraft and the Inquisition in Venice, 1551–1650', seminar paper delivered at the University of Kent, May 1981

Marx, A. 'The expulsion of the Jews from Spain: two new accounts', in his *Studies in Jewish history and booklore* (New York, 1944), pp. 77–106

Masini, Eliseo *Sacro Arsenale, overo Prattica dell' Officio della S. Inquisitione ampliata* (Genoa, 1625)

Meersseman, G. 'Études sur les anciennes confréries dominicaines, II: Les confréries de Saint-Pierre Martyr', *Archivum Fratrum Predicatorum*, 21 (1951), pp. 51–196

Menis, G. C., ed., *Mille processi dell' Inquisizione in Friuli, 1551–1647* (Udine, 1976)

Miccio, Scipione 'Vita di Don Pietro di Toledo, Marchese di Villafranca', ed. F. Palermo, *Archivio Storico Italiano*, 9 (1846), pp. 3–89

Milano, A. *Storia degli ebrei in Italia* (Turin, 1963)

Milano, A. *Il Ghetto di Roma: illustrazioni storiche* (Rome, 1964)

Molmenti, P. G. *Curiosità di storia veneziana* (Bologna, 1919)

Monter, E. W. *Witchcraft in France and Switzerland: the borderlands during the Reformation* (London, 1976)

Monticone, A. 'Albizzi, Francesco', in *Dizionario biografico degli Italiani*, II (Rome, 1960), pp. 23–6

Moore, K. *Those of the street: the Catholic Jews of Mallorca. A study in urban cultural change* (Notre Dame–London, 1976)

Morosini, Giulio *Via della fede mostrata a' gli ebrei* (Rome, 1683)

Mueller, R. C. 'Les prêteurs juifs de Venise au Moyen Age', *Annales: Economies, Sociétés, Civilisations*, 30 (1975), pp. 1277–1302

Muir, E. *Civic ritual in Renaissance Venice* (Princeton, 1981)

Musi, A. 'Pauperismo e pensiero giuridico a Napoli nella prima metà del secolo XVII', forthcoming in *Timore e carità* ...

Nahon, G. 'Les Sephardim, les marranes, les Inquisitions péninsulaires et leurs archives dans les travaux récents de I. S. Révah', *Revue des études juives*, fourth series, vol. 132 (1973), pp. 5–48

Netanyahu, B. *Don Isaac Abravanel, statesman and philosopher* (second edition, Philadelphia, 1968)

Netanyahu, B. *The Marranos of Spain from the late XIVth to the early XVIth century, according to contemporary Hebrew sources* (second edition, New York, 1973)

Niero, A. *I Patriarchi di Venezia da Lorenzo Giustinian ai nostri giorni* (Venice, 1961)

Niero, A. 'Ancora sull' origine del Rosario a Venezia e sulla sua iconografia', *Rivista di Storia della Chiesa in Italia*, 28 (1974), pp. 465–78

Paci, R. 'La scala di Spalato e la politica veneziana in Adriatico', *Quaderni Storici*, 5 (1970), pp. 48–105

Paci, R. *La 'scala' di Spalato e il commercio veneziano nei Balcani fra Cinque e Seicento* (Venice, 1971)

Parker, G. *The Dutch revolt* (London, 1977)

Paschini, P. *Venezia e l'Inquisizione romana da Giulio III a Pio IV* (Padua, 1959)

Pastor, L. von *The history of the Popes from the close of the Middle Ages*. ed. F. I. Antrobus and others (London, 1891 onwards)

Pastor, L. von 'Allgemeine Dekrete der römischen Inquisition aus den Jahren 1555–1597. Nach dem Notariatsprotokoll des S. Uffizio zum erstenmale veröffentlichet', *Historisches Jahrbuch*, 23 (1912), pp. 479–549

Pavanini, P. 'Abitazioni popolari e borghesi nella Venezia Cinquecentesca', forthcoming in *Studi Veneziani*

Peña, Francisco, ed., *Literae apostolicae diversorum romanorum pontificum, pro officio Sanctissimae Inquisitionis, ab Innocentio III Pontifice Maximo usque ad haec tempora* (Rome, 1579)

Peña, Francisco. See also Eymeric, Nicolau

Pirri, P., ed., *L'Interdetto di Venezia del 1606 e i Gesuiti: silloge di documenti con introduzione* (Rome, 1959)

Politi, G. *Aristocrazia e potere politico nella Cremona di Filippo II* (Milan, 1976)

Preto, P. *Venezia e i Turchi* (Florence, 1975)

Prodi, P. 'The structure and organisation of the Church in Renaissance Venice: suggestions for research', in *Renaissance Venice*, ed. J. R. Hale (London, 1973), pp. 409–30

Pullan, B. 'Wage-earners and the Venetian economy, 1550–1630', *Economic History Review*, second series, 16 (1964), pp. 407–26

Pullan, B. 'Service to the Venetian state: aspects of myth and reality in the early seventeenth century', *Studi Secenteschi*, 5 (1964), pp. 95–148

Pullan, B., ed., *Crisis and change in the Venetian economy in the sixteenth and seventeenth centuries* (London, 1968)

Pullan, B. *Rich and poor in Renaissance Venice: the social institutions of a Catholic state, to 1620* (Oxford, and Cambridge, Mass., 1971)

Pullan, B. 'The occupations and investments of the Venetian nobility in the middle and late sixteenth century', in *Renaissance Venice*, ed. J. R. Hale (London, 1973), pp. 379–408

Pullan, B. 'Catholics and the poor in early modern Europe', *Transactions of the Royal Historical Society*, 5th series, vol. 26 (1976), pp. 15–34

Pullan, B. '"A ship with two rudders": "Righetto Marrano" and the Inquisition in Venice', *The Historical Journal*, 20 (1977), pp. 25–58

Pullan, B. 'Poveri, mendicanti e vagabondi (secoli XIV–XVIII)', in *Storia d'Italia: Annali I. Dal feudalesimo al capitalismo*, ed. C. Vivanti and R. Romano (Turin, 1978), pp. 981–1047

Pullan, B. 'The Inquisition and the Jews of Venice: the case of Gaspare Ribeiro, 1580–81', *Bulletin of the John Rylands Library of Manchester*, 62 (1979), pp. 207–31

Pullan, B. 'Natura e carattere delle Scuole', in *Le Scuole di Venezia*, ed. T. Pignatti (Milan, 1981), pp. 9–26

Pullan, B. 'The old Catholicism, the new Catholicism, and the poor', forthcoming in *Timore e carità* ...

Pullan, B. 'Religious toleration and economic decline: Venice and the Marranos', forthcoming in *Journal of Italian History*

Rapp, R. T. *Industry and economic decline in seventeenth-century Venice* (Cambridge, Mass., and London, 1976)

Ravid, B. 'The legal status of the Jewish merchants of Venice' (Harvard University Ph.D. thesis, 1973)

Ravid, B. 'The establishment of the *Ghetto Vecchio* of Venice, 1541', *Proceedings of the Sixth World Congress of Jewish Studies*, II (Jerusalem, 1975), pp. 153–67

Ravid, B. 'The first charter of the Jewish merchants of Venice, 1589', *Association for Jewish Studies Review*, 1 (1976), pp. 187–222

Ravid, B. *Economics and toleration in seventeenth-century Venice: the background and context of the Discorso of Simone Luzzatto* (Jerusalem, 1978)

Ravid, B. 'The prohibition against Jewish printing and publishing in Venice and the difficulties of Leone Modena', in *Studies in medieval Jewish history and literature*, ed. I. Twersky (Cambridge, Mass., 1979), pp. 135–53

Ravid, B. 'The socioeconomic background of the expulsion and readmission of the Venetian Jews, 1571–1573', in *Essays in modern Jewish history: a tribute to Ben Halpern*, ed. F. Malino and P. C. Albert (Rutherford–Madison–Teaneck, 1982)

Repertorium Inquisitorum pravitatis haereticae in quo omnia quae ad haeresum cognitionem ac S. Inquisitionis forum pertinent continentur. Correctionibus et annotationibus praestantissimorum iurisconsultorum Quintilliani Mandosii ac Petri Vendrameni decoratum et auctum (Venice, 1588)

Révah, I. S. 'Les marranes', *Revue des études juives*, 117 (1959), pp. 29–77

Révah, I. S. 'Autobiographie d'un marrane. Édition partielle d'un manuscrit de João (Moseh) Pinto Delgado', *Revue des études juives*, 119 (1961), pp. 41–130

Révah, I. S. 'La religion d'Uriel da Costa, marrane de Porto (d'après des documents inédits)', *Revue de l'histoire des religions*, 166 (1962), pp. 45–76

Révah, I. S. 'Pour l'histoire des marranes à Anvers', *Revue des études juives*, 122 (1963), pp. 123–47

Révah, I. S. 'L'hérésie marrane dans l'Europe catholique du 15e au 18e siècle', in *Hérésies et sociétés dans l'Europe pré-industrielle: 11e-18e siècles*, ed. J. Le Goff (Paris–The Hague, 1968), pp. 327–39

Révah, I. S. 'Les marranes portugais et l'Inquisition au XVIe siècle', in *The Sephardi Heritage*, I, ed. R. D. Barnett (London, 1971), pp. 479–526

Rivkin, E. 'The utilization of non-Jewish sources for the reconstruction of Jewish history', *Jewish Quarterly Review*, 48 (1957–58), pp. 183–203

Rivkin, E. *The shaping of Jewish history: a radical new interpretation* (New York, 1971)

Roth, C. 'Leone da Modena and England', *Transactions of the Jewish Historical Society of England*, 11 (1924–27), pp. 206–27

Roth, C. 'Léon de Modène, ses *Riti Ebraici* et le Saint-Office à Venise', *Revue des études juives*, 87 (1929), pp. 83–8

Roth, C. *The history of the Jews in Venice* (Philadelphia, 1930; reprint, New York, 1975)

Roth, C. 'The religion of the Marranos', *Jewish Quarterly Review*, 22 (1931–32), pp. 1–33

Roth, C. *A history of the Marranos* (Philadelphia, 1932)

Roth, C. *The ritual murder libel and the Jew: the report by Cardinal Lorenzo Ganganelli (Pope Clement XIV)* (London, 1934)

Roth, C. 'The strange case of Hector Mendes Bravo', *Hebrew Union College Annual*, 18 (1943–44), pp. 221–45

Roth, C. *The House of Nasi: Doña Gracia* (Philadelphia, 1947)

Roth, C. *The House of Nasi: the Duke of Naxos* (Philadelphia, 1948)

Rotondò, A. 'La censura ecclesiastica e la cultura', in *Storia d'Italia*, ed. C. Vivanti and R. Romano, V (Turin, 1973), pp. 1399–1492

Santosuosso, A. 'Religious orthodoxy, dissent and suppression in Venice in the 1540s', *Church History*, 42 (1973), pp. 476–85

Sanuto, Marino *I Diarii*, ed. R. Fulin and others (58 vols., Venice, 1879–1903)

Saraiva, A. J. *Inquisição e cristãos-novos* (second edition, Oporto, 1969)

Sarpi, Paolo *Lettere ai protestanti*, ed. M. D. Busnelli (2 vols., Bari, 1931)

Sarpi, Paolo 'Sopra l'officio dell' Inquisizione (18 novembre 1613)', in his *Scritti giurisdizionalistici*, ed. G. Gambarin (Bari, 1958), pp. 119–212

Sarpi, Paolo 'In materia di crear novo inquisitor di Venezia. 29 ottobre 1622', in his *Opere*, ed. G. and L. Cozzi (Milan–Naples, 1969), pp. 1202–11

Savio, P. 'Il nunzio a Venezia dopo l'Interdetto', *Archivio Veneto*, serie v, vol. 56 (1955), pp. 55–110

Scarabello, G. *Carcerati e carceri a Venezia nell' età moderna* (Rome, 1979)

Scholem, G. *Sabbatai Ṣevi, the mystical Messiah (1626–1676)* (Princeton–London, 1973)

Schwarzfuchs, S. 'Les marchands juifs dans la Méditerranée orientale au XVIe siècle', *Annales: Économies, Sociétés, Civilisations*, 12 (1957), pp. 112–18

Scult, M. *Millennial expectations and Jewish liberties: a study of the efforts to convert the Jews in Britain, up to the mid-nineteenth century* (Leiden, 1978)

Secret, F. *Les kabbalistes chrétiens de la Renaissance* (Paris, 1964)

Segre, R. 'Il mondo ebraico nel carteggio di Carlo Borromeo', in *Michael: on the history of the Jews of the Diaspora*, I, ed. S. Simonsohn (Tel-Aviv, 1972), pp. 163–260

Sella, D. *Commerci e industrie a Venezia nel secolo XVII* (Venice–Rome, 1961)

Sforza, G. 'Riflessi della Controriforma nella Repubblica di Venezia', *Archivio Storico Italiano*, anno 93 (1935), vol. I, pp. 5–34, 189–216; vol. II, pp. 25–52, 173–86

Shuckburgh, E. S., ed., *Two biographies of William Bedell, Bishop of Kilmore* (Cambridge, 1902)

Shulvass, M. A. *The Jews in the world of the Renaissance*, transl. E. I. Kose (Leiden–Chicago, 1973)

Sicroff, A. A. 'Clandestine Judaism in the Hieronymite monastery of Nuestra Señora de Guadalupe', in *Studies in honour of M. J. Benardete (Essays in Hispanic and Sephardic culture)*, ed. I. A. Langnas and B. Sholod (New York, 1965), pp. 89–125

Simonsfeld, H. *Der Fondaco dei Tedeschi in Venedig und die deutsch-venetianischen Handelsbeziehungen: Quellen und Forschungen* (2 vols., Stuttgart, 1887)

Smith, L. P. *The life and letters of Sir Henry Wotton* (2 vols., Oxford, 1907)

Soranzo, G. 'Rapporti di San Carlo Borromeo con la Repubblica Veneta', *Archivio Veneto*, serie V, vol. 27 (1940), pp. 1–42.

Spampanato, V. *Vita di Giordano Bruno, con documenti editi e inediti* (2 vols., Messina, 1921)

Stella, A. *Chiesa e Stato nelle relazioni dei nunzi pontifici a Venezia: ricerche sul giurisdizionalismo veneziano dal XVI al XVIII secolo* (Vatican City, 1964)

Stella, A. 'Utopie e velleità insurrezionali dei filoprotestanti italiani (1545–1547)', *Bibliothèque d'humanisme et Renaissance: travaux et documents*, 27 (1965), pp. 133–82

Stella, A. *Dall' Anabattismo al Socinianesimo nel Cinquecento Veneto: ricerche storiche* (Padua, 1967)

Stella, A. *Anabattismo e antitrinitarismo in Italia nel XVI secolo: nuove ricerche storiche* (Padua, 1969)

Stella, A. 'La società veneziana al tempo di Tiziano', in *Tiziano nel quarto centenario della sua morte, 1576–1976* (Venice, 1977), pp. 103–21

Stern, M. *Urkundliche Beiträge über die Stellung der Päpste zu den Juden* (2 vols., Kiel, 1893–95)

Stow, K. R. 'The burning of the Talmud in 1553, in the light of sixteenth-century Catholic attitudes toward the Talmud', *Bibliothèque d'humanisme et Renaissance: travaux et documents*, 34 (1972), pp. 435–59

Stow, K. R. *Catholic thought and papal Jewry policy, 1555–1593* (New York, 1977)

Susannis, Marquardus de. *De Iudaeis et aliis infidelibus, circa concernentia originem contractuum, bella, foedera, ultimas voluntates, iudicia, et delicta Iudaeorum et aliorum infidelium, et eorum conversionem ad fidem* (Venice, 1558)

Tacchi Venturi, P. *Storia della Compagnia di Gesù in Italia* (2 vols. in 4, Rome, 1950–51)

Tassini, G. *Curiosità veneziane, ovvero Origini delle denominazioni stradali* (new edition, ed. L. Moretti, Venice, 1964)

Tenenti, A. *Cristoforo Da Canal: la marine vénitienne avant Lépante* (Paris, 1962)

Tenenti, A. *Piracy and the decline of Venice, 1580–1615*, transl. J. and B. Pullan (London, 1967)

Tessadri, E. *L'arpa di David: storia di Simone e del processo di Trento contro gli ebrei accusati di omicidio rituale, 1475–1476* (Milan, 1974)

Thiriet, F. 'Sur les communautés grecque et albanaise à Venise', in Beck and others, eds., *Venezia centro* ..., I, pp. 217–31

Timore e carità: i poveri nell'Italia moderna (Cremona, forthcoming)

Toaff, A. 'Nuova luce sui marrani di Ancona (1556)', in *Studi sull' ebraismo italiano in memoria di Cecil Roth*, ed. E. Toaff (Rome, 1974), pp. 261–80

Tramontin, S. 'La visita apostolica del 1581 a Venezia', *Studi Veneziani*, 9 (1967), pp. 453–533

Tucci, U. 'The psychology of the Venetian merchant in the sixteenth century', in *Renaissance Venice*, ed. J. R. Hale (London, 1973), pp. 346–78

Vanzan Marchini, N. E. 'Medici ebrei e assistenza cristiana nella Venezia del '500', *Rassegna mensile di Israel* (April–May 1979), pp. 132–61

Vanzan Marchini, N. E. 'Il dramma dei convertiti nella follia di una ex ebrea', *Rassegna mensile di Israel* (Jan.–Feb. 1980), pp. 3–30

Viaro, A. "La pena della galera: la condizione dei condannati a bordo delle galere veneziane', in Cozzi, ed., *Stato, società e giustizia* ..., pp. 379–430

Villani, P., ed., *Nunziature di Napoli* (Rome, 1962 onwards)

Wee, H. van der *The growth of the Antwerp market and the European economy (fourteenth to sixteenth centuries)* (3 vols., Louvain, 1963)

Wolf, L. 'Jews in Elizabethan England', *Transactions of the Jewish Historical Society of England*, 11 (1924–27), pp. 1–91

Wootton, D. *Paolo Sarpi, atheism and the social order: a case study in early modern irreligion* (forthcoming)

Yerushalmi, Y. H. *From Spanish court to Italian Ghetto. Isaac Cardoso: a study in seventeenth-century Marranism and Jewish apologetics* (New York–London, 1971)

Yerushalmi, Y. H. *The re-education of the Marranos in the seventeenth century* (Cincinnati, 1980)

Zanelli, A. 'Di alcune controversie tra la Repubblica di Venezia ed il Sant' Officio nei primi anni del Pontificato di Urbano VIII (1624–1626)', *Archivio Veneto*, serie v, vol. 6 (1929), pp. 186–235

Index